# of Hole in the Day

ANTON TREUER

**BOREALIS
BOOKS**

Borealis Books is an imprint of the Minnesota Historical Society Press.
www.mhspress.org

The Minnesota Historical Society Press is a member of
the Association of American University Presses.

Manufactured in the United States of America

10 9 8 7 6 5 4 3 2 1

∞ The paper used in this publication meets the minimum requirements
of the American National Standard for Information Sciences —
Permanence for Printed Library Materials, ANSI Z39.48–1984.

International Standard Book Number
ISBN: 978-0-87351-779-9 (cloth)
ISBN: 978-0-87351-843-7 (paper)
ISBN: 978-0-87351-801-7 (e-book)

Library of Congress Cataloging-in-Publication Data

Treuer, Anton.
The assassination of Hole in the Day / Anton Treuer.
p.   cm.
Includes bibliographical references and index.
ISBN 978-0-87351-779-9 (cloth : alk. paper) — ISBN 978-0-87351-801-7 (e-book)
1. Hole-in-the-Day, Chief, 1828–1868—Assassination.   2. Ojibwa Indians—Kings and rulers—Biography.   3. Ojibwa Indians—History—19th century.   4. Ojibwa Indians—Government relations.   5. Ojibwa Indians—Treaties.   6. Indian leadership—Minnesota—History—19th century.   7. Minnesota—History—19th century.   8. Minnesota—Race relations—History—19th century.
9. Ojibwa language.   10. Oral history.   I. Title.
E99.C6H648   2010
977.6'004970092—dc22
[B]
2010023347

Maps by David Deis. Image on page 19 by John Swartz. Images on
pages 120, 157, and 158 courtesy National Museum of the American Indian.
All other images in MHS collections.

For my father, Robert Treuer, who told me stories about the chiefs named Bagone-giizhig and sparked my interest in them, the field of history, and the pursuit of knowledge.

Contents

Maps

Ojibwe Band Locations in Minnesota

CANADA

Lake of the Woods

PEMBINA

RED LAKE

Rainy

Upper Red Lake

River

Lower Red Lake

WINNIBIGOSHISH

Lake Superior

Leech Lake

PILLAGER

RED River

NORTH DAKOTA

Mille Lacs Lake

LAKE SUPERIOR

MINNESOTA

MISSISSIPPI

Mississippi

SOUTH DAKOTA

Minnesota

River

River

WISCONSIN

IOWA

miles

0   50   100

Preface

Archives, Oral History, and the Ojibwe Language

> Should the future historian include in his annals a list of noted
> men ... few will be more conspicuous or attract more attention
> than that of Hole-in-the-Day.
> — "B," LETTER TO THE *ST. CLOUD TIMES,* JULY 11, 1868[1]

RESEARCHING AND WRITING ABOUT HOLE IN THE DAY

I first developed an interest in Bagone-giizhig (Hole in the Day) as a small child. Traveling with my family throughout Minnesota's lake country, I listened to my father's stories about the father and son chiefs, Fort Ripley, and other people and places of importance. As an adult I returned to those stories, people, and places determined to fill in the missing pieces and discover who really killed Bagone-giizhig the Younger and how the Ojibwe lost control of so much of the most beautiful land in the world.

As I delved deeper into the father and son named Bagone-giizhig and the history of Ojibwe-Dakota relations, treaties, and removals, I found a wealth of information by modern scholars and some of Minnesota's best-known early writers. Henry R. Schoolcraft, William W. Warren, George Copway (also known as Gaagigegaabaw [Stands Forever]), Samuel Pond, Johann Georg Kohl, and many other officials, missionaries, scholars, and politicians wrote about Bagone-giizhig the Younger. Some of them knew him and had witnessed him in action negotiating with American officials and Dakota leaders; others published biographical sketches or lengthy accounts of both men named Bagone-giizhig in journals and correspondence. Both the father and son had impressed the observers with their physical presence, intelligence, the way they spoke, and the substance of their political endeavors. I wanted to know more.[2]

I began digging in the Minnesota Historical Society and National Archives, searching the Aspinwall, Pond, Sibley, Bassett, Ramsey, Manney, Spears, and Whipple papers, as well as the personal correspondence of most of Minnesota's early politicians and military figures stationed in Minnesota. There was clearly enough material in the archives to write a biography of the younger Bagone-giizhig. However, in order to do him justice, I felt it necessary to know what Ojibwe people thought about him.

I am Ojibwe, a lifelong resident of the greater Leech Lake area, and a fluent speaker of the Ojibwe language. I traveled extensively throughout Minnesota and Wisconsin for many years to attend Big Drum ceremonies, apprenticed to Archie Mosay at summer Midewiwin initiations on the St. Croix Reservation, and researched Ojibwe language, history, and culture. I wondered if the respected elders I knew, the most eloquent Ojibwe language speakers alive today, had information or perspective on the chiefs I was studying and if their knowledge differed from the archival information. All I had to do was ask them.

I was both surprised and delighted at the depth of knowledge that many Ojibwe people retained about the lives of the long-dead chiefs. For example, when I visited Melvin Eagle, a Mille Lacs elder, to learn about the music and speeches of the ceremonial Big Drum, he was able to speak for two hours about Bagone-giizhig. Melvin Eagle is the grandson of Chief Migizi (Eagle), who was chief in Mille Lacs when Bagone-giizhig was chief in the Gull Lake region. Migizi and the head warrior from Mille Lacs, Niigaanigwaneb, had actually sent warriors to protect Fort Ripley in 1862 during the U.S.–Dakota Conflict because Bagone-giizhig had threatened to take over the fort and join the Dakota in a large-scale war with whites in Minnesota. Fort Ripley was not only the seat of U.S. military presence in Ojibwe country; it was also the focal point of a major military stand-off between the Ojibwe and the U.S. government in 1862 engineered by Bagone-giizhig the Younger while a larger conflict embroiled the Dakota and Americans. Melvin Eagle told me how his father and grandfather had been entrusted with keeping oral histories as part of their hereditary leadership duties. Now I had someone who could say not simply, "Here's what the elders say," but rather, "Here is what my grandfather told me about what he did, and here is why he did it." Melvin Eagle was a gold mine of information about Bagone-giizhig, the chief's contentious relationship with the leaders in Mille Lacs, and his actions in 1862, at treaty signings, and in attacking the Dakota.

Archie Mosay, who was born in 1901, also knew a great deal about Bagone-giizhig. His father had been born in a wigwam near Sandy Lake, where Bagone-giizhig the Elder and his people lived before settling new villages in the Gull Lake region. Mosay and Bagone-giizhig were cousins. The evidence Mosay presented was not merely anecdotal. It helped me better understand the nature of Ojibwe chieftainship and how the culture of the Ojibwe people informed leadership dynamics.

I spent a great deal of time speaking with Joseph Auginaush of White Earth, who shared stories about Bagone-giizhig. He showed me a copy of a grocery receipt for twenty-four dollars that the local trader had used to assume title to his father's original land allotment against the will of the Auginaush family and without a hearing, service of notification papers, or due process of law. This information confirmed allotment abuses at White Earth after Bagone-giizhig's assassination. The information would never have been accessible had I confined myself to archival research. I also had several conversations with Bagone-giizhig the Younger's great-great-granddaughter, Karen Fairbanks, and other relatives now living at White Earth. Their insights into his actions and legacy contributed greatly to my expanding understanding and evolving interpretations of the chiefs.

I spoke with forty-seven Ojibwe, Potawatomi, and Dakota elders and community members who were knowledgeable about Bagone-giizhig and the history of tribal warfare, treaties, allotment, and relocation. Thirty-five of them were fluent Ojibwe speakers whom I repeatedly interviewed in Ojibwe over a fifteen-year period. A detailed list of the people I interviewed, their home communities, and the language of the interviews is provided in this book's bibliography. Some of my oral history interviews were published as the bilingual anthology *Living Our Language: Ojibwe Tales and Oral Histories*. Others appeared in the *Oshkaabewis Native Journal.* Many more have yet to appear in print.[3]

Some historians have been quick to dismiss oral accounts as flawed, biased, easily disputed, and often refuted. However, I found agreement across space and time among all the oral accounts. William W. Warren's narratives from the mid-nineteenth century agreed with Archie Mosay's versions more than a hundred years later. Since Mosay was not literate in English, those earlier textualizations did not influence his accounts. The larger story of Bagone-giizhig's times is that of the Ojibwe people's loss of land and political power, which did not formally end until the Indian Reorganization Act of 1934, when the U.S. government ceased allotting tribal land and reaffirmed tribal sovereignty. This year was within most of my interviewees' living memories.[4]

The people I interviewed in the late twentieth century and early twenty-first century possessed an understanding of culture that was deep and authentic, but it was different from the understanding Bagone-giizhig and his contemporaries had in the nineteenth century. I did not want to "upstream" or use modern Ojibwe cultural understandings to describe nineteenth-century understandings, which could be quite different.[5] But the oral history I was collecting had tremendous value since the interviewees had deep knowledge about specific events. Their cultural knowledge complemented the work of William W. Warren, Henry R. Schoolcraft, and other primary source documents describing Ojibwe culture and politics. The linguistic information gleaned from my interviews and my own knowledge of the language also helped to flesh out the meaning of important political, military, and cultural concepts.

I wanted to write a book about the chiefs Bagone-giizhig that was unique not only by being the first historical monograph about them, but by using both oral and archival sources. Although Bagone-giizhig the Younger was assassinated, two major investigations brought no formal charges, indictments, or remedies. There were dozens of important figures with motive and opportunity for engineering his death. I wanted my work to be informed not just by the writings of white government officials and traders, but also by Bagone-giizhig's own people. My goal was to research Indian history in a new and different way that includes the archives and the Indians, and not just as nameless "informants." I hope that more historians will be inspired to investigate the broader issues of Ojibwe leadership, Ojibwe-Dakota relations, and the oral tradition, subjects that formed Bagone-giizhig the Younger and that he helped mold and change in his own day.

My experience in gathering these oral histories led me to several conclusions. Oral history is still vibrant in the Ojibwe communities of Minnesota and Wisconsin today. The oral histories contain much more information, analysis, and legitimacy than most historians have realized. Ojibwe interpretations of their own history and definitions of Ojibwe culture are alive and vital to understanding Bagone-giizhig's life. For example, white officials never understood why Ojibwe warriors from Mille Lacs took protective positions around Fort Ripley to deter Bagone-giizhig from attacking it in 1862, but Melvin Eagle and several other elders from Mille Lacs did.

Like oral history, linguistic analysis is a relevant source useful in any balanced exploration of Ojibwe history. Bagone-giizhig the Younger gave all of his speeches in Ojibwe. He dictated his letters in Ojibwe and had them translated as necessary for monolingual English speakers or Dakota speakers. Only the English versions of his letters are usually available, but occasionally Ojibwe versions have survived. The Ojibwe still have a vibrant language and many retained cultural traditions, so understanding linguistic and cultural concepts is extremely useful in this historical exploration.[6]

In addition to interviews with many Ojibwe speakers and knowledgeable oral historians, some written translations of oral histories have been important in exploring Bagone-giizhig's story. William W. Warren's *History of the Ojibways* (1885) offers the most thorough collection of Ojibwe oral history recorded and published in the nineteenth century. Some of the information he recorded and numerous legends and histories have been kept alive in the oral tradition of the Ojibwe people today, but much in his work is available only in the published history. Warren's work is especially important because Warren knew Bagone-giizhig the Younger well and had researched and planned to write about Bagone-giizhig the Elder.

Warren is also important because he was a key player in nineteenth-century Ojibwe history. A mixed-blood Ojibwe, he advocated removal of the Ojibwe from their homelands, represented the government during the 1850 Sandy Lake annuity fiasco (in which hundreds of Ojibwe died), and served as translator for Treaty of 1847 at Fond du Lac and other formal discourse between Indian leaders and the U.S. government. His personal relationships with Bagone-giizhig the Younger and other Ojibwe chiefs may have influenced his interpretations of the eighteenth- and nineteenth-century events he wrote about in newspaper articles, correspondence, and his book.[7]

One of Warren's letters to the editor was a direct response to Bagone-giizhig the Younger's public comments about Warren. Negwanebi, a hereditary chief at Mille Lacs when Warren was a translator for treaty negotiations, complained that Warren deliberately mistranslated treaty provisions to protect the Warren family's financial interests and ostracize the Mille Lacs leadership, with whom Warren was not on friendly terms. (Warren's family had traded with Indians prior to 1838, and his father continued to serve the American Fur Company.) Negwanebi's complaint about William Warren must be taken in the context of the negotiations themselves, and some Ojibwe people viewed Warren's role favorably. While Warren's *History of the Ojibway People* has many shortcomings — including extensive focus on warfare to the exclusion of other critical discussions and disdain for some elements of Ojibwe culture — the history contains important information. The larger oral tradition at its foundation offers a great deal more.[8]

George Copway's book *The Traditional History and Characteristic Sketches of the Ojibway Nation* (1850), republished as *Indian Life and Indian History* (1858), is another important work informed largely by Ojibwe oral accounts. (Copway used his Indian name, Gaagigegaabaw, or Kah-ge-ga-gah-bowh, on his early work.) Copway also published *The Life, History and Travels of Kah-ge-ga-gah-bowh* (1847) — expanded and slightly retitled in 1850. Copway, like Warren, knew both the Bagone-giizhigs and was especially close to Bagone-giizhig the Elder. Copway provided several important references to the elder chief, including evaluation of his character from personal experience and his religious views based on attempts to discuss Christianity. Although Copway's work was clearly influenced by his time and his agenda as a missionary, he had access to Ojibwe oral histories in the middle of the nineteenth century. Copway's work is a treasure for understanding the chiefs and their times.

Charles Eastman wrote an important article about Bagone-giizhig the Younger. Although Eastman was only eleven when the chief was assassinated he was something of an insider. Many years after the assassination, Eastman interviewed Reverend Claude H. Beaulieu, who knew Bagone-giizhig, and Bagone-giizhig's son Joseph L. Wood-bury. Eastman's essay thus has substantial merit, although he left no footnotes or evidence for others to follow his claims. Eastman's essay also speaks to the high level of fascination about Bagone-giizhig among Indians and non-Indians, scholars, and the general public.[9]

There is now a small but growing body of recent scholarship on Ojibwe leadership as well. While this book is about the history, not the historiography, of the chiefs Bagone-giizhig—scholarship can and should speak for itself— I have tried to engage with important recent works by Melissa Meyer, Janet Chute, Rebecca Kugel, and Theresa Schenck when appropriate.[10]

In writing *The Assassination of Hole the Day*, I've cited all sources and provided as much bibliographic information as possible about each oral-history interviewee because oral history offers a relatively new, underutilized, and powerful dimension to researching Ojibwe history. I have found good information in surprising places—rang-ing from archival references in Canada and England, where Canadian provincial authorities and the British Crown feared that Bagone-giizhig might start a pan-Indian rebellion in 1862, to paper and oral documentation from Bagone-giizhig's descendents alive today. I have tried to keep my work focused on the chiefs Bagone-giizhig and their roles as both agents and observers of change. This has forced me to limit the amount of information devoted to certain di-mensions of Ojibwe physical culture, art, social history, and gender. As much as possible I have tried to show how Ojibwe people influ-enced the world around them, or how they demonstrated "agency." Bagone-giizhig the Younger's agency is obvious, but I have also tried to show the power possessed and used by his wives, the role of the *berdache* (gays and lesbians) in the traditional leadership structure, and specific communication and interactions with women in order to illuminate the role of gender in Ojibwe culture.

LANGUAGE, ORTHOGRAPHY, AND TERMINOLOGY

Since there are multiple writing systems for Ojibwe, a few words on language presentation seems useful. Unless words are a direct citation or a quote, I have presented Ojibwe terms using the double-vowel orthography—the most consistent and widely used for south-western Ojibwe, the language of Bagone-giizhig. The double-vowel orthography was developed for Minnesota Ojibwe by Charles Fiero, and Earl Otchingwanigan (Nyholm) and John Nichols refined additional writing conventions.[11]

In this work, proper Ojibwe nouns and names are followed with a translation in parentheses at first reference and are not italicized. Exceptions are made for individuals known primarily by their English names, such as Charles Ruffee and Clement Beaulieu. Their Indian names appear in parentheses at first reference. Ojibwe vocabulary words appear in italics, followed by a gloss in parentheses.

The Ojibwe language is extremely complicated grammatically and divided into distinctly different verb categories and noun genders, commonly referred to as animate and inanimate. For example, the Ojibwe word meaning "to eat something inanimate" is *miijin.* The Ojibwe word meaning "to eat something animate" is *amo.* The two realms require radically different words and concepts for appropriate expression. This categorization appears to have no significant associated value — animate things are not more important than inanimate ones — but there are patterns to the distinction.

Ojibwe is further complicated by being a predominantly verb-based language. Two-thirds of Ojibwe words are verbs, whose conjugation is especially expressive. In English there is a first, second, and third person form in both plural and singular. Ojibwe has an additional obviative form, and the first-person plural has both inclusive and exclusive distinctions. All Ojibwe verbs can be conjugated in three forms — independent, dependent, or participle — and all three forms have different meanings and expressions. Furthermore, Ojibwe has tenses and other thought paradigms that are unique to Algonquian-family languages such as Potawatomi, Ottawa, Ojibwe, and Cree.

In addition to the language's complexity, it is important to note the high importance that Ojibwe people placed on oratorical expression. Bagone-giizhig and his father skillfully used their powers of oratory to create and maintain their chieftainships. Use of language was central to their political power.

To avoid confusion, it must also be noted that the word *Chippewa,* frequently used in reference to the Ojibwe, especially in the United States, is actually a corruption of the word *Ojibwe.* Europeans frequently missed subtleties of Ojibwe pronunciation, hardening sounds and omitting letters. The soft Ojibwe *j* was written down as *ch,* and the soft *b* was written as *p.* The *o* was not even written, and the *e* was written as a short *a.*

There have been numerous alternative spellings of the word *Ojibwe* itself. Ojibwe people today use *Ojibwe* as a tribally specific term of self-reference (Ojibwe only) but also use the term *Anishinaabe* to refer to all Indians — Ojibwe, Dakota, and others. The deeper meaning of these terms is discussed in Appendix D.

Bagone-giizhig called himself Bagone-giizhig. The name Hole in the Day was a translation used by nonnative contemporaries. In an effort to develop a closer understanding of Bagone-giizhig — not just his name, but his personality — I usually refer to him by the name he chose. I also engage his language whenever possible to try to access his thought patterns and the Ojibwe culture in which he existed.

In discussing other tribes, I've tried to use the spellings preferred by reservation tribal governments (Potawatomi, Menominee, Ottawa, Assiniboine, and Ho-Chunk [rather than Winnebago]).[12] Sometimes tribal-government spellings do not reflect the preferred spellings of tribal members or accepted orthographies. Indians know the most appropriate terms and spellings best.

Finally, I use the word *Indian* intentionally, with full knowledge of its shortcomings. Knowing that the word may offend some people, I find the ambiguity of the terms *native, indigenous,* and *aboriginal* equally problematic and even more cumbersome. As Sherman Alexie once remarked, "The white man tried to take our land, our sovereignty and our languages. And he gave us the word 'Indian.' Now he wants to take the word 'Indian' away from us too. Well, he can't have it."[13] As much as possible, however, I use *Ojibwe* and *Anishinaabe* in writing about the Ojibwe, because they are authentic terms of self-reference and rich with empowered meaning.

Exploring the legendary life of Bagone-giizhig has been a challenging task that I have tried to meet by grounding my research in oral history and supporting it with traditional primary sources. I hope that readers and future historians will find understanding and fruit for further study in the remarkable story of Bagone-giizhig's life, death, and legacy.

The Assassination of Hole in the Day

Prologue

Possessed of superior native talents and judgment, and an intuitive perception of the motives of men, he was a serious obstacle to the success of schemes of plunder, so ingeniously devised by unscrupulous men for the ruin of his people. He was killed by members of his own race tis true, but we know that no monarch was ever more loved by his subjects than was Hole-in-the-Day... When the whole truth is published and known, we predict that an infamy unparalleled will lie at the door of other than a Chippewa.
— "B," LETTER TO *ST. CLOUD TIMES*, JULY 11, 1868[1]

Bagone-giizhig the Younger, also known as Hole in the Day the Younger, acquired many enemies during his reign as a principal chief of the Mississippi Ojibwe (Chippewa) in central Minnesota. From the time he assumed his father's name and chieftainship until his assassination more than two decades later, Bagone-giizhig relied on his many friends and followers to keep his enemies at bay.[2] He shrewdly cultivated relationships with Americans and with Dakota and Ojibwe leaders to make himself an important treaty negotiator for his people and helped change the nature of Ojibwe leadership to accomplish that goal. When the U.S. government tried to force the Ojibwe from their villages onto a single reservation, however, Bagone-giizhig's personal enemies finally caught up with him.[3]

On June 27, 1868, Bagone-giizhig (pronounced Bug-oh-nay-gee-zhig) made final preparations for a trip to Washington, DC. He intended to redress or renegotiate the very unpopular Treaty of 1867, which provided for the removal of the Mississippi Ojibwe to a new reservation at White Earth. He and his bodyguard, a cousin named Ojibwe, gathered supplies in the village of Crow Wing (eleven miles south of present-day Brainerd, Minnesota), at the confluence of the Crow Wing and Mississippi rivers. Crow Wing, the northernmost European settlement on the Mississippi River, was populated equally with Ojibwe and Americans. As Bagone-giizhig and his cousin

PO-GO-NAY-KE-SHICK, (Hole in the Day.)
The Celebrated Chippewa Chief.

WHITNEY'S GALLERY, - - - - SAINT PAUL.

Bagone-giizhig the Younger, ca. 1865. The chief's regalia asserts his
leadership position in all realms: the otterskin turban of a civil chief, the
eagle feathers of an experienced warrior, the suit of a cooperative chief
with American influence, and the blanket of a traditional Indian.

approached the Gull River outlet a half mile from the Crow Wing agency, their horse-drawn buggy was accosted by Ojibwe men from Leech Lake. The group included Medwe-wiinind (He Who Is Heard Being Named), Baadwewidang (Coming Sound), Enami'egaabaw (He Who Stands Praying),[4] Naazhoobiitang (Two Waves), Wezowiikanaage (Tail Bone), Namewinini (Sturgeon Man), Odishkwe-giizhig (End of the Day), Dedaakamaajiiwaabe (Ebb and Flow), Gaazhagens (Cat), Ondinigan (Source), Biiwaash (Approaching Flight), and Gebesindang (Ever Present Being). Three others — Naawi-giizhig (Center of the Sky), Zhiibingogwan (Shaking Feather), and Mekadewikonayed (Black Robe) — may also have been there, since they had intercepted a village resident named Makoons (Little Bear) to learn the chief's exact location.

Medwe-wiinind and Baadwewidang approached Bagone-giizhig's wagon and pointed a shotgun and a rifle at the surprised chief. Bagone-giizhig shouted in Ojibwe, "You have caught me in a bad moment, for I am unarmed." For the first time in thirteen years he was not carrying the Colt 45 revolver given him by President Franklin Pierce in 1855. Medwe-wiinind hesitated for a moment, and then he and Baadwewidang each shot the chief — one in the head and the other in the neck. Bagone-giizhig fell from his carriage dead.

The assassins quickly took Bagone-giizhig's cousin Ojibwe hostage. Then Odishkwe-giizhig bent over the chief's body, firing one more time. The other assassins surrounded the body and shot Bagone-giizhig again and stabbed him. Then the chief was stripped of his clothes, watch, and other possessions. Ojibwe asked them to move the body into the shade so it would not heat in the summer sun and be full of maggots before it could be retrieved. The assassins obliged. Then they left the body and took Ojibwe to Bagone-giizhig's large two-story house a few miles away, where they pillaged the chief's belongings.[5] They absconded with two horses, a few rifles, and clothing. The presence of Bagone-giizhig's wives and Ojibwe prevented wholesale damage and looting, largely because the assassins feared retaliation if they attacked Ellen McCarty, Bagone-giizhig's third wife, a white woman. Later, the assassins tried to sell their loot, including the chief's watch, to Julia Warren Spears, sister of interpreter and historian William W. Warren. Spears reported seeing ten of the assassins loot the school at Leech Lake the day after the assassination and hearing the eldest assassin say, "Hole-in-the-Day is dead.

I killed him yesterday morning. I was chosen to fire the first shot and killed him."[6]

News of Bagone-giizhig's death spread quickly. Within thirty minutes of the attack, Crow Wing residents Charles Ruffee, Augustus (Gus) Aspinwall, and John Morrison retrieved the chief's body and brought it to the Indian agency. Newspapers as far away as New York City carried stories about the assassination. Throughout the Indian and non-Indian world, everybody seemed to be talking about the death of Bagone-giizhig. Everyone may have been talking, but they were not saying the same thing. Although there were two official government investigations immediately after the assassination and the whereabouts of the triggermen were known, U.S. officials had no authority to intervene in Indian-on-Indian crimes on tribal land. As a result the killers were not even interviewed, much less detained. For the next forty years they would carry many secrets, until an unrelated investigation of land fraud at White Earth gave them the opportunity to speak openly about the event. In the meantime, the men behind the killing and the reasons for the murder remained completely obscured.

After Bagone-giizhig's assassination, John Morrison, Charles Ruffee, Clement Beaulieu, Augustus Aspinwall, and their business colleagues in Crow Wing argued that Bagone-giizhig was killed by a group of Leech Lake Indians because of personal jealousy. Bagone-giizhig had arranged a special provision in the Treaty of 1867 that provided him and his heirs an annual stipend of one thousand dollars. Many Ojibwe people believed the chief's use of his political power for personal gain showed disrespect for Ojibwe leadership traditions and the increasingly impoverished Ojibwe people. The chief's decision to take a white woman as his third wife during his previous trip to Washington, DC, heightened this negative perception.

The decline of the fur trade and subsequent dispossession of Ojibwe through land cession treaties from 1837 to 1867 had pushed most Minnesota Indians into abject poverty and made them increasingly dependent on the U.S. government. Bagone-giizhig's role as a treaty negotiator during the years they lost their land also left many Ojibwe with an unfavorable impression of him. He was both a scapegoat and the object of legitimate criticism for his role in the treaties. In 1863, he wrote President Abraham Lincoln for permission to represent the U.S. government (not the Ojibwe) in its attempt to gain land cessions from the Red Lake Ojibwe in northwestern Minnesota, and then, when he was denied permission, he showed up uninvited at the treaty conference and claimed to represent the Red Lake and Pembina Ojibwe.[7] Because Bagone-giizhig asserted authority where he had no accepted rights, he alienated and infuriated chiefs from Red Lake, Leech Lake, and Mille Lacs. Some claimed that his assertion that he was head chief of *all* the Ojibwe pushed them to take action and end his intrusions into their sovereignty. Others argued that young men from Leech Lake killed Bagone-giizhig in retaliation for his attempts to manipulate the Leech Lake Ojibwe in 1862 during the U.S.–Dakota Conflict, an event of great importance for the Ojibwe as well as the Dakota. As Dakota Indians under Little Crow began their attacks on white settlers in southern Minnesota, Bagone-giizhig sent runners to Leech Lake with the message that whites were conscripting Indian men for the Union Army and that he was starting a war against whites. But Bagone-giizhig did not himself unleash or participate in any violence. Instead, he let the Leech Lake Ojibwe — who burned the Indian agency at Walker, took prisoners, and marched to Crow Wing — take most of the risks. Only later did they find that Bagone-giizhig had lied to them.

Religion may have been another factor in Bagone-giizhig's death. He was in the middle of a tense feud between Catholic missionaries including Francis Xavier Pierz and Thomas Grace and Protestant missionaries including Henry B. Whipple and John Johnson, also known as Enami'egaabaw (Stands Praying), over missions and political ambitions. Bagone-giizhig flirted with conversion to Catholicism but always maintained his traditional Ojibwe beliefs, to the chagrin and frustration of the missionaries. John Johnson married Bagone-giizhig's first cousin and was even adopted as a son by Bagone-giizhig's father, but the family relationship soured in the 1860s. Johnson eventually held Bagone-giizhig the Younger responsible for impeding his mission, threatening his life, and even killing his children, who died from exposure in 1862 while fleeing impending violence directed at the Gull Lake mission by Bagone-giizhig. Johnson wrote to the commissioner of Indian Affairs that he would not be safe in Minnesota until Bagone-giizhig was "disposed of."[8]

Still others claimed that Bagone-giizhig was killed because he frequently advocated keeping most mixed-blood Indians off the new reservation at White Earth and denying them annuity payments. He had already successfully stipulated a provision in the 1867 treaty denying payments to mixed-bloods not on reservations. Others claimed that his statements made him more powerful enemies among his closest colleagues at Crow Wing, the white and mixed-blood businessmen who collected annuities themselves and made small fortunes off real and falsified claims of debts owed by Ojibwe.[9]

The identity of the men who physically gunned down Bagone-giizhig was known, but the U.S. government could not legally prosecute Indian crimes against Indians. Tribal chiefs took no formal action because they feared retaliation from their own people and intratribal warfare. Yet the identity of the assassins and their unpunished murder was only a small part of the story. There were many more people involved in Bagone-giizhig's demise, and they had a list of motives and methods as long as the mighty Mississippi.

A powerful leader who incited both positive and negative passions, Bagone-giizhig wielded more influence among his own people and among American officials than any other Ojibwe leader of his time. Exploration of the story of his life and the mysteries of his death provides a window into Ojibwe history that is essential to understanding the profound changes occurring in Ojibwe leadership in the nineteenth century. Paradoxically, it is precisely these historic changes that made Bagone-giizhig's rise to power so hotly contested yet so easily achieved.

1

The Nature of Ojibwe Leadership

Fear of the nation's censure acted as a mighty band, binding all
in one social, honourable compact. They would not as brutes be
whipped into duty. They would as men be persuaded to the right.
—George Copway[1]

The assassination in 1868 of Mississippi Ojibwe chief Bagone-giizhig the Younger, one of history's best-known Ojibwe leaders, was one of the most intriguing stories of the nineteenth century. Many people had motive and the triggermen were known. But the conspiracy was a well-kept secret. Although Bagone-giizhig's untimely death created a stir in newspapers throughout the United States, the details of his legendary life and death have remained shrouded in a maze of inconclusive military reports and letters and Indian oral tradition. Most historians have found the records obtuse, inaccessible, and unreliable.

Ojibwe leadership was transformed in the nineteenth century in part because of Bagone-giizhig and his father. Bagone-giizhig's contested rise to power defied the accepted Ojibwe definitions of political leadership, which were hereditary and clan-based. Under Bagone-giizhig's leadership, political connections to outside groups including the Americans and the Oceti Sakowin (Seven Council Fires of the Sioux), especially the Dakota, grew in importance.[2] Profound changes occurred when the clan system no longer served as the primary credential for political leadership and when the once clearly divided realms of civil and military leadership blurred and blended. In addition, both Bagone-giizhigs defied the established custom wherein chiefs represented specific communities, not geographical regions. Furthermore, under their leadership American-Ojibwe diplomacy morphed from one-way American intervention in Ojibwe affairs. It became a complex two-way dynamic wherein chiefs also intervened in American affairs, inserting themselves into the government's negotiations with other groups of Indians over whom they had no formal claim of leadership.

THE MEANING OF A NAME

Bagone-giizhig is a powerful name carried by at least four prominent nineteenth-century Ojibwe leaders: one from Red Lake, Minnesota, who was present for diplomacy at the time of the Nelson Act of 1889; one from Leech Lake, who played a leading role in the country's last battle with an Indian nation, at Sugar Point, Minnesota, in 1898;[3] and the father and son chiefs of the Mississippi Ojibwe in central Minnesota. The younger chief, known as Hole in the Day the Younger, Hole in the Day II, or Bagone-giizhig II (with numerous alternative spellings), left an indelible mark on the Mississippi Band from 1847 to 1868.

While both chiefs Bagone-giizhig were well known by American leaders and citizens, interviews with Melvin Eagle, grandson of Mille Lacs chief Migizi, suggest that the younger was better known among the Ojibwe as well, though not necessarily better loved.[4]

The meaning of the name *Bagone-giizhig* is mysterious. The root word, *giizhig*, means both "sky" and "day." The word for white cedar tree, *giizhik*, sounds similar to *giizhig*. The prefix *bagone-* pertains to an aperture or hole, but it can also denote the process of opening or creating a hole. Several words in Ojibwe contain the morpheme *bagone-*, such as *bagonebiisaa* (the lake opens up [ice recedes]), *bagone'an* (to drill a hole in something), and *bagoneyaa* (there is a hole).[5]

Because of the diverse meanings of *bagone-* and *giizhig* and the guarded nature of Ojibwe naming protocol, the name has many interpretations, but there is general agreement that *Bagone-giizhig* means "Hole in the Day" or "Hole in the Sky." Explanations for that translation differ greatly. Some argue that it refers to an opening in the clouds where the sun shines through or even to an eclipse, while others say it refers to an opening in the sky through which the Great Spirit watches over the Indian people or an opening in the clouds or sky where the smoke and prayers from a pipe ceremony ascend to the Great Spirit.[6] It is unknown if Bagone-giizhig the Elder received

Important Places

CANADA

Lake of the Woods

Rainy River

Upper Red Lake

Lower Red Lake

Cass Lake

Lake Winnibigoshish

Lake Pokegama

Leech Lake

Sandy Lake

La Pointe

Lake Superior

NORTH DAKOTA

Red River

Bagone-giizhig the Younger's Second Home

Gull Lake

Rabbit Lake

Bagone-giizhig the Younger's First Home

Otter Tail Lake

Fort Ripley

Crow Wing

Mille Lacs Lake

MINNESOTA

St. Cloud

Mississippi

WISCONSIN

Minneapolis

St. Paul

Fort Snelling

SOUTH DAKOTA

Minnesota River

River

IOWA

- - - - - - Prairie du Chien boundary line, 1825

miles

0   50   100

his name from an elder member of the tribe through a traditional naming ceremony or if he acquired it through a dream while fasting as a young man.[7] Names were acquired both ways in the nineteenth century.

Naming was extremely important for the Ojibwe. Names were much more than words that other humans used to identify or speak to someone. A name represented spiritual identification and gave direction and meaning to one's life. Names had spiritual power and were divined, not invented. The person giving the name acquired it either directly from the spirits by fasting or dreaming or indirectly by giving one of his or her own names to the recipient. The name giver's own names offered just as much spiritual empowerment because they were divined by someone else through fasting or dreaming. A name symbolized a greater teaching—the vision or dream that it came from. Naming ceremonies were often elaborate affairs because each name giver—there were often several—had to tell the story behind the name he or she was giving, in addition to observing other protocol and feasting.

Names encoded secret meaning. Saying a name divulged to the spirits the entire depth of meaning behind the name but kept that information hidden from humans because humans do not "see" the way spirits do. People who heard the name could only guess at the whole story behind it.

Because a traditional name was so deeply personal and powerful, it was closely guarded. Ojibwe people believed that sharing the deeper meanings behind a name with persons other than the closest of family members would make the name holder spiritually vulnerable. Nineteenth-century Ojibwe Indians worried a great deal about "bad medicine"—spiritual or medicinal harm that could kill, sicken, or possess someone. It was believed that anything from simple jealousy to political rivalry could encourage enemies to use bad medicine. One of the strongest protections against it was to keep personal spiritual information and items secret from strangers and enemies. Ojibwe people only very rarely divulged details of the deeper meanings behind their names except in the twilight of their lives, when spiritual vulnerability was no longer of great concern.

So much effort was devoted to keeping spiritual information secret that many people chose not to divulge their true names or the names of their children in public. Sometimes sharing such details was unavoidable, because spiritual names had to be used when praying for someone at ceremonies and at funerals. However, this belief helps explain why many young men, including Bagone-giizhig the Younger, were not introduced to others by their true spiritual names. He was simply called *Gwiiwizens* (Boy) in public. Other common variations of Gwiiwizens were used as public names as well, including *Gwiiwizhenzhish* and *Maji-giiwizens* (both translated as Bad Boy). *Oshkinawe* (Young Man) was also a common public name used to avoid spiritual name identification.[8]

The name giver and the name receiver both used the word *niiya-we'enh* (my namesake) to refer to each other. *Niiyaw* (my body) carries the critical meaning in the word. When someone gave a name, the name giver took part of his or her spiritual essence and put it into the body of the name recipient, making them spiritually related for life. The name giver then functioned much like a godparent in Christian tradition, as a spiritually connected family member blessed with the same dream or vision that informed the given name.

Perhaps only the original Bagone-giizhig knew the true origin and meaning of his name. Yet the many interpretations and the cultural beliefs surrounding naming add to our understanding of Bagone-giizhig and his legacy among Ojibwe people today.

THE CLAN SYSTEM AND CHIEFTAINSHIP

In the nineteenth century, the Ojibwe were one of the most populous tribes of North America. Hundreds of Ojibwe primary villages spread out from Quebec in eastern Canada to Montana in the western United States and from the southern Great Lakes to northern Manitoba. Despite sharing many critical aspects of language and culture, the Ojibwe people did not function as one nation politically. Within each region of Ojibwe country were networks for shared political and military discourse and decision making, but there were no head chiefs, kings, or other top officials. Instead, there were numerous chiefs in each village who communicated with one another and made decisions in council. The dynamics of how Ojibwe leaders functioned were changing before either Minnesota chief named Bagone-giizhig was born and would have continued to change had they never existed. But their ascension to chieftainship significantly catalyzed dramatic cultural changes.

During what is known as the nineteenth-century "treaty period," when Indians were being forced to cede their land to the U.S. government, American officials customarily called Indians who lived in regions together "bands."[9] This was a Euroamerican construct, not an indigenous one. Nevertheless, the proximity of the villages grouped together as a band often had utility beyond formal treaty signings. Dialect variations among the Minnesota Ojibwe show that significant divergences in grammar and syntax often occur along band lines.

The Mississippi Band to which Bagone-giizhig belonged encompassed most of the Ojibwe villages in central Minnesota and along the Mississippi River watershed. The Mississippi Band included villages at Mille Lacs, Gull Lake (Bagone-giizhig's village), and Sandy Lake. Government treaties were negotiated with "head chiefs of the Mississippi Band." However, those chiefs had never made decisions about politics, economics, or warfare as a united group before the American government tried to convince them all to sell their lands. And although the Mississippi Band was Bagone-giizhig's band, he sometimes tried to assert influence over Ojibwe groups outside his regional political network.

Minnesota had several so-called bands. The Pembina Band lived along the Red River near Pembina, North Dakota, immediately adjacent the Red Lake Band, which occupied Upper and Lower Red Lake and areas north to Lake of the Woods. The Winnibigoshish Band, which lived around Lake Winnibigoshish and Bowstring Lake, was later grouped together on the Leech Lake Reservation with the Pillager Band, which stretched from Leech Lake in north-central Minnesota to Otter Tail Lake in western Minnesota. The Lake Superior Band lived near Duluth and along the shore of Lake Superior. The Ojibwe word for leadership—ogimaawiwin—literally means "to be esteemed" or "held to high principle." It comes from the morpheme ogi, meaning "high," found in other Ojibwe words such as ogichidaa (warrior), ogidakamig (on top of the earth), and ogidaaki (hilltop).

Among nineteenth-century Ojibwe there were three main types of leadership—civil, religious, and military. Each realm required different responsibilities and often involved different people. Sometimes a person of rare gifts could assume positions of authority in more than one area.[10]

Civil leadership positions were almost invariably held by men. The authority to assume civil leadership most often was inherited through the father's line. In this way, certain clans, such as the *maang doodem* (loon clan) and *ajijaak doodem* (crane clan), maintained leadership positions consistently for long periods. Although the nature and organization of clans changed over time, today's Ojibwe spiritual leaders note that taboos and protocols about clan changed relatively little compared to the amount of change in leadership patterns. Even today there is remarkable consistency to the spiritual, but not the political, configuration of clans and their patrilineal structure.[11]

Entrenchment of clan traditions are demonstrated in published accounts by captive John Tanner of his thirty-year experience of living among the Ojibwe. The same is true in the writings of William W. Warren and George Copway. Leadership dynamics in Ojibwe country underwent much more rapid change than the clan system that helped form those traditions.[12]

For Bagone-giizhig's predecessors, the clan system had been far more important to leadership authority than military prowess or oratorical ability. The Ojibwe clan system was totemic, from the Ojibwe word *doodem*, or clan.[13] The word *doodem* comes from the morpheme *de*, meaning "heart or center." The relationship between the words *ode'* (his heart), *oodena* (village), *doodem* (clan), and *dewe'igan* (drum) has caused considerable confusion among some scholars, who have occasionally claimed that one of these words was derived from another when in fact they simply share the same root morpheme *de*. *Ode'* (the heart) is the center of the body. *Oodena* (the village) is the center of the community, and *doodem* (the clan) is the center of spiritual identity. *Dewe'igan* (the drum) is the center of the nation, or its heartbeat.[14]

Among the Ojibwe, clans defined the core of one's spiritual essence. Just as *ode'* was the heart of one's physical being, *doodem* was the heart of one's metaphysical being. Originally, only Ojibwe people from certain families of the *maang doodem* (loon clan) and *ajijaak doodem* (crane clan) could be chiefs.[15]

Although the morphological composition of clan as the center of spiritual identity is the most widely held view of the elders I interviewed, it is still possible that that *doodem* (clan) and *oodena* (village) share both a cultural and a linguistic root. Certain clans dominated certain villages to the point that those villages were identified by their totemic assignations. Over time the difference in the concept of clan and village could have conflated in some areas. Originally two clans—*maang* (loon) and *ajijaak* (crane)—governed all of the chieftainships.[16]

Marriage between people of the same clan was one of the strongest taboos in Ojibwe culture, and people could be killed for violating it. According to Edward Benton-Banai, the *waawaashkeshi doodem* (deer clan) was completely exterminated for having violated this taboo. William W. Warren tells of a very similar story, although he identifies the exterminated clan as the *mooz doodem* (moose clan). If married couples and families lived in a village, there had to be at least two clans there; typically there were five or more.[17]

Ojibwe clans were a strictly patrilineal birthright.[18] Even when the Ojibwe intermarried with the French, British, and Americans, the patrilineal structure was not altered. Instead, as a birthright (not a ceremonial or legal adoption), children with a nonnative father were automatically adopted into an existing clan, although this practice varied somewhat by region. The *migizi doodem* (eagle clan) was the adopting clan for many of the communities along the western edge of Ojibwe territory, including most of Minnesota. It is still the dominant practice today in White Earth, Leech Lake, Red Lake, Mille Lacs, St. Croix, Fond du Lac, Bad River, Red Cliff, Lac Courte Oreilles, and Lac du Flambeau.[19]

In some communities of northwestern Ontario, the *waabizheshi doodem* (marten clan) is the adopting clan for children with a nonnative father. In some other Ontario communities, the adopting clan is determined at a *jiisakaan* (shake tent), where the practitioner divines the adopting clan. Throughout Ojibwe country, I have never encountered a knowledgeable elder, a reliable archival reference, or a tradition that claims patrilineal clan inheritance alters with introduction of a non-Indian father.[20]

Researching and writing about clans has proven difficult and confusing for many scholars because the clan system was not static. By the middle of the nineteenth century, the five or seven original clans had expanded to more than twenty. The clan system had also eroded as the primary factor in determining chieftainship.[21]

In some communities, clan function was deeply affected by missionary activity. Some Ojibwe and Ojibwe-Cree villages in northern

Ontario saw successive waves of missionaries who spoke tribal languages and achieved high rates of conversion to Christianity, occasionally nearing 100 percent. As a result, the importance of clan
became devalued and was eventually forgotten. In Bearskin Lake,
for example, Ojibwe language-fluency rates remain near 100 percent even today, but the clan system is virtually nonexistent. The
very meaning of the word *doodem* has changed as well. Instead of
"clan" or, literally, "spiritual heart or center," *doodem* means simply
"friend."[22] This helps explain why John Long, who stayed at Nipigon
(Ontario) from 1777 to 1779, believed that *doodem* meant "friend" or
"animal friend," rather than "clan" or "spiritual heart or center."[23]
The dynamic of religious and cultural change came early for some
of the eastern Ojibwe communities and did not necessarily follow
loss of the Ojibwe language. In Minnesota, however, the clan system
remained intact throughout the Bagone-giizhig chieftainships, and it
remains so, in changed form, today.

As late as the eighteenth century, clan was the primary determi-
nant of leadership status and function, and the *maang doodem* (loon
clan) and *ajijaak doodem* (crane clan) were hereditary recipients of
chieftainship. When disagreements arose between chiefs of these
clans, members of the *bineshiinh doodem* (bird clan) could intervene
to help settle disputes. *Makwa* or *noke doodem* (bear clan) members
had responsibilities pertaining to medicinal knowledge, healing, and
protection. Edward Benton-Banai, Lawrence Henry, Mary Roberts,
and other Ojibwe elders I interviewed attested to the special importance of medicinal knowledge. Ojibwe elders Eugene Stillday, Thomas
Stillday Jr., and Anna Gibbs placed greater emphasis on the role of the
makwa doodem (bear clan) in providing protection. William W. Warren's publications seem to support the latter interpretation, although
there is truth in both. The *waabizheshi doodem* (marten clan) held
rights for military protection.[24]

Clan designation was a birthright that established and reinforced
a spiritual connection with an animal, bird, or water creature.[25] Even
today, most Ojibwe people honor taboos about not eating their own
clan (animals or birds) and not marrying someone of the same clan.
The animal-human relationship is further reinforced by the common belief that a clan member assumes many of the attributes of his
or her clan. For example, I have heard people of the *migizi doodem*
(eagle clan) remark that they love fish because that's the favored

food of their *doodem.* I also heard a woman state that her protective treatment of her children reflected her being in the *makwa doodem* (bear clan), and mother bears are always watchful of their young.

As early as the seventeenth century, the clan system began to diversify as clans began breaking into several groups. Sometimes, new clans were introduced through marriage with outside groups. This was the case with the *ogiishkimanisii doodem* (kingfisher clan) and the *ma'iingan doodem* (wolf clan), both of which came to the Ojibwe through Dakota paternity in mixed marriages. Many offshoot clans such as the *ogiishkimanisii* (kingfisher), *ma'iingan* (wolf), *owaazisii* (bullhead), *bizhiw* (lynx), and *migizi* (eagle) clans became especially numerous among the Minnesota Ojibwe.[26]

The eighteenth and nineteenth centuries were very tumultuous times for the Ojibwe, and sustained periods of warfare with the Iroquois Confederacy to the east and the Dakota to the west gave the Ojibwe more territory in all directions. Increased friendship and joint occupation of certain areas with tribes such as the Cree and the Assiniboine led to wider dispersion of the Ojibwe population. New Ojibwe villages formed regularly throughout this period, but, increasingly, the supremacy of clan in determining chieftainship was challenged. Often, clans that dominated warfare, such as the *waabizheshi* (marten) and *makwa* or *noke* (bear), found themselves occupying new territory without significant representation of the traditional chieftainship clans. Ojibwe society was highly structured, and chieftainship rules began accommodating the new clan composition. Leadership remained a hereditary right after a village was established, but the rights dispersed among various clans as the pool of hereditary chiefs diversified.[27] Minnesota was on the Ojibwe "frontier" with the Dakota when Bagone-giizhig the Elder came to power, and this no doubt affected clan continuity.

The structure of clans in Ojibwe culture today cannot be used to explain day-to-day life in the nineteenth century, but it does shed light on how clan structure evolved and particular clans came to dominate certain groups. The overwhelming majority of Minnesota Ojibwe Indians are of the *makwa* (bear), *migizi* (eagle), *ma'iingan* (wolf), *waabizheshi* (marten), *owaazisii* (bullhead), and *mikinaak* (turtle) clans. Before Red Lake Reservation developed its tribal flag, leaders conducted a clan census in order to include a symbol of each clan on its flag. Although some clans may have been overlooked,

The Red Lake flag carries an emblem for each of the original reservation clans: bear, turtle, bullhead, otter, eagle, marten, and kingfisher. Absent from the flag are hereditary chief clans loon and crane. Red Lake certainly had chiefs, but they were selected from representatives of the other clans there rather than from "traditional" chieftain clans. The selection of new chiefs from different clans and the clan representation on the Red Lake flag evidence a changing pattern in Ojibwe leadership and the devaluation of clan as the primary indicator of chieftainship rights.

seven original Red Lake clans were found — *makwa* (bear), *mikinaak* (turtle), *owaazisii* (bullhead), *nigig* (otter), *migizi* (eagle), *waabizheshi* (marten), and *ogiishkimanisii* (kingfisher). The traditional leadership clans of the seventeenth and eighteenth centuries — *maang* (loon) and *ajijaak* (crane) — were not found, so they are not included on Red Lake's flag. Other clans are represented today at Red Lake, including *name* (sturgeon) and *adik* (caribou). But these clans were either underrepresented or unrepresented when the census was conducted. Marriage with people from other reservations probably accounts for expanded clan representation at Red Lake.[28]

The present-day composition of clans in Minnesota's Ojibwe communities is a reminder that traditional clan-based leadership paradigms could not continue as they had done for centuries in part because those chieftain clans were not well represented on the western edge of the Ojibwe frontier with the Dakota. In some cases they may even have been absent. This made a new leadership structure necessary, one which enabled men who lacked traditional claims to leadership to become chiefs by virtue of their military reputations and oratorical skills.

Although the authority to become an Ojibwe civil chief was considered hereditary, influence was not. A person earned influence through years of service to the people. This requirement helped many to assume civil leadership positions without the hereditary right of chieftainship. Moreover, religious and military chieftainships were not considered strictly hereditary rights. Therefore, individuals could rise to leadership positions in all three arenas of Ojibwe chieftainship.

The increasing fluidity of Ojibwe leadership in the nineteenth century helps explain how Bagone-giizhig's father came to such a powerful position among his people. Ironically, these changes in leadership dynamics did not completely erode hereditary considerations, thereby enabling Bagone-giizhig the Elder to pass his position on to his son. Heredity, clan, military prowess, religious knowledge, political savvy, oratorical ability, and personal charisma all played a role in determining who had political power.

Ojibwe missionary and historian George Copway wrote extensively about Ojibwe political structure and protocol during the lifetimes of Bagone-giizhig the Elder and Younger. In 1850, he noted: "The rulers of the Ojibways were inheritors of the power they held. However, when new country was conquered, or new dominions annexed, the first rulers were elected to their offices. Afterward, the descendants of these elected chiefs ruled the nation, or tribe, and thus power became hereditary." Explorers Henry Schoolcraft and Charles C. Trowbridge had similar perspectives on Ojibwe leadership. Writing in 1820, Trowbridge declared: "The Chieftainship descends from father to son, and the women are always excluded, so that the line becomes extinct on the death of the last male of the old line. When this happens to be the case (but I believe it seldom happens), the vacancy is filled by election of the man most valiant, brave and powerful, or the most celebrated for wisdom and eloquence; and he inherits the title of chief together with all the honors of the last in power." Trowbridge continued, "This practice is never deviated from except by some daring fellow, who usurping the authority holds the tribe in awe by his ferocity or the influence of numerous relatives devoted to his interest. Such a one however is soon disposed of by his enemies." James Duane Doty, a member of the 1820 Cass Expedition, made a remarkably similar observation.[29]

The need for a change in leadership paradigms in the nineteenth century came from a dramatic and rapid expansion in the territory the Ojibwe occupied. Attitudinal changes in the population, however, came more slowly. So although a new system arose for selecting chiefs in newly settled territories, the succession of chieftainship lines remained largely hereditary. Once a chieftainship was in place, it was passed on from father to son, much as it had been for centuries.

Historian Rebecca Kugel analyzes the differences between civil and war chiefs in *To Be the Main Leaders of Our People,* but she overstates the rigidity of those categories. The chiefs Bagone-giizhig were both — they led war parties and used that role to gain influence, and they also asserted civil positions, especially in dealing with the Americans. In fact, by the nineteenth century, most Ojibwe civil chiefs in the region had war experience and used it to reaffirm their civil positions. Similarly, war leaders used their experience to bolster their political ambitions. Furthermore, Red Lake and many other communities where there were no chiefs from traditional civil chieftain lineages (loon or crane clan) had leaders in both war and civil matters. There were not separate categories of civil and military chieftainship so much as there were different sources of empowerment for any chieftainship. The categories are meaningful for some discussions, but they overlap more than they differentiate, especially in the mid-nineteenth century, where Kugel describes an alliance between warrior chiefs and mixed-blood traders against civil chiefs that perhaps oversimplifies a very complicated and rapidly changing nexus of relationships that transcended categories.

In fact, all important Ojibwe decisions were made on a grassroots level. Council was the traditional medium for political activity. The most respected and powerful civil, religious, and military leaders would gather to share their thoughts, advice, and potential plans. The act of passing a pipe was central to any important meeting. The Ojibwe word for meeting, *zagaswe'idiwin,* literally means "a smoking."

Consensus had to be reached.[30] Then leaders saw to implementation of the council's will. Decisions were made not by one person but in consultation with all the political entities in a community as well as with metaphysical forces. Although French, British, and especially Americans tried to make consensus-oriented and cooperative Indians into chiefs by gifting showy medals and flags, those tokens did little to change perceptions among regular Indians. The American custom of calling them headmen or head warriors rarely trumped cultural belief in consensus and the value of hereditary right and clan designation.

Leaders could use their influence to help shape decisions made in council. But, especially when it came to war, they often had a hard time exerting that influence, prompting some outside observers to remark that chiefs had little tangible authority. This observation is not true — chiefs did hold significant sway — but their authority manifested itself differently than in nonnative societies. Ojibwe leadership did not involve powers of command and control so much as great powers of persuasion and influence. Oratorical skill was especially important. Paul LeJeune wrote of the Ojibwe, "All the authority of their chief is in his tongue's end, for he is powerful in so far as he is eloquent." Ascending to positions of Ojibwe leadership was difficult.[31]

Among leaders, accumulation of wealth was traditionally considered abhorrent, and chiefs frequently had fewer possessions than their followers. In the mid-nineteenth century Johann Kohl described this attitude:

> As long as a man has anything, according to the moral law of the Indians, he must share it with those who want; and no one can attain any degree of respect among them who does not do so most liberally. They are almost communists and hence there are no rich men among them . . . Frequently, when a chief receives very handsome goods, either in exchange for his peltry, or as a recognition of his high position, he will throw them all in a heap, call his followers, and divide all among them. If he grow[s] very zealous he will pull off his shirt and give it away, and say, "So you see, I have now nothing more to give; I am poorer than any one of you, and I commend myself to your charity."

In 1838, Anna Jameson noted, "The chief is seldom either so well lodged or so well dressed as the others."[32]

A chief's generosity with food, trade goods, and, eventually, annuities represented a critical part of his power within his own community. Paul LeJeune wrote in 1634 that a chief "will not be obeyed unless he pleases the Savages." Gabriel Marest reported in 1712 that a chief's power rested on his "wherewith to fill the kettle." Nicolas Perrot made similar observations.[33]

Generosity and oratorical skill were especially important for ascending to positions of leadership, whether civil, religious, or military. It was largely through exhibiting these attributes that Bagone-giizhig the Elder, Eshkibagikoonzh (Flat Mouth) the Elder, and other prominent figures in Ojibwe history achieved their positions.[34] At treaty negotiations in 1837, Eshkibagikoonzh of Leech Lake actually claimed that he derived his authority through his merits rather than through his bloodline. There are other cases where military accomplishments or oratorical abilities trumped heredity in the accession of political position and even cases where well-known and widely respected chiefs stepped down from office while still alive because they could no longer speak loudly and eloquently.[35]

RELATIONS WITH THE U.S. GOVERNMENT AND OTHER TRIBES

In 1819 the U.S. government began constructing Fort Snelling at the junction of the Mississippi and Minnesota rivers in order to establish a stable U.S. presence in the region. This event accelerated change in the dynamics of Ojibwe leadership. Although Ojibwe communities generally despised the accumulation of personal wealth among chiefs, it became possible for civil chiefs, through trade, land sales, and annuity distributions, to use the fleeting financial benefits of the fur trade and treaties to enhance their own positions by distributing valuable trade goods and money. A chief on good terms with American officials could become a financial power broker, negotiating terms for treaties and deciding who should be paid. Bagone-giizhig the Younger used this role extensively, adding mixed-blood trader friends to annuity roles when it suited his purposes and excluding them when they did not return his favors. Although the fur trade and then land sales generated most of the money that trickled into Ojibwe hands, chiefs received much of the credit when the money arrived and much of the blame when it did not. This made a chief's relationship with the U.S. government increasingly important.[36]

Chiefs actively sought recognition by the government because it enabled them to serve as intermediaries in the distribution of trade goods and to influence annuity-payment lists. But recognition also led to greater dissension among the Ojibwe because chiefs competed with one another for that acknowledgment and for the financial benefits attached to it.

The French, the British, and especially the Americans liberally gave "chief" medals and flags to Ojibwe people who seemed to have any kind of influence, not just to Ojibwe civil chiefs. They looked for hierarchies in Ojibwe culture that simply were not there and called anyone who spoke at formal meetings a chief, headman, or head warrior. Americans sought cooperative Ojibwe people to negotiate with and manipulate in land acquisitions. Many chiefs tried to limit the distribution of medals and flags to so-called headmen and head warriors because it diffused the perception of their own authority in American minds. Eshkibagikoonzh of Leech Lake strongly chastised Henry Schoolcraft for this, saying that it was "not proper to give medals to Indians to make them chiefs" based on American notions of hierarchy and cooperation.[37] Eshkibagikoonzh said that chiefs had to be recognized as such by the Ojibwe themselves. Despite American attempts to manipulate and sometimes circumnavigate Ojibwe leadership protocol, he continued, a chief's true merits, oratorical ability, consensus approval, and hereditary right should determine chieftainship.

In addition to leadership relationships with the U.S. government, relationships with other tribes became increasingly important. Nineteenth-century Ojibwe history is best understood in terms of the complicated web of intertribal politics the Ojibwe had spun with the Dakota, Nakota, Ho-Chunk, Assiniboine, Cree, Potawatomi, Menominee, and Ottawa, as well as relations between the Ojibwe, British, and Americans. Many historians have examined Ojibwe-American relations or Ojibwe-British relations, but few have wrestled with the question of intertribal diplomacy that defined Ojibwe political and military power. As a result, many historians have been unable to explain why Bagone-giizhig would threaten war with the United States in 1862 but be unwilling to strike the first blow and why he would choose instead to try to manipulate Ojibwe from other villages into attacking white settlements. An examination of Ojibwe relations with the Dakota and intratribal power dynamics among the Ojibwe helps to answer that question.

Many historians have asserted that the U.S. government intervened in Ojibwe affairs because it was powerful enough to do so—

that the Ojibwe had no choice but to comply. Yet a close look at inter-tribal diplomacy reveals that the Ojibwe intentionally intervened in American affairs, as well. They did so to influence Ojibwe-Dakota relations and acquire the trade goods and money that would strengthen their positions among their own people, rather than out of concern with U.S. expansionism. The Ojibwe and the Dakota both agreed to the Treaty of Prairie du Chien on August 19, 1825, and to subsequent separate land cessions in 1837 not out of necessity or be-cause they feared the Americans. They did so because they feared their Indian neighbors and sought to protect their territory from them with a white buffer zone in which both groups could still hunt and fish.

The same rationale was used by the Pillager Band in the Long Prairie Land Cession Treaty of 1847. The Pillager Band's desire to have the Ho-Chunk and Menominee relocated to Long Prairie in order to create a buffer from Dakota attacks explains the Pillager Ojibwe's willingness to cede an 890,000-acre parcel of land in exchange for only two hundred beaver traps, seventy-five guns, and an annuity of blankets with no financial compensation.[38]

While Ojibwe chiefs increasingly relied on the American govern-ment as a source of revenue and as an intermediary in their relation-ships with Dakota leaders, it is important to note that the Americans needed the Ojibwe as well for trade, land cessions, and preservation of peace. As a result, there were many mutual accommodations. For instance, first territorial governor of Minnesota Alexander Ramsey smoked a catlinite peace pipe with Bagone-giizhig the Younger and adopted Ojibwe protocol for meetings with Indian leaders. Indians were not simply pushed aside, then, when the white man entered Minnesota Territory.

GENDER AND THE ROLE OF WOMEN

Women's role in Ojibwe leadership and diplomacy is frequently mis-understood. While Ojibwe women rarely participated in general council, they contributed significantly to civil and especially religious affairs.[39] Men often consulted with women prior to formal council meet-ings, usually attended only by men. As wives, mothers, and grand-mothers, women wielded power, and male leaders sought their advice and consent in many important matters. All religious actions decided by council had to meet the approval of the *ogimaakwe* (head woman).[40]

Women and men usually sat on opposite sides at lodge gatherings for important ceremonial and political functions. This was not to show that women were subordinate to men. Instead, the seating division maintained proper balance, according to elder Mary Roberts in 1989. Gender division symbolically reinforced the notion that men and women each owned half of the lodge. Important community decisions could not be made by one sex alone. This protocol applied to the Midewiwin, the primary religious society of the Ojibwe, to drum ceremonies, and to many other religious events. Numerous elders whom I interviewed confirmed these beliefs, including James Clark (2000), Melvin Eagle (2002), Thomas Stillday Jr. (1996), Anna Gibbs (1996), and Mary Roberts (1991). These elders, who actively participated in recent ceremonies, carry this knowledge from their oral tradition as well.[41]

Although sociopolitical leaders were almost always male, women were not prohibited from being leaders. One notable woman who achieved highly respected leadership and influence was Gaagige-ogimaansikwe (Forever Queen) of the Pembina Band. Women leaders in this sphere were usually, but not always, lesbian. Though female, they functioned as men socially and politically, took other women as wives, hunted, and engaged in war.[42]

In the nineteenth century the role of women in Ojibwe leadership changed dramatically. For example, Ruth Flatmouth, Eshkibagikoonzh (Flat Mouth) the Younger's sister, served as a proxy at several significant diplomatic events when he was away from Leech Lake.[43]

Ojibwe society nevertheless had a strong division of labor by gender. Males hunted, trapped, and protected the group. Females carried water, cooked, tanned hides, gardened, and sewed. Females owned and governed the home. Henry Schoolcraft remarked of the divisions, "The lodge is her precinct, the forest his." Women could fight as well, especially if the village was being attacked, but they were required to use non-projectile weapons such as clubs. Female use of guns, spears, and bow and arrows were prohibited by taboo. Even on the rare occasions that women led men into battle, this seems to have been true. This taboo was often explained as necessary because projectile weapons penetrated the enemy's body, whereas other weapons crushed the enemy.[44]

Gender divisions among the Ojibwe extended to the spiritual realm. Women were considered to have a deep, sacred connection with water. Men had a special relationship with fire. These relationships structured many ceremonial functions, where men guarded and kept watch over the sacred fire and women always blessed the water. It was considered taboo for men to do women's work and vice versa.[45]

Sex usually determined one's gender and, therefore, one's work, but the Ojibwe accepted variation. Men who chose to function as women were called *ikwekaazo,* meaning "one who endeavors to be like a woman." Women who functioned as men were called *ininiikaazo,* meaning "one who endeavors to be like a man."[46] The French called these people *berdaches. Ikwekaazo* and *ininiikaazo* could take spouses of their own sex.[47] Their mates were not considered *ikwekaazo* or *ininiikaazo,* however, because their function in society was still in keeping with their sex. If widowed, the spouse of an *ikwekaazo* or *ininiikaazo* could remarry someone of the opposite sex or another *ikwekaazo* or *ininiikaazo.* The *ikwekaazowag* worked and dressed like women.[48] *Ininiikaazowag* worked and dressed like men. Both were considered to be strong spiritually, and they were always honored, especially during ceremonies.[49]

The role of *ikwekaazo* and *ininiikaazo* in Ojibwe society was believed to be sacred, often because they assumed their roles based on spiritual dreams or visions. Peter Grant, who traveled extensively among the Ojibwe in the early 1800s, reported: "They have the greatest faith in dreams, by which they imagine that the Deity informs them of future events, [and] enjoins them certain penances . . . I have known several instances of some of their men who, by virtue of some extraordinary dream, had been affected to such a degree as to abandon every custom characteristic of their sex and adopt the dress and manners of the women. They are never ridiculed or despised by the men on account of their new costumes, but are, on the contrary, respected as saints or beings in some degree inspired."[50]

French, British, and American officials made similar observations. Thomas McKenney, commissioner of Indian Affairs from 1824 to 1830, traveled extensively in Ojibwe country while negotiating the

1827 Treaty of Fond du Lac and other political and trade agreements between the United States and Ojibwe nations. Of the *ikwekaazo* among the Mississippi Ojibwe he observed in 1826:

> This singular being, either from a dream, or from an impression derived from some other source, considers that he is bound to impose upon himself, as the only means of appeasing his *manito,* all the exterior of a woman . . . So completely do they succeed, and even to the *voice,* as to make it impossible to distinguish them from the women. They contract even their walk; turn in their toes, perform all the menial offices of the lodge; wear, of course, petticoats, and breast coverings, and even go through the ceremony of marriage! Nothing can induce these men-women to put off these imitative garbs, and assume again the pursuits and manly exercises of the chiefs . . . [They] live, and die, confirmed in the belief that they are acting the part which the dream, or some other impression, pointed out to them as indispensable.[51]

One of the earliest extended visits to Ojibwe territory was made by Jesuit priest Jacques Marquette and Louis Jolliet in 1673 under a commission from the government of New France. They wrote that some men in both Algonquian and Siouan societies

> while still young, assume the garb of women, and retain it throughout their lives. There is some mystery in this, for they . . . glory in demeaning themselves to do everything that the women do. They go to war, however, but can use only clubs, and not bows and arrows, which are weapons proper to men. They are present at all the juggleries, and at the solemn dances in honor of the calumet . . . They are summoned to the councils, and nothing can be decided without their advice. Finally, through their profession of leading an extraordinary life, they pass for Manitous, that is to say, for spirits, or persons of consequence.[52]

Artist George Catlin witnessed the annual dance in honor of the *berdache* and remarked that they were "looked upon as medicine and sacred." Missionary Samuel Pond mentioned women who accompanied men to war and "resembled a woman only in form." Primary source documents contain numerous other references to acceptance of homosexuality in Ojibwe society. The *ikwekaazo* and *ininiikaazo* were clearly important both socially and politically.[53]

RELIGIOUS AND MILITARY LEADERSHIP

Among the Ojibwe, leadership in religious affairs was more highly valued than leadership in other spheres. Religious leaders received the highest esteem and respect, and it usually took many years of hard work to achieve this high status. Although religious leadership was not a hereditary right, as it was for political leaders, the prominence of one's family and close clan relatives improved chances of ascending to leadership. Aspiring leaders could apprentice to these relatives and acquire the skills necessary to officiate in ceremonial functions. Men and women had prominent religious duties, and many ceremonies required the guidance of both a male and a female leader.[54]

Both religious and sociopolitical chiefs had headmen, or helpers, usually referred to as *oshkaabewisag.* The *oshkaabewisag* played essential cultural roles, for they ensured the enforcement of decisions and usually oversaw much of the communication and summons to council.[55]

The third type of Ojibwe leader functioned in military matters. Military leadership was more fluid and more easily attained than religious or political leadership. While war chiefs were highly respected, they were not nearly as important or well known as religious and civil leaders. A young man of intelligence and courage could earn a reputation as a fighter and in a short time acquire enough influence to gather war parties and ascend to a position of some authority. Pursuits of war were almost entirely left to men.

It was as a military leader that Bagone-giizhig the Elder first made his mark. He quickly developed a reputation as a powerful commander through his bravery in battle and his charisma in council. His influence in other areas increased, too, and eventually he claimed broad representative powers among the Mississippi Ojibwe and asserted himself at literally every treaty signing involving the Mississippi Ojibwe in his adult life. Upon his death, Bagone-giizhig the Younger claimed that role as an inheritance from his father. Bagone-giizhig the Elder and his son, then, both earned reputations as skilled military leaders, and their prowess in battle reinforced their rise to political leadership.

Because of the importance of military leadership in the era of Ojibwe-Dakota warfare, it is critical to understand Ojibwe practices and beliefs pertaining to war and the environment in which military actions took place. Among the Ojibwe, powerful social obligations compelled a reaction when one's relatives or fellow clan members were killed. It was believed that the spirit of the deceased, when wronged by murder or war, needed to be appeased in order to release itself from this world and go to the spirit world. This appeasement could be accomplished in three main ways.

The first way of releasing a wronged spirit was to solicit a medicine man to conduct a medicine dance and set things right. This process was time-consuming and expensive, because it required numerous feasts and the giving of gifts.[56] The second option was to "cover the dead" (referred to as "paying the body" or "wiping off the blood"). The murderer, or representatives of that person's family or community, accomplished this by making an offering of numerous gifts and food, as missionary Baraga observed: "Sometimes the relatives of the killed are appeased by the relatives of the murderer, by great presents . . . They call it '*paying the body*.'" William Warren explained that the custom meant "to heal the matter *Indian fashion,* paying in goods for the lives lost." If the relatives of the slain person found the offering acceptable, a religious leader would pray over the event, send the spirit of the deceased on his or her journey, and present the offerings to the family of the deceased. Sometimes the offending party offered one of its own relatives to be adopted by the victim's family. These first two options were commonly practiced—though not always—when the murderer and murdered were from the same group or closely allied groups.[57]

When the offending party came from a neutral or a hostile group, a third option was usually taken—revenge. Revenge could entail taking a captive to replace the person who had been killed. More often, someone was killed, although revenge was not simply a bloodletting. Revenge was spurred by deep religious beliefs, and once a murder had been repaid in kind, the spirit of the person being avenged still had to be "sent on." Scalp dances were frequently used for this purpose. Scalp dances involved straight-beat singing (which was different from the syncopated beat reserved exclusively for social dancing) on large drums and animated dancing. Women took part in some of these dances. Henry Schoolcraft observed an Ojibwe scalp dance on July 10, 1832, that took place at the families' graves to demonstrate that the departed had been properly avenged.[58]

Revenge released a spirit that had been offended through murder or war. In 1661, Father Richard remarked that the Ojibwe believed "that their departed relatives will not rest in peace unless some human beings are sacrificed to them." Around 1800, Bizhiwoshtigwaan (Lynx Head), a Pembina chief, stated that once revenge was sought, the war party became responsible for the spirit they were seeking to release: "We bear with us . . . those that were our friends and children, but we cannot lay them down, except [when] we come into the camp of our enemies."[59]

The practice was relentless and brutal, as Baraga observed:

> When an Indian kills purposely some person or persons of his tribe, the relatives of the killed (the nearest first, and if there are none, also the more remote and collateral) have in their opinion a right to take the life of the murderer. They do it as soon as they can, without any previous ceremonies or formalities, and without any permission or assent of the chief . . . [If] the murderer flees, the relatives of the killed exercise retaliation in a very unproper manner on the *relatives* of the murderer, who had no share in the crime. And often it happens that three or four victims are sacrificed . . . No length of time is able to allay their revengeful resentment. I saw Indians who killed some person in a certain place, many years ago, and who never would go for any advantage to that place, for fear they would be killed by the friends of the person they had murdered.[60]

The practice of avenging deaths often kept tensions high between the Ojibwe and Dakota over long periods of time even when they were not engaged in territorial conflict. If an Ojibwe was killed, the entire population of Dakota could be held responsible. Even if the offending party was Nakota, Dakota people living two hundred miles away could be the target of revenge attacks. The Dakota would then be obligated to set things right in respect to their loss, frequently choosing military revenge over the option of ceremonial resolution. Thus, hostilities were often maintained between entire nations without significant material, political, or territorial incentives.

Large-scale military campaigns were also waged by both the Ojibwe and the Dakota for military, material, and territorial gain. The desire to claim or take back territory played an important role in Ojibwe-Dakota warfare. After the primary land battles for territory had occurred in the eighteenth century, eventually giving the Ojibwe control of most of northern Wisconsin and Minnesota, nineteenth-century warfare in Minnesota consisted mostly of small raids back and forth. These generally did not lead to large numbers of fatalities or territorial changes. Despite constant pressure on Ojibwe-Dakota borders, they changed very little in Minnesota after 1800, with a few notable exceptions.[61]

By the nineteenth century, territorial incentives were usually subordinate to spiritual and cultural norms of revenge. Land was still a key issue in tribal warfare, however, and missionary Samuel Pond described the economic importance of territory in Ojibwe-Dakota warfare: "If they were to live at all, they must have a country to live in; and if they were to live by hunting, they must have a very large country, from which all others were excluded. Such a country they had, not because their enemies were willing they should occupy it, but because they were able and willing to defend it by force of arms. If they had not resisted the encroachments of their enemies, they would soon have been deprived of the means of subsistence and must have perished. If they would have game to kill, they must kill men too."[62]

Dakota leader Little Crow believed that peace could easily be made between the Dakota and Ojibwe, but he did not advocate it. His reasoning highlighted the conundrum: "It is better for us to carry on the war in the way we do than to make peace. We lose a man or two every year, but we kill as many of the enemy during the same time. If we make peace the Chippewa [Ojibwe] will overrun all of the hunting grounds . . . Why then should we give up such an extensive country to save the life of a man or two annually?"[63]

A surprising aspect of ongoing hostilities between the Dakota and Ojibwe was the practice the Ojibwe called *biindigodaadiwin.* The word literally means "to enter one another's lodges." The practice amounted to temporary truces in order to hunt, arising largely out of economic need, but also out of the desire for peace. Even in the most heated periods of conflict, *biindigodaadiwin* was a common practice and one in which Bagone-giizhig and his followers frequently participated. It was a temporary truce that also resulted in joint Ojibwe-Dakota camps and hunting parties. People would literally enter one another's lodges, sleep in the same buildings, smoke the same pipes, frequently adopt one another, form friendships and even marriages, and then be at war again the next spring.[64]

Another often misunderstood aspect of military custom in Ojibwe country is the widely practiced custom of scalping. While the origins of the practice are extensively debated, it is certain that scalping did become a common Indian custom deeply embedded in indigenous ritual and religious belief for the Ojibwe and most of their neighbors by the end of the eighteenth century.[65]

For both the Ojibwe and Dakota, scalping after death was widely expected and always considered an honor. The Ojibwe around La Pointe complained to Alexander Henry in 1765 that in a recent battle with the Dakota their enemies did not scalp their fallen comrades. The Ojibwe said they "consider it an honour to have the scalps of our countrymen exhibited in the villages of our enemies, in testimony of our valour." Being scalped was deemed a far better fate than being killed and not scalped. Explorer Joseph Nicollet also noted that, "they consider it an honor to be scalped. Not to be scalped is a sign of contempt."[66]

Scalping was not simply vindictive mutilation. Scalps were taken as symbols of the enemy killed in battle and brought back to communities for important religious ceremonies. The scalp was seen to contain the spirit of the slain person, as Joseph Nicollet observed: "They take the individual for the scalp; for them the scalp is the same thing as the individual. Bringing back the scalp is as if they were going with the individual. In the scalp feasts they throw bits of food into the fire before eating." Food put in the fire during a scalp dance was an offering to the spirit of the deceased.[67]

The mere death of an enemy was not enough to satisfy the need for revenge. A symbol representing the slain enemy had to be brought forth to appease the spirit of the person for whom vengeance was sought. The scalp served this purpose. With the scalp properly prepared through prayer and dance, the offended spirit could be sent on to the spirit world.[68]

Among the Ojibwe, both men and women participated in the scalp dance. Members of the community who had lost relatives welcomed the opportunity to mourn, to authenticate the vengeance, and to honor the dead. The ceremony helped assuage grieving, and those who had lost loved ones to the enemy had to participate. Often, scalps were taken to several communities for scalp dances, and a single scalp could be used for a year or longer. Henry Schoolcraft observed one scalp that was sent from Leech Lake to Cass Lake and from there to the Red River, Pembina, and then back to Leech Lake. Scalps were tied to a stick and held in the air as a symbolic offering, to make the reasons for the war clear in the eyes of the creator. Usually the person who took the scalp held the stick.[69]

Because scalped enemies were seen to fulfill the scalper's important spiritual need, the scalped individuals received special treatment. Although successful war parties had much to rejoice about, the victorious warriors blackened their faces on their way home as a symbol of mourning for those they had slain. Often, successful Ojibwe warriors put tobacco down at the camp of their overrun enemies as an offering to the spirits whom they may have offended in exacting their revenge. Scalps might be kept for many years after the initial scalp dance and buried with the scalper as a revered sacred item. Because of the importance of the scalp in releasing the spirit of someone being avenged, it was considered a greater honor to scalp someone (regardless of who did the killing) than it was to actually kill an enemy.[70]

Ojibwe religious and political culture evolved in unique ways over hundreds of years without European influence, but by the nineteenth century, Ojibwe leaders were coming to power in a new era and would confront unanticipated challenges. The stage was set for the gifted leader Bagone-giizhig the Elder—and for his young son, who would watch, learn, and take those skills in unimagined directions. Their stories follow.

2

Becoming Chief

The Rise of Bagone-giizhig the Elder

[Bagone-giizhig's people] would quietly sit and listen with an
occasional murmur of approval of the truth of what he was saying;
but when it suited his purpose to appeal to their passions, he would
rouse himself up to all the fire and impetuosity of his nature, and
while his eye flashed and his features changed with the changing
emotions which glowed within his own breast, those passions and
emotions ran like an electric shock through his auditors, until unable
to restrain themselves, they would literally leap from their seats, and
in a frenzy of excitement, fill the air with their savage yells.

—JULIUS T. CLARK[1]

Bagone-giizhig (Hole in the Day) the Elder's rise to power and
prominence among the Mississippi Ojibwe could not have been
predicted. No Ojibwe leader before him had achieved comparable influence with so little claim to traditional sources of power. His
surprising ascension to chieftainship demonstrates the deep flux in
Ojibwe society and the complicated Ojibwe political arena dominated
by relations with the Dakota and the American government. He was
both an obvious agent of change and a product of his times.

COMMON MAN, UNCOMMON CHARACTER

Bagone-giizhig the Elder was born sometime around 1800 near La
Pointe, Wisconsin, on Madeline Island in Lake Superior.[2] The era was
one of complicated political and military relationships among the
Ojibwe, the Dakota, and the American and British governments.
Ojibwe territory, technology, and politics were undergoing funda-
mental and rapid change.

For hundreds of years, the Ojibwe people had been slowly migrat-
ing westward. Even before the arrival of Euroamericans, spiritual

and economic incentives had propelled the Ojibwe and their close allies the Odaawaa (Ottawa) and Boodawaadamii (Potawatomi) to push westward through the Great Lakes into present-day Wisconsin, Minnesota, and Ontario, where wild rice grew abundantly. My recent oral history interviews report that spiritual concerns were in part responsible for this migration to what the Ojibwe called "the land where food grows on water."[3]

In 1679 the Ojibwe made a historic agreement with the Dakota in a large council held near present-day Duluth. The Ojibwe, who were already in close contact with Europeans, agreed to act as middlemen in the trade between the French and the Dakota. In return, the Dakota allowed the Ojibwe to settle in northern Wisconsin, including the important villages of Lac du Flambeau and Lac Courte Oreilles.[4]

The Ojibwe-Dakota entente lasted almost sixty years. Eventually, however, the Dakota found other ways to acquire European trade goods, causing Dakota alliances with the Ojibwe, Ottawa, and Potawatomi to weaken. The construction of French trading posts in Dakota lands eliminated the need for the Ojibwe as middlemen. When Pierre Gautier de Varennes, Sieur de La Vérendrye, set up a base of operations for exploration and trade in Cree and Assiniboine territory, the Ojibwe were pressured by the Cree, Assiniboine, Ottawa, and Potawatomi to side with those tribes in their conflicts with the Dakota.

The Dakota-Ojibwe entente erupted into war in 1736.[5] Eventually, the Ojibwe, in concert with the Ottawa, Potawatomi, Cree, and Assiniboine, began to push the Dakota westward. Ojibwe territory expanded into the heart of what would eventually become Minnesota and beyond. New Ojibwe villages were established at Sandy Lake, Mille Lacs, and Leech Lake—formerly prominent Dakota communities.

In 1800 the Ojibwe and Dakota were still engaged in hostilities (especially along the Red River), but their territories in Wisconsin and central Minnesota were fairly well accepted. There were casualties every year, but not on the scale seen in the mid-eighteenth century, when entire villages were wiped out on both sides. Warfare and diplomatic missions with the Dakota were important endeavors for Ojibwe leaders at this time, and even Ojibwe diplomacy with the Americans and the British focused primarily on relations with the Dakota.

Bagone-giizhig the Elder's father was a common Ojibwe man named Bakwene (Smoke). His Ojibwe mother's name has been lost.

Bakwene's maternal grandfather may have been a chief at Madeline Island, but this probably would shed minimal light on his rise to power. Bagone-giizhig was born a common man.[6]

Around 1820, he moved to Metaawangaagamaag (Sandy Lake, Minnesota) with his new wife and his older brother Zoongakamig (Strong Ground). Bagone-giizhig the Elder killed a Dakota man in war at an early age, earning an eagle feather and a seat in war councils. Reinforcing this new status, he and his brother Zoongakamig rapidly acquired reputations as courageous, even reckless, participants in Ojibwe military actions against the Dakota.[7]

Missionary Alfred Brunson first met Bagone-giizhig in 1838 before Brunson became Indian agent at La Pointe. Based on encounters and conversations with Bagone-giizhig before he became a chief, Brunson commented in depth about Bagone-giizhig's character and force of personality:

> [He] was distinguished for his eloquence, wisdom, and force of argument. His daring exploits on the war-path, the chase, and in personal encounters, as well as his boldness and force in council, naturally drew around him the young men of his tribe, who admired such feats and traits of character, and who acknowledged him as a leader. Like other demagogues, in their aspirations for distinction and notoriety, he moulded the minds of his admirers and adherents as he desired, and his superior talent and tact at this, and his success in it, could hardly fail to create in him an ambition for position and distinction among his own people, even if it had not been born in him.[8]

Intelligent, brave, loquacious, and ambitious, Bagone-giizhig made a universally powerful impression on nearly everyone he met. Brunson speculated, "Had Hole-in-the-Day been favored with an education, he would have been distinguished among the great men of the world." In *Harper's New Monthly Magazine,* John George Nicolay, Abraham Lincoln's private secretary and biographer, wrote about him: "Originally he had been a common Indian; but by his prowess on the war-path against the Sioux, the hereditary enemies of his tribe, by his daring in battle, and his oratory in council, he became an O-ge-mah [chief]."[9]

In the early 1820s, the principal chief of the Sandy Lake Ojibwe was Babiizigindibe (Curly Head). He was a member of the crane clan, which had totemic and hereditary claims to chieftainship. Although he had a lifetime of experience gathering the support of his people, he had no children.[10] Babiizigindibe began to pay special attention to Bagone-giizhig and Zoongakamig, giving them extra responsibilities and honors as his *oshkaabewisag,* a clearly established position in nineteenth-century Ojibwe society. The word *oshkaabewis* has been translated as "messenger," "helper," and "official." Bagone-giizhig the Elder and Zoongakamig carried Babiizigindibe's pipe to official functions, served as his messengers in gathering war parties, and accompanied the chief everywhere. Babiizigindibe grew increasingly attached to them and treated them as his own children.

At Sandy Lake, Bagone-giizhig married into two highly respected families. He married the daughter of Bookowaabide (Broken Tooth), another prominent Sandy Lake chief, and he also married Zaagaji-wekwe (Coming Over the Hill Woman), the daughter of highly respected Leech Lake chief Eshkibagikoonzh (Flat Mouth).[11]

Polygamy, a common practice among the Ojibwe at the time, was a custom born out of necessity. Male mortality rates were high because of warfare, travel, and activities such as fishing on thin ice, and the gendered division of labor placed serious work demands on women who needed help with all their responsibilities. It was more common for a man to marry two or three sisters rather than women from different families.[12] Most likely Bagone-giizhig also used two marriages in part as a way to advance his political aspirations. His son would do the same thing when he became an adult, causing one of the hereditary chiefs from an adjacent community to remark, "If I was a woman, you would marry me."[13]

Through his position as *oshkaabewis* to Babiizigindibe and through his marriages, Bagone-giizhig began to acquire status and a reputation among his people. He was still far from having extensive authority as a war or civil chief, but he was becoming recognized as a leader.

In 1820, Bagone-giizhig the Elder gained wide, but exaggerated, attention for his role in a showdown between British and American forces at Sault Ste. Marie, which the Ojibwe called *Bawatig,* meaning "the rapids." (Primary source materials often use Ojibwe terms, including the locative form of the name — *Bawatigong,* meaning "at the rapids.") A large Minnesota Ojibwe expedition went to Sault Ste.

Marie (where Lake Superior connects with Lake Huron) to treat with American officials, including expedition leader Lewis Cass (governor of Michigan Territory), Henry Schoolcraft (geologist), Dr. Alexander Woolcott Jr. (Indian agent from Chicago), Captain David B. Douglass (U.S. Army Corps of Engineers), Charles C. Trowbridge (assistant to Captain Douglass), James D. Doty (expedition secretary), and others.[14] Bagone-giizhig still served as *oshkaabewis* to the principal Sandy Lake chief, Babiizigindibe, at this time. Trowbridge later claimed that Bagone-giizhig did not accompany the expedition. Cass, Doty, and Schoolcraft did not report on Bagone-giizhig's presence or role at the event. But Alfred Brunson, who was not there, claimed that Bagone-giizhig not only was present, but that he took charge. Although it seems likely that Bagone-giizhig was in attendance but not a conspicuous participant, Brunson's account became very popular and influenced later perceptions among Americans.[15]

After the War of 1812, the British had continued to pay annuities to Indians in the United States to ingratiate them and maintain their allegiance in the event of another war with the United States.[16] To stymie the payment in 1820 and to assert American presence along the Canadian border, Lewis Cass, the superintendent of Indian Affairs for the Northwest, led the expedition of forty-two American soldiers, interpreters, and domestic attendants to Sault Ste. Marie to intercept a British trade shipment to the Ojibwe, including Sandy Lake residents.

When Cass arrived at Sault Ste. Marie, he found a large Ojibwe encampment of two or three thousand people waiting for their promised annuity payments. A British flag flew overhead. Cass stormed into the camp, tore down and trampled the British flag, hoisted the American flag, and demanded that Indians loyal to the United States step up and help him defend the Stars and Stripes. This was foolish. Most Ojibwe had sided with the British in the War of 1812, and those gathered at Sault Ste. Marie in 1820 were looking forward to their British annuities. If the Minnesota Ojibwe from Sandy Lake had not intervened, Cass and his entire entourage may well have been killed.

According to Cass, the Sandy Lake Ojibwe delegation did not favor trade or close diplomatic ties with the Americans over the British. They had never met Cass and had no reason to protect him. But they had seen trade goods in the American canoes, they knew the power of the United States, and they sensed Cass's influence as its representative.

After Cass's dramatic declaration, the Sandy Lake chiefs and *oshkaabewisag* saw an opportunity, and they acted. About a hundred men rushed to Cass's side. Since most of the Ojibwe assembled did not want to fight other Ojibwe people, Cass was spared, and the British were not allowed to land. Some Canadian Indians hoped later to capture and steal the contents of the warehouse and navy boat, but the Sandy Lake delegation's support of the Americans prevented looting.[17]

Cass promptly returned the favor to the Sandy Lakers. He distributed the trade goods he had brought among the Indians who had not sided with the British. Cass rewarded Bagone-giizhig's people with "a liberal distribution of goods."[18]

Lewis Cass knew that the Sandy Lake Ojibwe had saved his life, forced British officials to stay in Canada with their goods, and promoted American interests among other Ojibwe delegations. The reputation and status of the entire band and its chiefs and *oshkaabewisag* was elevated with the Americans and other Ojibwe groups. Brunson's probably apocryphal account of the event gave special, if unwarranted, credit to Bagone-giizhig the Elder for avoiding a serious confrontation: "Discovering that Hole-in-the-Day was not a regular or hereditary chief, and feeling that his daring, bravery, and evident influence over the tribe demanded recognition and reward, he [Cass] elevated him to that rank and dignity, and gave him a flag and a medal in presence of them all." According to Brunson, Bagone-giizhig the Elder, a mere *oshkaabewis* to Babiizigindibe, was awarded a chief's medal and an American flag.[19]

Years later Bagone-giizhig the Elder would proudly display the medal and flag given the Sandy Lake delegation. Whether he was present or he simply acquired the flag and medal as an inheritance from his chief, Bagone-giizhig used the fabled event to bolster his own reputation with both American and Ojibwe leaders. He was beginning to acquire a reputation among American officials as someone of importance, and this perception would later help him gain leverage at treaty negotiations. His bravery in battle and his emergence as an orator would further enhance his reputation, but he was still far from being considered a chief. It would take one more major event in 1825 for Bagone-giizhig the Elder to establish himself in that role.

CLAIMING POSITION: BAGONE-GIIZHIG AND THE
1825 TREATY OF PRAIRIE DU CHIEN

Following the War of 1812, American military officials sought to so-lidify control of the Great Lakes region, which was all unceded Indian land that had been an exclusively British trade zone since the Revolutionary War. American officials conveniently ignored the fact that Indian people throughout the territory had ceded nothing in the course of British-American hostilities. As a part of the post-1812 assertion of American presence, U.S. officials were willing to trade and treat with the Indians and eventually gained permission from the Dakota to establish Fort Snelling near present-day Minneapolis. Construction of the fort began in 1819 under Lieutenant Colonel Henry Leavenworth and was finished under Colonel Josiah Snelling in 1825. Once completed, the fort was garrisoned and staffed with U.S. soldiers and a new Indian agent—Major Lawrence Taliaferro.[20]

In his first seven years on the job, Taliaferro arranged no fewer than ten separate Ojibwe-Dakota peace conferences.[21] Although every effort ended in miserable failure, his exertions had major repercussions on Ojibwe-Dakota relations and Bagone-giizhig's rise to power.[22] Taliaferro's council held at Prairie du Chien in 1825 proved especially noteworthy, more because of who came and what the various Indian delegates said than for the importance of the document they signed.[23] It was the Treaty of Prairie du Chien, signed August 19, 1825, and the death of Babiizigindibe only a few weeks later, on September 5, that projected Bagone-giizhig the Elder into the center of Ojibwe diplomacy and prepared people for his ascendancy to the status of chief.

In 1825, Bagone-giizhig the Elder and Zoongakamig accompanied Babiizigindibe to Prairie du Chien as his *oshkaabewisag.* The chief had been summoned by U.S. officials who wanted several tribes to treat with one another and with the government. Lewis Cass and William Clark (commissioner of Indian Affairs, explorer, soldier, and territorial governor) hoped that through establishing a lasting peace between the Ojibwe and Dakota, a profitable trade could be more easily maintained and white settlement could advance westward more easily.[24]

Since Europeans had first entered the Great Lakes region, the Ojibwe had engaged in steady trade with the Americans, who were successfully asserting control over most of the trade south of the Great Lakes by the 1820s. The Ojibwe were dependent on trading first with the French, then with the British, and finally with the Americans in order to maintain their technological advantage in manufactured weapons against the Dakota. The Ojibwe also sought to maintain their standard of living, which had been buoyed by the influx of domestic trade goods such as metal traps, tools, containers, and woven cloth. The Ojibwe accepted Americans as players in Ojibwe politics because trade was important to the Ojibwe livelihood.

While the Treaty of Prairie du Chien appeared to be the first major occasion that the Ojibwe allowed the United States to intervene in Ojibwe affairs, the Ojibwe themselves saw the treaty not so much as an intervention but as a chance to impress American officials with their military and diplomatic power and to protect their trade relationship. The treaty would cede no territory to the United States; it merely would draw lines between Ojibwe and Dakota lands.

Bagone-giizhig made his first marks as an official diplomat when the treaty commissioners Lewis Cass, who knew Bagone-giizhig by reputation and personal acquaintance, and William Clark (commissioner of Indian Affairs) tried to agree upon boundaries between Ojibwe and Dakota territories to the east of the Red River. At the meeting, however, Bookowaabide (Broken Tooth) claimed Ojibwe possession of all of the Rum River, Crow Wing River, Red River, Sheyenne River, and Devils Lake (North Dakota). This was equivalent to the Ojibwe drawing a line from Fort Snelling to Minot, North Dakota, and claiming all the land north of it (including present-day St. Cloud and the entire Otter Tail Lake region). Cass seemed surprised at the large claim and asked by what right the Ojibwe claimed such a massive expanse of Dakota land. Bagone-giizhig the Elder rose and proclaimed, "My father! We claim it upon the same ground that you claim this country from the British King—*by conquest.* We drove them from the country by force of arms, and have since occupied it; and they cannot, and dare not, try to dispossess us of our habitations." Cass, who seemed heavily influenced by Bagone-giizhig's bold statement, immediately replied, "Then you have a right to it." When concluded, the Treaty of Prairie du Chien drew boundaries on terms highly favorable to the Mississippi Ojibwe.[25]

Bagone-giizhig the Elder claimed later in life that if the Treaty of Prairie du Chien had not been drawn up, the Dakota would have been pushed completely out of Minnesota. Ojibwe missionary and historian George Copway reported in 1850 that Bagone-giizhig "used to confidently affirm that he would have made his village at St. Peters, and the hunting grounds of his young men would have extended far into the western plains of the Siouxs."[26]

The successful U.S. diplomatic mission to Prairie du Chien turned sour after the various parties dispersed. On their way home, many of the Indian delegates got terribly sick, and rumors of intentional food poisoning by American officials spread rapidly. One of Bagone-giizhig's wives, his father (Bakwene), and Sandy Lake chief Babiizig-indibe perished. Just before he died on September 5, 1825, Babiizi-gindibe's entourage stopped at Lake Pepin. There Babiizigindibe called his *oshkaabewisag* to his side and told them to watch over his people after he departed for the spirit world. Babiizigindibe was buried above the Falls of St. Anthony (in present-day Minneapolis) in accordance with Ojibwe war custom, sitting up and facing west.[27]

Returning to central Minnesota, Bagone-giizhig the Elder and his brother Zoongakamig began to assert power among the Sandy Lake Band. Although their claims to leadership were not based on tradi-tional Ojibwe hereditary ascension, most people from Sandy Lake were unwilling to dispute the dying words of their childless former chief.

It is not known just how the people of Sandy Lake formally trans-ferred leadership. George Copway referred to an Ojibwe system of electing a new chief in newly conquered territory, and Charles Trow-bridge, who accompanied Henry Rowe Schoolcraft's expedition in 1820, claimed that a particular system was used not just to elect a chief for new territory but also when a hereditary chief's bloodline had expired. Trowbridge noted the importance of wisdom and elo-quence in a chief's election.[28]

Bagone-giizhig had those qualities in abundance, but there is no evidence of elections like those described by Copway and Trow-bridge. There is also no evidence of serious attempts to promote a more distant blood relative or someone of the same totemic clan. Bagone-giizhig's ascension would be a break with custom, but the culture of leadership was changing, and Bagone-giizhig would play a role in molding the change himself. Because of his diplomatic talent, his reputation in war, and the dying wish of the last hereditary chief of his band, he claimed leadership.

Julius T. Clark, who did not meet Bagone-giizhig the Elder until 1843, claimed that Bagone-giizhig was "head chief" of his band as well as the entire region. Clark wrote that Bagone-giizhig "did not occupy this position by hereditary right, but by the common voice of the nation, aided by his own restless ambition and love of distinction. For . . . the Indians while nominally recognizing the hereditary nature of chieftainship, are by no means confined to it, and a man of aspiring and really superior character, has it . . . in his power to reach the goal of his ambition, irrespective of the accidents of birth." Clark's statement suggests that Bagone-giizhig's chieftainship enjoyed the support of his people's "common voice" and that even if no election process was involved, the chief exerted some effort to build consensus.[29]

From 1825 to 1843, Bagone-giizhig must have worked hard at building that base of support, since it would not have happened automatically. Clark's personal observances of the chief also suggest strong character, oratorical ability and intelligence that was unique and, in Clark's estimation, extraordinary. Exercising his claim to leadership and acquiring the respect of his constituents was a long process for Bagone-giizhig the Elder. Since Ojibwe chieftainship was traditionally passed down paternally from father to son, Bagone-giizhig may have married into the families of chiefs and even been treated like a son by at least one chief, but he did not have a traditional claim, in spite of the powerful and respected families with which he was linked. Bookowaabide (Broken Tooth) and Gwiiwizhenzhish (Bad Boy) were considered the traditional chiefs of the Sandy Lake Ojibwe, and the positions of Bagone-giizhig the Elder and Zoonga-kamig were significant but culturally subordinate.[30]

Bagone-giizhig ascended in position slowly and carefully, apparently conscious not to upset other Ojibwe leaders in the early years of his civil and war chieftainship. He and his brother always acted in concert with Bookowaabide and Gwiiwizhenzhish, but through his almost reckless bravery in war and his charisma in council, Bagone-giizhig the Elder won the respect and loyalty of many Indian people from Sandy Lake and elsewhere.

Oratorical prowess seems to have been especially influential. Clark heard Bagone-giizhig speak on several occasions, and he described the chief's powerful oratory this way:

When [Bagone-giizhig] began to speak, he was very deliber-
ate, and his voice calm, and his manners mild and gentle as
a woman's; but as he continued speaking, his animation and
energy increased, until he finally poured forth a torrent of elo-
quence, such as I had never heard before. As his chest heaved
and eye glowed with the fervor of his thoughts, his right arm
bare and extended, and his mantle, like a Roman toga, hanging over the other shoulder and around his body, he looked
the personification of *eloquence* itself... [His people] would
quietly sit and listen with an occasional murmur of approval
of the truth of what he was saying; but when it suited his
purpose to appeal to their passions, he would rouse himself
up to all the fire and impetuosity of his nature, and while
his eye flashed and his features changed with the changing
emotions which glowed within his own breast, those passions
and emotions ran like an electric shock through his auditors,
until unable to restrain themselves, they would literally leap
from their seats, and in a frenzy of excitement, fill the air with
their savage yells.

Clark further wrote in his reminiscences that "the greatness of ge-
nius is inherent, and not the result of nationality or of any factitious
circumstances of birth or education. Quickness of perception, firm-
ness of purpose, comprehensiveness of mind, incorruptible fidelity,
nobleness of disposition—these, and other like qualities, make the
truly great man, whether civilized or savage; and the career of Hole-
in-the-Day... developed these traits of character."[31]

Modern-day oral history interviews with Ojibwe elders Melvin
Eagle of Mille Lacs and Archie Mosay of St. Croix expressed remarkably similar recollections of Bagone-giizhig. Both reported that he
was a gifted and intelligent speaker, that he was proud and even
vain, that he was cautious about offending other Ojibwe leaders, and
that he tried to work with Ojibwe who held traditional positions of
power at Sandy Lake.

Bagone-giizhig the Elder used the flux in Ojibwe leadership
paradigms to empower himself. When the time came, he would be
able to pass along that position, as well as many of his most notable
character traits, to his son, Bagone-giizhig the Younger. This is one
of the paradoxes of the Elder's chieftainship. He thwarted and bent
ancient customs of leadership and came to power outside them. At

the same time, he successfully used Ojibwe concepts of leadership and tradition to reinforce his political position and pass it on within his own bloodline. He was both a product and an agent of cultural and political change, steadfastly traditional and overtly modern. He was self-serving yet sensitive to the needs of his constituents.

Had Bagone-giizhig the Elder been born in the 1700s, he would not have been able to ascend in political authority in the same way. Membership in a particular clan had been far more important to leadership authority than military prowess or oratorical ability. Only men from certain families of the *maang doodem* (loon clan) and *aji-jaak doodem* (crane clan) could become chiefs. Bagone-giizhig was of the *noke doodem* (bear clan) and lacked traditional leadership lineage. And as Bagone-giizhig's influence grew, other Ojibwe leaders, especially from Mille Lacs, began to resent his rise to power because it was not grounded in Ojibwe tradition.[32]

Brunson, an outsider, observed that "the chieftainship is hereditary; but, like greater monarchies, sometimes a man of superior prowess enthrones himself. This was the case with Hole-in-the-Day, now the most influential chief of the [Ojibwe] nation." But neither the oral tradition nor archival records validate Brunson's claim that Bagone-giizhig was the most influential chief, and many other men had positions of power and influence in the Ojibwe communities of the day. Moreover, Bagone-giizhig had not simply enthroned himself. He had been asked by his dying chief to help lead the people. There must also have been some truth in Brunson's interpretation. If not the most influential chief in the eyes of the Ojibwe, Bagone-giizhig was certainly an influential leader in the eyes of American officials. Those officials wanted to negotiate with people who would serve their purposes, and Bagone-giizhig seemed willing to do that. His central role in many treaty negotiations reflected his assertion of authority and American recognition of that claim, more than any widespread support among Ojibwe people.[33]

While Bagone-giizhig's rise to prominence surely represented a break with Ojibwe tradition, it is possible to argue that his acquisition of chieftainship also indicated ways in which non-Indian culture and politics began to heavily influence Ojibwe society and reshape leadership paradigms. As clans were devalued as a condition of leadership, political connections outside the community became increasingly valued. Assent to civil chieftainship became more fluid, and Bagone-giizhig the Elder used that fluidity to his advantage.

WAXING POWER: BAGONE-GIIZHIG'S CHIEFTAINSHIP BEFORE THE LAND CESSIONS

Between the Treaty of Prairie du Chien in 1825 and the Treaty of 1837, Bagone-giizhig the Elder's political energies focused on the complex relationship between the Ojibwe, Dakota, and American nations. Known for his boldness, Bagone-giizhig killed perhaps forty Dakota with his own hands in his lifetime. One of his daring exploits included an incident near Fort Snelling in which he approached a group of Dakota alone and in broad daylight, caught a straggler, killed, and scalped him. He then fled his pursuers by canoe, swimming, and finally hiding behind sheets of water at Minnehaha Falls. He was not a single-mindedly belligerent leader, however, and from 1825 to 1837 he often worked diligently to establish and maintain Ojibwe-Dakota peace.[34]

In 1826, a peace conference was held at Fond du Lac to gain wider acceptance of the Prairie du Chien agreement.[35] Shortly thereafter an Ojibwe group approached Fort Snelling on a mission of peace. Women and children were among the native delegation, a new development heralding the great degree of security felt by the Ojibwe. They were ambushed by a group of Dakota within view of the fort, and several Ojibwe were killed. According to eyewitness William Joseph Snelling, son of the Fort Snelling commander, "Men, women and children were indiscriminately butchered." The reasons for the Dakota attack are not known, but the reactions to the event are well documented.[36]

On May 28, 1827, a party of two dozen Ojibwe including Bagone-giizhig the Elder, Eshkibagikoonzh (Flat Mouth), Zoongakamig (Strong Ground), and their families approached Fort Snelling.[37] (Bagone-giizhig had an especially close relationship with his first wife and eldest daughter, whom he frequently brought with him on trips despite travel hardships and danger.) The group had come mainly to seek redress for the killing of the Ojibwe in the previous year. The party was willing to forego vengeance and seek recompense through "covering the dead," a custom in which the deceased's family was offered tribute, usually trade goods and blankets.[38]

The Ojibwe delegation was well received by Indian agent Law-rence Taliaferro and Colonel Josiah Snelling and it took shelter within the fort while preparing for council. Dakota chief Shakopee and nine others approached the fort, and Eshkibagikoonzh invited them for a feast of meat, corn, and maple sugar. The Dakota stayed until dark, sharing their pipes and socializing with their Ojibwe hosts. As they prepared to leave, one of the Dakota held the door open while others fired a volley into a seated Ojibwe group. One man was murdered. Eight were wounded, including Bagone-giizhig, who suffered a life-long spinal condition from his injuries. His young daughter was mortally wounded in the groin and died six weeks later. Bagone-giizhig's heart ached for revenge—a feeling so strong that it influenced his actions for years to come. The Ojibwe delegation could barely restrain the grieving chief.[39]

The Ojibwe were also deeply disturbed because they believed they had been under the protection of the Americans and had gath-ered in peace. Zoongakamig told Colonel Snelling: "Father, you know that two summers ago we attended a great council at Prairie du Chien, where by the advice of our white friends we made peace with the Sioux. We were then told that the Americans would guarantee our safety under your flag. We came here under that insurance. But fa-ther, look at your floor, it is stained with the blood of my people, shed under your walls. I look up and see your flag over us. If you are a great and powerful people, why do you not protect us? If not, of what use are all these soldiers?"[40]

Although there were only eight Dakota perpetrators, Snelling immediately dispatched Major Nathan Clark to gather up as many Dakota as possible. Thirty Dakota men were quickly arrested and imprisoned in the fort. On May 29, a large group of Dakota who came to the fort witnessed a brutal example of frontier justice. The thirty Dakota prisoners were paraded before the Ojibwe visitors, and two identified assailants were given to the Ojibwe. The prisoners' hands were tied, and they were made to run. The Ojibwe then shot them dead outside the fort, stabbed them, wiped their blood on the faces and blankets of the Ojibwe dead, and scalped the prisoners.

Colonel Snelling instructed American soldiers to dispose of the bodies, which they threw over the bluff into the Mississippi River. Among the Dakota prisoners was an elder named Eagle Head, whose nephew had just been killed. He feared that the Americans were prepared to turn the remaining Dakota prisoners over to the Ojibwe, although in William Joseph Snelling's version of the story, Eagle Head was more frightened by the prospect of losing his own life. Eagle Head told Colonel Josiah Snelling that the two men just killed were not responsible for the attack and that he would find and bring in the men who were. The colonel released him.

Eagle Head found the leader of the Dakota attack in his teepee and told him: "You have acted like a dog...Some one must die for what you have done and it is better that your lives should be taken than that others should die for your folly. There are no worse men than you in our nation. Go with me like men or I will kill you where you sit." Eagle Head then cocked his gun and, holding his war club in the other hand, brought the two young men back to Fort Snelling. They offered no resistance. When the two were presented to the Ojibwe, Eshkibagikoonzh claimed that no further retribution was needed because two Ojibwe and two Dakota had been killed, thus evening the score. Eshkibagikoonzh feared that the Dakota would be enraged by further violence and that the Ojibwe might be ambushed and slaughtered on their way home.[41]

Bagone-giizhig and some of his entourage had different thoughts. Zhimaaganishens (Little Soldier) said that he had no such fear and that the Dakota had killed his brother the year before. He told the Dakota to run for their lives, and when they did, he executed them, just as the other two Dakota men had been killed the day before. After the grisly episode was over, the Ojibwe managed to return home in safety.[42]

Events that summer caused a series of reactions that greatly worsened Ojibwe-Dakota relations. Colonel Snelling and Taliaferro's poor handling of the affair increased the animosity of the Ojibwe and Dakota for each other and for white neighbors. The Ojibwe were upset about having been attacked twice at Fort Snelling, once under the explicit protection of the Americans. The Dakota were upset about four of their number having been sacrificed for the killing of two Ojibwe.[43]

As a direct result of the 1827 Dakota-Ojibwe violence, the United States implemented a new policy designed to minimize future interactions between the two tribes. The policy transferred the official site where the Minnesota Ojibwe would interact with the U.S. government from Fort Snelling to distant Sault Ste. Marie at the Michigan-Canada border. Explorer, scholar, and Indian agent Henry R. Schoolcraft

Lawrence Taliaferro, ca. 1830. Taliaferro, Indian agent stationed at Fort Snelling, played a central role in Ojibwe-Dakota war and peace. Bagone-giizhig the Elder and Taliaferro met and communicated frequently.

opened a subagency at La Pointe, Wisconsin, and put his brother-in-law in charge there. While La Pointe was somewhat closer, the trip was still long and difficult for Minnesota's Sandy Lake, Leech Lake, and Red Lake Ojibwe. They had to make a much more arduous trip to consult with the American government and collect government gifts and annuities, and they were furious. Because many Minnesota Ojibwe distrusted the Indian agent at La Pointe and did not want to deal with an intermediary to Schoolcraft, they opted to go to Sault Ste.

Marie when necessary. Since Taliaferro and Schoolcraft were bitter rivals, the change of venue also infuriated Taliaferro. Eshkibagikoonzh
and other Ojibwe, however, believed that Taliaferro had incited the
Dakota to violence against the Ojibwe. Schoolcraft made the most of
their suspicions by ensuring that every important official active in
Indian affairs was aware of the allegations.[44]

Although the Ojibwe were angry about the Fort Snelling attacks
and the transfer of their agency, Bagone-giizhig the Elder restrained
his desire for retribution for his daughter's death. He and his brother
refused to participate in vengeance and encouraged their followers
to do likewise, hoping to maintain peace with the Dakota. Bagone-
giizhig's nonbelligerent attitude reflected his belief that peace brought
benefits in terms of life and livelihood. He also knew that the Americans were replacing British trade networks across the continent
and that traders and public officials were less likely to go into areas
that were violent. The Ojibwe's economic future depended on this
trade.

Eshkibagikoonzh (Flat Mouth) the Elder did not campaign for
peace like Bagone-giizhig the Elder. Most of the Leech Lake and Red
Lake Ojibwe, as well as some Sandy Lake and Gull Lake Ojibwe, continued to press and attack the Dakota in 1828 and 1829. In fact Bagone-
giizhig the Elder told Taliaferro that his own people attempted to kill
him for trying to prevent retaliation against the Dakota.[45]

While publicly urging peace in 1827 and 1828, Bagone-giizhig the
Elder himself wrestled with personal despair because of his first
wife's and daughter's deaths. He was gripped by mental depression
for nearly a year. He largely retreated from diplomacy and war. Then
a life-affirming event shook him from his fog of sorrow. One of his
wives gave birth to a son, Gwiiwizens (Boy). Bagone-giizhig doted
on Gwiiwizens and brought him on most of his diplomatic missions
as soon as he was old enough to travel. Gwiiwizens would learn firsthand from his father the tribulations and challenges of Ojibwe leadership, accumulating experiences at a young age that would later
help mold him into the powerful leader Bagone-giizhig the Younger.

The death of Sandy Lake's Bookowaabide (Broken Tooth) in 1827
carried consequences for Bagone-giizhig. Although Gwiiwizhenzhish
(Bad Boy) had claimed hereditary right to the principal chieftainship
there, the community was factionalized, and many did not follow
him as passionately as they had Babiizigindibe or Bookowaabide.

Bookowaabide's passing created a power vacuum that Bagone-giizhig the Elder tried to fill. With a son to whom he could bequeath his power one day and with room to increase the scope of that power, Bagone-giizhig shook off the despair that had gripped him after his losses and pushed himself further to the forefront of Ojibwe politics.

In 1829 Bagone-giizhig temporarily dropped his peace efforts after Dakota attacks. In one of the small attacks, largely along the Crow Wing River and Otter Tail Lake, Bagone-giizhig the Elder's uncle and cousins were killed. He and other Mississippi Band Ojibwe decided to seek revenge. Bagone-giizhig's personal desire for revenge combined with his rediscovered political ambition. He would satisfy his people's need for justice at the same time that he sought to improve their political foundation with the Americans. Bagone-giizhig the Elder himself killed and scalped a lone Dakota hunter in the Crow Wing River country in 1830. He was compelled to take action to right the loss of his uncle, cousins, and daughter, but he did not wish to create greater animosity than already existed, especially with the Americans. To this end, he proved to the Americans and his own people that he was as bold in effecting peace as he was in engineering war. Bagone-giizhig went to Fort Snelling, confessed his actions, and submitted to whatever punishment Taliaferro might mete out. To the surprise of many Americans, Taliaferro said: "I know that you have been wounded yourself, your daughter shot before your face—by the Sioux; you lost your father here and your wife and uncle and two cousins. You have behaved well, and done but one bad act in ten years. You now give yourself up to me and have acted with bravery and goodwill. I will let you return to your family."[46]

Bagone-giizhig returned home. He now commanded a stronger leadership position among his people and a strengthened relationship with Taliaferro. He continued to visit with American officials at Fort Snelling despite the Ojibwe agency's transfer to La Pointe. With assurances of support from Taliaferro, he once again pressed for peace and sought to dissuade his people from waging war against the Dakota.

Ojibwe-Dakota relations were diplomatically complex, however, and even Bagone-giizhig could not control their outcome. White traders active in Ojibwe and Dakota territory often exacerbated tensions between the two tribes and occasionally sought to escalate hostilities in order to disrupt their competition's trade, in spite of the risks to the stability of their own trade networks. William Aitkin, a prominent trader among the Ojibwe, for instance, had a personal feud with Joseph Renville Sr., a French-Dakota trader in the Minnesota River country. Aitkin had married an Ojibwe woman, and Renville had married a Dakota, and through their family connections and power as weapons traders, they used the tense situation between the Ojibwe and Dakota to get at each other.

In 1829, Aitkin offered the Sandy Lake Ojibwe a large supply of trade goods and ammunition if they would send a war party of a hundred or more men against the Wah'petonwan Dakota at Lac qui Parle, thereby disrupting Renville's trading operations there. In addition to the Ojibwe and Dakota competing for resources in the land between Lac qui Parle and the Crow Wing River, Aitkin and Renville competed for their business in the Otter Tail Lake region, where the Ojibwe had begun to trade with the Dakota and with the latter's traders at Lac qui Parle and Lake Traverse. Aitkin felt threatened by the possibility of his business being further undercut, and by sponsoring the attack at Lac qui Parle, he hoped to increase Ojibwe-Dakota tension, thereby making it harder for friendly trade between the Ojibwe and Renville at Otter Tail and Lac qui Parle. The Ojibwe attack, which was temporarily successful, was one of many occasions in which private and public traders abused their positions of authority in order to increase Indian bloodshed for personal gain.[47]

Ojibwe-Dakota warfare continued through the 1830s. In spite of continued tribal conflict, Bagone-giizhig the Elder and the Dakota leader Little Crow began to correspond through scribes and interpreters about how to arrange lasting peace between their nations. The Dakota, however, had no choice but to focus most of their time and energy on the escalating pressure from the United States to cede their territory.[48]

The 1830 Treaty of Prairie du Chien focused on peace and land cessions from the represented tribes. The Ojibwe were not officially involved, and many Dakota did not participate. In fact, a Mdewakantonwan Dakota leader named Medicine Bottle led a contingent of Dakota warriors up the St. Croix River against the Ojibwe at the very time the official Dakota delegations were smoking the peace pipe at Prairie du Chien. Nevertheless, the Treaty of Prairie du Chien ushered in a new era in the region. All tribes would have to focus more and more energy on slowing American demands for their land.

Although Ojibwe-Dakota warfare continued, events would have been much more sanguine if the Ojibwe and Dakota had not been so concerned about American expansion.[49]

For the next two years, warfare between the Ojibwe and Dakota persisted but slowed considerably. Red Wing's Dakota community at Lake Pepin relocated to a safer position at nearby Sturgeon Lake, the only major shift in Ojibwe and Dakota village sites in Minnesota during this period. The occasional skirmishes between Ojibwe and Dakota forces that did take place were largely constrained to the Long Prairie River war road in central Minnesota. The Long Prairie River was one of the primary routes through which the Mississippi Ojibwe traveled to attack the Sisitonwan Dakota and the Ihanktonwan Nakota.[50]

The only large Ojibwe-Dakota battle in the early 1830s took place along this river. During the winter of 1832–33, Zoongakamig decided to break ranks with his brother Bagone-giizhig the Elder, who still advocated peace. Zoongakamig led an Ojibwe force from Sandy Lake. At the present-day Minnesota town of Long Prairie, they encountered a large group of Wah'petonwan Dakota. The Ojibwe killed nineteen and wounded forty. No Ojibwe died in the attack.

This was an especially large number of casualties for the Dakota, and the event led to escalation of Dakota-Ojibwe violence. There were several Dakota counterattacks directed primarily at Ojibwe villages at Sandy Lake and Mille Lacs. Tensions continued to escalate as the Dakota sought to avenge the loss of relatives. In 1835, a large group of Wah'petonwan Dakota approached an Ojibwe camp in the Crow Wing area under a flag of truce and then attacked, killing five Ojibwe. This further eroded the trust between nations that Bagone-giizhig the Elder and other Ojibwe leaders had tried to build.

Frustrated with the escalating violence, Bagone-giizhig began to increase pressure on Henry Schoolcraft, Lawrence Taliaferro, and other U.S. officials to assist him in trying to reduce tensions and bring peace. When Schoolcraft visited Ojibwe communities in 1832, he spoke at length with Eshkibagikoonzh (Flat Mouth) of Leech Lake. Bagone-giizhig was not present, but his advocacy helped Eshkibagikoonzh make a strong stand and thus indirectly influenced Schoolcraft. At Eshkibagikoonzh's insistence, Schoolcraft began preparations to demarcate the lines between Ojibwe and Dakota territory that had been agreed upon in the 1825 Treaty of Prairie du Chien.

Bagone-giizhig and Eshkibagikoonzh felt that this might help clarify territories, dissuade the Dakota from trespassing on Ojibwe lands, and discourage white officials and traders from instigating inter-tribal warfare. Eshkibagikoonzh in particular had complained to Schoolcraft at length about Dakota attacks and the role of Lawrence Taliaferro, William Aitkin, and Joseph Renville in encouraging and instigating intertribal violence.[51]

It took years of persistent diplomacy for Bagone-giizhig to have his request honored. In 1825, the first Treaty of Prairie du Chien had established the dividing lines between Ojibwe and Dakota territory. In 1832, Bagone-giizhig began to seriously petition U.S. officials to draw those lines. But it was not until 1835, almost eleven years after the treaty and four years after Bagone-giizhig's request, that survey-ors finally staked out a dividing line between the tribes. Perhaps not surprisingly, both tribes expected the line to be drawn differently than it eventually was, and they were unhappy with the result. Some from both tribes pulled up the surveying stakes. Bagone-giizhig and other advocates of peace had to seek other ways to achieve a dip-lomatic end to Ojibwe-Dakota violence, since treaties negotiated with white men seemed to be ineffective in changing Ojibwe-Dakota relations.[52]

From the death of Babiizigindibe after the 1825 Treaty of Prairie du Chien to the 1835 marking of the Ojibwe-Dakota boundary estab-lished in that treaty, Bagone-giizhig had helped limit intertribal war-fare in certain areas. He gained widespread recognition from U.S. officials and his own people as a powerful leader. Bagone-giizhig was fully equipped for decisive political action.

NEW BASE OF POWER: THE MOVE TO THE GULL LAKE REGION

From 1825 to 1835, Bagone-giizhig had demonstrated the caliber of his leadership potential to the Ojibwe, the Dakota, and the Americans through diplomatic and military savvy. The greatest boost to his posi-tion, however, came through a change at Bagone-giizhig's village of Sandy Lake that transformed Ojibwe leadership dynamics through-out Minnesota.

Sandy Lakers had wintered in the vicinity of Gull Lake, fifty-five miles southwest, as early as 1810 but never established a perma-nent village there. Babiizigindibe (Curly Head) considered himself a Sandy Laker throughout his life. However, in 1836, Bagone-giizhig moved from Sandy Lake to Swan River in the Gull Lake region near present-day Brainerd, Minnesota, and established a new Ojibwe village there. He and other Ojibwe leaders had frequented Gull Lake for twenty years, especially to hunt and fish in the winter months, but because Gull Lake was only thirty miles from the Treaty of Prairie du Chien line dividing Ojibwe and Dakota lands, in the summer months most Ojibwe found it too dangerous and so they stayed in Sandy Lake, Leech Lake, or Mille Lacs.

Bagone-giizhig's relocation was bold and risky, but he stood to benefit from it in significant ways. Although other Ojibwe leaders such as Gwiiwizhenzhish would continue to try to discredit Bagone-giizhig's claims to chieftainship, no longer would there be any in his home community to challenge him. He would be the undeniable primary leader of the new Ojibwe communities around Gull Lake.

Contests and resentments about his leadership became less vociferous and widespread. Ojibwe people began expanding throughout the Gull Lake region, setting up new villages at Rabbit Lake (north of Mille Lacs, west of Sandy Lake), Gull Lake, Swan River, the Crow Wing River, the Leaf River, and the Mississippi River. Counter to a common historical assumption that tribal land bases decreased after contact with the United States, the land base occupied and used by the Ojibwe under Bagone-giizhig increased throughout the early contact period.

Rich in game and fish, the Gull Lake region was strategically located near central Minnesota's major rivers that served as highways for trade, war, and diplomacy. Bagone-giizhig occupied the geographic center of political, economic, and military activities for the Mississippi Ojibwe. Because of Gull Lake's excellent location, white traders migrated to the area as well, establishing a new white settlement and trade center nearby at Crow Wing when the land was ceded in 1837. It became the northernmost white settlement on the Mississippi River and was populated equally with Ojibwe and whites. Because of the ease of transporting goods to Crow Wing, traders were able to offer Bagone-giizhig's people supplies at greatly reduced prices compared to those offered by Lake Superior–based traders.[53]

Other Ojibwe people from Sandy Lake, Mille Lacs, and Leech Lake began to flock to the Crow Wing and Gull Lake district. As the community grew, so did the influence and power of Bagone-giizhig the Elder. His brother Zoongakamig (Strong Ground) also joined the new village at Gull Lake. From this point on, however, Zoongaka-mig, though influential and older, functioned as a secondary leader who deferred to his brother on all important decisions. Bagone-giizhig also was gaining favor and influence with local traders and missionaries, and he forged friendships and even family relation-ships with them. Half-Ottawa missionary John Johnson, also known as Enami'egaabaw (Stands Praying), married Bagone-giizhig's niece Biiwaabiko-giizhigookwe (Iron Sky Woman) several years after John-son's arrival in Minnesota in 1834. Bagone-giizhig's power was grow-ing in all directions.[54]

The Ojibwe settlements at Gull Lake became permanent when Bagone-giizhig the Elder moved there in 1836. Through a strong de-fense against Dakota attacks, careful diplomacy, and a steady stream of new Ojibwe settlers, by 1838 Bagone-giizhig could claim undisputed control over a large area ranging along the Prairie du Chien line from the Crow Wing River to Long Prairie and north along the Mississippi almost to the greater Leech Lake region.[55]

Bagone-giizhig's move to the Gull Lake area brought major changes to the structure of Ojibwe communities in the entire region. Previ-ously, Ojibwe villages had been the nexus of political and economic interactions, and each village had a separate group of hereditary civil chiefs. However, Bagone-giizhig asserted chieftainship over a large region that contained many different villages, even Crow Wing, which was equally populated with whites. He traveled the area ex-tensively and went beyond his domain of natural influence to main-tain his position as regional chief. Never before had an Ojibwe leader claimed or successfully exerted a leadership position over so much territory, so many villages, or so many people.

With a new seat of power in the Gull Lake region and numerous followers, Bagone-giizhig the Elder continued to press for peace with some success. Although Ojibwe-Dakota warfare persisted through-out the 1830s, he was instrumental in slowing the tide of violence. In-dian agent Lawrence Taliaferro reported that during the 1830s there were far more instances of the Ojibwe and Dakota hunting together peacefully than fighting. In 1836, missionary Gideon Pond wrote, "There is not much war carried on between these two nations, yet they kill now and then."[56]

Helping Bagone-giizhig's peace efforts with the Dakota was a background escalation in Dakota hostilities with the Fox along the

16. EN-ME-GAH-BOWH. Who stands by his People. Rev. John Johnson.

Enami'egaabaw (Stands Praying), also known as John Johnson, ca. 1865. A missionary at Gull Lake and White Earth, Johnson was good friends with Bagone-giizhig the Elder, who adopted him as a son. He also married the chief's niece, Biiwaabiko-giizhigookwe (Iron Sky Woman). His relationship with Bagone-giizhig the Younger was far more strained and eventually became adversarial.

Iowa border that caused greater anxiety among the Mdewakanton-wan and other Dakota.[57] Moreover, frustration and disgust with the fatalities and stress of warfare were widespread among the Ojibwe and Dakota, both of whom were economically strained during the 1830s. Weakening demand for fur-bearing animals meant declining fur prices. Heavy harvesting had depleted fur-bearing animals in parts of Minnesota. The first Minnesota land cession treaties were also beginning to have an effect on fur and food harvesting. Adding to these factors was a surge in white settlement, which meant more competition for fewer resources in the same area. All these developments led to a decline in the economic status of both the Ojibwe and the Dakota, as well as less warfare. Tribal leaders had more pressing concerns such as maintaining adequate food supplies for their communities.

The two tribes continued to use much of the border region between their lands jointly. Both groups would hunt there, especially in the winter. But because the Ojibwe had greater numbers in the immediate area, they increased control over this region and pushed the joint-use area farther south. By 1838, when Bagone-giizhig had consolidated control over the Gull Lake region, the joint hunting area had shifted south to the Sauk and Crow rivers. At the same time, the Ojibwe from Leech Lake had pushed west, gaining exclusive use of Otter Tail Lake and eventually establishing a large settlement there. The growing Ojibwe settlement at Otter Tail Lake northwest of Gull Lake further strengthened Bagone-giizhig's communities in central Minnesota.[58]

Exactly when Ojibwe presence at Otter Tail Lake became secure is a subject of some debate. Most primary source documents say that the Ojibwe village was large and well established by 1830, but that it was constantly under threat of attack from the nearby Dakota and Nakota. In addition, there are numerous reports of the Ojibwe hunting a full day's march west of the Red River on the prairies of North Dakota and South Dakota. The Ojibwe and Dakota contended for possession of the Bois de Sioux River (just north of Lake Traverse on the western edge of present-day Minnesota).[59]

The Ojibwe, especially the Leech Lake Pillagers and those under the leadership of Bagone-giizhig the Elder, had found ways to press their domain farther south and west with a minimum of direct warfare with the Dakota. They did so by occupying joint-use areas and establishing new village sites closer and closer to the edge of Dakota lands. In many places, the joint-use areas had shrunk, with the bulk of the land going to the Ojibwe. In some cases, the joint-use area moved farther south. Although Bagone-giizhig advocated peace with the Dakota, he felt no qualms about keeping pressure on their lands. The Ojibwe expanded farther down the Mississippi River, with a new village established at the mouth of the Elk River in Morrison County, Minnesota (not the Elk River in Sherburne County, Minnesota). Between that location and the larger settlements around Gull Lake, the Mississippi Ojibwe had also established new villages at the mouth of the Nokasippi River and at the mouth of the Crow Wing River. The St. Croix and Mississippi Ojibwe had also set up new villages along the Snake River and farther down the Rum River, in addition to increasing their strength at Rice Lake in Aitkin County, Minnesota, and at Pokegama Lake. Leech Lake, Mille Lacs, Sandy Lake, Gull Lake, and newcomer Crow Wing remained the principal Minnesota Ojibwe settlements during this time, but Ojibwe domain was increasing, largely because of the peaceful yet purposeful dispossession of Dakota lands and joint-use areas.[60]

The decrease in Ojibwe-Dakota hostilities was not to last, however. Tensions always existed, even when they were at peace, so a small spark could light a large fire. Traders William Aitkin and Joseph Renville Sr., never on favorable terms, had become even more hostile toward each other from 1835 to 1836. Aitkin's business had become less profitable, and the increasing peace between the Ojibwe and the Dakota enabled Renville to outpace his rival. The Ojibwe who settled at Otter Tail Lake and Red Lake were regularly hunting far out on the prairies along the Sheyenne River (North Dakota). The Pillager Band Ojibwe at Otter Tail Lake had developed a good relationship with a large group of Wah'petonwan Dakota, with whom they hunted regularly. Large rendezvous of Ojibwe, Nakota, Dakota, and Assiniboine were common in the mid-1830s at Lake Traverse, Big Stone Lake, and Lac qui Parle. The relative peace between the Ojibwe and Dakota and Nakota in this region made it possible for the Ojibwe to trade with the Indians of the Oceti Sakowin (Seven Council Fires of the Sioux) and the white and mixed-blood traders among them. In 1836, Aitkin wrote to Ramsay Crooks, president of the American Fur Company, that he was withdrawing the American Fur

Company trading post from Otter Tail Lake because of competition from Lake Traverse, where the Ojibwe were trading at the Dakota post.[61]

Renville had been getting the upper hand in his feud with Aitkin, but Aitkin would not quietly give up. He had already paid one Ojibwe war party to attack Renville's post and was prepared to instigate further attacks. The feud between these traders eventually sparked widespread violence between the Ojibwe and the Dakota.

In 1835, Renville's brother was killed by a group of Ojibwe. It is not known if Aitkin instigated the attack, but he was not upset by it. Renville, for his part, blamed the Ojibwe and treated even the most peaceful of them trading at his post in a manner described by visitor George Featherstonhaugh as "obnoxious." Renville sponsored a revenge attack against the Ojibwe living in Aitkin's trading district in which, Bagone-giizhig reported, three Ojibwe people were killed and scalped at Elk Lake. One was a relative of Bagone-giizhig the Elder. Several other minor battles between the Ojibwe and the Dakota resulted from the feud between these two traders as well.

These incidents led many Ojibwe leaders from Leech Lake and Sandy Lake in particular to feel that American officials were as dangerous as Dakota leaders and that Ojibwe could trust neither whites nor other Indians to strive for peace. War seemed inevitable to some Ojibwe, and if there was to be one, they would fight to win. Large war parties formed at Leech Lake and Sandy Lake to seek vengeance for the Dakota attacks in the mid-1830s.[62]

Bagone-giizhig the Elder was deeply disturbed by the loss of his relative, and it stirred his lasting grief over the deaths of his wife, daughter, and uncle several years before. He was also disturbed by the willingness of white traders to meddle in Ojibwe affairs and the potential for escalating violence. He wanted a profitable peace and control over affairs in his land. Although pressured persistently to choose the warpath and by a growing sense of concern about Dakota attacks, he determined to give peace one more try.

So the Gull Lake Ojibwe did not join the Leech Lakers and Sandy Lakers in great numbers in war. Instead, Bagone-giizhig convinced the Dakota to "cover the dead" instead. In an unusual arrangement, the Dakota sponsoring the ceremony offered Bagone-giizhig's band usufructary or use rights to Dakota and Nakota lands in present-day

North Dakota and South Dakota as the Dakota payment to avoid further bloodshed and keep the peace.[63] The Ojibwe would be able to hunt there for several years in return for promising not to avenge the previous Dakota attacks on Gull Lake Ojibwe. The Ojibwe accepted the offer, and Bagone-giizhig the Elder and his followers began hunting on the prairies west of Lake Traverse. In 1837, Bagone-giizhig told the Wah'petonwan: "All nations as yet continue the practice of war, but as for me, I now abandon it. I hold firmly the hand of the Americans. If you, in the future, strike me twice or even three times, I will pass over and not revenge it. If wars should continue, you and I will not take part in them ... There shall be no more war in that part of the country lying between Pine Island and the place they called 'They shot them in the night.' Over this extent of country we will hold the pipe firmly."[64]

Bagone-giizhig the Elder's rise to power represented a remarkable triumph. Lacking the clan associations that would have facilitated his consolidation of power and overcoming the deaths of his daughter, wife, uncle, and other relatives, he showed intelligence and innovative strategies in leadership that brought peace, expanded territory, and, ultimately, changed the nature of Ojibwe leadership. In addition he built the villages in the Gull Lake region with speed and centrality of leadership never before seen by the Ojibwe. Now in his late thirties, he was personally evolving, and his people would be the primary beneficiaries. But his power as a leader and his success as a diplomat were soon to be tested. White men wanted Ojibwe land.

3

Testing His Mettle

Bagone-giizhig the Elder in the Early Treaty Period

> Hole-in-the-Day was the only man in the nation who was feared by
> the traders and Government officers. I do not mean that they feared
> personal injury, or were in danger of coming into personal conflict
> with him; but they feared his influence with his people.
> —JULIUS T. CLARK[1]

U ntil the late 1830s, American officials lacked the military power and diplomatic groundwork to seize Indian lands in Minnesota. But the declining fur trade put pressure on Indian communities to find other ways to acquire trade goods. Fort Snelling had established a firm American military presence near present-day St. Paul. Perhaps even more importantly, American treaty negotiators had come to know Minnesota's Ojibwe leaders and established a useful rapport with them.

THE TREATY OF 1837 AND ITS AFTERMATH

On July 29, 1837, the first major land cession treaty was signed with the Minnesota Ojibwe. The Treaty of 1837 was negotiated at St. Peters, near Fort Snelling, and signed by large delegations of the Ojibwe leadership from central and eastern Minnesota and western Wisconsin. Bagone-giizhig the Elder was prominent among the delegates. Although only one of his formal speeches was recorded, his diplomacy played an important role in intratribal negotiations and the Ojibwe's final acceptance of the treaty.[2]

The negotiations were dramatic. The Ojibwe delegations from Lac Courte Oreilles and Lac du Flambeau arrived late, only to find that the Mississippi Ojibwe had begun negotiations for the sale of

Wisconsin Ojibwe lands without the presence of any delegates from Wisconsin other than St. Croix. This upset them, the traders who arrived late with them, and some American officials.

More than fifty traders made financial claims against the payments intended for the Ojibwe. Trader Lyman Warren, based at La Pointe, Wisconsin, demanded large quantities of the 1837 Ojibwe annuity payments to cover debts incurred at his post. Both Warren and William Aitkin represented the American Fur Company and had especially large claims. Warren was following an established European trader practice of inflating Indian debts, creating false claims, and using them to gouge money from the Indians' government annuities. This ultimately forced Indians to buy the goods they needed with credit, not with cash, which started the vicious cycle again.[3]

At the treaty signing Warren also served as interpreter for many of the Wisconsin bands, even though his business interests were counter to those of the Ojibwe. His claims were so outrageous and forcefully stated that Indian agent Lawrence Taliaferro pulled his revolver and threatened to kill Warren if he did not sit down. It is impossible to tell how much Taliaferro's dramatic actions were a response to false trader claims and how much to his mistake of having allowed negotiations to begin with so many important people absent. Bagone-giizhig was indignant at the outrageous trader claims and undoubtedly concerned that the arrival of so many Indians from regions beyond his influence would detract from his central role in the negotiations. "Shoot him, my father," he yelled to Taliaferro. Henry Dodge, the governor of Wisconsin Territory, intervened before events turned bloody.[4]

Bagone-giizhig was impressed with Taliaferro's public stand against Warren. That trust, along with abundant good food and liquor, led Bagone-giizhig to advocate strongly for accepting the terms of the Treaty of 1837. Although Bagone-giizhig was only one of forty-seven chiefs and warriors who signed the treaty—he was not noted as a principal chief or speaker in the treaty record—his advocacy had a significant impact.

Traders engaged in gouging unjustified amounts from U.S. government annuity payments to Indians plagued the Ojibwe at every successive treaty signing and annuity payment. Many traders had mixed Ojibwe and European heritage. Typically, however, they did not identify as Indians, did not participate in traditional native religious ceremonies, and did not live in Indian villages. But when Indians were being paid for sale of tribal lands, the traders made sure that they and their families received payments as if they were regular village Indians and partial owners of the land being sold. These payments were garnered in addition to payments from their employers for their inflated claims of Indian credit purchases and payments from the government for services rendered as witnesses, interpreters, and scribes. The Warren and Aitkin families were only two of many mixed-blood trader families who received government annuity payments while serving private companies that benefited from the treaties and serving the government that gained possession of the Indian land.[5]

The Treaty of 1837 was not favorable to the Ojibwe. Ojibwe leaders were misled about its exact provisions. Hunting rights were explained to them as tantamount to ownership rights. According to Ojibwe people in Mille Lacs today, their ancestors believed that they were only selling the part of the land that grew above the ground, the trees and bushes, for example.[6] The treaty did not force Indians to relocate, and they were allowed to continue to use the land for hunting, fishing, and living. These usufructary rights built into the treaty overshadowed the issue of land tenure and ownership. Linguist John Nichols brilliantly analyzed issues related to English-Ojibwe translation in the 1837 treaty, including key phrases such as "privilege of," "pleasure of the president," "relinquish and convey," and "right, title and interest," and concluded that Ojibwe treaty signers did not comprehend terms of the treaty well and that the United States was probably neither able nor willing to convey those understandings.[7]

The precise terms of the treaty were probably much less important to the success of obtaining signatures than were the political climate of the meeting, the dramatic actions of agent Taliaferro, and the rhetoric of Bagone-giizhig. According to Lyman Warren, who was also present at negotiations and fluent in both Ojibwe and English, the Ojibwe were not properly compensated, and when certain chiefs raised critical questions about treaty provisions, they were "cowed down by the braggadocia" of Bagone-giizhig.

Ultimately, title to all Ojibwe land east of the Mississippi River below the mouth of the Nokasippi River (in present-day Crow Wing County) as far east as the Wisconsin River was ceded. The Ojibwe retained usufructary or use rights. Whites were legally allowed to settle on the land, however, and although federal law prohibited the sale of alcohol to Indians, white traders could legally establish "wet" trading posts and bars on ceded land adjacent to Indian communities. Breaking Indian liquor laws was thus even easier than before.[8]

The effect of the 1837 treaty on relations between the Ojibwe and the Dakota was immediate and pernicious. Friendly visits to traders east of the Mississippi River by both groups and joint hunting excursions were common. With alcohol now widely available, tensions often boiled over into violence.[9]

As land opened up east of the Mississippi River, the Ojibwe and Dakota had to contend with white settlers as well as with government and trade officials. This put new demands on Indian behavior, land, and resources, making Indian-white relations increasingly tense. The taking of treaty payments to cover real and sometimes fabricated debts to traders became official policy. In addition, the new settlers in 1837 brought with them a new wave of smallpox, which struck Ojibwe and Dakota communities.[10]

While Bagone-giizhig the Elder made a favorable impression upon U.S. officials during negotiations for the 1837 treaty, many of his own people were upset with him and the treaty. As white traders and settlers started to pour into old hunting grounds south of Mille Lacs and Gull lakes, Ojibwe sometimes resented Bagone-giizhig for his role in convincing other Ojibwe leaders to sign the treaty. In addition, the Dakota were angry with him because the treaty brought white settlers through their lands en route to the newly opened Ojibwe territory. Undeterred, the chief continued to advocate peace and restraint with the Dakota and the Americans—until the human landscape changed in the winter of 1837.

BLOODBATH: BAGONE-GIIZHIG'S WAR WITH THE WAH'PETONWAN

Although Bagone-giizhig had advocated peace for more than a decade, it is the sanguine events following the 1837 treaty for which Bagone-giizhig the Elder became best known.[11] In the winter of 1837–38 the Gull Lake Ojibwe and the Wah'petonwan Dakota from Sauk Lake held a joint hunting camp. There they practiced *biindigodaadiwin*, living in lodges, hunting, and fishing together and sharing the harvest along the border region between their lands.[12] Bagone-giizhig's

Ojibwe settlements around Gull Lake and Swan River had maintained long-lasting and friendly relations with the Wah'petonwan for several years.

That winter Wah'petonwan chief Rattling Cloud summoned Bagone-giizhig and his brother Zoongakamig to a council to discuss plans to fight whites for possession of Dakota lands in southern Minnesota. The Dakota chief invited Bagone-giizhig to join them in a military campaign. Bagone-giizhig declined the offer, citing the difficulty and danger of the task as well as the large number of whites and mixed-bloods already living among the Ojibwe. He and Zoongakamig left the hunting camp and returned to the Gull Lake region, while many other Ojibwe stayed behind.

When Bagone-giizhig reached Swan River, however, runners caught up with him and delivered shocking news. His band had been attacked at the joint hunting camp, shattering the trust built between the Wah'petonwan Dakota and the Gull Lake Ojibwe. Bagone-giizhig's stepson, nephew, and cousin were killed.

Infuriated, Bagone-giizhig raised a large war party of 150 and set out against the Wah'petonwan Dakota living at Sauk Lake, west of Mille Lacs. William Aitkin's half-Ojibwe son was among the willing war party, but Aitkin pulled his son from the ranks and fought with him. Humiliated, the son withdrew. Aitkin apparently had no qualms about Ojibwe and Dakota people killing one another as long as his own children did not participate.

When Bagone-giizhig's force approached the Wah'petonwan village at Sauk Lake, the Dakota invited them to a feast and begged for forgiveness. The Dakota offered to cover the dead and give the Ojibwe many guns with powder and ammunition. They also offered the right to hunt deep into Dakota territory on the prairies where there were abundant buffalo. Bagone-giizhig accepted their offer, and the war party left in peace. It seems that he harbored little ill will toward the Dakota and wanted to stabilize the peace between their bands. A time for shared hunting was arranged for the spring, and Bagone-giizhig returned to Gull Lake.[13]

In spring 1838, Bagone-giizhig traveled to Lac qui Parle for his rendezvous with the Wah'petonwan to receive the promised gifts and hunt for buffalo. He brought along a number of important Ojibwe leaders including Zoongakamig and Waabojiig (White Fisher) the

Younger. Also in the party was his eleven-year-old son, Gwiiwizens (who later assumed the name Bagone-giizhig). Gwiiwizens was already considered an *oshkaabewis* to his father and recognized as his leadership heir. On April 11, 1838, the Ojibwe arrived at the Dakota camp on the bank of the Chippewa River in western Minnesota's present-day Chippewa County (between Lac qui Parle and Benson).

The Dakota received the Ojibwe cordially. They feasted in the Wah'petonwan lodges and slept in the same structures. In the evening, however, after the Dakota had fallen asleep, Bagone-giizhig led an attack. One Dakota woman was taken captive by Bagone-giizhig and another escaped. All eleven other Dakota were stabbed to death—three men, four women, and four children. Bagone-giizhig goaded his son to join in the killing. According to the account by missionary Gideon Pond, who buried the dead, when Gwiiwizens shied away from killing a Dakota girl, Bagone-giizhig the Elder said, "If you are afraid, I'll whip you." At age eleven, under pressure from his father, Gwiiwizens took a life in battle and brought home his first scalp.[14]

The Wah'petonwan were infuriated about the killings and the capture. Alfred Brunson, who had his first encounter with Bagone-giizhig in July 1838, just after this event, noted that the Dakota were sending runners throughout the region to gather warriors for a reprisal, and the Ojibwe were in council frequently to discuss preventative measures. Brunson was trying to build a mission in the midst of the crisis when he stumbled across a council of Ojibwe people near Little Falls. Bagone-giizhig was the sole dissenting voice in the council, which wanted to return the Dakota captive to ease tensions. Bagone-giizhig, according to Brunson, was "the dirtiest, most scowling and savage looking man in the crowd" and said, "I hate the Sioux. They have killed my relatives, and I'll have revenge. You call me chief, and so I am, by nature as well as office, and I challenge any of these men . . . to dispute my title to it."[15]

After Taliaferro and other American officials exerted pressure on Bagone-giizhig, he released the Dakota captive as a peace offering. He also sent a letter to Wah'petonwan chiefs. (Communicating by letter was becoming common practice among both Ojibwe and Dakota leaders in this era. Letters were dictated to interpreters and scribes in native languages, translated and written in English, and then translated back into Ojibwe or Dakota.) Bagone-giizhig the Elder wrote with apparent contrition for his deed: "I have done what I was sorry for—but four times was I struck by you on the same ground where I found opportunity to revenge the loss of my people...I am sorry for what has happened but I could not help it...I promise never to strike another blow and to kill the first of my nation who should dare to break the peace—provided the Sioux are willing to stop at once. I have begged to go down and give myself up. I am ready to die at any time."[16]

But Bagone-giizhig the Elder's letter did not please the Dakota. A group of Wah'petonwan chiefs, including He Who Walks Running, He Who Touches the Feathers of a Bird's Wing, Warclub That Shows Itself, Cloud Man, Rattling Cloud, and He Who Talks to the Eagle, replied:

> You have written another letter. We have seen it. You say that last spring you did something bad and that you are sorry about it. Truly, how could you not be sorry about it? That action wasn't that of a man, but of a woman. This action is not the only one for which you should be sorry. There are many others as well. Be sorry for all of them together. But you still say we will be relatives. Where are the names of the chiefs, where are the names of the soldiers? We do not see any. Your name is the only one that appears. It isn't that of a chief; it isn't that of a soldier; but it is the name of a woman. This is why we will not say more.[17]

(Since women typically did not engage in war, the reference may have been a way to label someone a coward, although the use of gender as an insult was not especially common among either the Ojibwe or the Dakota.) The letter's most important feature is its tangible anger. Tensions between the Dakota and Ojibwe, at least as far as Bagone-giizhig the Elder was concerned, had escalated steeply, and the events of the next several years reflect a context of animosity.[18]

On August 2, 1838, only four months after the killing of the Wah'petonwan Dakota, Bagone-giizhig, Waabojiig (White Fisher), two Ottawa Indians, and an Ojibwe woman approached Fort Snelling to treat with Lawrence Taliaferro. Many Ottawa had been moving westward with the Ojibwe from Sault Ste. Marie, and it was not uncommon for members of these tribes to live together and even to conduct joint diplomatic ventures.[19]

Bagone-giizhig had not wanted to release the prisoner he had taken, and his desire for vengeance against the Dakota was still unsatisfied. He knew that his visit to Fort Snelling would start trouble, and that seems to be exactly what he wanted. A group of Mdewakantonwan Dakota from Lake Calhoun, aware of the killing of the Wah'petonwan Dakota, learned of Bagone-giizhig's arrival and approached Fort Snelling to attack his party. Taliaferro intercepted them and told them they were free to kill Bagone-giizhig only if they did so when he was on his way home and not within the walls of the fort.

The Mdewakantonwan agreed, but then three of them returned to the fort and attacked the Ojibwe-Ottawa party just as Taliaferro arrived. One Ottawa was killed on the spot and the other wounded. The dead Ottawa had exchanged clothes with Bagone-giizhig, possibly to protect the chief, and the two were mistaken for one another when the attack commenced. Waabojiig killed one of the Dakota, and the Mdewakantonwan Dakota attackers withdrew.

Taliaferro was visibly shaken by the event and upset that the Dakota dared to attack the Ojibwe at Fort Snelling. He insisted that the Dakota perpetrators be turned over to him for punishment because they had committed homicide on fort property, which he termed "sacred ground." The Dakota felt that Taliaferro's demands were unjust because only one of the attackers was still alive, the attacks were within the accepted Indian protocol for revenge, and, especially, in view of the fact that Bagone-giizhig had been involved in the attack against the Wah'petonwan earlier that year.

Ultimately, Taliaferro and Major Joseph Plympton, commanding officer of the 5th Infantry at Fort Snelling, accepted the Dakota offer to punish the young men themselves. Plympton ordered their release, and Dakota leaders had the two young men's blankets, leggings, and breechcloths cut into tiny pieces and cut their hair, an especially humiliating punishment. Then they were publicly and mercilessly flogged. Neither was killed (as Taliaferro had originally planned), but Plympton voiced satisfaction with the punishments: "I never saw the ceremony before—in fact it was new and novel and interesting to all present. This unfortunate affair was thus amicably settled. The Indians, relations and all quite satisfied it was no worse. And soon all dispersed, and all was again tranquil—one Chippewa killed and one Sioux killed—*even*."[20]

Everything was not even, however, in the minds of the Indian groups concerned. Both felt unjustly treated by the other and by the

Americans. In addition to grievances about the series of attacks in 1838, the Dakota were upset with American efforts to punish them for carrying out ancient war customs, and the Ojibwe were distressed with the Americans' failure to offer appropriate protection while they visited officials at Fort Snelling.

DAKOTA REVENGE: THE MASSACRES OF 1839

In the summer of 1839, Indian-white tensions and Ojibwe-Dakota tensions came to a head at Fort Snelling in the most violent event of the decade. Bagone-giizhig and Zoongakamig led a delegation of more than nine hundred Mississippi Ojibwe to Fort Snelling. Included were large numbers of Gull Lake, Crow Wing, Sandy Lake, Mille Lacs, and St. Croix Ojibwe. Even Pillager Band Ojibwe from Leech Lake— not included in the Treaty of 1837—attended. Everyone in the party believed that they would receive annuities from the 1837 treaty at Fort Snelling, not at La Pointe. Many women and children accompanied the expedition under assurances of peace from the Dakota and the Americans. Many Dakota came to the fort at the same time, suggesting that despite recent tensions, the two peoples had genuine peace. They fraternized in the Indian custom. Horse races, foot races, and lacrosse dominated the social events, together with councils of peace, pipe ceremonies, and feasts. But peace was not to last.[21]

On June 2, it became clear to all present that Ojibwe annuities could only be collected at La Pointe. The Ojibwe prepared to return home, except for two young men from Bagone-giizhig's band who remained behind in order to avenge a previous loss. When the two killed a Dakota near Lake Calhoun, Dakota response was rapid and furious. Fifty Dakota immediately ran to the site of the ambush and found the Ojibwe men there, but their cover was so advantageous that many Dakota would have died trying to kill them. Rather than run this risk, the Dakota prepared a larger expedition to exact a more favorable revenge. Their plan would prove devastating to the Ojibwe.[22]

Red Bird led the Dakota attack. Runners were sent in all directions. Since agent Taliaferro had previously given the Dakota permission to attack the Ojibwe if any Dakota were killed and since the Dakota were still incensed about Bagone-giizhig's attack in 1838 and hostilities in the previous two years, the Dakota elected to seek terrible vengeance. Three hundred Dakota warriors under Little Crow,

Shakopee, Good Road, Black Dog, and Red Bird gathered at the Falls of St. Anthony. Dakota chief Shakopee later told Taliaferro that all they could think about were "the many insults offered our people and the murder in cold blood of the three lodges of our women and children last year by Hole-in-the-Day."[23]

Because two Ojibwe from Bagone-giizhig's band had earlier been seen at Fort Snelling weeping over the grave of an Ojibwe man, the Dakota suspected that these were the two who were responsible for the ambush. But the Dakota decided not to attack Bagone-giizhig's party because they thought the group would be expecting an attack. One party of Dakota warriors pursued the Ojibwe returning to Mille Lacs, and another followed the Ojibwe headed toward the St. Croix region. Neither of these Ojibwe groups had been involved in the ambush, but they were the easiest to catch. Besides, it was within proper custom to exact vengeance from any enemy, not just those responsible for the initial attack. Red Bird was so incensed that he ordered no captives be taken and no lives be spared.

Dakota overtook the Mille Lacs Ojibwe near the mouth of the Rum River. Men had gone ahead to forage for food, while women and children were traveling more slowly with their possessions. None suspected an attack because of the recent peaceful visit with the Dakota and because they knew nothing of the earlier Ojibwe ambush at Lake Calhoun. When the Dakota broke through a clearing and commenced the attack, one Dakota man saw his Ojibwe lover among the group he was attacking. She crossed her arms in a sign of surrender, but, remembering Red Bird's order that no prisoners be taken, he simply touched her with a spear and left her to be killed by the next warrior. By the time the Ojibwe men returned after hearing the gunfire, the Dakota had already fled. The few Ojibwe men who had remained behind put up a spirited defense but had only limited success. Dakota leader Red Bird lost one of his sons, but other Dakota losses were minimal. Seventy Ojibwe, mainly women and children, perished.

The second contingent of Dakota avengers overtook the St. Croix Ojibwe at present-day Stillwater, Minnesota, at a ravine (near the current state prison). By this time trader William Aitkin, who had joined the Ojibwe in order to gain advantage in future trade and sold them alcohol, had succeeded in intoxicating most of the Ojibwe. The

Dakota saw Aitkin and waited to attack until he had left the group. A surprise volley by the Dakota then killed twenty-one and wounded twenty-nine. The Ojibwe managed to put up a defense and even drove the Dakota a short distance away. The total death toll was more than one hundred Ojibwe and fewer than twenty Dakota. George Copway, who visited the site shortly after the bloody event, reported that the battlefield was littered with the bodies of Ojibwe families.[24]

In total triumph, the Dakota forces returned home to mourn the Ojibwe they had killed and conduct the scalp dance. Elated and confident though they were, they knew Ojibwe retaliation was sure to come. They soon abandoned the Lake Calhoun settlement, which Americans called Eatonville, as well as the Lake Harriet Mission (in present-day Minneapolis). Missionaries at Lake Harriet claimed the Dakota there would sound a false alarm almost every morning, saying, "The Chippewas are coming! They are here, they are here! Perhaps we shall all be dead tomorrow." When the anxiety proved too great, the Dakota simply abandoned the entire area.[25]

Agent Taliaferro at Fort Snelling was disgusted with the events, but his disgust seems somewhat hypocritical since he had sometimes encouraged the Dakota to attack the Ojibwe. Still, he appeared genuinely upset by his inability to secure peace between the Ojibwe and Dakota. He was also disheartened at the abandonment of Eatonville because he considered it not just a Dakota village, but also a promising American experiment in converting the Dakota to Christianity and an agrarian lifestyle. In 1840 he resigned his position and returned to Pennsylvania, leaving his Dakota wife and mixed-blood children behind in Minnesota.[26]

Other government officials were also frustrated with the situation. For a while in the early 1840s, they tried to withhold annuity payments to ensure peace, but this plan only increased the animosity between Indians and whites.[27] Indian-white relations continued to deteriorate with the collapse of the American Fur Company posts in Minnesota and a decline in the fur trade due to dramatic gluts and shortages of furs from restructuring in the business, overharvesting, and changes in European fashion which governed demand for furs.

The Ojibwe sought retribution for the 1839 Dakota attacks but were never able to inflict comparable damage. In 1841 and 1842,

Bagone-giizhig the Elder instigated a series of actions designed to punish the Dakota and push them farther south. He tried to establish a new village at the Little Elk River near Little Falls, directly on the Prairie du Chien boundary line between the tribes, from which he hoped to expand his territory and punish the Dakota. Frequent Dakota attacks, however, forced him to retreat from that location and the Mississippi Ojibwe village at the mouth of the Little Elk River. Rabbit Lake and eventually Lower and Upper Whitefish Lake, northeast of Gull Lake, became the new Ojibwe population centers in the region because most of Bagone-giizhig's band felt safer there.[28]

In 1841, Bagone-giizhig raised a large war party of two hundred, but after he proposed to attack Dakota leader Little Crow's village southeast of St. Paul on the Mississippi, probably the strongest Dakota village at the time, all but two of his warriors deserted. Undaunted, the remaining three pressed on and fired into lodges in the main village, killing the son of a chief. The Dakota chased them as far as the St. Croix River, but all three escaped. Missionary Samuel Pond witnessed the event. From this attack, Bagone-giizhig the Elder achieved even greater fame, because it was considered a brave act.[29]

The next year he raised a war party of 160 and set a careful ambush for Little Crow's band. They killed twelve Dakota and wounded sixteen others, losing five of their own in the process. This was a triumph for Bagone-giizhig, which he exploited to his benefit. His visit to La Pointe for annuities that year became a celebratory victory parade.

THE TREATY OF 1842, INTERTRIBAL WARFARE, AND EARLY MISSIONARIES

At treaty negotiations in 1842 at La Pointe, Bagone-giizhig expanded his political capital based on his military actions of the preceding year.[30] Alfred Brunson reported that at the meeting Bagone-giizhig "displayed the skill of a general, and the wisdom of a statesman." To impress participants, he had his warriors construct a large, elevated scaffold on pontoons for a grand entry. They paddled to the site with Bagone-giizhig riding on top of the platform holding an American flag. Warriors sang his personal song — composed by Bagone-giizhig — which included the words, "Surely, I will have great praise." His

entourage sang, danced, and fired guns. The spectacle enhanced his
reputation among the Americans as a man of importance among the
Ojibwe and a flag-carrying friend of the United States.[31]

While the Ojibwe leadership already assembled surely thought
his actions unnecessary and boastful, how could they challenge his
young warriors after their triumphant excursion against the Dakota?
Missionary John Johnson wrote to Henry Whipple years later: "The
celebrated warrior Hole-in-the-Day was the most conspicuous and
prominent chief among them and was in his prime manhood. His
name had reached far and wide and it was the biggest object to see
him walk independently before the non-combatants—his head covered with the finest eagle feathers waving beautifully on his head,
which tell the numbers of scalps taken and the number killed of his
hereditary enemy. Yes, it was an object of sight indeed."[32]

Although the 1842 treaty did not directly affect his band's territory, it proved to be a significant event in Bagone-giizhig's chieftainship. That he had any formal involvement at all in the proceedings
demonstrates his influence outside of his band. Ojibwe chiefs from
other areas kept their resentments about his chieftainship and the
nature of his arrival at La Pointe to themselves. Although he was not
a primary treaty negotiator, he played a diplomatic role and was allowed to speak and influence decisions about land and money that
were clearly beyond his rightful claim. American officials were eager
to work with any Ojibwe leader willing to sign land cession treaties,
but Bagone-giizhig went out of his way to win their favor and influence them. When a delegation of Ojibwe from Sault Ste. Marie arrived
at La Pointe for its share of the annuities, Alfred Brunson stalled
until he could be sure that the group legitimately deserved them.
When the group prepared to take their annuities by force, Bagone-
giizhig intervened and protected the annuity warehouse with more
than a hundred warriors. Once again, grateful traders and American
military and government officers were impressed with the chief's
power, prowess, and pro-American disposition. He would continue
to curry their favor in other diplomatic encounters.[33]

For the rest of his career, Bagone-giizhig the Elder was involved
in skirmishes with the Dakota, seeking vengeance for the damage
inflicted upon his people in 1839.[34] Many other groups joined him
in this effort. In 1840, a Dakota named Long Foot and his wife were

killed between Mendota and St. Paul. Ojibwe also killed two Dakota at Lac qui Parle in the fall of 1841. The next year, Ojibwe attacked Little Crow's village, killing two girls. The Ojibwe also attacked Big Thunder's village at Pig's Eye Lake, killing ten men, two women and one child. Another Dakota was killed at Lake Traverse. The Dakota reciprocated when attacked, so the battles went back and forth with no clear winners or losers. Both groups suffered; neither group was significantly displaced or depopulated.

In 1841, the Dakota mounted an attack against the Ojibwe settlement at Lake Pokegama that eventually led the Ojibwe to abandon their village. Most skirmishes were small, however, and did not affect the territorial holdings of either group. As time passed, tensions cooled, and by the mid-1840s, relations returned to a state of troubled truce, with some minor skirmishes.

Throughout his adult life, Bagone-giizhig the Elder had been a leader. For more than a decade, he had successfully guided the Ojibwe toward peace. When Ojibwe-Dakota violence erupted in the late 1830s, he proved himself a remarkable leader in times of war as well. By the 1840s, he was at the height of his power and respected by Ojibwe, Dakota, and whites alike. According to Julius T. Clark, "Hole-in-the-Day was the only man in the nation who was feared by the traders and Government officers. I do not mean that they feared personal injury, or were in danger of coming into personal conflict with him; but they feared his influence with his people."[35]

Bagone-giizhig was powerful, in part, because he was perceived to be powerful. His influence stemmed from his skills at persuasion and instilling fear more than from control or love. As his power and influence grew, he began to proclaim himself head chief of all the Ojibwe Indians, even though no such position existed. Alfred Brunson said, "He was not acknowledged the *head* chief, yet he exerted a greater influence among his people, and with the whites, than any other chief among them." Trader Lyman Warren believed he was not well loved outside his home Gull Lake region, and this statement is supported in modern oral histories collected at Mille Lacs, where his claim to head chieftainship was strongly repudiated.[36]

Missionaries tried to persuade Bagone-giizhig to convert to Christianity and lead his people down the white man's road. While he promised to educate his son Gwiiwizens in the white man's tradition and guide Ojibwe people toward these pursuits, his promises were calculated to keep missionaries interested in courting him and to manipulate them into establishing missions, trading, and giving presents to his constituents. He never intended to give up his indigenous religion or control over his son's education.

In the spring of 1841, for instance, Ojibwe missionary and historian George Copway stopped at Rabbit Lake to visit Bagone-giizhig, as he had done several times over the years. Bagone-giizhig gave Copway eighty pounds of maple sugar, and Copway tried to engage the chief in a discussion of religion. Copway reported on their conversation: "While conversing with the chief on the importance of true religion, he became much troubled, and admitted that his own religion was not as good as the religion of the Bible; but, said he, 'I will embrace your religion when I have returned from one more battle with the Sioux; and I will then advise my people to embrace it too.' What a struggle the poor fellow had within!" Bagone-giizhig, who was a brilliant politician and manipulator, likely chose his words to hold Copway's interest and then focused the communication on his people's economic and political betterment more than their spiritual transformation.[37]

In spite of Copway's unsuccessful efforts to convert Bagone-giizhig to Christianity, the two men maintained a strong and trusting friendship. In 1841, Copway left his wife with Bagone-giizhig while he traveled from Rabbit Lake to St. Peters in an effort to collect provisions and support for the Rabbit Lake Mission. While gathering the provisions, Copway ventured a trip to Little Crow's village and stumbled into preparations for a full-scale war expedition against the Ojibwe. Little Crow told Copway, "Tell Hole-in-the-Sky, I am coming for his scalp." Copway, fearing for his wife and for his friend Bagone-giizhig, covered the entire distance from Little Crow's village to Bagone-giizhig's in three days, in part on horse but mainly by running on foot. Copway wrote in his journal, "I was so anxious . . . that I had no appetite for eating . . . having walked two hundred and forty miles, forded eight large streams and crossed the broad Mississippi twice. My coat and pantaloons were in strips." Copway promptly warned Bagone-giizhig, who quickly moved all of his people from the area and took precautions for the rest of the summer that probably saved hundreds of Ojibwe lives.[38]

Gaagigegaabaw (Stands Forever), also known as George Copway, 1850.
A well-known scholar and missionary, Copway knew both Bagone-
giizhigs but was especially good friends with Bagone-giizhig the Elder,
whom he visited on numerous occasions and wrote about in his books.

Bagone-giizhig cultivated personal relationships with many white,
mixed-blood, and Indian people in positions of power. Missionary
John Johnson and Bagone-giizhig spent time together during his
tenure as chief. On at least two occasions in 1840 and 1841 Johnson
took refuge from Dakota war parties with Bagone-giizhig the Elder.
In 1846, Bagone-giizhig adopted Johnson as his son.[39]

THE TREATIES OF 1847 AND THE ALCOHOL TRADE

After the Treaty of 1837 ceded ownership of central Minnesota Ojibwe land to the U.S. government, private traders and even government officials deliberately began weaving alcohol use and abuse into the fabric of Indian communities. As the Ojibwe faced new and profound challenges, alcohol became a common crutch for many Ojibwe people — with terrible and long-lasting consequences. Although the depth and breadth of alcohol abuse in Ojibwe communities was primarily a reaction to negative economic, political, and social change, rather than a biological predisposition to alcoholism, once it became an ingrained part of Ojibwe social experience, the damage caused by abuse was passed on through the generations and still haunts many Ojibwe people today.

When the American Fur Company pulled out of Minnesota in 1842, independent traders quickly increased Indian peoples' access to alcohol. Some traders such as William Aitkin used whiskey as a tool for negotiating for furs, food, and land.[40] With the decline in fur trading and increased pressure on Indians to sell land for trade goods, money, and food, many Indian people despaired and turned to the poison offered by unscrupulous traders. Even prosperous, powerful leaders like Bagone-giizhig and his brother Zoongakamig abused alcohol with a frequency that increasingly affected their ability to lead.

In 1845, Zoongakamig (Strong Ground) died from alcohol poisoning. After leading numerous wars against the Dakota, and losing two sons and one wife in conflicts with the Dakota, he died from drinking too much whiskey. He was survived by one son named Ojibwe (1820–1911), who was a bodyguard to Bagone-giizhig the Younger, who relocated to White Earth, and who became a primary informant for Frances Densmore's research on Ojibwe culture and music. Bagone-giizhig the Elder, who also drank heavily, now had to face the complicated arena of Ojibwe diplomacy without his trusted brother.[41]

The mid-1840s saw continuing Ojibwe-Dakota hostilities. In 1844, the Dakota killed Babiizigindibens (Little Curly Head), a prominent Ojibwe leader. Gull Lake Ojibwe attacked Lac qui Parle that winter, and the next spring a group of Dakota killed four Ojibwe on the Rum River. In 1845 Bagone-giizhig the Elder and a contingent of Mississippi Ojibwe approached Fort Snelling and negotiated a peace with the Dakota that attempted to soothe Ojibwe anger about the death of

Babiizigindibens. The endeavor was moderately successful, although two Leech Lakers instigated an attack against the Dakota in the area at the same time, which greatly undermined peace efforts.[42]

In 1847 and 1848, a series of diplomatic developments irrevocably altered Ojibwe-Dakota and Ojibwe-American relations. A new government plan to decrease violence between the Ojibwe and Dakota and, at the same time, open large areas of Indian land to white settlers called for relocating the Wisconsin Ho-Chunk (Winnebago) and Menominee to reservations in central Minnesota. There the two tribes would serve as a buffer between the Ojibwe and the Dakota, and the lands they had occupied in Wisconsin would then be opened for white settlement.[43]

The government's first step was to gain land cessions from the Mississippi, Lake Superior, and Pillager Band Ojibwe to create a place for the Ho-Chunk and Menominee. Bagone-giizhig, who believed that the paltry sum of money being offered would be sufficient if the cession would bring about peace between the Ojibwe and the Dakota, traveled extensively for months to build support before the formal treaty signings. The Ojibwe would eventually agree to the cessions in the form of two separate treaties in hopes that the move would bring about greater peace, not significant financial compensation.

In fact, the Pillager Band eventually agreed to extinguish their land title, without any financial compensation, for the paltry payment of seventy-five guns, two hundred beaver traps, and a five-year annuity of blankets because they wanted the other tribes there as a buffer from the Dakota. With the Menominee and the Ho-Chunk living between the Ojibwe and Dakota, much of the jointly used Ojibwe-Dakota area would be off-limits to both groups, resulting in less competition and conflict in the border regions. Some of the major war roads would also be blocked by the proposed changes. The Ojibwe would eventually cede a large section of their territory and the joint-use area between them and the Dakota, including the land south of the Crow Wing River between the Mississippi River and Otter Tail Lake as far south as the Swan River. The cession west of the Long Prairie River was to be for the Menominee; the cession east of the river was to be for the Ho-Chunk. Treaties were scheduled with the Mississippi and Lake Superior Ojibwe at Fond du Lac and the Pillager Ojibwe at Leech Lake in August 1847.

Knowing that peace between the Ojibwe and the Dakota was contingent upon the Menominee and the Ho-Chunk moving to Long Prairie, Bagone-giizhig paid a visit to Ho-Chunk leaders in Prairie du Chien, Wisconsin, in May 1847. His mission was to learn how they felt about the treaties and to convince them to accept the treaties and move to Long Prairie. By constantly engaging the Americans and leaders of four Ojibwe bands and several tribes in diplomacy, Bagone-giizhig became a true intertribal and international Ojibwe politician.[44]

On his way back to Gull Lake from Wisconsin, Bagone-giizhig stopped at the Falls of St. Anthony to visit traders there and drink several shots of whiskey. Sometime later, as his horse-drawn cart crossed the Mississippi River at Little Falls one hundred miles away, he fell out of the wagon in a stupor. The wheel ran over his chest, aggravating spinal wounds incurred in 1827. He was brought to the home of an Ojibwe family nearby and died a few hours later.[45]

Although born without traditional claims to chieftainship, Bagone-giizhig the Elder had attained more status and power than many traditional hereditary chiefs. The constant flux in Ojibwe-Dakota relations and the burgeoning military and economic power of the United States created rapid change in Ojibwe communities, and Bagone-giizhig the Elder was able to use that climate and his undeniable charisma, oratorical power, and diplomatic savvy to build a powerful chieftainship for himself—not a traditional, hereditary chieftainship, but a powerful position nonetheless. Ironically, he was also able to use the existing respect for heredity in Ojibwe culture to pass that position on to his son, Gwiiwizens. In spite of his humble roots, Bagone-giizhig the Elder had risen to a position of great power among the Mississippi Ojibwe. His career was at times peaceful, at times violent, but always pursued with grace, passion, and prowess. His life was cut short in 1847, lost fighting the disease of alcoholism rather than fighting for the rights of his people.

As the great chief lay dying, he summoned his son Gwiiwizens to his side and told him, "Take the tribe by the hand. Show them how to walk."[46] At age nineteen, Gwiiwizens thus inherited his father's role as principal leader for the Gull Lake Ojibwe. Bagone-giizhig the Elder's diplomatic career was over, but his legacy would live on through the tumultuous period of his son's rule. Bagone-giizhig the Elder was dead, but Bagone-giizhig the Younger would take the Ojibwe forward.

4

Pride and Power

Bagone-giizhig's Inheritance

In his home [Bagone-giizhig the Younger] had many white servants
and henchmen and really lived like a lord. He dressed well in
native style with a touch of civilized elegance, wearing a coat and
leggings of fine broadcloth, linen shirt with collar, and, topping all,
a handsome black or blue blanket. His moccasins were of the finest
deerskin and beautifully worked. His long beautiful hair added
much to his personal appearance. He was fond of entertaining and
being entertained and was a favorite both among army officers and
civilians. He was especially popular with the ladies.
—CHARLES A. EASTMAN[1]

Alternately a despot and subject, landholder and agrarian,
aristocrat and communist, citizen and savage, now invoking and
now defying the law, a civilized barbarian who goes scalp-hunting
by stage, and an apostate heathen...[Bagone-giizhig the Younger]
will be a potent instrument for good or evil so long as he remains
on the border, subject to the accidental influence of good or bad
surroundings and impulses.
—JOHN GEORGE NICOLAY[2]

Gwiiwizens (Boy) was asked by his father, the first Bagone-giizhig, to carry on as a leader of the Mississippi Ojibwe. But
his father's acquisition of power had not been universally
welcomed, especially by traditional hereditary Ojibwe chiefs from
Mille Lacs and Sandy Lake, and the teenager's right to inherit his
father's position would be challenged. Gwiiwizens asserted himself
forcefully and proved his mettle as a leader, eventually surpassing
even his father in influence, vanity, and fame.

FROM GRIEF TO CHIEF: BECOMING A LEADER

Gwiiwizens was deeply disturbed by the death of his father, with
whom he had a close emotional bond. Bagone-giizhig had always

kept Gwiiwizens in his company, demonstrating tactics in diplomacy and war and thus equipping his son for a future leadership position among the Mississippi Band.

Gwiiwizens had fasted at age ten. A year later he took his first scalp under his father's direction. He was expected to be precocious, fearless, and exceptional in preparation for becoming a warrior and chief. His father insisted he keep bear cubs as pets, rather than a dog or crow, which was more common. By the time he was nineteen, Gwiiwizens had been included as a signatory to two treaties negotiated by his father. Gwiiwizens wore several feathers for military honors by killing or scalping Dakota. He was being groomed for the chieftainship, and throughout his period of apprenticeship he came to love and admire his father as no other member of his family had.[3]

As a young boy at Gull Lake, Gwiiwizens once caught such a large fish that it pulled his canoe. Unable to land the fish, he yelled to his father for help. His father, fearing a Dakota attack, came running and rebuked his son for making so much noise about a fish: "If a mere fish scares you so badly, I fear you will never make a warrior."[4]

For weeks after the death of his father, the teenage Gwiiwizens mourned and moped. He felt unready and unworthy of the mantle bestowed upon him by his father on his deathbed. Ojibwe leaders such as Waabojiig (White Fisher) and traditional hereditary chief Bookowaabide's son Nenda-miiniked (Berry Hunter) were prepared to fill the vacuum left by Bagone-giizhig the Elder's passing, but Gwiiwizens was too proud of his father to give up his father's request.

After his father was buried at Lookout Hill (Hole in the Day's Bluff) near Little Falls, his "ghost feed" four days later, and proper mourning rituals begun, Gwiiwizens stepped into his father's moccasins and decided to travel to Fort Snelling. There was tribal business to attend to, and there was a new chief to attend to it. The young Bagone-giizhig's claim to authority was highly contested throughout his life, especially by traditional chiefs from Mille Lacs and Sandy Lake, but Bagone-giizhig undauntedly assumed his father's role.[5]

Family members warned Gwiiwizens that he would probably be attacked and killed by the Dakota if he went to Fort Snelling, but he replied, "My father walked here, and I like to walk where he did."[6] When he arrived at the fort he boldly introduced himself not as "Gwiiwizens" but as "Bagone-giizhig." Assuming a father's name was not a common practice among the Ojibwe. Some tribes, including

WAH BO JEEG. (WHITE FISHER.)
Chief Gull Lake Band Chippewas. An old Warrior, once taken prisoner by the Sioux, and speaks the language.

WHITNEY'S GALLERY, SAINT PAUL.

Waabojiig (White Fisher) the Younger, ca. 1860. Waabojiig the Younger and his father were among the most experienced and celebrated war leaders of the Ojibwe, although Waabojiig the Younger also asserted a civil chieftainship subordinate to that of Bagone-giizhig.

the Dakota, passed on names from father to son, but the Ojibwe did not traditionally do this, nor was it traditional for a son simply to assume his father's dream name. But Bagone-giizhig the Younger, like his father, was not a traditional leader, and he did not adhere to ancient protocols. He claimed the name, and from then on he was almost invariably called Bagone-giizhig, Bagone-giizhig the Younger, Hole in the Day, or Hole in the Day the Younger.

Although Bagone-giizhig's assumption of his father's name was a break with Ojibwe custom, a few other well-known Ojibwe leaders, including Eshkibagikoonzh and Waabojiig, did the same thing. They were Bagone-giizhig the Younger's contemporaries, so it is unlikely that they were following his example or vice versa. It seems more probable that some young leaders began to change naming traditions in order to capitalize on the recognition and political capital that their fathers' names commanded with outsiders, especially the Americans. At age nineteen Bagone-giizhig was less likely to be disregarded by the Americans when he introduced himself using his father's name. Thus, his break with naming protocol was both an indication of broad change happening in Ojibwe leadership and culture and also a major factor driving those changes. He was affected by cultural changes, and he himself created changes. He exerted personal choice in assuming his father's name that was neither common nor customary but not completely anomalous.

As little more than a youth, Bagone-giizhig caught Indian and white people's attention and began winning their support. Claude Beaulieu, a local trader, described him as "a man of distinguished appearance and native courtliness of manner. His voice was musical and magnetic, and with these qualities he had a subtle brain, a logical mind, and quite a remarkable gift of oratory. In speech he was not impassioned, but clear and convincing, and held fast the attention of his hearers."[7]

Julia Warren Spears, missionary and sister of William W. Warren, had a similar impression of the chief: "I was surprised indeed to see such a noble looking Indian . . . He wore a green blanket around him which by the way, he always wore and underneath the blanket he wore a black broadcloth coat and vest, and a pink calico shirt, the color he always wore. He was very fond of pink. Beaded leggings and moccasins completed his costume. His hair was cut short in front. His back hair braided in two large braids and he wore a head dress

Earliest known daguerreotype of Bagone-giizhig the Younger, ca. 1855
(possibly much earlier). Note the two chief medals received as an
inheritance from his father. Eagle feathers were given for proven feats in
war (killing, wounding, or scalping), and the small number of feathers
displayed marks Bagone-giizhig in the earliest stages of his career as
both chief and warrior.

of feathers and brightly colored beads. He always carried a loaded
revolver. I remember very distinctly just how he looked."[8]

Many accounts suggest that Bagone-giizhig dressed this way
every day, not just for major public events and photographs. Certainly he designed his attire to present himself as a leader in every
regard. He wore an otterskin turban on his head—customary for

civil chiefs only. Tucked in that turban he proudly displayed eagle feathers, each one earned in battle—common for military leaders but not for civil chiefs. In addition he wore the elaborate beadwork of a traditional Ojibwe religious leader. Finally he wore a frock coat and trousers to emphasize his modern and civilized American position. It was as if Bagone-giizhig was saying that he was a legitimate leader in the Ojibwe civil, military, and religious traditions and in the white man's tradition. Such a claim did not have to be voiced; it was evident from his appearance. His clothing suggests his awareness that politics was all about impressions. According to missionary Alfred Brunson, "No one strutted, or seemed to feel his consequence, more than he did."[9]

Newspaper and magazine accounts suggest the powerful impression he created by his mere presence. The *New York Tribune* in 1851 observed that "young Hole-in-the-Day is . . . well formed, with a thoughtful and even melancholy expression of countenance. He is said to be exceedingly ambitious, and utterly regardless of danger." In 1858 the *Prairie du Chien Courier* wrote: "He is a splendid specimen of manhood, well proportioned, and walks with a grace that would become a Roman Emperor in the palmy days of Rome." *Harper's New Monthly Magazine* described him as "standing erect, walking, moving his arm, with extended forefinger in emphatic gesture, his eye full of fire, and his features full of expressive energy . . . Hole-in-the-Day was a very model of wild masculine grace—a real forest prince, bearing upon his whole figure and mien the seal of nobility." Upon his death, the *St. Paul Pioneer Press* would note: "There is something almost romantic in his reckless daring on the war path. He was the Chippewa Cid, or Coeur de Lion, from the gleam of whose battle-axe whole armies of Saracen Sioux fled as before an irresistible fate. His exploits would fill a book."[10]

THE 1847 TREATY OF FOND DU LAC

After meeting with white authorities at Fort Snelling, the young Bagone-giizhig learned the details of the U.S. plan to treat with the Mississippi and Lake Superior Band Ojibwe at Fond du Lac. The purpose was a land cession around Long Prairie, just west of Bagone-giizhig's villages in the Gull Lake area. The Pillager Band claims to that region would be dealt with in a separate treaty later that month.

The Mississippi Band included Ojibwe villages from Mille Lacs, Sandy Lake, Rabbit Lake, and Gull Lake. The Lake Superior Band included Ojibwe villages from Fond du Lac, northern Wisconsin, and the Arrowhead region of northeastern Minnesota. The Pillager Band included Ojibwe villages from Leech and Ottertail lakes.

Big changes were coming to Ojibwe country. Wisconsin Territory had been organized in 1836 to include all of present-day Minnesota east of the Mississippi, which was still unceded Indian land. However, Wisconsin was about to become a state (which happened in 1848), Minnesota Territory was about to be organized (which happened in 1849), and the federal, state, and territorial governments wanted Indian land to realize their ambitions. The U.S. Army presence at Fort Snelling was growing, and there was a new plan to build Fort Ripley just a few miles from Bagone-giizhig's village at Gull Lake (which happened in 1848). U.S. government proposals focused on land cessions but also included the possibility of moving annuity stations throughout the region and even relocating some Ojibwe communities.

Bagone-giizhig the Elder had worked hard in the months before the treaty signings to convince Ho-Chunk, Menominee, and especially Ojibwe people of the merits of relocating other tribes to buffer lands the Ojibwe would cede in order to facilitate Ojibwe-Dakota peace. Other pressing matters were building up, too. After his death at this critical time, the Ojibwe needed strong leadership. But Bagone-giizhig the Younger was an unproven teenager who had walked only in his father's shadow.

In the summer of 1847, the younger Bagone-giizhig left for Fond du Lac, arriving there on August 1. Other Ojibwe chiefs and white officials did not expect the young Bagone-giizhig to play much of a role at the treaty site. He was only nineteen, and although he was well liked by his own people, he did not have a reputation like that of his father. His support was limited to his home community. Ojibwe leaders from Mille Lacs, in particular, did not support his claim to a leadership position, especially over larger groups of Ojibwe people, but they underestimated him. He had a striking appearance, physical charisma, and intelligence in abundance. To everyone's surprise, he would somehow dominate the treaty negotiations.[11]

When Mississippi and Lake Superior Band Ojibwe leaders were finally seated in council at Fond du Lac, the pipe smoked, and delegates ready to discuss the treaty, Bagone-giizhig rose to his feet.

This preempted the other Ojibwe chiefs present. Then, according to historian Edward Neill, he boldly and aggressively addressed the assembled leaders with these words:

> Our Great Father instructed you to come here, for the purpose of asking us to sell a large piece of land, lying on and west of the Mississippi River. To accomplish this you have called together all the chiefs and headmen of the nation, who to the number of many hundreds are within hearing of my voice; that was useless, for they do not own the land; it belongs to me.
>
> My father, by his bravery, took it from the Sioux. He died a few moons ago, and what belonged to him became mine. He, by his courage and perseverance, became head chief of all the Chippewas, and when he died I took his place, and am consequently chief over all the nation. To this position I am doubly entitled, for I am as brave as my father was, and through my mother I am by descent legal heir to the position.
>
> Now, if I say sell, our Great Father will obtain the land; if I say no, you will tell him he cannot have it. The Indians assembled here have nothing to say; they can but do my bidding.[12]

While we do not have the original Ojibwe text of Bagone-giizhig's speech, a version published in the *St. Paul Pioneer Press* nearly twenty years later reported Bagone-giizhig's remarks this way:

> The country our Great Father sent you to purchase belongs to me. It was once my father's. He took it from the Sioux. He, by his bravery, made himself the head chief of the Chippewa nation. I am a greater man than my father was, for I am as brave as he was, and on my mother's side I am hereditary head chief of the nation. The land you want belongs to me. If I say sell, our Great Father will have it. If I say not sell, he will do without it. These Indians that you see behind me have nothing to say about it.[13]

The discrepancies between the versions of this important speech are significant. If the young Bagone-giizhig believed and claimed that he was greater than his father, we are left with a different perception of the chief's ego and his relationship with his father. In addition, Bagone-giizhig's claim to chieftainship through his mother's line was untrue, since there was no such tradition in Ojibwe culture.

Bagone-giizhig claimed that his mother was the daughter of a Leech Lake chief. This may not have been true, as the genealogical records of the Skinaway family show she came from Sandy Lake. But either way, the chief's mother never held a formal position herself.

In his first public speech, the young Bagone-giizhig obviously showed little respect for the many assembled Ojibwe chiefs. In both word and action he dismissed them and discounted their authority. For a young chief making a disputed claim to leadership, this must have seemed foolish. Perhaps Bagone-giizhig was emotional after the recent passing of his father. Most likely, however, he wanted his speech to impress the American officials present, not to gain favor with the Ojibwe, who probably found it infuriating. Moreover, the substantive issues of the treaty negotiation—land sales and payments—appeared to be of little concern to Bagone-giizhig.

Amazingly, nobody seemed to challenge the young Bagone-giizhig. His claims to head chieftainship and to ownership of the land were ludicrous. The Lake Superior Ojibwe in particular had never interacted with him, except during annuity payments at La Pointe. Even within Bagone-giizhig's domain, Waabojiig (White Fisher) and Gwiiwizhenzhish (Bad Boy) disputed his claim to the title. Waabojiig in fact signed the treaty with the title "first chief" next to his name. Yet nobody challenged Bagone-giizhig publicly at the treaty council. The other chiefs remained silent, in keeping with older, nonconfrontational traditions. The assembled chiefs were probably surprised by his words but unwilling to cross the young leader, whose power now seemed quite tangible.

Later that year, some Mille Lacs chiefs did formally repudiate his claim to grand chieftainship of all the Ojibwe. In a letter to the president of the United States, dictated through an interpreter, Mille Lacs chief Negwanebi (Resting Feather) and other chiefs made it clear that Bagone-giizhig did not represent them or their communities. By failing to address the issue when it first came up and challenge Bagone-giizhig at the treaty negotiation, however, their counterclaim did little to disempower his discourse in 1847 or on any subsequent treaty between the Minnesota Ojibwe and the U.S. government. (In fact, insult was added to injury for Chief Negwanebi, who signed the receipt for his treaty payment only to learn that the commissioner had designated the money for Bagone-giizhig, leaving Negwanebi empty-handed.)

While Bagone-giizhig's bold action won him the attention of the United States, it heightened tensions between his family and the Mille Lacs leadership.[14]

In reporting on the 1847 treaty-signing event, the *St. Paul Pioneer Press* was as astounded as the Ojibwe leaders by Bagone-giizhig's words and actions:

> The change in the face of things at the appearance of Hole-in-the-Day showed his bravery and commanding influence... Here were powerful chiefs of all the Chippewa tribes, some of them seventy or eighty years old, who, before his coming spoke sneeringly of him as a boy who could have no voice in the council, saying there would be no use in waiting for him, but when he appeared, they became his most submissive and obedient subjects; and this in a treaty in which a million acres of land were ceded. The terms of the treaty were concluded between the Commissioners and young Hole-in-the-Day alone.[15]

Although this account exaggerates and is not completely supported by the treaty journals, it contains an important truth. Bagone-giizhig the Younger insisted that U.S. treaty negotiators speak with him alone, an uncommon request and even more uncommonly granted. However, American officials must have been excited at the possibility of gaining vocal Ojibwe support for their proposals. After lengthy discussion, Bagone-giizhig indicated Ojibwe acceptance of the treaty. The other assembled Ojibwe leaders seemed willing to sign as well. Although this does not mean that Bagone-giizhig dictated terms of the treaty by himself, some Americans surely received the impression that his counsel was more important than that of the other chiefs. Adding to that perception, Bagone-giizhig insisted that all other chiefs sign the document first so that his mark would appear last, separate from the lesser chiefs and common people. Remarkably, that is exactly what happened.[16]

DIPLOMATIC CONNECTIONS WITH THE UNITED STATES AND THE DAKOTA

After the Fond du Lac treaty, Bagone-giizhig returned to Gull Lake brimming with confidence and determined to fill his father's moccasins beyond his father's expectations. He worked to strengthen the village on the northeast shore of Gull Lake and expand his band's control over Rabbit Lake, Crow Wing, and other sites in the region. Like his father, Bagone-giizhig the Younger successfully asserted himself as chief of the region rather than chief of a particular village. No other Ojibwe leader in history so successfully affirmed authority over such a large swath of land, number of villages, and population of native inhabitants. He even claimed to be chief of Crow Wing, which was half populated with whites. The importance of being a resident of a particular village to assert leadership thus became less important in Bagone-giizhig's chieftainship. The nature of Ojibwe leadership and the composition of Ojibwe communities were changing quickly, and Bagone-giizhig was helping drive that change.[17]

Bagone-giizhig soon became deeply involved in altercations with the Dakota and with traders and timber and land speculators. He was a busy man. *Harper's New Monthly Magazine* noted: "His shrewdness and intelligence attracted the attention of the white traders and officials who came in contact with him. The notice which they bestowed upon him to secure his friendship, and through him that of his band and tribe, gave him much influence with the Indians, and excited his vanity and ambition to become the recognized head chief of the whole Chippewa nation."[18]

While Fond du Lac treaty commissioners Isaac A. Verplank and Henry M. Rice were upset with Bagone-giizhig's bullying demeanor at the negotiations, he had made a tremendous impression on other white officials and traders. This impression, together with other political and economic considerations, soon made his request for an annuity-payment station on his home turf into a reality. In order to protect white settlers and try to keep the peace between the Ojibwe, Dakota, and Ho-Chunk, the Americans built Fort Ripley in 1848–49 near the confluence of the Mississippi and Nokasippi rivers, several miles south of present-day Brainerd, Minnesota. The fort and the new annuity station at Sandy Lake (an easy walk or canoe trip from all of the villages in Bagone-giizhig's region) made it easier and safer for the Ojibwe to treat with the Americans by reducing their need to travel to Fort Snelling and through Dakota territory. With the stronger American presence and growing populations of white settlers between the Ojibwe and the Dakota, warfare between them generally decreased in frequency and intensity.

Ojibwe-American relationships and the nature of Ojibwe chief-tainship were being manipulated and changed by the Americans, the Ojibwe, and in particular Bagone-giizhig. Charles Cleland, who re-searched tribal leadership for the Mille Lacs Ojibwe, observed:

> Hole-in-the-Day's rise to a position of leadership and influ-ence was part of a pattern of larger change. With the cooling of hostility between the Dakota and the Chippewa and the advent of American settlement in the 1840s, war chiefs began to lose influence. This was also in part due to the decline in the fur market, which not only increased the importance of annuities but also enhanced the position of civil chiefs who were able to secure more annuities by consolidating their followers and accommodating American demands. In this situation the government tried to manipulate Ojibwa politics by channeling treaty-stipulated goods and services to "coop-erative" chiefs. The result was that those chiefs who could acquire more goods for their people built their prestige.[19]

Bagone-giizhig made the most of the new dynamic. He saw the Americans not just as invaders, but as sources of revenue and power. He used the dispersal of annuities as a political mechanism, reward-ing loyal followers and buying support from mixed-blood traders. The chief's effort to insert himself into treaty negotiations in the region was not simply an effort to shape political decisions about the land and people. It was an effort to control the flow of money through his hands and to his people. Similarly, he intervened in all major decisions about the location of annuity stations (Fort Ripley, Sandy Lake, La Pointe, Fort Snelling) because those decisions could have a tremendous impact on the political and economic power of a chief. Geographic proximity to annuity stations meant ease of access and control.

Bagone-giizhig saw the growing American presence in his peo-ple's homeland as potentially beneficial. Easier access to American trade goods, reduced fatalities from war with the Dakota, greater ease of diplomacy, and money channeled through his hands were represented improvements. But the land cessions that made this change possible also set the stage for eventual economic and po-litical disempowerment of the Ojibwe. No Ojibwe leader, including Bagone-giizhig, could foresee what the future would hold until it was too late. But for the time being, Bagone-giizhig reaped the benefits and focused diplomatic attention on the Americans and the Dakota. For him, they were sources of economic and political empowerment.

Ojibwe-Dakota warfare continued to decline gradually but did not cease after the building of Fort Ripley.[20] In 1848, Mdewakanton-wan Dakota near Sauk Lake killed Bagone-giizhig's brother, Gichi-noodin (Great Wind). Bagone-giizhig raised a large war party to avenge the attack, but most of the warriors deserted him because of the boldness of his plan. With twenty-eight men, Bagone-giizhig led an assault on Shakopee's village and killed a medicine man there. The Dakota in turn attacked Sandy Lake to avenge the killing of their spiritual leader. Bagone-giizhig later said of the attacks and Ojibwe-Dakota warfare in general:

> With the Indians, as well as with the whites, there is an ambition to excel, and those who go to war generally delight in punishing their enemies. When I go, I do the same, and have revenge. I do not hate the Sioux; I love them, as I do every one on the continent who has a red skin. Of course, as I go to St. Paul very often, I frequently meet the Sioux and also the Winnebagoes. I shake hands with them, and, reminding them that the Indian once owned the continent, ask them where they are now. I tell them this every time I see them, that, when they fight, they punish themselves and not the whites. I am a friend of peace.[21]

Bagone-giizhig clearly questioned the need for Ojibwe-Dakota warfare, and he also resented white encroachment. Although Bagone-giizhig's sentiments were sometimes inconsistent with his actions, these themes emerged more strongly as he matured as chief.

PERSONAL CONNECTIONS:
WIVES, MISSIONARIES, AND TRADERS

As a young chief, Bagone-giizhig busily built a power base through diplomatic and familial arrangements. Charles Eastman asserted that "[Bagone-giizhig the Younger] was an astute student of diplomacy. The Ojibways allowed polygamy, and ... he made political use of it by marrying the daughter of a chief in nearly every band. Through these alliances he held a controlling influence over the whole Ojib-way nation." There are many reasons to doubt that Bagone-giizhig's influence was a controlling one, but it was undoubtedly substantial. Bagone-giizhig did use marriage to advance his political objectives. He married at least three women from different Ojibwe bands (although one died), and a white woman as well. He had many children by his marriages, including Ignatius, Louise or Louisa, Adeline, Ohbezzum, Erlenmon, Calin, Rose, Elizabeth, Ida, Julia, Belle or Madeline, and Joseph.[22]

Bagone-giizhig also worked hard at maintaining friendly relationships with missionaries John Johnson, George Copway, and to a lesser extent Henry Whipple. He encouraged Johnson to build St. Columba Mission at the village site on the northeast shore of Gull Lake.[23] He also cultivated close personal ties with traders, including most of the Beaulieu brothers in Crow Wing, William W. Warren, Augustus Aspinwall, Charles Ruffee, and most of the Fairbanks brothers. The papers and correspondence of each of these men have numerous references to their relationships and encounters with Bagone-giizhig the Younger.

Bagone-giizhig also added traders Clement Beaulieu, Paul H. Beaulieu, and William McCarthy to the tribal roll and insisted that they be paid "an equal share of the money paid to these Indians" from treaties.[24] Bagone-giizhig did not involve a formal council for this but simply used his personal influence with treaty officials to add members of the growing Crow Wing trading cohort to the annuity rolls. He did so despite the fact that they did not live or identify with the Ojibwe people and often served the government as translators and witnesses for treaty signings. According to Ma'iingaans (Little Wolf), a longtime resident of the village at Crow Wing, "The whiskey was always present right there at Crow Wing, was always on hand, and Hole-in-the-Day used to drink all the time, for the reason that [the traders] gave him drinks . . . thanking him because Hole-in-the-Day had enrolled them on the annuity pay-rolls."[25]

Being "a man of means and influence," Charles Eastman reported, Bagone-giizhig "was listened to with respect by scattered white settlers in his vicinity." In fact, through the advocacy of his white friends, Bagone-giizhig became a U.S. citizen before any of his constituents by special act of the Minnesota State Legislature. He was a staunch Republican who voted in state and local elections, and his name appears in the voter registration poll book for Crow Wing as "H. Day, Esq."[26]

Agidajiwekwe (Coming Over the Top of the Mountain Woman), wife
of Bagone-giizhig the Younger and mother of Ignatius and Madeline
Hole-in-the-Day, ca. 1865

Bagone-giizhig tried to maintain a reputation of affluence in order to build networks with white power brokers. The *St. Paul Pioneer Press* noted: "He spent with profusion, for he was as great a prodigal as he was a warrior. Disdaining the humble bark wigwams of his tribe, he lived in a good house near Crow Wing, and kept horses, and surrounded himself, while his means lasted, with luxuries."[27] The *Prairie du Chien Courier* reported that one day he bought thirty-two pairs of shoes, determined that his wives and family members would have all the accoutrements of "civilized" life. There was no subsequent report about whether his family found heeled shoes practical while doing their daily work on the bare ground of their wigwam villages. Bagone-giizhig also tried to learn English, but he never mastered it. He was once heard courting white settlers and businessmen in a heavy accent with the words, "Chentimen, you Pemicans [Republicans], come out and drink!"[28]

There were blemishes in Bagone-giizhig's courtship of traders, especially when he was drinking and his temper flared. This propensity for aggressive behavior manifested itself in many ways, including in his personal life. As a young man he killed many Dakota in war, threatened white settlers, and even killed people in bar-room brawls at Crow Wing. On February 2, 1849, Charles H. Oakes, a Crow Wing trader, reported to Indian agent Jonathan E. Fletcher that Bagone-giizhig had killed a mixed-blood named John Fairbanks Jr. (brother of trader William Fairbanks) in cold blood.[29] Violence between Indians usually received little attention from white officials, and no formal investigation was opened. Bagone-giizhig offered to turn himself in to the white authorities and submit to American justice, although the sincerity of his offer was never tested. Fletcher dismissed the event as an accident, and no action was taken. It is not clear if the killing was accidental or intentional, although Bagone-giizhig did feel remorse and even tried to have the mother of John Fairbanks Jr. adopt him as a son and accept payment in a traditional "covering the dead" ceremony. The family found his offer insincere and rejected it.[30]

Despite the Fairbanks killing, Bagone-giizhig was successfully building his base of support among Ojibwe, Dakota (with whom he both fought and engaged in diplomacy), mixed-blood traders, missionaries, and U.S. officials. He used marriage as a tool to strengthen his political position and his role as financial arbiter in the annuity-based economy to buy political allies among mixed-blood traders. Throughout, he used his affable charm and intellect to build rapport with anyone he perceived to be in a position of power.

A NEW ECONOMY: ANNUITIES, TIMBER, AND FARMING

Throughout his chieftainship Bagone-giizhig was involved in many treaty negotiations with the United States. In fact, he tried to insert himself into almost every Minnesota Ojibwe treaty negotiation between 1847 and 1867.

The Menominee and Ho-Chunk removal attempts were only forerunners to major land grabs by the United States in central Minnesota. Because the fur trade had dwindled significantly throughout the first half of the nineteenth century, Ojibwe people were forced to adapt their resource-intensive economy. Initially, the sale of timber and minerals helped compensate for lost income. In addition to these annuities, the Ojibwe increasingly planted gardens and sold excess produce to white settlers in the area.[31]

Yet even these changes were insufficient at times. With the whites continually pressing to acquire land, not just the timber, mineral, and food resources on the land, the Ojibwe began to sell it off in treaty after treaty. Doing so forced them to depend more on the treaty annuities for their livelihood. It was a vicious cycle, as land moved to nonnative control and the Ojibwe had fewer resources with which to sustain themselves. This created pressure to sell more land.

With the escalating poverty of the Ojibwe in central Minnesota came new tests to their relationship with white settlers. Sometimes settlers chased Indians off land at gunpoint. This even happened on occasions when white settlers were squatting on legitimate reservation land and despite the retained usufructary (use) rights of the Ojibwe to the 1837 treaty area. As tensions between white settlers and Ojibwe people increased, Bagone-giizhig became an active diplomat and leader.

Bagone-giizhig pursued diplomatic channels with American officials with some success. Article 5 of the 1847 treaty at Fond du Lac, for example, had guaranteed that annuity payments would be dispensed near Fort Ripley, but the article was stricken from the document after Bagone-giizhig had signed. The chief complained bitterly in a formal petition to the president of the United States that blasted the government's paternalistic language ("Great White Father," "Little Red Children"), challenged illegal alterations of signed agreements without Indian consent, and expressed doubts about the trustworthiness of the American government. Jonathan Fletcher, who was serving as Indian agent for the Ho-Chunk at the time, presented Bagone-giizhig's petition and a letter of his own supporting the petition's content. This correspondence resulted in the annuity agency being relocated to Sandy Lake and Fletcher being assigned there as Indian agent for the Mississippi Ojibwe. Bagone-giizhig's success in getting the annuity station moved closer to his people greatly enhanced his prestige among all of the Mississippi Ojibwe.[32]

In November 1850, while numerous Ojibwe from throughout the region descended on Sandy Lake in hopes of receiving their annuities, Bagone-giizhig stayed behind for several weeks to deal with another intrusion on his band's sovereignty. Eight soldiers from Fort Ripley had trespassed onto Indian land near Bagone-giizhig's village. Under army orders, they began cutting trees for the fort. Bagone-giizhig sent warriors to stop the woodcutters and demand compensation for the timber harvested. The soldiers refused, and Bagone-giizhig's men confiscated the team of oxen being used to skid the logs out of the woods. The soldiers returned to the fort. Bagone-giizhig displayed skillful tact, force, and diplomacy in handling the issue. Two of his letters on the matter to Governor Alexander Ramsey and Captain John B. S. Todd survive, as do numerous references to his conversations with army officers and American diplomats.[33]

Bagone-giizhig was polite, but firm. He wrote to army and government officials that he wanted no trouble but that the Americans had to respect Ojibwe land and sovereignty. The Americans had trespassed and the Ojibwe only wanted compensation for the timber that was illegally taken. "Do not think hard of me," he wrote to Todd, "but I do as others would—the Timber is mine." He refused to turn over the confiscated oxen until his people were compensated. Todd tried to get Indian agent John S. Watrous to withhold annuity payments to pressure Bagone-giizhig into returning the oxen without compensating the Ojibwe. Bagone-giizhig's letter to Ramsey produced more effective results. Ramsey wrote Todd that withholding the annuities was too extreme and that Bagone-giizhig should have been paid first, although Ramsey added that the chief "should have appealed to his agent, and not have taken summary redress into his own hands." What is most interesting in Ramsey's communication is that he accepted Bagone-giizhig's position on the sovereignty of the Ojibwe and their right to compensation. In that regard, Bagone-giizhig had won an important diplomatic battle. Ojibwe sovereignty over land and resources was affirmed by the chief's actions and words. Ramsey formally reprimanded the Indian agent for not preemptively paying the Indians and for disregarding Indian timber rights even when the wood was "wanted for Government purposes."[34]

Ramsey then dispatched trader and treaty commissioner Henry M. Rice to deal with Bagone-giizhig. Rice eventually convinced Bagone-giizhig to release the oxen in return for a promise to compensate the Ojibwe for the lumber and to provide formal notice and payment in advance for future cuttings. Ultimately, the Ojibwe did receive money for the timber. Even more important, Ramsey promised Bagone-giizhig that the United States "will always see that your rights are not infringed, or if they should be, that you receive proper remuneration."[35]

Bagone-giizhig's firm stance set a precedent for U.S. timber harvests on Indian land, not only for his own band but for Indians throughout the region. When timber on Dakota land was needed at Fort Snelling later that year, the Indian agent was directed as follows: "Whenever it was necessary to cut timber on Indian lands for government purposes, that [the Indians] should be compensated." The chief's skills as a diplomat and his willingness to take a firm stance against the government set parameters for government intrusions on Indian land and created a template for his future dealings with government officials.[36]

Bagone-giizhig had successes as an advocate for his people. He pressured and threatened at just the right times to win compensation for the illegal timber harvest and to move the annuity station to Sandy Lake. In 1850, however, the celebrated move had disastrous consequences when the U.S. government manipulated the station's relocation to coerce the permanent removal of the Ojibwe from Wisconsin and the Upper Peninsula of Michigan to Minnesota.

THE 1850 SANDY LAKE ANNUITY FIASCO

By 1850 the Ojibwe were feeling tremendous pressure on their liveli-hoods and land. Minnesota had been organized as a territory the year before, and territorial officials saw tribal control of the land as an obstacle to the goal of statehood. In this rapidly changing economic situation, the government relentlessly pursued acquisition of indige-nous land by any means. Alcohol was often employed by government officials to coerce or manipulate people into signing treaties. Where manipulations failed, disease and violence produced even greater pressures.[37]

In 1850, President Zachary Taylor signed an order for the removal of the Ojibwe from Wisconsin and the Upper Peninsula of Michigan to Minnesota. The agency at La Pointe, Wisconsin, was closed, and the station at Minnesota's Sandy Lake became the only place the Wisconsin and Michigan Ojibwe could receive their annuities from earlier treaties. As the pace of white settlement and state and ter-ritorial ambition grew, so did the intensity of efforts to concentrate and relocate the Ojibwe.

The government's plan backfired at the first annuity payment to the eastern Ojibwe at Sandy Lake. The government had summoned the Indians there to receive their annuities, but somehow it failed to have either the cash annuities or adequate food rations for the Ojibwe who arrived there. While waiting for their promised pay-ments, three thousand Ojibwe were fed moldy flour and spoiled meat. Major outbreaks of food poisoning and measles ensued.[38]

Julia Warren Spears, William W. Warren's sister, who was en-trusted with communicating the removal plan to the Indians, wrote that the Ojibwe "waited about three weeks before the money came. They suffered with cold, and hunger, pork and flour was issued out to them but not sufficient, for so many. The measles and other sick-ness broke out, a great many children died and a number of Indians, it was a very distressing time."[39]

While the Americans claimed the catastrophe was accidental, the Ojibwe believed otherwise. Some 150 people died immediately, and four hundred more perished on the way home, mainly of food poisoning. The *Minnesota Pioneer* commented on the Sandy Lake an-nuity fiasco on November 21, 1850, stating, "Here now, it is winter, and not a dollar of their annuities, which by the solemn treaty stipulations of the government, ought to have been paid months ago, have any of these destitute tribes received."[40]

Bagone-giizhig arrived at Sandy Lake after most of the spoiled provisions had already been consumed. (He later reported that four, five, or six people died every night while he was there.) When it became clear that annuity payments were not immediately forthcoming, he left. The Sandy Lake tragedy was reported in the *Minnesota Democrat* that winter and is referred to frequently in the personal correspondence of several chiefs, Governor Ramsey, Henry H. Sibley, Julia Warren Spears, and William W. Warren.

Eshkibagikoonzh (Flat Mouth) had his speech at Sandy Lake transcribed and sent to Governor Ramsey. It contains a scathing indictment of the government's response to the tragedy and the land cessions:

> We have been called here, and made to suffer by sickness, by death, by hunger and cold. I lay it all to him. I charge it all to our Great Father the Governor. It is because we listened to his words that we have now suffered so much. We were poor before but we are poorer now... We have been taken from our country at the most valuable season of the year for hunting and fishing, and if we had remained at home we should have been far better off... Tell him I blame him for the children we have lost, for the sickness we have suffered and for the hunger we have endured... The Governor promised to feed us while here. He has not done it... It makes our hearts sore to look at the losses we have sustained while at Sandy Lake. You call us your children, but I do not think we are your children... You are not our Father and I think you call us your children only in mockery. The *earth* is our Father and I will never call *you* so... We did not sell the ground to our Great Father. We gave it to him in order that he might follow our example and be liberal to us.[41]

After the disaster Bagone-giizhig demanded a council with the white authorities to seek reparations and an increase in annuity payments. Showing consciousness of diplomacy, he gave a speech on January 8, 1851, to the congregation of the Presbyterian Church in St. Paul to build white support for his reparation requests. William W. Warren served as his interpreter. Warren had suffered along with the Indians for a significant share of the time at Sandy Lake, and the diseases had engulfed his family as well. The chief and Warren were

Alexander Ramsey, ca. 1848. Ramsey, the first governor of Minnesota Territory, was actively involved in the Sandy Lake tragedy in 1850 and several Ojibwe diplomatic events and treaties. He and Bagone-giizhig the Younger knew one another well.

good friends, but Warren's service to the Office of Indian Affairs and defense of Ramsey stressed their friendship for years.[42]

Bagone-giizhig's speech received a great deal of attention, including press coverage and a formal rebuke from Governor Ramsey, who was chagrined by the growing criticism of the government's handling of the Sandy Lake annuity fiasco. Several members of the legislature were present and heard Bagone-giizhig harshly criticize Ramsey. The governor was clearly uncomfortable with the negative attention published in newspapers. John S. Watrous, the government's removal agent, was especially upset. He tried to stop Bagone-giizhig from giving further speeches to whites, writing Ramsey in 1851, "You will oblige me by preventing him if possible as he only goes to create difficulty as he cannot have any other business."[43]

William W. Warren spoke briefly after Bagone-giizhig at the Presbyterian church and gave at least several speeches independently from Bagone-giizhig, reiterating his sorrow about events at Sandy Lake but defending Ramsey, Watrous, and the Office of Indian Affairs. Warren was working for the U.S. government and had tried unsuccessfully to engineer two removals of the Lake Superior Ojibwe. But he was deeply upset about the failure of the government to make his job possible and the damage it did to his reputation in the Indian community. Prior to the Sandy Lake disaster, Warren and the chief had a growing friendship, although Warren's comments were always less confrontational and served a different agenda.[44]

When Bagone-giizhig learned that Warren had defended Ramsey, Watrous, and the government, he was furious. He wrote an open letter to Warren that he succeeded in having published in the *Minnesota Pioneer*. He blasted the government's handling of the fiasco and also viciously attacked Warren's motives and character:

> Had I understood Mr. Warren at the time, I certainly would have proved to the meeting, his double way of acting . . . and explained the truth in favor of the Indians, who have given him bread since he has been born. To those very Indians he owes his livelihood, but no, he is one of those men who can be bought at any time for a small sum of money. I have said, and say still, that the bad provisions killed the Indians. I also say that the usual quantity of provisions we did not receive; I also say that the agent refused to have the bills and invoices

William W. Warren, ca. 1851. A trader, historian, and Indian Affairs officer, Warren knew both chiefs Bagone-giizhig and was good friends with Bagone-giizhig the Younger, who called him *nisayenh* (older brother). His relationship with them was that of both insider and outsider. At times he served as interpreter for treaty signings, worked for the government, and used his position to help the American Fur Company gouge Ojibwe annuities. Yet he also interpreted for the chiefs, accompanied Bagone-giizhig on diplomatic missions, and wrote letters defending Ojibwe military and diplomatic positions.

> compared with the goods and provisions brought to us. The Chippewas were compelled to sign papers through hunger and want.

Bagone-giizhig even noted in his letter that "a dog had died from the effects of eating rotten provisions."[45]

Warren defended himself with information and personal attacks. His letter to the editor of the *Minnesota Democrat* reported, among many other things, that Bagone-giizhig "is known to, and recognized as chief but by a fraction of the tribe." Warren spent a significant amount of time over the next two years trying to discredit Bagone-giizhig's claim to chieftainship. Warren wrote to George P. Warren, for example: "Governor Ramsey thanked me for the course I had taken and refuses any longer to recognise Hole in the Day as chief." He instructed him, "If the chiefs are handy by you, write a strong letter for them to the Governor... Mention also that Hole in the Day they do not recognise as being chief."[46]

Warren's attempts to discredit Bagone-giizhig's claim to chieftainship met with little success. While he and the chief reconciled, many Ojibwe leaders, including Bagone-giizhig, never fully forgave him for his role in the Sandy Lake annuity fiasco or his later efforts to remove the Ojibwe. In spite of their conflict in 1850, however, the peace Warren and Bagone-giizhig made in 1852 was genuine. According to Julia Warren Spears, the two were close friends, and Bagone-giizhig customarily called Warren *nisayenh* (older brother). When Warren died in the summer of 1853, Bagone-giizhig remarked that "he had lost his elder brother and best friend."[47]

In spite of Ramsey's distress about being publicly lambasted at the Presbyterian Church and Bagone-giizhig's temporary falling out with Warren, officials at Fort Snelling were willing to meet with Bagone-giizhig about the fiasco at Sandy Lake. A special committee was formed that included Henry M. Rice (trader, treaty commissioner, and now an aspiring territorial politician), Justus Ramsey (the territorial governor's brother), and Charles Borup. The committee limited their work, however, to soliciting reparations for Bagone-giizhig's band instead of a general redress of the deaths and annuity problems for all Ojibwe people. President Zachary Taylor's 1850 order for the removal of the Michigan and Wisconsin Ojibwe to Sandy Lake was retracted in 1851 because of the tragedy at Sandy

Lake, but this did little to ease tensions. Bagone-giizhig requested a private audience with President Taylor and the commissioner of Indian Affairs through William Warren, but Ramsey succeeded in having the request denied by his friends in the Office of Indian Affairs.[48]

Bagone-giizhig continued to solicit support for further reparations, larger annuities, and closer annuity stations and Indian agencies. He gave speeches, wrote letters, and traveled tirelessly to advance his concerns. In a letter to the editor of a St. Paul paper, he wrote, "Though it may cost me my liberty, it is my duty, and I will continue to speak and act also, till the wrongs of my people shall be righted."[49]

OJIBWE-DAKOTA RELATIONS: MANIPULATING THE AMERICANS

Bagone-giizhig's call for a large conference to address annuity concerns and Ojibwe-Dakota warfare began to receive additional support following several small Dakota attacks on Ojibwe settlements in Minnesota and Wisconsin before and after the Sandy Lake annuity fiasco. On March 23, 1850, prior to the Sandy Lake catastrophe, Dakota Indians killed and scalped the son of Gull Lake chief Waabojiig (White Fisher). Waabojiig appealed for help to William W. Warren, who presented his request for redress to Jonathan Fletcher, the Indian agent at Long Prairie, and then to Governor Ramsey. U.S. officials refused to take action, citing Ojibwe attacks against the Dakota as having provoked the killing of Waabojiig's son.[50]

On April 2, 1850, a group of Dakota from Red Wing and from Kaposia, Little Crow's village opposite Pig's Eye Lake, attacked an Ojibwe sugar camp at Apple River, Wisconsin, northeast of Stillwater, Minnesota. Fourteen Ojibwe were killed and scalped, and one nine-year-old boy was taken prisoner. On April 3, the Dakota paraded their scalps and prisoner through the streets of Stillwater to the horror of white settlers there. The *Minnesota Chronicle and Register* published a series of articles defending the Dakota attacks, with contributions by local traders and even Reverend Gideon H. Pond. William Warren defended the Ojibwe, publishing a response in two parts titled, "Dakotah and Chippewa Wars." While the letters probably had little effect on anyone's belief about moral justifications for the violence, some American officials began to realize that Bagone-giizhig's call for a peace conference might be the best way to stem the violence and calm the fears of the settlers, missionaries, and traders.[51]

While advocating for the peace conference, Bagone-giizhig responded to growing Ojibwe distress with his own escalation of hostilities. With his cousin Ojibwe and two other Mississippi Band members, he traveled to St. Paul in May 1850 and killed and scalped a Dakota north of town. They escaped by canoe in full view of the man's family. William W. Warren had seen Bagone-giizhig leave in preparation for the attack and unsuccessfully tried to stop him. Warren wrote to Alexander Ramsey: "Hole in the Day has personally visited Leech, Winnepeg, Pokagama and Sandy Lakes, and by the 15th of June they will probably collect between four and five hundred warriors . . . [I] just returned from Crow Wing in pursuit of a [war party] headed by Hole in the Day, who with three others have gone . . . to the St. Peter's River. I did not succeed in catching them. Hole in the Day has gone contrary to his solemn promise."[52]

The violence of 1850 vexed American authorities, especially because the Dakota attack at Apple River had frightened many white settlers. Governor Ramsey agreed to summon a peace conference at Fort Snelling. Bagone-giizhig would have a chance to voice his concerns about annuity payments and Ojibwe-Dakota violence. Many Dakota leaders were invited as well. William W. Warren had doubts about the prospects for peace and warned Ramsey: "It will be difficult to pacify the Chippeways, as they are very much exasperated."[53]

The Ojibwe delegation arrived on June 9, 1850, to a stir of excitement in the press. One reporter noted: "We have never seen a finer looking body of men assembled, than these Chippewas. There is scarcely one among them that would not be considered a model of grace and perfection by an artist." The Dakota showed up the next day with more than three hundred warriors. Many of St. Paul's elite came to the meeting, as did Ramsey's entire staff.[54]

The meeting commenced on June 10 failed on the spot. Ramsey, who was completely ignorant of indigenous protocol in peace making, brought two white women to the formal council. Many Dakota and Ojibwe leaders were extremely upset by this breach of custom, and the blunder on Ramsey's part destroyed his chance to forge a diplomatic solution.[55]

Bagone-giizhig, however, was willing to ignore the breach as long as he maintained a central diplomatic position. He actually offered the women a seat with his delegation, saying, "The Ojibway chiefs will feel highly honored if the ladies will consent to sit on our side." The *New York Tribune* reported an even coyer version of his overture, claiming "that he was happy to see so many sweet women there, and that they were all welcome, with their angelic smiles, to sit on his side." Other Ojibwe chiefs, however, and all the Dakota leaders present were upset, and many delegations returned home, disgusted with Ramsey and the Americans. After the women eventually left, discussions resumed the next day.[56]

Bagone-giizhig seized the upper hand. He stated that the Ojibwe were the aggrieved party and that if the Dakota paid them twenty-nine thousand dollars from their annuities, he would use the money to "cover the dead" and resolve the recent conflicts peacefully. Bagone-giizhig was shrewd. He could not possibly have expected the Dakota to agree that the Ojibwe were the only party with a grievance or to accept all responsibility for recent violence. Although he was demanding compensation from the Dakota, he did not expect that either. He did, however, understand the concerns of American officials and their personalities. As he anticipated, the Dakota leadership was outraged by the proposal, which caused major disruptions to the proceedings. This uproar made Bagone-giizhig look reasonable.[57]

When the council resumed once again, Bagone-giizhig simply said that he trusted Alexander Ramsey to make a fair and equitable resolution and proposed a binding arbitration. The remaining Dakota agreed to let the United States make a final decision based on what all Indian delegations had said at the meeting. Bagone-giizhig knew this was a safe move because he was the only chief who made a request for financial reparation. Although the Dakota had rebuked that request and repudiated the claim that they were the perpetrators of the worst violence, they never made a counterclaim against the Ojibwe. For the Ojibwe, the worst that could happen was that they would get no money, and the best outcome was that they would get exactly what they asked for. The most likely outcome would be somewhere in between, and that is precisely what happened.

Ramsey agreed with Bagone-giizhig that the Dakota were the primary aggressors and that the Ojibwe had lost more people. He also agreed to garnish the Dakota annuities to the tune of five thousand dollars (an amount later reduced to fifteen hundred dollars). Although the final result did little to preserve peace between the Ojibwe and the Dakota, it showed Bagone-giizhig's skill at political chess. He killed Dakota Indians with his own hands after swearing to uphold the peace. Then, with nothing more than smooth rhetoric and well-timed requests, he got the Dakota to pay reparations for the chain of violence that ensued.[58]

Bagone-giizhig was involved in at least two additional attacks on Dakota Indians. In January 1858 he led a war party that was later seen with two fresh Dakota scalps. In 1860 he again led a small expedition against the Dakota that killed five people. John George Nicolay reported in *Harper's New Monthly Magazine* that there were six Dakota fatalities and that Bagone-giizhig had shot each one with his Colt 45 revolver, although he shared the scalps with his men: "When the battle was over, and the party counted the slain Sioux, five of the scalps belonged beyond question to the chief with his revolving gun. The sixth Indian corpse also contained his ball; but as it had likewise been hit by buckshot from the gun of one of his warriors, he generously gave him the scalp." It was reported that two more slashed their own throats rather than be taken prisoner, although this is a suspicious report since the Ojibwe rarely took adult prisoners in war, especially males. Bagone-giizhig was wounded in the leg in the last attack.[59]

Despite Bagone-giizhig's direct involvement in conflict with the Dakota, the level of warfare was waning in central Minnesota. The troubled truce that dominated Ojibwe-Dakota relations during this period was continually being tested, broken, and reforged. But despite the frequency of attacks, they were less and less debilitating. With the exception of the bloody events of 1839, Ojibwe-Dakota violence claimed fewer than twenty lives per year in Minnesota.

LAND CESSIONS AND RESERVATIONS:
THE TREATIES OF 1854–55

Bagone-giizhig was disappointed at the failure of the peace conference. In spite of his unsuccessful attempt to gain support from white authorities for larger and timelier annuity payments, he did convince them to hold back further plans for land cessions from the Ojibwe. In fact, it was not until 1854 and 1855 that U.S. officials again approached Ojibwe leaders with plans for additional cessions in Minnesota.[60]

Bagone-giizhig acted as both statesman and warrior in his political endeavors—trying to win friends in positions of power and

fighting anyone who got in his way. His oscillations between conciliation and resistance baffled officials. He advocated U.S. citizenship
for all Ojibwe, flirted with American culture and religion, and even
advocated construction of the St. Columba Mission at Gull Lake, although he himself never participated directly in mission activities or
church services. It is doubtful that he actually intended to convert to
Christianity, although his requests for citizenship seem sincere and
consistent with his diplomatic agenda.

Massive pressure was building, however, for land cessions from
the Ojibwe and the Dakota in Minnesota. White settlers were starting to pour into Indian lands. Usufructary rights guaranteed in treaties were being ignored. Treaty annuities were being withheld, a
common government practice that created leverage for more Indian
land cessions and served as a tool for paying off Indian debts to traders, whether real or fabricated.

Bagone-giizhig spent a great deal of time negotiating for and demanding payments promised in treaties. In 1854, he even threatened
Indian agent David Herriman that he would burn down the agency
warehouse in Crow Wing if the annuities inside were not dispersed
to his people. When the annuities were not distributed, the agency
warehouse burned, with no witnesses to the arson. In fact, there
were three separate cases of arson against government buildings
in Crow Wing over the next year. Herriman had Bagone-giizhig arrested and imprisoned at Fort Ripley, but Willis Gorman (the second territorial governor of Minnesota) ordered that the chief be
released when no evidence of his direct involvement could be found.
Nevertheless, the government's year-and-a-half delay in paying the
annuities and distrust of Bagone-giizhig heightened tensions with
Ojibwe leaders.[61]

In 1854 and 1855 two significant land treaties altered Ojibwe life
forever. Before the treaties, most Minnesota Ojibwe still lived in numerous villages on unceded land, as they had for centuries. After
the treaties most Minnesota Ojibwe would live on reservations that
were scattered islands surrounded by a sea of white settlers and
white timber, mining, and railroad operations. The ability of native
people to provide for themselves by traditional harvesting of wild
rice, fish, and game was significantly reduced, creating the need for
further adaptation. Chief Bagone-giizhig the Younger played a paramount role in the negotiations for both treaties.[62]

On September 30, 1854, Bagone-giizhig signed the first of these large land cession treaties at La Pointe, with the words "head chief" next to his name. The 1854 treaty divided Minnesota's Arrowhead region between the Mississippi and Lake Superior Ojibwe and ceded most of northeastern Minnesota to the government. Bagone-giizhig's villages were unaffected, but all of the Lake Superior Ojibwe were now confined to reservations. In spite of the location of the land cessions and the bands affected, Bagone-giizhig was instrumental in negotiations and encouraged the Lake Superior Band leadership to cede their portion to the United States. Again, Bagone-giizhig upset and alienated other tribal leaders but earned the respect and praise of government officials and returned home with the promise of further annuities to his people. Bagone-giizhig led a delegation to Washington, DC, to discuss terms for the 1855 treaty, which was to follow. The government wanted the Mississippi, Pillager, and Winnibigoshish Ojibwe to cede all of their lands in Minnesota and Wisconsin, but that was an impossible request. Bagone-giizhig conceded that the Ojibwe would have to make adaptations to their economy and lifestyle but argued that it would take time and the government's dedication of tremendous economic resources to make that happen.

Commissioner of Indian Affairs George W. Manypenny and Bagone-giizhig sparred for hours over treaty terms, payments, and changes in the Ojibwe economy. By the time negotiations concluded and the document was signed, Bagone-giizhig was largely responsible for enabling the Ojibwe to hold on to a portion of their homeland in the form of eleven different reservations, but the overwhelming majority of Ojibwe land in Minnesota was now in white hands.

Bagone-giizhig was promised a personal payment from the 1855 treaty, although Congress blocked this payment when the treaty came before the U.S. Senate for ratification. Bagone-giizhig did receive a private land grant of 640 acres as part of the treaty. The grant was one of several moves that provided financial compensation or personal benefit to Bagone-giizhig while Ojibwe people were losing land, economic resources, and political power. Although he gained the short-term benefit of increased personal wealth, the long-term effect was erosion of the trust and confidence of many of his constituents. The rift between Bagone-giizhig and his people slowly widened as his actions became more and more out of sync with those of his people. After the 1855 treaty signing, Major H. Day wrote to Manypenny, "[Bagone-giizhig] often passed a sleepless night... from the mortification of being accused of betraying or sacrificing the interests of his nation."[63]

Bagone-giizhig was not alone in receiving criticism and distrust from the people he represented at the treaty negotiations. The venerated and greatly respected Eshkibagikoonzh (Flat Mouth) of Leech Lake had his life threatened by his own warriors. They did not harm him, but they killed the horse he rode from Leech Lake to St. Paul on his way to Washington for the 1855 negotiations.[64]

A POLITICIAN APART: BAGONE-GIIZHIG'S HOUSE AND LAND

After the 1855 treaty Bagone-giizhig initiated another major change in the structure of his chieftainship. He had lived in the village at Gull Lake for many years and had positioned himself as a village chief who could speak for Ojibwe people throughout his region. Although his claim to represent other Ojibwe leaders was never accepted, he had a large and loyal following from Gull Lake.

Once he received his private land grant, however, he made plans to build his own house on his private land and not live with the people in his village. There were, of course many villages located throughout the Gull Lake region, including large ones at Rabbit Lake, Gull Lake, and Crow Wing. But his private land grant was on the opposite side of the river from the village at Crow Wing, which the Ojibwe called Gichi-mashkodeng (Big Field).[65]

Thereafter Bagone-giizhig did not claim to be a village chief or to represent one village. Instead, he claimed to be the chief and representative of the entire Gull Lake region, including the villages at Crow Wing, Gull Lake, and Rabbit Lake. Eshkibagikoonzh (Flat Mouth) of Leech Lake claimed to represent the Pillager Band at Otter Tail Lake in addition to the main village at Leech Lake where he lived, but Bagone-giizhig's claim to be a band and regional chief while not living with his people represented an anomalous development in Ojibwe leadership paradigms. Although he was certainly not the only chief to receive a private land grant, Bagone-giizhig was the only chief claiming to be a strong regional or band chief who lived outside an Indian community.

Gwiiwizhenzhish (Bad Boy), who had been in a subordinate position to Bagone-giizhig when they lived in the village at Gull Lake, now claimed to be Gull Lake's village chief. His ascendancy was initially accepted by Bagone-giizhig, who saw Gwiiwizhenzhish's growing power as subordinate, and this acquiescence continued until 1862. Similarly, Gwiiwizhenzhish, Aazhawaa-giizhig (Crossing Sky), and other village chiefs in the Gull Lake region did not publicly challenge Bagone-giizhig's claim to now be a regional and band chief. Their tacit acceptance was a major departure from the leadership tradition that had persisted for centuries in Ojibwe country among civil, military, and religious leaders.

Bagone-giizhig's claim to be a regional chief met with mixed responses among the Mississippi Ojibwe. Mille Lacs chiefs repudiated his claim to regional and band representation. They even asserted that the Mille Lacs Indians were independent and not part of the Mississippi Band to clarify that Bagone-giizhig did not and could not be a Mille Lacs leader. Within the Gull Lake region, Bagone-giizhig went unchallenged until 1862, when Gwiiwizhenzhish, Aazhawaa-giizhig, and Waabojiig (White Fisher) the Younger called his claim into question.

Bagone-giizhig used his new location across the river from Crow Wing to build his relationships with white and mixed-blood traders and with businessmen, missionaries, and the staff of the Indian agency after it was relocated there. A consummate politician, he traveled tirelessly in the Gull Lake region and frequently visited John Johnson and the chiefs, villagers, traders, and agents in the area.

At the same time, Bagone-giizhig industriously farmed his private land grant on an agricultural site north of his new house and sold hundreds of dollars worth of crops and vegetables as early as the fall of 1855. He told his people: "This my brethren is the result of my farming. While you have been wandering, pursuing the uncertain chase, I have been laboring; you are poor, I am rich; I have no fears with winter, as I have sufficient food to carry me through; profit by my example." While he was doubtless seeking to model how Ojibwe should adapt to the shrinking land base and growing white economy, he alienated many people with his words and actions. His large house, his ostentatious clothing, and his large income—from annuities, his chief stipend, and farming—encouraged some Indians

QUI-WI-SAIN-SHISH, (BAD BOY,)
Chief of Gull Lake Chippewas.
Who to escape the vengeance of the Indians when they discovered his
friendship for the whites, in the outbreak of 1862, was obliged to seek
protection in Fort Ripley.

WHITNEY'S GALLERY, SAINT PAUL.

Gwiiwizhenzhish (Bad Boy), ca. 1860. Gwiiwizhenzhish assumed
the position of primary civil chief at Gull Lake when Bagone-giizhig
left the village and asserted himself as chief of the entire region.
Gwiiwizhenzhish's role was cooperative with and subordinate to
that of Bagone-giizhig until 1862, when rifts in Ojibwe leadership led
Gwiiwizhenzhish to challenge Bagone-giizhig's authority and eventually
move to Mille Lacs to distance himself.

to believe that he was profiteering from their displacement and land loss.[66]

By 1860, most Ojibwe resented white settlers in their lands more than they had the scattered attacks by Dakota warriors of the previous decades. The new annuity-based economy was difficult for most Ojibwe. It meant a declining standard of living, less freedom to live where and how they wished, and less control over their own affairs. Tensions continued to escalate until they boiled over in 1862, when unusual events earned Bagone-giizhig more fame and more enemies. His pivotal role in the events of that year made him a marked man in that life-altering moment of Ojibwe history.

5
The Art of Diplomacy
Bagone-giizhig and the Conflict of 1862

[He] told us in full detail how their land belonged to the Sioux and
Ojibbeways, and how the white men had torn it from them by force:
how the pale faces were always extending further and growing
more dangerous . . . He said that the danger was pressing: either the
giant must be strangled in the cradle, or he would trample on all
the Indians far and near.
— Johann Georg Kohl[1]

Are you the smartest man that our Great Father could send in a
trying time like this? Because, if you are the smartest man the Great
Father has got, I pity our Great Father.
— Bagone-giizhig[2]

In 1862, irate Ojibwe took dozens of white prisoners and destroyed
white churches, trading posts, and houses at Leech Lake, Crow
Wing, and Ottertail City. These events have been overshadowed
by the more widespread concurrent violence of the U.S.–Dakota Conflict in southern Minnesota. Exploring how the U.S.–Ojibwe Conflict
developed and why it stopped without large-scale loss of life brings
to life relations between American settlers, the Ojibwe, the Dakota,
and Bagone-giizhig, the primary Ojibwe leader involved in the event.[3]

BAGONE-GIIZHIG, LITTLE CROW, AND
OJIBWE–DAKOTA COOPERATION BEFORE 1857

Tensions leading to the U.S.–Ojibwe Conflict of 1862 had been develop-
ing for decades. Many important Ojibwe and Dakota leaders, especially
Bagone-giizhig and Little Crow, had communicated about the possibility of uniting their nations in common resistance to the whites. Although united action did not occur, frequent communications between
these leaders and the plans they discussed undoubtedly influenced

events in 1862. Bagone-giizhig was well aware of the tensions in Dakota country and the potential for widespread violence there. He also knew Little Crow's thoughts on those tensions intimately. Bagone-giizhig used this information to exploit events to his advantage.[4]

Little Crow had participated in discussions of joint violence against white authorities and settlers prior to the U.S.–Dakota Conflict in 1862, even though the actual conflict was not planned. Once it began, however, he tried unsuccessfully to gain military support from the Ojibwe. Major Edwin Clark wrote to the *Minneapolis Journal* years later that he had received "the bead belt and pipe sent by Little Crow to the head chief of the Chippewas of Red Lake, requesting the Chippewas join the massacre." It is probable that other solicitations were sent to other Ojibwe chiefs, as well.[5]

The story of the U.S.–Dakota Conflict of 1862 has received considerable historical attention for many reasons. The conflict caused the deaths of anywhere from four hundred to eight hundred white men, women, and children. The American response resulted in the expulsion of most Dakota and Ho-Chunk people from Minnesota, as well as new attempts to relocate the Ojibwe. Government efforts to round up the Dakota, hold them in a winter camp at Fort Snelling, and relocate them out of the state in turn killed hundreds of Indians. The event also heralded the largest mass execution in American history, with thirty-eight Dakota men hanged simultaneously at Mankato, Minnesota. The U.S.–Dakota Conflict also led American troops onto the plains in search of Dakota "renegades" and ignited wars there between several native nations and the United States. Two regiments of union soldiers were called to Minnesota from the front lines of the Civil War to put down the "Indian uprising." Historians of the U.S.–Dakota Conflict including Angela Wilson, Roy Meyer, Gary Clayton Anderson, and others have uncovered new research and offered critical perspective on the event. (Wilson's use of oral history is especially useful in documenting Dakota experiences and interpretation of events.)[6]

The U.S.–Dakota Conflict was largely a spontaneous development. The Dakota were starving under the new annuity-based economy. U.S. officials withheld annuities and traders refused to give Indians goods based on credit. One trader went so far as to say, "If they are hungry, let them eat grass or their own dung." Fearing large-scale loss of life from starvation and an increasingly unresponsive, oppressive U.S. government having control over their affairs, the Dakota took up arms to fight the whites.[7]

This picture of the 1862 U.S.–Dakota Conflict is largely true, but Dakota leaders were concerned about much more than the immediate needs of their people. They knew the size and power of the American government. Many had even journeyed to Washington—seeing with their own eyes hundreds of sizable American towns. They knew what would happen if they attacked the government, although some Dakota leaders, especially Little Crow, hoped for Ojibwe involvement in their resistance. This wish may have been unrealistic, but the Ojibwe nearly did become involved, and Bagone-giizhig alone could have pushed events that far had he chosen to do so.

Dakota leaders knew that the united strength of the Ojibwe and Dakota would be sufficient to expel many whites from Minnesota, at least for a time. Indians outnumbered whites in Minnesota by about six to one in 1862. Dakota leaders also knew that, if necessary, many Dakota could seek refuge among the Ojibwe in Canada. While they hoped this would not be necessary, it was an option. Both the Ojibwe and the Dakota were aware of the extent to which the Civil War was straining military resources and diverting troops to campaigns far from Minnesota.[8]

On the same day that the U.S.–Dakota Conflict erupted, another conflict between whites and the Mississippi Ojibwe flamed up almost two hundred miles away. While the events played out differently, evidence suggests that cooperative communication between Little Crow and Bagone-giizhig prior to 1862 significantly impacted the actions of the Dakota and Ojibwe.

Premeditations of large-scale attacks on the American forts and white settlers in Indian lands had begun long before. In 1837–38, Bagone-giizhig the Elder and Zoongakamig (Strong Ground) made peace between the Mississippi Ojibwe and the Wah'petonwan Dakota. The Ojibwe frequently visited Dakota friends for council and joint hunting expeditions. During one friendly visit in the spring of 1838, the Dakota invited the Ojibwe to a secret council where Dakota leader Wapeassina rose and addressed Bagone-giizhig the Elder and Zoongakamig. He told them "in full detail how their land belonged to the Sioux and Ojibbeways, and how the white men had torn it from

Bagone-giizhig the Younger, ca. 1856. This photograph is one of just a few in which Bagone-giizhig did not display a pipe, blanket, or eagle feathers.

them by force: how the pale faces were always extending further and growing more dangerous...He said that the danger was pressing: either the giant must be strangled in the cradle, or he would trample on all the Indians far and near."[9]

The Dakota spokesman went on to reveal a plan for all the Oceti Sakowin (the Seven Council Fires of the Dakota, Nakota, and Lakota) to bring their forces together in order to destroy Fort Snelling. He then petitioned Bagone-giizhig and Zoongakamig to join with them, saying, "Help us, brothers, let our quarrel be at last utterly forgotten, and ally yourselves with us. Send us warriors, and come yourselves, at the appointed time, and let us secure the freedom of our country by our united strength!"[10]

Bagone-giizhig the Elder responded that it would be difficult to gain the support of all Ojibwe people for such a plan because there were so many whites and mixed-bloods living with them. Because of that, he and Zoongakamig could give no answer, but they promised to keep their council secret. Bagone-giizhig did not in fact keep the affair secret. He told a mixed-blood surveyor at Fort Snelling who worked with Johann Kohl, who then recounted the story.[11]

Ojibwe-Dakota relations turned violent in 1838 and extremely bloody in 1839. This seriously dampened any Dakota ideas to focus military energies on the whites. The 1838 council, however, showed that the Dakota and Ojibwe understood they had a great stake in each other's future, the high degree of trust between them, and their mutual deep distrust of the whites. Although it would be twenty-four years before the conflicts took place, the idea of intertribal co-operation and war with whites had been circulating for many years. Bagone-giizhig the Younger's role would prove to be especially important when the moment finally arrived.

INDIAN-WHITE TENSIONS BEFORE 1857

Indian-white tensions continued to escalate, and by the 1850s relations in Minnesota, Wisconsin, North Dakota, and South Dakota were increasingly stressed. Ojibwe and Dakota people occasionally killed the livestock and destroyed the property of white settlers and missionaries. Attacks and violence against Indians by white settlers escalated. In one incident in 1850, a white man "attempted some liberties" with an Indian woman near Chippewa Falls, Wisconsin.

Bagone-giizhig the Younger, ca. 1858. The weapon emblem on the pipe suggests its use in war summons and council. It appears in several pictures of the chief: likely it was his personal pipe.

When her Indian husband fought the white man, a group of settlers intervened and killed the Indian. The incident was reported to the Indian agent at La Pointe, but no action was taken. Bagone-giizhig, who was traveling in Wisconsin at the time, somehow convinced the murdered man's family members not to "take the matter into their own hands."[12]

Tensions mounted on both sides throughout the 1850s. In 1856, a small Wisconsin newspaper reported: "It is hard for the industrious and poor white settler to have his wood and stacks of hay burnt up, his traps and their booty stolen, and his game shot down, and much of it wasted." The white settlers obviously did not understand or respect the treaties between their government and the native nations, whose people retained hunting and fishing rights on ceded land. Indians did the same to whites who settled on legitimately titled Minnesota land, as well as to those who squatted illegally on Indian land. Sometimes the Indians purposely hunted around white settlements to make life more stressful for the settlers. Some reports, though exaggerated, claimed that twelve hundred white-tailed deer were killed each week in some areas of Wisconsin.[13]

THE CORNSTALK WAR AND THE INKPADUTA CONFLICT

In 1857 events in Ojibwe and Dakota country turned violent for a time, foreshadowing the large-scale violence that would erupt five years later. The Cornstalk War for the Ojibwe and the Inkpaduta Conflict for the Dakota manifested the brewing Indian-white tensions in Minnesota and Wisconsin.

The Cornstalk War was a farcical event involving six Ojibwe men burning the haystacks of a white settler named Jemmy Burns. In response a force of thirty government light cavalry charged to the St. Croix River country where the farm was located. Expecting to meet a large, organized Ojibwe army, they found six Ojibwe men fleeing through the cornstalks for their lives. The Americans killed one of the men, and, returning fire, the Ojibwe killed one of the Americans. The Ojibwe surrendered and were marched to St. Paul. The five Ojibwe prisoners rightly pleaded self-defense. Amazingly, four were released immediately. The other was ordered to stand trial for murder of a white man, but he managed to escape as he was taken from the sheriff's house to the courthouse at Taylors Falls.[14]

The Inkpaduta Conflict, sometimes called the Spirit Lake Massacre, was more serious than the Cornstalk War. Thirty white settlers in northern Iowa and southern Minnesota were killed by a small number of Wah'pekute Dakota Indians led by Inkpaduta. They escaped punishment by leaving Minnesota and joining a group of their Titonwan Lakota relatives on the Missouri River. Some returned later, including Inkpaduta's immediate family. The Inkpaduta Conflict terrified white settlers but did not increase the resolve of the United States to come to terms with Indian concerns and animosities.[15]

Both the Cornstalk War and Inkpaduta Conflict of 1857 reflected an atmosphere that led to large-scale conflicts in 1862. Indians did not suffer for those two events the way they would later, but the small incidents did nothing to repair increasingly poor Indian-white relations or even to vent the mounting anger of the Indian people.

VIGILANTE VENGEANCE: THE CROW WING LYNCH MOB

In August 1857, the same summer as the Cornstalk War, Mississippi Ojibwe began to express growing resentment of white encroachment around Fort Ripley. Some cattle belonging to the mission at Gull Lake had been killed, and tensions were running high. Then a series of events plunged the entire white and Indian population of the area into a state of fear. A German man traveling near Gull Lake was killed, and three Ojibwe men were arrested and charged with the murder. White settlers in Swan River took the law into their own hands. They formed a vigilante posse that threatened the sheriff and his deputies (to the point of securing a noose around the neck of one of them), hanged the three Ojibwe men, and buried them handcuffed to one another.[16]

Bagone-giizhig was furious at white settlers for the lynchings and at the U.S. government for failing to enforce its own laws. He asked Aandegoo-miigwan (Crow Feather) and another Ojibwe man to go to Crow Wing, kill the first white man they met, and then burn down the mission buildings at Gull Lake. According to Reverend Solon W. Manney (the army chaplain at Fort Ripley), Bagone-giizhig had also paid men to kill the Ottawa mixed-blood missionary John Johnson, also known as Enami'egaabaw (Stands Praying).[17]

Bagone-giizhig and his father had had many friendly relationships based on mutual respect with area missionaries, including

George Copway and John Johnson, who was adopted as a son by Bagone-giizhig the Elder. By the 1860s, however, Bagone-giizhig the Younger's view of Johnson and other missionaries had changed. He frowned upon Johnson's role in treaty negotiations, removal, and economic discussions at Crow Wing and St. Peters. Johnson sometimes directly thwarted Bagone-giizhig's efforts, and Bagone-giizhig saw Johnson as an agent working for acculturation of his people and government intrusion in his chieftaincy. This probably played into his threats against Johnson, who escaped harm but never trusted Bagone-giizhig again.

The possible murder and arson incident was concluded after Clement Beaulieu, a local storeowner, businessman, and trader, intercepted Aandegoo-miigwan and somehow dissuaded him from carrying out his deed. Whether this happened by an appeal to his reason, by bribe, or by threat is unknown. Some property was destroyed in 1857, but the Gull Lake mission remained intact, and no more people were killed. The white settlers in Swan River and Crow Wing and the army soldiers stationed at Fort Ripley, however, remained terrified about the possibility of an Indian attack. Reverend Manney, the chaplain at Fort Ripley, noted in his journal: "We may now expect personal violence, and murders, and the destruction of property on the ceded lands, and all along the frontier."[18]

Bagone-giizhig and Clement Beaulieu, who had been good friends and neighbors for several years, never got along well after the events of 1857. In March 1858, Beaulieu's store in Crow Wing was set afire by a group of Ojibwe. One of the arsonists was killed and another wounded. It is not clear whether Bagone-giizhig was behind the arson attempt, but the prospect of Beaulieu's store burning down would surely not have upset him. Beaulieu held Bagone-giizhig responsible.

THE OPPOSITIONAL DYNAMIC: BAGONE-GIIZHIG 1857–62

As animosity toward the Americans grew, both the Ojibwe and the Dakota hoped to improve their circumstances with some sort of resistance that would bring change.[19] Matters worsened in 1861, when Lucius C. Walker became the new Indian agent for the Ojibwe. Walker had — and would continue to — embezzle thousands of dollars of Ojibwe annuity payments and sold Ojibwe treaty goods to white traders for his personal profit. Clark Thompson, the agency superintendent, refused

Clement Beaulieu, ca. 1890. A store owner and trader at Crow Wing and White Earth, Beaulieu became a neighbor to Bagone-giizhig when the chief built a house on his private allotment at Gichi-mashkodeng (Big Field), across the river from the village at Crow Wing. Their longtime friendship soured during the last several years of the chief's life.

to take action against Walker and, in fact, may have been receiving a cut from Walker's schemes. Indian agent David B. Herriman was also believed to be taking goods meant for the Ojibwe from the annuity storehouse and selling them for personal gain.[20]

After the Civil War began, the government did not keep up with its responsibilities to provide annuity payments to many different tribes on time because of problems with revenue, transportation, reallocations to war efforts, and basic communications. The government's failure to expeditiously honor financial obligations to tribes across the country struck blows to Indian-white relations (including the sworn allegiance of some Oklahoma Indian tribes to the Confederacy). The abuses of Walker and Herriman in Minnesota were especially egregious, however, and were well known to both Indians and white officials.

Bagone-giizhig made repeated trips to St. Paul and even Washington, DC, to complain about Walker, Clark, Herriman, and the general treatment and condition of his people. Clement Beaulieu, George Day, George Morrison, and Peter Roy joined the voices complaining about Walker and Thompson. Many traders and officials also preyed on the annuity economy to the detriment of Indians, and most people were well aware of the developments.

The Ojibwe became so upset about annuity abuses, falsified trader claims, and the cooperation of the government in those abuses that they burned several warehouses and annuity stations between 1855 and 1862 rather than lose their goods and money to the traders. After a barrage of letters and visits, commissioner of Indian Affairs William P. Dole finally agreed to investigate, but he did not follow through. In 1860, the government still owed the Ojibwe eighty-one thousand dollars in past-due annuity payments from treaties in the 1850s, but it made no effort to make the payments or address abuses. Bagone-giizhig was incensed.[21]

The chief was also upset with Lucius Walker for refusing to give him a larger share of annuities than he gave other Indians. Bagone-giizhig had become accustomed to receiving a chief's bonus, but Walker refused to supply it, which further escalated tensions. This refusal did not lessen the legitimacy of complaints about treaty abuses, but Bagone-giizhig's personal agenda became further intertwined with the band's welfare.[22]

Bagone-giizhig frequently went to St. Paul to council with the Dakota, especially with Little Crow. He had established good rapport despite the earlier hostilities and Little Crow's statement to George Copway in 1841 that he was coming for Bagone-giizhig the Elder's scalp.[23]

According to Gwiiwizhenzhish (Bad Boy), the Gull Lake chief who moved to Mille Lacs after 1862, Bagone-giizhig made plans with the Dakota in the summer of 1861 to make a joint war against the whites: "Hole-in-the-Day's headman came to me and told me that Hole-in-the-Day was about to make a treaty with the Sioux, and that they were to fight the whites together... Afterward, I met Hole-in-the-Day and had a talk with him. He said ... 'I want your assistance in my undertaking.' He told me we were going to kill all the Indians that join the whites ... He also told me they were going to attack the fort [Ripley] and then fall back to the British Possessions, and then get the Indians up there to help us." Since Bagone-giizhig and Little Crow did communicate frequently, white settlers were not unwise to worry about the possibility of a joint Ojibwe-Dakota campaign against them. Cooperation between the two leaders was not supported strongly enough by other Ojibwe and Dakota leaders, however, to bear fruit.[24]

Bagone-giizhig himself had concern about the difficulty of mobilizing the entire Ojibwe nation against the whites since many whites and mixed-blood people lived with the Ojibwe as loved and protected family and community members. But the events of 1857 and 1858 suggest that he was willing to consider engaging in hostilities. His councils with the Dakota and his well-documented attempts to convince other Ojibwe leaders to take a hard stand indicate that hostilities were jointly deliberated by some Ojibwe and Dakota leaders.

In 1861, Joseph Goiffon, a missionary at Pembina, wrote that a Dakota runner passed through the area on his way to the western plains with a war summons in preparation for a conflict with the Americans. From frequent observations of the Ojibwe and the Dakota, Goiffon also wrote, "I saw clearly, from their discourses, that they wanted to make war on the Americans." Fort Ripley would likely be on the edge of the war zone, especially since large parties of Dakota warriors were reported to be in the vicinity frequently. The entire stretch of Ojibwe and Dakota country was bracing for possible conflict with the United States.[25]

Bagone-giizhig the Younger, ca. 1860. Note the chief's evolving regalia. Here he displays an otterskin turban, typically worn only by civil chiefs, but with a growing arrangement of eagle feathers, typically displayed only by experienced warriors. He also employs a blanket in addition to his suit, reinforcing his influence in native and nonnative circles.

While there were large segments of both groups who wanted nothing to do with hostilities with the Americans, they knew that trouble was brewing. John Johnson wrote to Henry Whipple after the depredations of 1862 had commenced: "[Bagone-giizhig's] project and plan was and has been fairly understood by the two tribes, Chipways and the Siouxs to combine their warriors together and make general [war against] the whites." In November 1862 the Office of Indian Affairs confidently declared: "From these reports it became the universal belief that a preconcerted and general uprising of all the Indians of the State was at hand and the State was to become the arena of a most formidable Indian war." Indian agents such as Lucius Walker were also convinced "that there was a general and preconcerted rising of all the Indians of the country." John Johnson had the same impression.[26]

In August 1862, the United States began to recruit soldiers for the Union Army in earnest. Fair numbers of Ojibwe, especially mixed-blood people, joined up. Some, however, were manipulated to do so while intoxicated. This activity raised the ire of Bagone-giizhig and other Ojibwe leaders. Walker's embezzlement of Indian annuity goods had never been addressed, and anxiety was extremely high.

Bagone-giizhig must also have been heavily influenced by the waning economic strength of the Ojibwe people. Simply put, they were running out of land to sell. Land cession treaties had become the staple of Bagone-giizhig's personal affluence and the annuities that sustained his people. He was aware that his bargaining position with the government was severely weakened by his inability to produce more land or other resources for the government in negotiations. This knowledge helps explain his increasing belligerence in dealings with the United States and with his longtime white and mixed-blood trader friends from Crow Wing. As he had less land to sell, traders had less interest in him. According to Charles Eastman, "[Bagone-giizhig] made a desperate effort to regain lost prestige, and turned savagely against the original betrayers of his confidence, the agents and Indian traders."[27]

THE U.S.-OJIBWE CONFLICT OF 1862

On August 17, 1862, the same day that the Dakota commenced hostilities against the whites along the Minnesota River, the Ojibwe had a major altercation with white authorities and settlers more than two hundred miles away on the Mississippi River, at Leech Lake, and at Otter Tail Lake.[28] A powerful chain of events pushed along the conflict in Dakota country, where Little Crow, who had opposed violence, soon found himself leading Dakota forces. In Ojibwe country, the impetus for conflict came not from a chain of hard-to-control events but from the calculated manipulations of one man — Bagone-giizhig. According to Bishop Henry Whipple, "this outbreak among the Ojibwa was entirely due to a personal grievance of Hole-in-the-Day."[29]

Bagone-giizhig anticipated the arrival of William P. Dole, commissioner of Indian Affairs, that summer and saw a unique opportunity to rivet the commissioner's attention on Ojibwe concerns. He was also well informed about events in Dakota country. He knew exactly when to act. Despite his lengthy premeditations, councils, and war summons, he had limited success in gaining the support from other Ojibwe leaders for a plan to launch a war against the whites. Unable to convince them, he decided to manipulate them.

Bagone-giizhig used Ojibwe frustration and anger with Walker's annuity thefts and the uninvited recruitment of Ojibwe soldiers for the Civil War to achieve his end. Julia Warren Spears had reported that an entire company of Indian men enlisted at Crow Wing in 1862 under the influence of alcohol. John Johnson personally observed several young Indians being paid enlistment bonuses of fifty to one hundred dollars while completely inebriated and then being taken to Fort Snelling for induction into the U.S. Army. Traders received payments for each Indian they convinced to enlist. Johnson reported that three sons of the head warriors from Leech Lake were among those manipulated to enlist while under the influence of alcohol. (Johnson, by his own admission, took a twenty-five-dollar bribe from Henry Rice to convince the Ojibwe families not to kill the traders.)[30]

Bagone-giizhig decided to act. On August 17 he sent runners from Gull Lake to Leech Lake with the following message: "Our Great Father intends to send men and take all the Indians and dress them like soldiers, and send them away to fight in the south, and if we wish to save ourselves, we must rise and fight the whites, take the whites prisoners, who are at the lake, and take their horses and goods from them."[31]

Taking this message to heart, Pillager Band Ojibwe gutted the mission school and trading post at Walker, Minnesota, and at Ottertail City. At Gull Lake, the cattle at the Indian agency were killed.

Lucius C. Walker, ca. 1858. Walker, a member of the first state legislature in Minnesota and an Indian agent in 1862, used his position to embezzle Ojibwe annuities, inciting the dramatic events of the U.S.–Ojibwe Conflict.

Similar events occurred at other white stations and settlements at Leech Lake and along the Mississippi River. The Ojibwe took several prisoners, including missionaries John Johnson and D. Moore, although they soon escaped and made their ways to Fort Ripley.

On August 19, nearly two hundred white settlers took refuge at Fort Ripley, and the tiny command prepared for battle with the Ojibwe. Indian agent Lucius Walker brought his family to the fort and then ordered Bagone-giizhig's arrest. Lieutenant J. B. Forbes took twenty soldiers to Bagone-giizhig's house to find him, but the chief ran into the forest where he knew the trails intimately and easily eluded them. He returned home after the soldiers left and took his family to the river. The soldiers spotted them crossing in canoes and fired on them. No casualties ensued, though there was an erroneous report that Bagone-giizhig had been wounded.

The enraged Bagone-giizhig sent new runners to Leech Lake and as far away as Lake Superior with the claim that the Gull Lakers under his leadership were now preparing to massacre the whites at Crow Wing, Fort Ripley, and St. Cloud, after which they would join the Dakota in their war. The runners petitioned all Ojibwe to join the Gull Lakers. White settlers across Ojibwe country were terrified by the reports. Distorted rumors included the misinformation that many people had been killed and the Ojibwe warriors at Mille Lacs were riding on horses to the Gull Lake region to join their comrades.[32]

LEADERSHIP RIFTS DURING THE U.S.–OJIBWE CONFLICT

Cooler heads prevailed. Chief Bizhiki (Buffalo) of Leech Lake, who had assumed greater authority after Eshkibagikoonzh (Flat Mouth) the Elder's death, dissuaded the Leech Lakers from killing whites until they were better informed about the war. The Leech Lake Ojibwe deferred now to Eshkibagikoonzh (Flat Mouth) the Younger and to Bizhiki, as did many other Ojibwe people in the region. Bizhiki and a contingent of Ojibwe warriors from Leech Lake went to Gull Lake and then on to Crow Wing to investigate and, possibly, join the war against the whites. Finding no hostile activity, they had a brief, angry conference with Bagone-giizhig, George Sweet, Clement Beaulieu, and other white and mixed-blood settlers and officials. When Bagone-giizhig realized that he was losing the active support of the Leech Lakers under Bizhiki, he had one of his warriors, Gegwej (He

Who Endeavors), cut the ferry rope at Crow Wing with an ax so U.S. troops could not cross to arrest him or attack his people.[33]

The Ojibwe then agreed to a four-day truce—contingent on their concerns about annuities, treaty goods, Lucius C. Walker, and the recruitment of Ojibwe men in the Union Army being addressed by Commissioner Dole in person. Bizhiki wanted to smooth over Leech Lake's relations with the Americans, and he later told Ashley Morrill, special Indian agent (Walker's temporary replacement), "Hole-in-the-Day stole the senses of our young men and led them to do bad deeds to the whites."[34]

Of even greater significance for Bagone-giizhig's leadership status was the refusal of the Mille Lacs Ojibwe to support his manipulations. In fact, the Mille Lacs leadership sent warriors to surround Fort Ripley and protect it against possible Ojibwe attack by Bagone-giizhig. Mille Lacs hereditary chief Migizi (Eagle) and the head warrior there, Niigaanigwaneb (First Seated Feather), orchestrated several actions to protect Fort Ripley and several white trade posts and settlement communities. Their actions are well documented in the records of white officials at Fort Ripley, as well as in the oral tradition of the Ojibwe.[35] Bishop Henry Whipple reported that "More than a hundred Mille Lacs warriors went at once to the fort and before Hole-in-the-Day could begin war the massacre was averted." The commissioner of Indian Affairs reported: "I feel confident that this diversion of nearly one-half the followers upon whom Hole-in-the-Day doubtless relied, went far in enabling us finally to effect a settlement of the Chippewa difficulties without a resort to arms."[36]

Rifts in the Ojibwe leadership of Minnesota were becoming more and more obvious. Even though Bagone-giizhig and other Ojibwe chiefs were on opposite sides in this conflict, they needed to use both strategies—opposition and conciliation—to be successful. Rebecca Kugel's *To Be the Main Leaders of Our People* masterfully appraises the success of this leadership dynamic. The Mille Lacs chiefs could not have gained favor with the United States if Bagone-giizhig had not directly opposed the government, and Bagone-giizhig could not have gained favor with frustrated Ojibwe if the Mille Lacs chiefs had not supported the government. Internal tensions were escalating, and divisions between leaders were becoming so severe that even the white newspapers picked up on the dissension. One newspaper reported of rival chiefs: "Hole-in-the-Day was regarded by them as a *parvenu*—a kind of usurper—but his pretensions have always been supported with so much boldness, and he has won such pre-eminence as a warrior, that they have not heretofore dared openly contest his position."[37]

UNINTENDED CASUALTIES

Although Bagone-giizhig did not succeed in manipulating the Ojibwe into a war against the United States, his actions had unintended casualties. Missionary John Johnson panicked when he heard about Bagone-giizhig's actions. Bagone-giizhig had threatened his life in 1857, and he further imagined that his entire family in the Gull Lake district was in grave danger, especially when he was briefly held prisoner on August 17, 1862, with other missionaries at the outset of the U.S.–Ojibwe Conflict. Although Bagone-giizhig had personally communicated to Johnson that he and his family would not be harmed, Chief Aazhawaa-giizhig (Crossing Sky) of Rabbit Lake reportedly told Johnson: "I am come to advise you to prepare to flee away to Fort Ripley. Hole-in-the-Day is going to march with his warriors to the Agency in two days from today, and massacre all the whites. Be sure to flee away. For when he returns he will be so ugly and spare no one whom he knows has sympathy with the whites."[38]

That evening, Johnson quickly dispatched a messenger to Mille Lacs, a development that may have contributed to the speedy response of the Mille Lacs leadership in sending warriors to protect Fort Ripley. When Bagone-giizhig and a large group of warriors scouted Fort Ripley on August 17, 1862, Johnson felt that his family was in mortal peril. He worried that Bagone-giizhig would blame him for warning whites that they were in danger. Johnson then put his wife and children in a canoe and dragged the canoe by hand all night long down the Gull River. The next day they reached Fort Ripley, where he warned the soldiers and settlers and sought protection for his family. He left his mission in such haste that two of his young children died from exposure on the trip in unseasonably chilly weather.

Lucius C. Walker had a mental breakdown while traveling to St. Paul. On August 20, he sent his wife ahead of him by stagecoach, and at Monticello he ferried himself across the river and then cut the

Biiwaabiko-giizhigookwe (Iron Sky Woman), Bagone-giizhig the Elder's niece and John Johnson's wife, ca. 1870

lashings, explaining to a very perturbed ferryman that there were hundreds of Indians chasing him. On August 22, he shot himself in the head just south of Big Lake and died instantly.[39]

COUNCIL AT CROW WING

The death of the unpopular Walker and Commissioner Dole's willingness to treat with the Ojibwe in person greatly reduced Ojibwe-white tensions. Lieutenant J. B. Forbes observed that Walker's death helped calm the Ojibwe because "one cause of their trouble was removed." Bagone-giizhig released most of his white prisoners and declared a truce. He feared a trap on the part of the Americans and did not entirely trust the Leech Lakers, who were upset about Bagone-giizhig's lies and manipulations. He must have also been concerned about the Mille Lacs Ojibwe resisting his belligerent overtures and protecting white settlers and soldiers. Bagone-giizhig refused to meet Dole at Fort Ripley, and an alternate council was scheduled at Crow Wing.[40]

The council at Crow Wing on September 10, 1862, provided the stage for one of Bagone-giizhig's craftiest diplomatic maneuvers.[41] Most Ojibwe leaders from Leech Lake, Sandy Lake, and Mille Lacs were upset with the chief for lying to them. American officials wanted the "trouble-maker" arrested or killed. John Johnson was especially vocal about his desire to see Bagone-giizhig executed and wrote bluntly: "Put a string around their necks." Chief Gwiiwizhenzhish (Bad Boy) and Johnson both wrote to the commissioner of Indian Affairs that there would never be peace in Minnesota "until he is dispose [sic] of." But Bagone-giizhig was an expert at getting what he wanted even when he seemed to have no remaining leverage.[42]

Commissioner Dole promised to come to the meeting unarmed and with no soldiers, but he secretly planned to capture Bagone-giizhig and put him in prison. Bagone-giizhig suspected trouble and planned accordingly. Dole arrived with one hundred soldiers and twenty-five white officials and settlers. Bagone-giizhig brought one hundred loyal Ojibwe warriors of his own. Dole curtly demanded that all white captives held by the Ojibwe be turned over immediately. Captain Hall tersely added that if the Ojibwe did not acquiesce, they would be "blown to hell in five minutes." Bagone-giizhig gestured to the hundred Ojibwe warriors seated at the council and then to the other hundred that appeared behind the American troops, effectively surrounding and outnumbering the American forces two to one. He said he was a friend of peace but that he could not stop his men from defending themselves. Dole, chagrined and embarrassed at being outmaneuvered, said that he would be glad to hear the Ojibwe grievances and then addressed the Ojibwe at some length. Trader Augustus Aspinwall, who attended the meeting, reported that Dole "got up and gave them a short nice speach [sic] telling them how glad he was to see them but I would bet he was wishing himself all the time that [he] was in his good arm chair in his office in Washington."[43]

Bagone-giizhig gave a lengthy address of his own. The official government report said, "During the council he was insolent, defiant, and disrespectful." According to one account, Bagone-giizhig took apart Dole's speech "from beginning to end, word for word, and when he got through, it was like a stocking that has been unraveled—there was nothing left of it." Bagone-giizhig concluded: "Are you the smartest man that our Great Father could send in a trying time like this? Because, if you are the smartest man the Great Father has got, I pity our Great Father. You have been talking to me as if I was a child. I am not a little child. I have grey hairs on my head ... [Y]our talk sounds to me like baby talk ... You say the treaty reads so and so. Now that is a lie and you know it."[44]

Bagone-giizhig got up to leave. Some of the soldiers approached to arrest him, but they were entirely surrounded, and when it looked like a fight might break out, he was allowed to go, much to the disappointment and anger of Dole, the soldiers, and other American officials. Bagone-giizhig refused to treat with Dole after that, as Dole had ordered more soldiers to Fort Ripley and did not seem ready to give in to the chief's demands. Dole had appointed Crow Wing postmaster Ashley Morrill as interim special Indian agent after Walker's suicide. Now he left Morrill in charge of finding a solution to the crisis and returned to Washington on September 10, immediately after the conference in Crow Wing.

Tensions increased dramatically the next day when two white Crow Wing residents, Peter Kelly and Ezra Briggs, burned down Bagone-giizhig's house. The chief believed that it was done with the knowledge and even the authorization of the army, and he was fuming. Bagone-giizhig demanded recompense for the act of arson and ten thousand dollars in annuities and trade goods for the Ojibwe to rectify the robbing of annuity payments by Walker, Herriman, and Clark. Again he threatened to attack Crow Wing. Some leaders, most notably Bizhiki, Gwiiwizhenzhish, Migizi, and Niigaanigwaneb, stopped him. The threat was enough, however, to convince federal officials and the Minnesota state government to appease Bagone-giizhig's demands.

The government's fear of a widening Indian conflict throughout the region increased when correspondence arrived from the British government in Canada indicating that Bagone-giizhig had made contingency plans that included the Canadian Ojibwe and a refuge in Canada should the Gull Lakers become embroiled in a war with the Americans. Joshua R. Giddings, the U.S consul general for the British North American provinces, wrote to Secretary of State William H. Seward: "There is little doubt that that the recent outbreak of the Chippewa Indians in the northwest has resulted from the efforts of secession agents, operating through Canadian Indians and fur-traders. My present object is to inform the Executive that a gentleman holding an honorable position under her Majesty, a halfbreed, but educated, is a cousin of the celebrated chief 'Hole-in-the-Day.'"[45]

Amid the increased fear and scrutiny of the U.S. and Canadian governments and ongoing violence in southern Minnesota, Bagone-giizhig's threats worked. On September 15, Henry M. Rice and Governor Alexander Ramsey both met with the chief, thus usurping Morrill's authority, and acquiesced to Bagone-giizhig's demands. There would be no reprimand or punishment. A treaty was negotiated with Bagone-giizhig and signed on September 15, 1862. It was not presented for formal ratification, in part because it involved no transfer of land and in part because Dole was chagrined that he was not able to punish Bagone-giizhig. Rice and Ramsey promised payment of overdue annuities within thirty days, a provision written into the treaty. Even more amazingly, the annuities were actually paid on October 27, 1862. Bagone-giizhig and other Ojibwe leaders were officially exonerated from all crimes or wrongdoing. Finally, officials promised an investigation of corruption by Indian agents, to be conducted by a commission independent from the U.S. Department of the Interior.[46]

With little support from other Ojibwe leaders and confronted with a hostile American government, Bagone-giizhig had successfully won a victory and imposed his demands over a powerful group of U.S. government officials. Morrill reported that Bagone-giizhig "went out of the council with his influence restored." Although not well loved by most whites or even many Ojibwe people, Bagone-giizhig proved to be a powerful diplomat and leader.[47]

In addition to the concessions that Bagone-giizhig extracted at the council, he was later reimbursed with five thousand dollars for the burning of his house.[48] Although there was no investigation of the arson, Bagone-giizhig wrote the president of the United States and the commissioner of Indian Affairs in 1863 about the two men (Peter Kelly and Ezra Briggs) who had burned his home and belongings.[49] He implied that they did it with the knowledge and authorization of the government, although he stopped short of a direct accusation and simply insisted that the government make reparations. Eventually, the United States assumed responsibility for Bagone-giizhig's financial losses and compensated him with five thousand dollars directly out of subsequent treaty provisions "for depredations committed in burning his house and furniture in 1862."[50]

Ashley Morrill was furious at his disempowerment in the ensuing negotiations and at the terms Bagone-giizhig and his supporters secured from the special commission. The government had committed a grave error, Morrill reported, "granting to them better terms than they could receive from the general government; in fact, rewarding them for the outrages committed upon white persons instead of letting them understand that they must suffer for it." John Johnson, who feared Bagone-giizhig and held him responsible for the death of two of his children, was flabbergasted: "Hole in the Day is a smart man . . . The white man never could punish Hole in the Day." Even Bagone-giizhig's enemies were astounded by his shrewd diplomatic triumphs during the Ojibwe hostilities of 1862.[51]

GROWING POWER, GROWING ENEMIES

While Bagone-giizhig achieved short-term goals in 1862, he permanently ruined his relationships with several former diplomatic allies. He terrified the missionaries around Leech Lake and Gull Lake. In 1863, Johnson, Peake, and other missionaries focused their efforts elsewhere and closed the mission at Gull Lake. Although many Ojibwe people must have said good riddance, the missions had been incorporated into the larger Ojibwe economy and their absence did affect Ojibwe livelihoods. Since missionaries usually advocated a diplomatic, not military, approach to Indian matters, their departure meant the government had less local resistance to more coercive strategies for Ojibwe relocation.

More importantly, Bagone-giizhig added to the growing rift between himself and Ojibwe leaders from Mille Lacs, Gull Lake, and, now, Leech Lake. Some chiefs from smaller villages in the Gull Lake area relocated to Mille Lacs to further distance themselves from Bagone-giizhig. Gwiiwizhenzhish (Bad Boy) was the most high-profile defection from Bagone-giizhig's constituency. The Mille Lacs leadership went so far as to send the government a petition (with a significant number of chief signatures) that read, "We the undersigned chiefs of the Mille [Lacs] Lake Band wish to express hereby our mind, that we don't agree in any way with the plans of [Bagone-giizhig]." Further accentuating the rift between Bagone-giizhig and other Minnesota chiefs, the Indians at Mille Lacs and its satellite communities began receiving their annuity payments separately from Bagone-giizhig and the rest of the Mississippi Ojibwe. This preserved internal peace among the Ojibwe but undermined Bagone-giizhig's Indian support and the perception of that support among American officials.[52]

The events of 1862 strengthened the oppositional dynamic in Ojibwe politics. Bagone-giizhig did not get along well with the civil chiefs from Mille Lacs. Those chiefs used his belligerent diplomacy and actions to gain position and favor with the U.S. government, and Bagone-giizhig used their complacent positioning to gain favor with his people when the government withheld annuities or treated them unfairly. Increasingly, Bagone-giizhig would use a more aggressive stance to gain favor, money, and good terms from government officials, traders, missionaries, and his own people. The strategy, though counterintuitive, worked.[53]

A NEW AGE IN OJIBWE-DAKOTA RELATIONS

The U.S.–Dakota Conflict of 1862 erupted on the same day as the U.S.–Ojibwe Conflict but had a much different outcome. Hundreds of whites and Dakota Indians were killed. The war spilled over to the plains, continued for years, and did not reach its brutal conclusion until long after the American Civil War ended.

Slight differences in the Ojibwe conflict could have greatly altered its outcome. If Bagone-giizhig had killed even one white person, as he apparently had planned, hostilities would have escalated and involved the Mille Lacs and Leech Lake Indians. The Ojibwe might have also killed hundreds of whites, perhaps joined the Dakota in great numbers, and lost many of their own people as well. These points are not entirely moot, even if they are now unchangeable. Bagone-giizhig had the power to force a certain chain of events in Ojibwe country but decided not to.

Ojibwe-Dakota relations entered a new stage in the 1862 conflicts. Both groups had to adjust to a rapidly increasing and more powerful white presence in their lands. For the Dakota, Nakota, and Lakota, there followed a brutal series of conflicts with the American government, the execution of thirty-eight Dakota at Mankato, and forced removal to Indian Territory and new reservations. For generations, the Oceti Sakowin (the Seven Council Fires of the Dakota, Nakota, and Lakota) had served as their primary intratribal diplomatic engine. The Dakota were the largest group numerically and the focus of greatest concern and diplomatic attention by the Americans. However, after the violence in 1862–63, the western Lakota began to dominate tribal relations with the Americans. The eastern Dakota never recovered in terms of population, territory, or political clout.

Many Dakota people escaped the wars in their homelands and took refuge among the Ojibwe in Canada or with other bands of Nakota and Lakota farther west and north. Although some Dakota returned to Minnesota years later, many remained among the Ojibwe of Canada. Several Canadian Dakota, Nakota, and mixed Ojibwe-Dakota communities today date to the refugee surge in 1862.

While some Canadian Ojibwe harbored resentments against the refugee Dakota because of recent Dakota-Ojibwe hostilities, most Dakota people were warmly received. The minor tensions that persisted tended to manifest themselves in lingering prejudice, rather than violence. Some people harbored prejudices for a long time, and even at the turn of the twentieth century some Dakota parents at Devils Lake, North Dakota, complained that their children were forced to go to schools where there were too many Ojibwe.[54]

Ojibwe-Dakota warfare had dwindled to minor border skirmishes and revenge attacks in the preceding two decades in the central Minnesota lake region and in at least one decade on the plains. The 1862 conflicts forced the tribes to deal with far more important concerns: how to hang on to the remains of their homelands, feed their families, and create a brighter future for their grandchildren. There were no major Ojibwe-Dakota wars after 1862.

In 1863, a peace conference north of Devils Lake between the Ojibwe and the Nakota and Dakota helped to further define boundaries between their peoples, permitting many Dakota who had not already done so to seek refuge with the Ojibwe and make a truly lasting peace. After one-and-a-quarter centuries of alternating periods of belligerence and peace, from 1736 to 1862, Ojibwe-Dakota wars ceased forever.[55]

Of great importance to both tribes was the Dakota presentation to the Ojibwe of a ceremonial Big Drum. The event took place in the early 1860s, probably in 1864.[56] The drum ceremony represented a peace offering that spread throughout Ojibwe country and even to other tribes. According to the legend of the drum's origin, it was against the will of the Great Spirit for the Ojibwe and the Dakota to kill one another. The drum was to provide both peace and protection to the families and communities that served as caretakers. The drum ceremony's role in helping cement peace between the tribes is undeniable. The ceremony is still widely practiced among the Ojibwe in White Earth, Mille Lacs, East Lake, Lake Lena, Hertel, Round Lake, Lac Courte Oreilles, Lac du Flambeau, and Mole Lake, as well as among the Menominee, Potawatomi, and Kickapoo in Wisconsin, Oklahoma, and Kansas.

Ceremonial drums served as central, unifying cornerstones in Ojibwe communities for generations, symbolizing and encouraging peace, health, and generosity. These drums also helped sustain Ojibwe leadership paradigms, even after hereditary civil chiefs had been stripped of their real power in later years and after the U.S. government had assumed control of Ojibwe reservations. Individual positions on ceremonial drums were appointed for life and passed on hereditarily. Originally, all male Ojibwe drum members had killed Dakota Indians, yet the role of warriors as peace-keepers was also a critical teaching of the drums. The respect given to drum chiefs represented a continuation of the Ojibwe religious leadership pattern. While the drums made and preserved peace between the Ojibwe and

Dakota, they also reaffirmed the role of ceremonial leaders, heredity, and warriors in Ojibwe culture.

A NEW AGE IN OJIBWE-AMERICAN RELATIONS

After the Ojibwe and Dakota events of 1862, the government would exert enormous pressure upon the Ojibwe to relocate and give up possession of their Minnesota homelands. Initially, officials wanted to remove all Indians in Minnesota to Isle Royale in Lake Superior, near Thunder Bay, Ontario. Eventually, officials decided to move the Dakota and the Ho-Chunk (who had nothing to do with the conflict) to Nebraska. The Ojibwe would be concentrated at Leech Lake in Minnesota and then later at White Earth. Arguably, fear of a major conflict with the Ojibwe seemed to keep the United States from exercising as heavy a hand with the Ojibwe as it had with the Dakota. Whether it was his true intention or not, Bagone-giizhig's threats probably echoed in the minds of American policy makers.[57]

Ojibwe and Dakota leaders had discussed the possibility of joining forces in conflict with the Americans for decades. The conflicts in 1862 were ignited by spontaneous events in southern Minnesota, but those sparks lit a fire that had been kindled by Ojibwe and Dakota leaders for twenty-five years. The U.S.–Ojibwe Conflict of 1862 showed that Indian resentment of white encroachment and American government policies was not confined to the Lower Sioux Agency. The conclusion of the conflicts ended hostile Ojibwe-Dakota relations and ultimately strengthened pan-Indian sentiment.

By his personal diplomatic challenges to the government, which were largely unsupported by other Ojibwe leaders, Chief Bagone-giizhig emerged victorious from the events. He secured promised annuities for the Ojibwe people. He obtained funds to replace his torched house. He was never arrested, imprisoned, or hurt. No Ojibwe people were killed in the U.S.–Ojibwe Conflict. Bagone-giizhig knew exactly when to forge friendships, lie, threaten, cajole, bully, and back down in his dealings with the Americans, the Dakota, and his own people. He proved his savvy as a diplomat, and he helped to retain the sovereign power of his people. In one of the great paradoxes of the 1862 events, Bagone-giizhig's triumph shows the fragility of Dakota, Ojibwe, and American power in Minnesota.

6

The Enemy Within

Assassinating Bagone-giizhig

Though it may cost me my liberty, it is my duty, and I will continue
to speak and act also, till the wrongs of my people shall be righted.
— BAGONE-GIIZHIG[1]

If we did kill anybody them days, it was no crime; you couldn't hang
a man for killing ten Indians.
— JOHN G. MORRISON[2]

The events of 1862 had serious long-term consequences for the
Ojibwe in Minnesota. The Dakota and the Ho-Chunk were
removed, the United States increased its military presence,
and the pace of white settlement escalated dramatically.[3] For a time
Bagone-giizhig and other Ojibwe leaders seemed confident of their
future in Minnesota, but pressure on them to cede land and abandon
their culture built at a furious pace. Soon the entire Ojibwe leadership was embroiled in an enormous battle with the government—a
battle fought not with war clubs and guns but with words and pens,
a battle to hold on to identity and sovereign power. It was to be
their toughest fight yet. Most of the Indian land base and some critical elements of Ojibwe culture would perish in the conflict, along
with some of the brightest Ojibwe leaders, including Bagone-giizhig.
Bagone-giizhig's trajectory from the height of his power to his untimely death paralleled the transition of the Ojibwe in Minnesota
from undisputed sovereignty to removal and reservation life.

LAND, MONEY, EVANGELISM, FEAR

Following the events of 1862, Bagone-giizhig was flush with political
power. His people continued to live around Gull Lake, confident of

their abilities to fight or negotiate for their needs. Still, many were concerned about the Americans, who seemed consumed with anger and greed. The Ojibwe worried about the Dakota, who were being hunted down and imprisoned or killed. The Ojibwe worried about the Ho-Chunk, who had not participated in violence against white settlers but were being herded onto boats and moved to Nebraska. What would the Americans try to do to the Ojibwe? The answer to that question was not long in coming.

Land prospects, money, evangelism, and fear combined to bring out the worst in American settlers, speculators, politicians, and priests in their treatment of Indian peoples. Few cases illustrate this fact more clearly than the attempts to remove the Minnesota Ojibwe from their homelands onto the White Earth Reservation. The White Earth removal was and is a tragedy—a relentless, calculated swindling of Ojibwe land and a systematic erosion of Indian sovereignty.

Removal was not a new concept in U.S. Indian policy, but there was something anomalous about the situation at White Earth. In the second half of the nineteenth century, the railroad and logging industries fueled American economic growth. Ojibwe lands in northern Minnesota contained some of the richest iron ore deposits and finest stands of white pine in the world. The Ojibwe also held some of the best agricultural land in the country along the Red River Valley on Minnesota's western border. The economic interests of railroad and timber tycoons and white settlers brought unprecedented pressure on the Ojibwe to cede their homelands in northern Minnesota.

Removal of the Minnesota Ojibwe was seen by many American politicians as the fastest way to gain access to large tracts of Ojibwe land. The call for removal also came from missionaries including Henry B. Whipple, John Johnson, George Copway, and others who had sought for years to concentrate the Ojibwe in one area so they could more easily proselytize their faiths and make them into Christian yeoman farmers. The missionary assimilationist imperative helped drive the call for Ojibwe removal.

Added to the economic and assimilationist incentives for removal was a profound fear lingering from the violence of 1862. The U.S.–Dakota Conflict of 1862 had resulted in the death of from four to eight hundred white men, women, and children. Although the Ojibwe did not join the Dakota, the Ojibwe did burn missions and annuity agencies and take several white prisoners at Leech Lake and Gull

1859.

Henry B. Whipple, 1859. Missionary Whipple was an instrumental
advocate for Ojibwe removal to White Earth.

Lake. Most white and mixed-blood settlers, however, feared all In-dians in Minnesota as a result of the events in 1862. Four years after the conflict trader George Bonga wrote about Indian-white tension, "I am really fearful it will bring on another 1862." Ironically, white fear that the Ojibwe were too powerful became a major contributing factor to tribal disempowerment.[4]

The first calls to remove all Ojibwe people to Isle Royale in Lake Superior made by many settlers and missionaries, including mixed-bloods like John Johnson, went unheeded. In a letter to President Abraham Lincoln, Bagone-giizhig complained that the U.S. govern-ment was trying to relocate his band "as far as possible from the white people." Ultimately, economics, assimilation, and fear — in that order — were the driving forces behind Ojibwe land cessions and removal.[5]

Bagone-giizhig himself was not opposed to the idea of removal, but he opposed any political or social change that might disempower the Ojibwe people or lead to a decrease in their standard of living. Although he had been a principal treaty negotiator for the Missis-sippi Ojibwe for many years, the political and social environment in which he operated after 1862 would be completely different. His style of leadership would change and harden in response.

REVIEW OF OJIBWE LAND CESSIONS BEFORE 1863

The Ojibwe's first land treaty in 1837 ceded a triangular section of land north of the Mississippi River and south of Mille Lacs Lake, adja-cent to the St. Croix River. There were few white settlers in Minne-sota at this time, and the Ojibwe retained usufructary rights over the ceded territory, so the treaty had little impact on Ojibwe daily life.[6]

There were, however, many problems with the administration of annuity payments and the signing of treaties between the Ojibwe and the United States. Article 4 of the Treaty of 1837 provided trad-ers William A. Aitkin and Lyman M. Warren each more than twenty-five thousand dollars. Both represented the American Fur Company, which helps explain their especially large claims against annuities (although they were probably inflated). In addition, more than fifty other traders present at the 1837 negotiations also laid claim to Ojibwe annuities. Besides representing the American Fur Company and advocating for his claim, Lyman Warren served as one of the principal U.S. government witnesses for the Ojibwe signatories and helped to interpret for the Lac du Flambeau and Lac Courte Oreilles delegations at the treaty negotiations.[7]

In the 1847 treaty with the Pillager Band, signed shortly after the death of Bagone-giizhig the Elder, the Ojibwe ceded a large section of land along the Long Prairie River in central Minnesota with the understanding that the Ho-Chunk (Winnebago) and Menominee Indians would relocate there. The Ojibwe believed that their presence would provide a buffer from Dakota attacks. The Ojibwe leaders' desire for protection was so strong that they agreed to the massive land cession with no financial payments or annuities and in exchange for only blankets, cloth, and "two hundred warranted beaver traps and seventy-five northwest guns."[8]

The 1847 treaty with the Mississippi and Lake Superior Ojibwe—which marked Bagone-giizhig the Younger's first major diplomatic foray—opened for white settlers the large tract of land in central and eastern Minnesota from the Long Prairie and Crow Wing rivers north and east. The Mississippi Ojibwe were party to the treaty, but most still lived on unceded lands in other parts of the state. The annuity fiasco at Sandy Lake in 1850 created tremendous tension in the Ojibwe communities, but daily life, village locations, and sovereignty were largely unaffected until the next round of treaties.[9]

The first major land-cession treaties with the Mississippi Ojibwe that created reservations were signed in 1854 and 1855. The 1854 treaty signed at La Pointe, Wisconsin, involved the Lake Superior Band of Ojibwe. In addition to its effects in Wisconsin, the treaty established Minnesota Ojibwe reservations at Grand Portage (in the far northeast corner of the state), Vermilion Lake (north of Virginia), and Fond du Lac (near present-day Duluth). The 1855 treaty, signed with the Mississippi, Pillager, and Winnibigoshish bands, ceded much of the heart of Ojibwe country in Minnesota and established separate Ojibwe reservations at Cass Lake, Lake Winnibigoshish, Leech Lake, Lake Pokegama (White Oak), Sandy Lake, Rabbit Lake, Gull Lake, and Mille Lacs Lake. There were eleven Ojibwe reservations in Minnesota in 1855.[10]

The 1837, 1847, 1854, and 1855 treaties had a tremendous impact on the Minnesota Ojibwe. Although people continued to live in their original villages and initially exercised usufructary rights to the resources on the land around their villages, profound economic and social changes had begun. The most important of these was the closing of the fur trade economy and the beginning of a new annuity-based economy. During the years of the fur trade, the Minnesota Ojibwe grew, gathered, and killed their own food and manufactured most of their own clothing, producing a large enough surplus to trade and maintain a comfortable standard of living.

Contrary to the experience of many tribes, the Ojibwe actually increased their territory—at the expense of other tribes—and increased their standard of living throughout the French, British, and early American regimes. Only after the United States established a presence at Fort Snelling in 1819 and gained the first land cessions from the Ojibwe in 1837 did Ojibwe territorial and economic expansion stall and then decline.

As Ojibwe lands were ceded and settled by non-Indians, the economy of the fur trade collapsed because of lost land on which to trap, over-trapping, and a declining market for furs. Annuities from land sales initially helped compensate for losses and maintain the Ojibwe standard of living, but then the Ojibwe were boxed in. They became increasingly dependent on annuities, which then created incentives for more and more land cessions. By the time the shortfalls of the annuity system became evident—the denial of treaty-stipulated usufructary rights, the escalating encroachment of whites on Indian land, the fleeting financial gains, and the failure of the United States to deliver on its promises—it was too late. With decreased demand, prices, populations of fur-bearing animals, and access to those animals, the fur trade had failed the Ojibwe people, and land cessions promised financial gains that might keep them afloat. Faced with this dilemma, the Minnesota Ojibwe listened to the first serious proposals for their removal.

THE TREATIES OF 1863:
LEECH LAKE REMOVAL AND OLD CROSSING

On March 11, 1863, a small delegation of Mississippi, Winnibigoshish, and Pillager Ojibwe leaders negotiated a treaty in Washington, DC, that called for concentrating the Mississippi Ojibwe at the Pillager stronghold of Leech Lake. Bagone-giizhig refused to attend the meeting or participate in the treaty. He was afraid that Commissioner Dole might try to have him arrested again, and he knew that only the presence of his warriors and his shrewd maneuvers had kept him

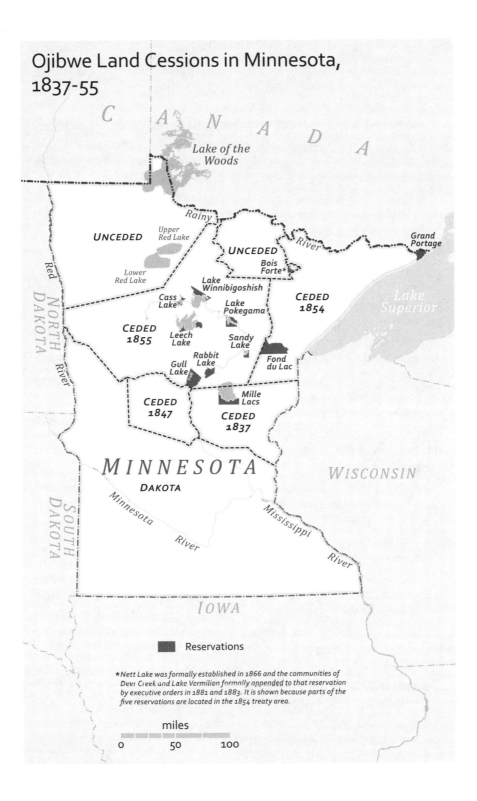

Ojibwe Land Cessions in Minnesota, 1837-55

CANADA

Lake of the Woods

UNCEDED

Upper Red Lake

Rainy

UNCEDED

River

Lower Red Lake

Bois Forte*

Grand Portage

Lake Winnibigoshish

Cass Lake

Lake Pokegama

CEDED 1854

Lake Superior

CEDED 1855

Leech Lake

Sandy Lake

Rabbit Lake

Fond du Lac

Gull Lake

RED RIVER

NORTH DAKOTA

Mille Lacs

CEDED 1847

CEDED 1837

MINNESOTA

DAKOTA

Minnesota River

Mississippi River

WISCONSIN

SOUTH DAKOTA

IOWA

■ Reservations

*Nett Lake was formally established in 1866 and the communities of Deer Creek and Lake Vermilion formally appended to that reservation by executive orders in 1881 and 1883. It is shown because parts of the five reservations are located in the 1854 treaty area.

miles

0   50   100

out of jail the previous year. He also suspected that the Americans wanted to remove the Ojibwe, as they were doing to the Ho-Chunk, who had also stayed out of the Dakota Conflict.[11]

Bagone-giizhig's suspicions were correct. In Washington, treaty commissioners offered the Ojibwe a reservation encompassing the Winnibigoshish reservation at Lake Winnibigoshish and the smaller Pillager reservations at Cass Lake and Leech Lake. All Ojibwe in Minnesota and Wisconsin were to relocate there. The older reservations established in the 1855 treaty — Gull Lake, Rabbit Lake, Lake Pokegama (White Oak Point), Mille Lacs, and Sandy Lake — were ceded to the government. In his absence, Bagone-giizhig's entire domain was ceded.

Not surprisingly, the Ojibwe chiefs who negotiated the treaty returned to a cool reception in Minnesota. Bagone-giizhig and others would reserve judgment until the terms of the treaty became clear, but they were suspicious of the way it was negotiated, of who represented them, and of the treaty itself. There was good reason.

Because the government was meeting greater resistance to treaties among Minnesota's Indian leaders, it began adding enticing provisions that would benefit chiefs. Thus, Article 4 of the 1863 treaty included allocations to chiefs of private land parcels not available to their own people. Article 4 further provided signing chiefs with funds to build personal two-story log homes. Article 8 provided an annual monetary payment to each chief. Clearly, the agency superintendent, Clark W. Thompson, treaty negotiator Henry M. Rice, and commissioner of Indian Affairs William Dole, who represented American interests at the treaty negotiation, were trying to buy the support of the Ojibwe leadership.

Less than half a year after the Mississippi, Winnibigoshish, and Pillager bands agreed to be concentrated at the enlarged Leech Lake Reservation, a second concentration and land-cession agreement was arranged with two other important bands. Leaders of the Pembina and Red Lake Ojibwe signed a treaty on October 2, 1863, referred to as the "Old Crossing Treaty," that ceded the northwest corner of the state. (The treaty would be renegotiated in Washington, DC, with different monetary terms and re-signed on April 12, 1864.)[12]

Initially, Bagone-giizhig sought to represent the U.S. government in obtaining land cessions from the Red Lake leadership. When his request was denied, Bagone-giizhig tried to insert himself into the treaty negotiations representing the Indians, but the Red Lake chiefs chased him out of the conference. Bagone-giizhig was not accus-tomed to being denied the center stage at a treaty negotiation, but he attended the event with little support. Numerous Red Lake chiefs and *oshkaabewisag* had assembled with their war clubs, chief bon-nets, and otterskin turbans, displaying feathers earned in battle, so he had to back down or risk a physical confrontation. They invited him back shortly thereafter, but as a guest observer, not a negotiator. Because the Old Crossing Treaty did not directly involve the Mis-sissippi Ojibwe, Bagone-giizhig's attempt to grasp control met with resistance.[13]

Bagone-giizhig's motives for trying to assert power at the nego-tiations were threefold: he sought to gain financial payment for his band and himself, to impress American officials with an eye on future leverage, and to expand his authority in white and Indian circles, all of which he had done successfully before. Although the Red Lake and Pembina chiefs did not support him, in many respects he did not fail in his endeavor. He was engaged in the diplomacy at the event even if his position was not decisive. After the Old Crossing Treaty, a large portion of the Pembina Band moved to the unceded territory surrounding Upper and Lower Red Lake. Other Pembina Band mem-bers moved farther north and west in North Dakota and Canada to Roseau River, Pembina, Turtle Mountain, and other locations.

Pressure was being put on Ojibwe lands as never before, and Bagone-giizhig shrewdly used Indian opposition to both treaties in 1863 as a way to catapult himself back to the forefront of diplomatic power brokering. He had successfully negotiated for payment of an-nuities from earlier treaties in 1862, and the Mississippi Ojibwe had generally been pleased. But as the terms of 1863 Leech Lake removal and Old Crossing treaties became clear, the Mississippi Ojibwe grew increasingly upset and even violent. Three Ojibwe leaders from Rab-bit Lake were killed because of their involvement in negotiating the treaty, among them Aazhawaa-giizhig (Crossing Sky), a growing rival of Bagone-giizhig, who had warned John Johnson in 1862 that he was in danger. The Ojibwe of central Minnesota could not have sent a stronger message of no confidence in their leaders who negotiated the 1863 treaty terms. The Pembina and Red Lake bands had not had to relocate in especially large numbers, even though they had ceded a significant section of their hunting territory. On the other hand, almost all of the Mississippi Ojibwe were being asked to leave their

Aazhawaa-giizhig (Crossing Sky), ca. 1863. Aazhawaa-giizhig was a cooperative chief from Rabbit Lake and a subordinate to Bagone-giizhig, although Aazhawaa-giizhig eventually undermined Bagone-giizhig's position. He was murdered by his own people in response to his signing of the land cession treaty that closed the Rabbit Lake reservation and ordered their removal to Leech Lake in 1863.

homes and move to Leech Lake, which was already a populous Indian settlement.[14]

Seizing the moment, Bagone-giizhig claimed that the 1863 Leech Lake removal treaty was invalid. He said he was the head chief of the Mississippi Ojibwe and that he had not been consulted in its signing. He wrote letters to President Lincoln and traveled throughout Minnesota to muster support. Because dissatisfaction with the treaty became so widespread and so few people had actually been relocated, the United States agreed to renegotiate the treaty in 1864.[15]

TREATY OF 1864: REVISITING REMOVAL TO LEECH LAKE

For the renegotiation, Bagone-giizhig was selected to lead the Ojibwe delegation to Washington, DC. He agreed to the trip because he felt that the timing was right for him to reenter the diplomatic stage, because the Americans and his own people were frustrated with the previous treaty negotiations, and because most leaders on both sides still feared the power he claimed.[16]

Bagone-giizhig used that diplomatic climate to shape the fundamentals of the 1864 treaty negotiations. He first requested that the 1863 Leech Lake removal treaty be annulled. Because the Ojibwe population had been so unhappy with the original terms and because U.S. officials feared further violence, they quickly gave in to Bagone-giizhig's demands. The removal terms of the 1863 treaty were voided and new parameters for Ojibwe relocation were set.

The main provisions of the new treaty were identical to the earlier one with two major exceptions. The new document provided a substantial enlargement of the Leech Lake Reservation in order to accommodate the number of people who would relocate there. The enlarged Leech Lake territory extended west to the unceded lands surrounding Lower Red Lake and encompassed part of the present-day White Earth Indian Reservation and all of the present-day towns of Bemidji and Bagley. In addition, although the Mississippi Ojibwe were still required to move to Leech Lake, the Mille Lacs and Sandy Lake Ojibwe were allowed to stay on their old reservations, apparently because of their "heretofore good conduct" in 1862.[17] The United States apparently saw this clause as a reward to the Mille Lacs and Sandy Lake Ojibwe for stopping Bagone-giizhig from killing whites during the 1862 hostilities.

The language of the 1864 treaty created an ambiguity in the status of the Mille Lacs and Sandy Lake Ojibwe. The Mississippi Ojibwe had ceded all of their reservations except the new one at Leech Lake, yet they were free to live at Mille Lacs and Sandy Lake. This ambiguity would continue through the policies of allotment and removal, the 1889 Nelson Act, and numerous presidential orders until the 1934 Indian Reorganization Act, which formally recognized the sovereignty of these groups as continuous from the 1855 treaty.[18] Bagone-giizhig was able to negotiate better terms in the 1864 treaty, but not good ones. The Mississippi Band had still given up most of their reservations in Minnesota, including Gull Lake, Rabbit Lake, and Pokegama. To avoid the wrath of his own people and maintain his own status, he had to play a hard hand with the U.S. government. Bagone-giizhig agreed to sign the treaty in 1864, but he did not himself plan to move to Leech Lake. Doing so would have disempowered him. He knew he was not well liked there and that the best village locations were all occupied. He agreed to the treaty not because he was willing to relocate but because he had a plan to gain more power and recognition for himself and his people.

Bagone-giizhig knew that the United States would not launch a major military campaign to move him and his followers to the reservation. By agreeing to the treaty but not actually moving, he hoped to be able to manipulate increases in annuity payments as well as gain additional provisions for Ojibwe settlements in Leech Lake and Gull Lake. After the treaty was signed, he continued to voice his opposition to removal, telling John Johnson, "It is for us to say wether [sic] we shall move or not."[19]

Personal land grants were included in the 1864 treaty for John Johnson, who had been a primary advocate for relocation and concentration of the Ojibwe, and for the only Ojibwe leaders who signed the treaty, Bagone-giizhig and Miskwaadesi (Painted Turtle). Bagone-giizhig also successfully negotiated reparation of five thousand dollars for the burning of his house in 1862. The treaty contained additional provisions for housing for the chiefs of the Mississippi Band communities who were not present, a government gesture to reward cooperative chiefs and missionaries and buy the complacency of other Ojibwe chiefs.

Bagone-giizhig used his shrewd abilities as a diplomat for personal gain as well as for the benefit of his people. But he paid a dear

Tribal delegation to Washington, DC, February 23, 1867, including Ojibwe, Dakota, Nakota, Mesquakie, Ottawa, Kickapoo, and Miami chiefs. Bagone-giizhig the Younger's ability to impress American officials and occupy a central position in large diplomatic ventures is well attested in his position in the photograph, next to President Johnson (between the middle two pillars) and separate from other chiefs.

price for personalizing his politics, losing significant support from his constituents and inflaming his Ojibwe enemies. It is surprising that Bagone-giizhig and the government considered the 1864 treaty a valid agreement between three bands of Ojibwe and the U.S. government when only two Ojibwe leaders, both from the Mississippi Band, participated and signed. No chiefs from the Pillager or Winnibigoshish bands were present at negotiations of the treaty that would dramatically affect their lands and people.

Although Bagone-giizhig and Miskwaadesi had agreed to removal by signing the 1864 treaty, they did not encourage anyone to move when they returned home. In addition to being attached to their homelands and fearing the disruption that relocation would cause, the Ojibwe resisted removal politically. Cognizant of the increasingly desperate attitude of U.S. officials involved in the removal treaties, Ojibwe leaders realized that they could manipulate officials by pushing off removal to future negotiations and that they would

PO-GO-NAY-KE-SHICK, (HOLE IN THE DAY.)
The Celebrated Chippewa Chief.

Bagone-giizhig the Younger, ca. 1864. The growing number of feathers displayed marks Bagone-giizhig as an experienced warrior, while the rest of his attire reinforces the perception of his role as chief.

be weakened politically if they moved immediately. Moreover, the promised annuity payments had yet to be delivered. By not moving, they had greater political leverage in securing their annuity payments. The removal effort stalled.

With his payment from the 1864 treaty (ratified March 20, 1865), Bagone-giizhig built himself a new house by Gull Lake close to the old Indian agency. In 1855 he had moved out of the village and across the river to Gichi-mashkodeng (Big Field), next door to trader Clement Beaulieu. The siting of his new house distanced him from white authority, including traders, and set his roots deeper and deeper in his homeland, albeit on a personal land grant. If the government wanted to convince him to lead his people to Leech Lake or another removal location, officials would have to pay dearly. Bagone-giizhig knew what he was doing.

THE TREATY OF 1867: REMOVAL TO WHITE EARTH

U.S. officials were exasperated by the failure of the 1864 Leech Lake treaty, but they were unwilling to try to force removal so soon after the 1862 conflicts. The new plan for the White Earth Reservation in northwestern Minnesota, officials hoped, would help assimilate the Indians and ease lingering white fears after the conflicts. It was supported by Episcopal bishop Henry Whipple, Roman Catholic bishop Thomas Grace, and missionaries Thomas Wilkinson, John Johnson, and George Copway.[20]

U.S. policy makers had many reasons for selecting White Earth as the new reservation site. There were several Ojibwe settlements in the area when the land was first ceded in 1855, but it was not as densely populated as Leech Lake. For most of the early nineteenth century, Ojibwe and Dakota hunters jointly used the entire area. Large villages were not established because of the occasional hostilities that erupted between those two peoples and the proximity to populous Dakota settlements at Big Stone Lake, Lake Traverse, and Lac qui Parle to large Ojibwe settlements at Red Lake and Leech Lake. By the 1860s, the Pillager Ojibwe, who had a sizeable village at Otter Tail Lake south of the current reservation, were the land's primary beneficiaries, frequently visiting to hunt and fish at Rice, Elbow, Long, Lost, Strawberry, White Earth, Round, Bad Medicine, and Twin lakes. Many Pillager Ojibwe already lived there throughout the year, and a

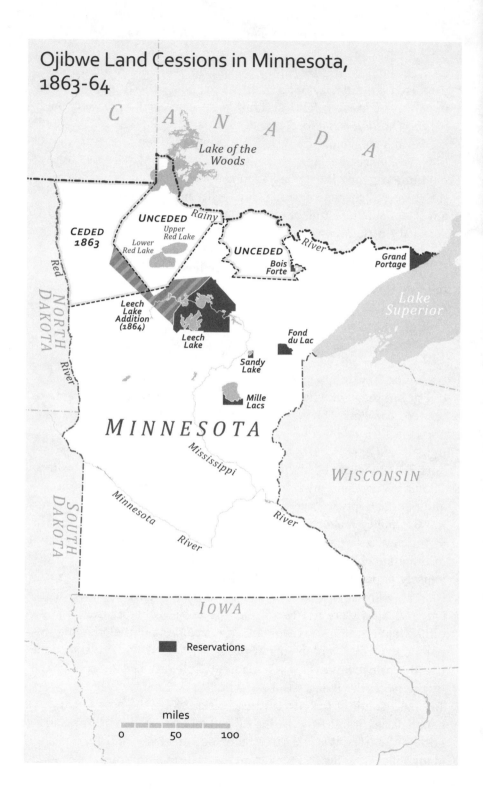

Ojibwe Land Cessions in Minnesota, 1863-64

CANADA

Lake of the
Woods

CEDED
1863

UNCEDED

Upper
Red Lake

Lower
Red Lake

Rainy

UNCEDED

Bois
Forte

River

Grand
Portage

NORTH
DAKOTA

Red

River

Leech
Lake
Addition
(1864)

Leech
Lake

Sandy
Lake

Fond
du Lac

Lake
Superior

Mille
Lacs

MINNESOTA

Mississippi

WISCONSIN

SOUTH
DAKOTA

Minnesota

River

River

IOWA

■ Reservations

miles

0   50   100

substantial number of those Ojibwe stayed on after the land cession treaty. The Otter Tail Lake Pillagers continued to inhabit Otter Tail Lake and surrounding areas, according to a report by Ashley Morrill, although "their presence was a great annoyance to the settlers."[21]

American officials also believed White Earth would be a perfect relocation area because the land suited the goals of policy makers. The eastern part had a bounty of wild rice and game and numerous lakes and rivers. The western part, where the tallgrass prairie and plains began, had good agricultural soil. The eastern lakes might help entice Ojibwe reluctant to give up hunting and gathering. The western plains were easily converted to farmland, offering a perfect place for an experiment in assimilation.

In March 1867, ten Ojibwe chiefs from the Mississippi and Pillager bands, including Bagone-giizhig, traveled to Washington, DC. There they voiced disgruntlement with the government's non-payment of annuities and with encroachment by whites on Indian lands. The chiefs received assistance in their demand for prompt payment from Bishop Whipple, an advocate for removal to White Earth, who wrote the commissioner of Indian Affairs in 1866: "Unless the government desires to destroy its influence with the entire body of Chippewas, they are bound to recognize to the fullest extent all its pledges to the Indians.[22]

A new treaty signed on March 19, 1867, promised payment of annuities and an investigation into other concerns. Most important, however, it reduced the size of the Leech Lake Reservation and created a large new reservation at White Earth. The treaty further stipulated that the Ojibwe would move to White Earth only after the government constructed roads, a sawmill, a gristmill, and a house for each Ojibwe family. According to the treaty, all of the Mississippi Ojibwe were to move to White Earth. U.S. treaty commissioners also hoped that the Pillager and Lake Superior Ojibwe would relocate there as well, although the reservations at Leech Lake, Grand Portage, and Fond du Lac were not formally ceded to the government.[23]

Some special provisions were added to the treaty as Bagone-giizhig again wielded his persuasive powers for personal gain. Officials seemed willing to do almost anything to gain his support, however unscrupulous.

Bagone-giizhig still maintained his personal feud with one-time friends Clement Beaulieu and other mixed-blood traders at Crow

Wing, whom he believed had encouraged Peter Kelly and Ezra Briggs to burn his house and commit other depredations in 1862. In order to ostracize mixed-bloods who did not live in Indian communities, Bagone-giizhig forced an addition to the treaty, Article 4, which stipulated that "no part of the annuities provided for in this or any former treaty with the Chippewas of the Mississippi bands shall be paid to any half-breed or mixed-blood, except those who actually live with their people upon one of the reservations." Ironically, Bagone-giizhig himself had lived off the reservation in a private house on private land from 1855 to 1862, and he did not seem to view that move as disconnecting from his people, whereas any mixed-blood following that path now should relinquish annuities for doing the same thing. Article 4 was clearly designed as a political move rather than a racial or residency statement. Most likely Bagone-giizhig wanted to keep his mixed-blood political opponents from settling at White Earth in order to disempower them politically and economically.[24]

Bagone-giizhig also had a provision added to the treaty that gave a monetary stipend of one thousand dollars a year to him and his heirs. These actions of personal politics and greed predictably would further erode his support base and anger his opponents within the Ojibwe leadership, though he was not the only power broker to abuse the 1867 treaty.

The government was clearly culpable in the treaty abuses of 1867 when it gave private land grants not only to chiefs Mino-giizhig (Fine Day) and Bagone-giizhig but also to Truman A. Warren, a private trader and occasional government representative at treaty signings. The government was buying support from mixed-blood and white people in positions of power as well as from Ojibwe leaders. Truman Warren, brother of William W. Warren and Julia Spears, in addition to being a beneficiary of Article 5 of the Treaty of 1867, also served as the sole interpreter working for the government during 1867 treaty negotiations. Self-serving interests were preying upon Ojibwe land and financial resources from every direction.

ROMANTIC DETOUR: A NEW WIFE

Bagone-giizhig's bold diplomacy was matched by bold actions in his personal life. While in Washington for treaty negotiations, he met a young white chambermaid named Ellen McCarty and formed

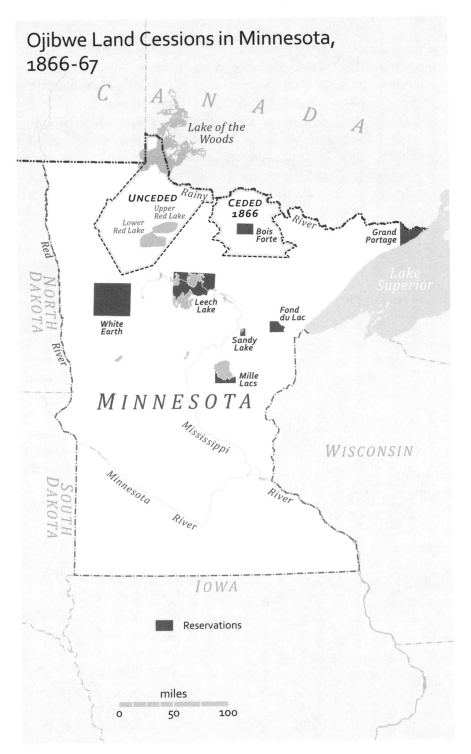

Ojibwe Land Cessions in Minnesota, 1866-67

a romantic relationship with her. When she approached the chief outside the U.S. Treasury Building in Washington to ask if she could interview him for a paper she was writing, he reportedly replied, "If the beautiful lady is willing to risk calling on the chief at his hotel, her request will be granted." According to Charles Eastman, "The lady went, and the result was so sudden and strong an attachment that both forgot all racial biases and differences of language and custom." When the treaty negotiations concluded, Bagone-giizhig initially left her in Washington because her family disapproved of the union, but she deserted them and eventually caught up with him in Chicago. She became his third wife after they were married by a Catholic priest in St. Paul before returning to Crow Wing. According to Julia Warren Spears, who observed them in public on a number of occasions, Bagone-giizhig "was very proud of his white wife, and treated her very kindly." They had one child named Joseph.[25]

FRACTURE: REMOVAL TO WHITE EARTH BEGINS

Ojibwe reaction to the 1867 treaty was mixed. Bagone-giizhig and other Ojibwe leaders seemed content to wait for the annuities to be paid and the houses, mills, and roads to be constructed at White Earth. However, Waabaanakwad (White Cloud), Niibiniishkang (He Who Treads the Earth in Summer), also known as Isaac Tuttle, Manidoowab (Sitting Spirit), and other Ojibwe leaders were disgusted with Bagone-giizhig's personal gains through treaty provisions and the increasing rate of alcoholism, gambling, and murder at Crow Wing and other border towns. On June 4, 1868, Waabaanakwad and a contingent of approximately two hundred impatient Mississippi Ojibwe formed a caravan to head for White Earth.[26]

Bagone-giizhig approached the group and threatened to kill the first person to leave for the new reservation. One of the men pulled a knife on Bagone-giizhig and said, "I see salvation for my children in that place — White Earth — and I see it nowhere else. I will bury this knife in the breast of the first man who attempts to stop me from saving my children, be he whom he may." Bagone-giizhig stepped aside, and the first removals to White Earth were under way.[27]

Aside from this small contingent under the leadership of Waabaanakwad, nobody else seemed ready to defy Bagone-giizhig and leave

WA-BON-AU-QUOT. (*White Cloud.*)
Chief of Gull Lake Chippewas.

From Martin's Gallery of Indian Portraits, St. Paul.

Waabaanakwad (White Cloud), ca. 1865. Waabaanakwad was a widely respected civil chief who also had religious leadership responsibilities and some limited war experience. He was the first chief from central Minnesota to challenge Bagone-giizhig openly, and he ultimately led the first Ojibwe relocatees to White Earth in 1867.

for White Earth. Bagone-giizhig himself was chagrined by the show-down and the challenge to his authority from within his own community. If there was a mass exodus to White Earth, he knew his power as a diplomat and leader would evaporate. Without followers, he would have no leverage in dealing with American officials. Believing there was still time to solidify his power base again, he decided to make another trip to Washington, DC, to make sure that treaty provisions would be enforced. He explicitly wanted to stop certain mixed-blood traders such as Clement Beaulieu from receiving annuities, a move which would keep his political opponents from using the removal process to orchestrate a coup d'état.

BAGONE-GIIZHIG'S ASSASSINATION

On June 27, 1868, Bagone-giizhig began his seventh long trip to Washington, DC. His first cousin, Ojibwe (son of Zoongakamig), accompanied him as he prepared to leave Crow Wing. Because he needed funding for the trip, Bagone-giizhig stopped by the homes of Joel Bassett, Augustus Aspinwall, and John G. Morrison. There he met Charles Ruffee, Charles Beaulieu (Clement's brother), who served as interpreter, and several other people. Both Aspinwall and Ruffee helped to finance the trip, although Ruffee's motive for doing so was unclear. Aspinwall had frequently funded Bagone-giizhig's travel and been reimbursed by claim out of the chief's annuities.[28]

Bagone-giizhig alluded to working privately on another new diplomatic plan. At Gull Lake he told Peter Roy, a mixed-blood trader and interpreter living in the Indian community, to avoid moving to White Earth until his return. He told Roy that they might move to White Earth or to a new reservation at Long Prairie or stay in the Gull Lake region. Everything depended on the results of Bagone-giizhig's diplomacy in Washington.[29]

Bagone-giizhig finished his business in Crow Wing and set out for St. Paul. From there he planned to take a train to Washington. But outside Crow Wing, near the annuity agency, he was accosted by Medwe-wiinind, Baadwewidang, Enami'egaabaw, Naazhoobiitang, Wezowi-ikanaage, Namewinini, Gebesindang, Odishkwe-giizhig, Dedaakamaajiiwaabe, Gaazhagens, Ondinigan, and Biiwaash—and then assassinated. The powerful chief was dead.[30]

Augustus Aspinwall heard the shots that felled Bagone-giizhig and set out to investigate. Messengers from Bagone-giizhig's wives carried the news of the chief's death. Aspinwall summoned Ruffee, and together they loaded Bagone-giizhig's body into a wagon and hauled it to the agency.

Two days later, Bagone-giizhig was buried at the Catholic cemetery in Crow Wing over the protests of some family members. He was forty years old. Bagone-giizhig had flirted with the idea of converting to Catholicism but was never baptized, and he most likely sought only to ingratiate himself with Christians in Crow Wing. He was never a very pious man, but he held on to his traditional Ojibwe religion.[31]

In spite of his personal beliefs, Bagone-giizhig was buried as a Christian by Father Francis Xavier Pierz. Attending the funeral were some the chief's associates from Crow Wing, including John Morrison. Although some Ojibwe people worried that the chief's spirit was offended by his send-off in the white man's custom, most people believed that Bagone-giizhig's body at least now rested in peace at the cemetery in Crow Wing. But like his life and death, Bagone-giizhig's departure to the spirit world was full of secrets that remained hidden for decades.

THE INVESTIGATION AND AFTERMATH

A few days after the funeral, Indian agent Joel Bassett personally led a force of twenty-two soldiers from Fort Ripley to Leech Lake in a halfhearted attempt to find the murderers. Bassett was unable to locate the Indians involved, and he received no cooperation from Eshkibagikoonzh (Flat Mouth) the Younger, a principal chief at Leech Lake with Bizhiki. Bassett declared the assassination an affair between Indians and impossible to prosecute under U.S. law. This was technically accurate because the Bassett investigation took place long before the *Ex Parte Crow Dog* case, decided by the U.S. Supreme Court in 1883, or the Major Crimes Act in 1885. The government had not yet forged a legal mechanism for interfering in Indian-on-Indian crimes. Bassett, however, could easily have conducted a more thorough investigation and satisfied American officials and Indian people about the truth of the chief's murder.[32]

Niigaani-bines (Head Bird), also known as Eshkibagikoonzh (Flat Mouth) the Younger, ca. 1896. Like Bagone-giizhig, he displayed the turban of a civil chief and the eagle feathers of an experienced warrior.

Newspapers as far away as New York carried articles about Bagone-giizhig, but none had the full story. Some reported personal jealousies of the chief over matters ranging from his three wives and his white wife to his personal enrichments by treaty provisions. Others cited his 1862 manipulations as a cause for the murder. Some reports mentioned conflict over the removal to White Earth.

Tensions in the Indian community were high about Bagone-giizhig's assassination, ongoing fraud in the Office of Indian Affairs, and pressure for removal. The government feared violence between Bagone-giizhig's people and the Leech Lakers or another "Indian uprising" over removal and fraud. To calm things down it appointed Dr. A. Jobe in the fall of 1868 to investigate the assassination and fraud at the agency, including that of agent Joel Bassett. Like Bassett, Jobe traveled to Leech Lake to meet with Eshkibagikoonzh and the Pillager Band Ojibwe. Jobe's investigation was far more thorough than Bassett's. Through his meetings with Eshkibagikoonzh, the assassins themselves, and numerous white missionaries, traders, and officials, Jobe unearthed evidence of Bassett's fraud and also discovered much of the truth behind Bagone-giizhig's assassination.[33]

The truth was shocking. Jobe reported to the commissioner of Indian Affairs: "At one time I thought I could make my report without using Mr. Ruffee's name ... I *certainly* desire to do no injustice to any man. But when I look at the interests involved, and the consequences, which are to flow out of this tampering with the Indians if unrestrained, I cannot feel that I would discharge my *whole duty* if I fail to mention *all* the facts ... I feel no unkindness toward Mr. Ruffee by declaring it as my opinion, from all the evidence I could obtain, that he has inspired, and organized this whole trouble."[34]

Jobe's report on the assassination has often been overlooked by historians because his most damaging statements about Charles Ruffee can be interpreted to pertain primarily to Ruffee's effort to take Bassett's job. But Jobe did suspect and implicate Ruffee in Bagone-giizhig's death as well. Jobe also obtained several letters that Ruffee had written to Bishop Whipple making it clear that he had a hand in the plot to assassinate Bagone-giizhig and the attempts to undermine Indian agent Bassett's authority.[35]

The press had already started to discover that Bagone-giizhig's assassination was more than a simple Indian squabble. As early as July 11 the *St. Cloud Times* had carried a letter to the paper, written on

June 30, which read: "Possessed of superior native talents and judgment, and an intuitive perception of the motives of men, [Bagone-
giizhig] was a serious obstacle to the success of schemes of plunder, so ingeniously devised by unscrupulous men, for the ruin of his
people. He was killed by members of his own race tis true, but we
know that no monarch was ever more loved by his subjects than was
Hole-in-the-Day... When the whole truth is published and known,
we predict that an infamy unparalleled will lie at the door of other
than a Chippewa."[36]

After investigating the situation, Jobe wanted to make formal
charges against the assassins and against Charles Ruffee as the primary conspirator in the chief's death. He seemed to have ample evidence. However, Leech Lake chief Eshkibagikoonzh (Flat Mouth) the
Younger refused to turn over the assassins to American authorities
for questioning or trial, perhaps rightly fearing that they would be
hanged and that Ruffee and his co-conspirators would be absolved
of any wrongdoing. Jobe commented in October about the Leech
Lake reticence, "I see they have not moral strength to bring Hole in
the Day's murderers to justice and have them punished, and there
seems to be no authority given to our government, in the treaty to
take the matter in hand, so these scoundrels are to go free." Neither
Bassett nor Jobe were able to bring the Leech Lake assassins to justice because they lacked legal authority to do so. However, without
statements from the assassins to corroborate Ruffee's letters to Whipple and Jobe's 1868 indictment of Ruffee, formal charges were never
filed against Ruffee either.[37]

Justice for Bagone-giizhig was elusive, and the chief's death remained on everyone's mind. The primary assassins, Medwe-wiinind
and Baadwewidang, were too afraid of imprisonment, hanging, or
retribution from Bagone-giizhig's relatives to speak about their role
for several years.

Not until 1873 did the assassins and their families start to speak
privately about a conspiracy by Charles Ruffee, John Morrison, and
Clement Beaulieu—the "business elite" of Crow Wing. The first reliable information that could be used to corroborate Jobe's 1868 report
came from Mizhaki-giizhig (Humid Day), who was an uncle of two
of the assassins and a chief from Rabbit Lake. He later testified that
seven of the assassins, including his nephews, approached him in
1873 at his house in White Earth (ironically, the former residence of

Charles Ruffee). They confessed to their crime and asked Mizhaki-giizhig to help them get their money from Clement Beaulieu Sr., whom they identified as the person who had promised to pay them. They claimed that Clement Beaulieu had promised them two thousand dollars, rather than one thousand dollars, as reported in some other accounts. Mizhaki-giizhig begged them to forget about the whole affair and keep it quiet: "You had better not try and get your pay... for fear that there shall be an outbreak, and your relatives will be killing one another on this reservation [White Earth]."[38]

They took his advice, and the truth about the assassination remained hidden. By 1873, Ruffee was the Indian agent at White Earth and Morrison was the chief of police. They suppressed ongoing rumors and statements by the assassins and stymied formal action by the Indian Police and the Office of Indian Affairs.

Bagone-giizhig's people still chafed at his assassins and the men who hired them going free. The injustice was all the more unbearable because the conspirators now controlled the new economy and political offices at White Earth where most of Bagone-giizhig's people lived. The assassins themselves felt terribly betrayed by Ruffee, Beaulieu, and Morrison, in part because they were never paid for their act but also because they had become victims of the new situation at White Earth along with everyone else. Assassins Namewi-nini and Medwe-wiinind realized soon after the assassination that Bagone-giizhig had been right in his assessment of the duplicity of the mixed-blood traders from Crow Wing. Although it was too late to change what they did, they deeply regretted the loss of Bagone-giizhig—not because of the immorality of his murder but because he had kept the Beaulieu-Ruffee-Fairbanks-Morrison clique from dominating the economic and political activities of the Mississippi and Pillager Ojibwe. Every member of that clique played a conspicuous role in the negotiations around allotment and removal.

In fact, the assassins could barely conceal their feelings of economic and political betrayal by the conspirators who hired them. In 1887, in the presence of Clement H. Beaulieu, Namewinini told Bishop Henry Whipple, John V. Wright, and Charles F. Larrabee that Beaulieu was selling out the Indians: "I do not hate the half-breed, but he is the man that is trying to lead us to ruin... In every place where the Indian is found you will find these half-breeds, they follow and pursue us."[39]

It was not until 1911, forty-three years after the killing of Bagone-giizhig, that the truth was finally recorded and documented in a manner that could be used to bring the conspirators to justice. It happened somewhat by accident through the auspices of a major investigation of land fraud, blood-quantum (a proven percentage of biological Indian heritage) rules, and tribal enrollment at White Earth. Even then, the truth behind Bagone-giizhig's assassination would not have surfaced if Clement Beaulieu and Charles Ruffee had actually paid their debt to the assassins they hired. Increasingly disgruntled about being cheated, the assassins began to talk openly and, during the course of the investigation from 1911 to 1915, offered sworn testimonies about it.[40]

Some of the investigators in 1911 used the formal inquiry to try to purge the Fairbanks and Beaulieu families from the tribal rolls, reflecting a larger power struggle at White Earth. The surviving assassins and their families, however, used the hearing as an opportunity to divulge long-hidden secrets. They wanted to attack the Clement Beaulieu family's reputation just as much as they wanted the truth of the assassination to be known, and they had motive to lie when they impugned him in Bagone-giizhig's death. However, because Bagone-giizhig was still loved by people at White Earth, their willingness to risk retaliation by speaking publicly lends credence to their stories. Even more important in evaluating the reliability of the testimonies is the consistency of the assassins' accounts with one another, with the Bassett and Jobe reports, with the eyewitness accounts of Bagone-giizhig's bodyguard, Ojibwe, and with the correspondence and journals of Ruffee and Whipple. Considered together, the accounts provide enough information to accurately describe who planned Bagone-giizhig's assassination and why.

When compelled to testify, some of the conspirators could barely conceal their involvement in Bagone-giizhig's death or their feelings that it was justified. The perpetrators defended their actions more than they denied involvement. John Morrison said, "If we did kill anybody them days, it was no crime; you couldn't hang a man for killing ten Indians." Augustus Aspinwall, the agency trader from Crow Wing and later a trader at White Earth, said, "The Government done nothing with the murderers as it was the policy of the Government not to interfere with the Indians in their own fights . . . It was much easier for the agents to get along with these Indians after Hole-in-the-Day's death, as he was the smartest Indian chief the Chippewa Indians ever had."[41]

Motives were obvious. The men who arranged the chief's death had the most to gain. After Bagone-giizhig's death, Charles Ruffee eventually became the Indian agent at White Earth. Clement Beaulieu became the annuity and allotment officer for the White Earth Reservation. John G. Morrison became the police chief at White Earth and later a court judge. With Bagone-giizhig out of the way, these men quickly ascended to power and exploited their positions to their personal benefit and the detriment of the Indians living there.

In spite of the sworn statements by the assassins, the affidavit and an interview from the chief's bodyguard, Ojibwe, the letters and statements collected by Jobe and Bassett, the sworn statements of conspirators, and the circumstantial evidence that still existed, none of the assassins or the conspirators who hired them were ever prosecuted or punished for the murder of Bagone-giizhig. By 1911, many of the conspirators were either dead or very old. The government had a vice grip on White Earth and had no further interest in investigating the death. But Bagone-giizhig's people missed their former chief—and the political power he had maintained for his people. They did get one consolation: the truth.

THE TRUTH REVEALED: ASSASSINATION CONSPIRACY

By 1867, Bagone-giizhig had made many enemies. American officials were annoyed by his firm diplomacy and resistance to removal after having agreed to the 1864 and 1867 treaties. Some Leech Lake and Mille Lacs Ojibwe were upset about his manipulations during the U.S.–Ojibwe Conflict of 1862, when he had lied to many chiefs and tried to get them to take great risks in conflict with white settlers. Many Gull Lake Ojibwe, such as Waabaanakwad, considered him too tolerant of alcohol and gambling on and near Ojibwe lands. Most Mississippi Ojibwe were unhappy with the special allowances provided to Bagone-giizhig and his heirs by the 1867 treaty and his accumulation of personal wealth, which conflicted with prevailing Ojibwe mores. Missionary John Johnson saw Bagone-giizhig as a threat to his own life and held him partly responsible for the deaths of two of his children. But it was the enemies Bagone-giizhig made by trying to ostracize the mixed-blood traders and deny them annuities that proved to be fatal.[42]

Bagone-giizhig's conflict with the Crow Wing trader cohort was not primarily about race or mixed racial heritage so much as it was about class and political power. There were many mixed-blood people living in Ojibwe villages who identified themselves as Ojibwe, and Bagone-giizhig considered them his people. However, both the white and the mixed-blood traders, businessmen, and government officials who worked to defraud the Ojibwe people and impede Bagone-giizhig's leadership identified themselves as white—not as Ojibwe and not as Métis. While some fine historians like Melissa Meyer use the term Métis loosely to mean mixed-blood, in fact that term was only used by certain mixed-bloods who had their own language (Michif), culture, customs, and leaders (such as Louis Riel) that distinguished them from Indians, whites, and other people of mixed racial ancestry.[43] Evidence abounds that the cohort of white and mixed-blood traders who vied for power in and around Minnesota Ojibwe communities for many decades prior to the establishment of White Earth did not consider themselves as Métis or Ojibwe, but rather as *white.* They never saw Bagone-giizhig as their leader or themselves as members of the Ojibwe community except when it was time to collect annuities. The divisions between the mixed-blood trading cohort and Ojibwe were profound, deep, and ancient—stemming from age-old intermarriages between French men and Ojibwe women at the start of the fur trade, strengthening throughout the American treaty period, and one of the primary causal factors in the new ethnic, economic, and political divisions. The schism was based on class and economic role more than race, though it was often incorrectly explained as a racial division. Both Bagone-giizhig and mixed-blood traders considered mixed-ancestry people living in Ojibwe villages who deferred to Chief Bagone-giizhig and self-identified as native to *be* Ojibwe. Mixed-ancestry people not living in Ojibwe villages who neither deferred to Bagone-giizhig as chief nor self-identified as native were *not* Ojibwe. Bagone-giizhig's dispute was with mixed-blood *traders, businessmen,* and *officials,* rather than *mixed-bloods.* Treaty terminology and government and tribal discourse has often made clarity about these assumptions in speech and writing impossible, rendering all labels problematic.

Bagone-giizhig's escalating feud with the white and mixed-blood traders of Crow Wing was well known at the time to Indians, government officials, and settlers. The Crow Wing traders had profited enormously from trade and annuity swindles with the Mississippi Ojibwe, so the entire business and trading community at Crow Wing was furious with the proposed removal of the Ojibwe to White Earth. Removal was sure to break up the traders' monopoly and cost them dearly. Bagone-giizhig had long-established friendly relationships with traders and businessmen Clement Beaulieu, Charles Ruffee, John Morrison, George Fairbanks, Robert Fairbanks, and Augustus Aspinwall, as well as Julia Warren Spears, William W. Warren, and missionaries George Copway and John Johnson. Those relationships were strained by events in 1862 and the removal effort, however, and Bagone-giizhig began to resent their predatory role. In advocating removal, Bishop Whipple wrote, "The people of Crow Wing are very much opposed to the removal of the Indians. [Crow Wing] is the depot now of the Indian trade and I am sorry to say of the infamous whiskey traffic, which carries death to the Indians and ourselves."[44]

Charles Ruffee had been feuding with the Indian agent over his clique's monopoly and hoped to extend it westward.[45] He had been campaigning for appointment to the post as agent himself for many years in order to increase control over trade with the Ojibwe. He was once actually appointed to the position, but missionaries had thwarted his confirmation by campaigning against him. Trader and interpreter Peter Roy also weighed in on the matter firmly when he wrote to Whipple: "I demand of you as a friend of the Chippewas if [it] lies in your power to prevent the appointment of Charles A. Ruffee for the office of Chippewa Agent. Major Bassett is going to be removed for defrauding the Indians, which no doubt that's due . . . [Ruffee] is very wild in his motives and a very dangerous man to be in that position . . . He would skin the Indians alive."[46]

Ruffee worried he might lose his entire business through the removal to White Earth, and he was prepared to do everything in his power to prevent it — or at least make sure he got a large piece of the profits from relocation. Initially, he and Clement Beaulieu claimed to be friends of the Indians and brought attention to the corruption of agent Joel Bassett, who had embezzled funds, defrauded government building contracts for Indian housing on the new reservation, given the Ojibwe spoiled food for annuities, and failed to have White Earth land prepared for farming. However, Ruffee and Beaulieu were most concerned about losing their trade with the Indians and their political clout. They helped bring Bassett into disrepute because he was an impediment to their ambitions. When their attacks on Bassett failed to alter the removal policy, they switched their focus to Bagone-giizhig. He seemed the biggest obstacle to them maintaining powerful economic and political positions after removal to White Earth.

Bagone-giizhig had become increasingly vocal about his former friends' scheming and manipulating of annuities. Although he had lobbied to include mixed-blood traders in annuity payments for many years from 1847 to 1863, he now advocated that they be excluded, even to the point of having this stipulated in the 1867 treaty. While drinking in Crow Wing he even got into a fistfight with some of the traders. Ma'iingaans (Little Wolf), a community member from Mille Lacs, was in Crow Wing in 1867 when the fight occurred. He claimed to have seen Bagone-giizhig exit a saloon with one eye swollen shut, saying, "See what my relations, the mixed-bloods, were doing to me. I can hardly see. Wait awhile. I shall get back at them. After a while they will not receive their annuity payments any more."[47]

Bagone-giizhig had been in violent barroom brawls before. He shot mixed-blood trader John Fairbanks to death in a Crow Wing bar in 1849. On April 26, 1864, he had a major altercation with his nephew Gaa-kanawaab (Looks Around) in which Bagone-giizhig was shot in the face and neck and nearly died. Though severely wounded, the chief opened a pocketknife and slashed Gaa-kanawaab across the face. Both parties lived and there was no escalation, but the event did reveal something of Bagone-giizhig's nature. He was starting to drink more often and more excessively. Julia Spears had claimed a few years earlier that he "did not drink" at all, but by 1867, many observers had a different impression. The fight with the mixed-bloods demonstrated not just Bagone-giizhig's (changing) nature but the heightened tension between him and the trading cohort from Crow Wing.[48]

Evidence shows that Charles A. Ruffee, a white man, schemed and planned Bagone-giizhig's assassination with mixed-bloods Clement H. Beaulieu, Charles Beaulieu, George Fairbanks, Robert Fairbanks, John G. Morrison, George D. Morrison, William MacArthur, Peter Roy, and other mixed-blood traders and businessmen over at least two years.[49] Even though Ruffee was white, his ambi-

Robert Fairbanks, ca. 1880. The Crow Wing trader and White Earth
storekeeper married Catherine Beaulieu, Clement Beaulieu's sister.

tion to be Indian agent and a trade profiteer was being thwarted by
Bagone-giizhig the same way that the chief impeded the opportun-
ism of the mixed-blood trading cohort with whom he used to work
and associate. Upset with the possibility of losing their power with
the Indian community and their annuity rights (if they were denied
settlement at White Earth) and vexed by Bagone-giizhig's intention
of going to Washington to bring that about, they tried to hire local
Indians to kill him. When that failed, they found several willing assassins from Leech Lake. Each killer was to receive one thousand
dollars from Clement Beaulieu, and each killer was guaranteed the
favor of Charles Ruffee, who was likely to become the Indian agent
at White Earth once Bagone-giizhig had been disposed of. The conspirators held at least three meetings to plan the assassination. Each
meeting involved several witnesses.

The first meeting occurred in June 1866 at the home of Aabita-
akiwenzii (Half Old Man) in Crow Wing at midnight. Gaagigeyaash
(Forever Flying), who moved from Gull Lake to White Earth six years
after the 1867 treaty, testified that he was at the meeting. He claimed
that he was summoned there along with Gabenangwewe (Sounds to
the End), Ge-gwekigaabaw (He Who Shall Turn Standing), and Jiing-
wabe (Rumble). Gaagigeyaash said that Clement H. Beaulieu Sr. (Gemaa
Akiwenzii), Charles Ruffee (Gaadookan), George Fairbanks, Robert Fairbanks, William MacArthur, John G. Morrison (Biiyaniish), George D.
Morrison, Peter Roy (Pierre-ish), and Bwaanens were also present.
They were promised one thousand dollars each to kill Bagone-giizhig,
and each assassin was to receive a team of horses and recognition as
a chief by the future White Earth Indian agent (presumably Ruffee).
Gaagigeyaash testified that Clement Beaulieu told him: "We want to
employ you, [this] is the reason why we tell you to come here . . . We
want you to kill Hole-in-the-Day . . . If you will kill Hole-in-the-Day, we
will give you a thousand dollars each, and a house built for you, and
a team of horses, and you will be made chiefs . . . If Hole-in-the-Day
is killed, everything will be open . . . If Hole-in-the-Day is not killed he
will be like a great log, high enough that you can't get over him." The
conspirators also claimed, "If we kill Hole-in-the-Day, all of the Indians will be prosperous, rich, or better, and everything." When Gaagigeyaash asked for half his payment before the deed, he was told
he would not be paid until afterward. He declined the offer, fearing
that he would never be paid. While the traders failed to hire assas-

sins from Crow Wing at this June 1866 meeting, they did not give up. Eventually, they found Pillager Band Ojibwe from Leech Lake willing to accept their terms.⁵⁰

The second known meeting planning the assassination took place at Gete-oodena (Old Village) on the Leech Lake Reservation two years later on June 19, 1868. The original conspirators had finally convinced some Leech Lake Indians to do what the Crow Wing Ojibwe would not. Leech Lakers Medwe-wiinind (He Who Is Heard Being Named), Wezowiikanaage (Tail Bone), Namewinini (Sturgeon Man), and Gebesindang (Ever Present Being) were speaking in hushed tones together when Medwe-ganoonind (He Who Is Heard Talking) and Niigaani-binesens (Small Head Bird) were discovered eavesdropping and allowed to observe the conversation under a promise of secrecy. (Medwe-ganoonind was a nephew to Medwe-wiinind and a cousin to Wezowiikanaage, which explains why they were allowed to listen in.) Medwe-ganoonind later testified that his uncle, Medwe-wiinind, told the others at the meeting:

> Hole-in-the-Day is going to be killed... because he is not going to allow the mixed-bloods to enter upon the reservation, the White Earth Reservation; and the person that is back of this assassination is Clement H. Beaulieu, Sr., Kah-do-kun [Charles Ruffee] and Be-yun-eesh [John Morrison]. The reason Kah-do-kun is helping to put this thing through is because he going to be put in as an Indian Agent, United States Indian Agent, and he is going to use us right, if he becomes an Indian Agent; and he is also going to give rifles, sixteen-shooter rifles—even everything that was promised in the Treaty, Kah-do-kun shall give; whatever was promised to the Indians is to be given to them, according to the agreement.⁵¹

Medwe-ganoonind and Niigaani-binesens stayed in Leech Lake, even though they had witnessed the meeting of the assassins. Medwe-wiinind, Namewinini, Wezowiikanaage, and Gebesindang gathered the rest of the assassins, who had not attended the first meeting observed by Medwe-ganoonind: Baadwewidang (Coming Sound), Enami'egaabaw (He Who Stands Praying), Naazhoobiitang (Two Waves), Odishkwe-giizhig (End of the Day), Dedaakamaajiiwaabe (Ebb and Flow), Gaazhagens (Cat), Ondinigan (Source), and Biiwaash (Approaching Flight). Naawi-giizhig (Center of the Sky), Zhiibingog-wan (Shaking Feather), and Mekadewikonayed (Black Robe) may have participated in the assassination as well. Soon after the meeting they left for Crow Wing.[52]

The assassins held their final planning meeting on June 27, 1868, just before Bagone-giizhig was killed. Enami'egaabaw described his firsthand observations:

> We saw May-dway-we-nind loading up a gun. When he was loading the gun, he remarked, "This is the day that Hole-in-the-Day is to die." Day-dah-cum-ah-je-wabe asked him who wanted to kill Hole-in-the-Day? He never answered. Way-zow-e-ko-no-gay spoke up—he was the son of Pe-pe-ge-we-zaince—he said, "Hole-in-the-Day must—will have to be killed to-day..." I said, "What is he getting for this, to kill Hole-in-the-Day?" He answered me kind of shortly, roughly, and said, he is to get a thousand dollars, and a house built for him, a nice house. I asked him, "Who is it that is hiring you to kill Hole-in-the-Day?" He answered me more shortly and rough, this Way-zho-e-ko-no-gay did, and said, "It is Ka-do-kun [Charles Ruffee], and Gay-mah-ke-wen-zie [Clement Beaulieu] and Be-yun-eesh [John Morrison]"; those are the names he mentioned... And, I asked him, "Why do they want to hire some one to kill Hole-in-the-Day?" In reply, he said, "It is for the reason that... he does not want to permit mixed-bloods on the reservation, the White Earth Reservation; that is the reason they hired someone to kill him, because he won't let them in."[53]

The assassins' and conspirators' motives, planning, and actions—the *who* and the *why*—are clear. Yet there remained a burning question about the *how*. Could the depth of Bagone-giizhig's betrayal have extended to his cousin and bodyguard Ojibwe? Bagone-giizhig was completely unarmed when he was accosted, but he wore his Colt 45 revolver everywhere, even at treaty negotiations. He had used that revolver with deadly force to successfully fend off Dakota attackers, in confrontations with mixed-bloods at bars in Crow Wing, and to intimidate people of every tribe and race he encountered. He knew he had enemies all over Minnesota. It seems completely out of character that he would have ventured out without his revolver. Could Ojibwe, his bodyguard, have taken it from him? It seems strange that Ojibwe himself never fired a shot when the chief was attacked. The chief and Ojibwe were accosted, not ambushed. He was the chief's bodyguard. Why didn't Ojibwe shoot at the assassins? Had the chief been armed and his bodyguard truly been defending him, the assassination attempt might have failed. Why wasn't Ojibwe harmed? In the heat of the moment, it seems strange that he would have avoided injury. Ojibwe did sign an affidavit in 1868 in which he said that he had been disarmed at gunpoint, and over the years none of the assassins claimed that Ojibwe was part of the plot at any level. Ojibwe lived a long life, much later serving as one of musicologist Frances Densmore's primary informants on Ojibwe music, but he never confided any further secrets about Bagone-giizhig in all of their interviews and work together.[54] Some answers were buried at White Earth.

THE PARADOX OF BAGONE-GIIZHIG: ASSESSING HIS LIFE

Though the motives and identity of Bagone-giizhig's killers are known, the mystery of Bagone-giizhig's life is far more complicated. How do we assess the life of this paradoxical man?

Bagone-giizhig dressed in the finest suits, meeting the president of the United States and other high-ranking officials, yet he also wore traditional Ojibwe attire and danced at war and scalp dances. He gave some of the most stunning speeches that government officials had ever heard, swaying leaders with the power of his thoughts, yet he held enormous influence with his own people and even the Dakota listened earnestly to his counsel. For decades he successfully led the Ojibwe toward peace with the Dakota, yet he killed and scalped many Dakota people with his own hands. He assured white traders and missionaries that he was interested in Catholicism, but he never strayed from his traditional Ojibwe beliefs or practices. Though not a hereditary chief, he was a traditional leader with enormous, undeniable power. He used that power on behalf of his people, but he also used it for personal gain. While much is known about Bagone-giizhig, interpreting that knowledge is a daunting task. He espoused and practiced many conflicting beliefs. He lived in two worlds, yet he was a complete and functioning individual.

Bagone-giizhig's leadership persona was manifest in all his dealings. He and his father before him successfully asserted chieftainship over a multi-village region, whereas other civil chiefs held position only in individual villages. This development was largely anomalous in Ojibwe leadership patterns. For a time Bagone-giizhig maintained his authority even while living in a private residence outside of any

Ojibwe village. He walked into treaty negotiations for a different band of Indians, successfully took over, and dictated treaty terms for both sides. He convinced Dakota leaders to pursue both peace and land cessions. He used force against the U.S. government (confiscating oxen in 1850 and taking white prisoners in 1862) and then convinced the leaders who wanted him arrested or executed to give him more annuities and personal financial allowances. Bagone-giizhig wielded tremendous power, and he used it liberally. Although he was not liked by some contemporaries who frequently challenged his authority, Bagone-giizhig still commanded their respect.

Bagone-giizhig had intelligence and charisma in abundance, and he knew it. He was proud and vain. He was incredibly bold — in war, in council, and in his personal life. He somehow led an attack against a primary Dakota village with only two supporters; he called U.S. treaty commissioners stupid children when they came to arrest him; and he took a white woman as his third wife while visiting Washington, DC, to negotiate the important Ojibwe removal to the White Earth Reservation. Bagone-giizhig was always a conspicuous figure. Though not grand chief of all the Ojibwe Indians, as he sometimes claimed, he was one of their most powerful leaders. He embodied the potential of his people to be successful in two worlds, demonstrate intelligence, and acquire and use political power wisely. He died young, but his people live on. Bagone-giizhig lives on with them — not just among his numerous descendants at White Earth and Sandy Lake today, but among all Ojibwe people — in spirit.

Epilogue

The Leadership Vacuum and Dispossession

The government done nothing with the murderers... It was much
easier for the agents to get along with these Indians after Hole-in-
the-Day's death, as he was the smartest Indian chief the Chippewa
Indians ever had.

—AUGUSTUS ASPINWALL[1]

Never stoops the soaring vulture on his quarry in the desert, on the
sick or wounded bison, but another vulture, watching from his high
aerial look-out, sees the downward plunge, and follows; and a third
pursues the second, coming from the invisible ether, first a speck,
and then a vulture, till the air is thick with pinions. So disasters
come not singly; but as if they watched and waited, scanning one
another's motions, when the first descends, the others follow,
follow gathering flock-wise round their victim, sick and wounded,
first a shadow, then a sorrow, till the air is dark with anguish.

—HENRY WADSWORTH LONGFELLOW[2]

Some residents of the White Earth Reservation in northern Minnesota today believe that Bagone-giizhig placed a curse on
the community just before his death because Waabaanakwad
(White Cloud) and other chiefs broke their loyalty to him and moved
to White Earth over his objections. They believe White Earth's terrible
conditions, poverty, high suicide rate, alcoholism, and drug abuse are
connected to the Ojibwe's removal from other parts of Minnesota and
to the actions of their earlier leaders.[3]

COMPLETING THE COUP D'ÉTAT

Whether cursed by their former chief or not, the people of White
Earth today are still deeply affected by the men who led them before removal. Although Ojibwe leadership traditions had been in flux
long before Bagone-giizhig the Younger was born, he and his father,

Bagone-giizhig the Elder, significantly contributed to the transformation from a clan-based, hereditary system to a more fluid one in which oratorical abilities, military skills, and political connections with outside groups such as the Dakota and the Americans became paramount. After Bagone-giizhig the Younger's assassination, the shape and strength of Ojibwe leadership changed again, and his people were overwhelmed.

Many historians have characterized the power shift at White Earth as a case of the U.S. government taking control from the Ojibwe and disregarding Indian interests. In *The White Earth Tragedy,* Melissa Meyer adeptly shows how government and corporate interests combined to impoverish the Ojibwe and usurp their sovereign power. But there was much more to the story. Although the government pushed for land cessions and removal to reservations as part of its broad national Indian policy, it was not the government or corporate interests that carried out the evisceration of the Ojibwe people at White Earth. From the earliest phase of removal through the land-allotment period and beyond, it was the white and mixed-blood traders who had Bagone-giizhig killed who also worked with the greatest effort and effect to undermine and supplant existing Ojibwe leadership traditions among the Mississippi Ojibwe. Traders staged a coup d'état that had broad and irrevocable consequences.

Bagone-giizhig's assassination clearly crippled the Mississippi Ojibwe leadership. Although pressures to cede land and relocate to White Earth had been mounting since 1862, Bagone-giizhig had slowed the process and shaped the terms and timing for the Ojibwe's benefit. Even after he had signed the removal treaty in 1867, he told people not to leave their homes until the U.S. government had built them the new houses, a sawmill, and a gristmill at White Earth as promised in the treaty. Without his shrewd diplomatic maneuverings, the Mississippi Ojibwe quickly lost control over where and how they were to live. His assassination left a leadership vacuum that quickly plunged his people to the nadir of their history.

The relationship between the Ojibwe and U.S. government also transformed after Bagone-giizhig's death. The Ojibwe were quickly coerced into removal, despite the fact that a few decades earlier they had been respected as valuable military and trade allies. In 1871, three years after the chief's death, treaty making ended. Indian nations were no longer considered separate sovereign countries, merely subjects of diplomacy. Before long, even the idea of tribal land ownership at White Earth was demolished through the policy of allotment, which broke the reservation itself into small parcels of privately owned land, most of which was sold to outsiders. Ojibwe leaders were ignored by the government, and Indian agents made decisions about land, people, and payments that had previously been the purview of the chief. Courts of Indian Offenses, which were operated and controlled by the U.S. government, began meting out justice on the reservation, while traditional tribal councils were ignored. Indian Police enforced the will and ruling of the Indian agents and court. Ojibwe nationhood itself was eroded, made possible in no small measure by Bagone-giizhig's passing.

After Bagone-giizhig was killed, many mixed-blood traders, their families, and their associates wasted little time in moving to White Earth and collecting their annuities. Many had powerful trade and business connections that gave them advantages in establishing new enterprises on the reservation. The exodus to White Earth escalated. James Bassett observed, "when Hole-in-the-Day was killed, the mixed-bloods were spilled into the reservation. If Hole-in-the-Day was living, there would not have been a single mixed-blood [there]."[4]

With Bagone-giizhig out of the picture, mixed-blood traders and businessmen inserted themselves into positions of power at White Earth. Among them were the people who had plotted Bagone-giizhig's murder—Clement Beaulieu, Charles Ruffee, and John G. Morrison. Also included were William W. Warren's siblings Julia Warren Spears, Sophia, Julia, Charlotte, and Truman Warren. Although William Warren had died, his adult children and their families also settled at White Earth. Robert Fairbanks, George Fairbanks, Paul H. Beaulieu, Frank Roy, Peter Roy, William MacArthur, Augustus Aspinwall, and John Johnson—all of whom had knowledge of Bagone-giizhig's assassination before it happened—also relocated their families, missions, and businesses.[5]

The people who arranged Bagone-giizhig's murder had the most to gain from his death, and subsequent events went according to plan. Charles Ruffee became the Indian agent and used this position of authority to put Clement Beaulieu and his sons, especially Gustave (Gus) H. Beaulieu, in charge of the annuity and allotment lists. The

Gustave H. Beaulieu, ca. 1910. A son of Clement Beaulieu, Gustave assumed his father's central position in the new economy at White Earth.

white and mixed-blood traders and saloon owners of Crow Wing became the allotment officers, timber and land speculators, bankers, publishers, and storeowners at White Earth. Once entrenched, Charles Ruffee and the Beaulieu, Fairbanks, and Morrison families held a tight grip on their power for decades.

The U.S. government's formal 1916 investigation at White Earth, sometimes known as the Graham Report, identified Charles Ruffee and Clement Beaulieu's son Gustave as the primary beneficiaries of land speculation there. Ruffee had been replaced as Indian agent, but Gustave Beaulieu ensured that Ruffee still received a cut of the land speculation profits and government appropriations. In just one of many schemes, Ruffee and Gustave Beaulieu each received substantial private funds appropriated by a congressional act on May 27, 1902. The funds were intended for Indians from Mille Lacs who relocated to White Earth as compensation for improvements to the lands they had left behind. The Graham Report detailed the response to the misappropriated forty-thousand-dollar trust:

> When the Indians learned what was going on they commenced suit against Beaulieu to recover the $11,020 which he had deposited to his personal credit and checked on as his own money. Beaulieu compromised by giving their attorneys $1,000 of the funds and leaving $6,600 in the bank for the Indians, thereby increasing his personal share of the plunder by $3,120. Out of this $6,600 an attorney received a $500 fee and the remainder was prorated among the Indians. Beaulieu thereupon published charges in a paper printed on the reservation to the effect that the present Indian agent, John R. Howard [Ruffee's replacement], had misappropriated the $40,000 fund of the Mille Lac Indians.[6]

Gustave Beaulieu was the owner and publisher of the reservation newspaper, *The Tomahawk* (formerly *The Progress*), which he used to scapegoat Ruffee's replacement and cover his own embezzlement. No further remedy was available to the Indians, who received only $6,100 of their $40,000 trust fund.

The coup d'état was complete. Bagone-giizhig and his family were no longer leaders of the Mississippi Ojibwe. The traders, translators, agents, missionaries, and businessmen took control. They were able to overwhelm even traditional chiefs such as Waabaanakwad (White Cloud) because Bagone-giizhig's constant challenges and defiance did not keep them at bay. According to one witness, "They got land and money... and when they had spent the money and sold the land ... they are robbing us of the little property we have left." Many of Bagone-giizhig's other enemies, fearful that they might be blamed for his death, moved to White Earth as well to avoid possible revenge killings. After the first exodus to the reservation, which included many mixed-bloods, the main Indian population moved piecemeal over many years.[7]

LEADERSHIP DYNAMICS IN TRANSITION

The loss of Bagone-giizhig was painful for most people in Ojibwe country, including his enemies. Chiefs who had cooperated with the government needed an oppositional chief for their diplomatic posture to be effective. No new people with comparable charisma, connections, and diplomatic savvy emerged to fill the leadership vacuum. The Ojibwe still had leaders, of course, and many were honorable servants of their people, but Bagone-giizhig had brought fire to the negotiating table. He knew how to get what he wanted, whether it was from Ojibwe, Dakota, or American leaders. After the removal to White Earth, the Ojibwe simply lost much of their power to negotiate. American officials did not need or want much from the Ojibwe at first—they had already acquired most of their land and moved them off to White Earth. There the Ojibwe had to fend for themselves while often isolated in small communities and families with little support from tribal leaders who lacked resources to help.

Bagone-giizhig's assassination and the White Earth relocation greatly strengthened the role of the Indian agent in controlling and managing affairs on the reservation. Indian leaders no longer told the government who should receive annuities. They no longer negotiated treaties. They could not use the oppositional dynamic the way Bagone-giizhig had done to win government concessions. They could not use the cooperative dynamic that chiefs at Mille Lacs and others had used to get what they needed. The departure of Bagone-giizhig from the diplomatic stage weakened both leadership strategies. The government and its agents controlled the reservations through the Office of Indian Affairs, Courts of Indian Offenses, and the Indian Police.

Any influence the chiefs at White Earth retained was greatly undermined by the fact that the reservation was home to many different bands and many chiefs trying to exert control with a larger population of Indians on a much smaller tract of land. Pillager, Mississippi, Pembina, and Lake Superior Ojibwe had followed some of their chiefs to White Earth. No one would be chief over them all. Indians at White Earth did not always get along. Waabaanakwad (White Cloud) had split from Bagone-giizhig, and his people were the first substantial contingent of Ojibwe to relocate there. He did not look favorably on the arrival of potential rivals such as Ojibwe (Bagone-giizhig's cousin and bodyguard), Miskwaadesi (a Mississippi chief who was Bagone-giizhig's subordinate), or Bagone-giizhig's son Mino-giizhig (Fine Day), also known as Ignatius Hole-in-the-Day. Under these circumstances, the traditional use of council gatherings to arrive at consensus was virtually impossible. Government by consensus had been a critical component of Ojibwe leadership dynamics — despite Bagone-giizhig and other Ojibwe leaders eroding its importance at times — but the divisions were now too deep to overcome. Rifts between Ojibwe leaders made it easier for government officials and mixed-blood businessmen to control the money and the land at White Earth. The money flowed through the hands of the men behind Bagone-giizhig's death to whomever they favored, instead of the hands of hereditary chiefs responsible to their people. With every new allotment, timber harvest, and government act, the chiefs became less and less important in deciding the affairs of their people.

REMOVAL: THE ECONOMICS AND POLITICS
OF DISEMPOWERMENT

Most of the migrants to White Earth in 1868 found terrible conditions. Bagone-giizhig's warning not to move before the government had built the promised houses proved prescient. The new migrants spent the winter in tents and wigwams with tiny government rations on which they could barely subsist. Although some houses were eventually built and some roads cleared, the treaty guarantee of a house for each Ojibwe family relocating to White Earth never materialized.[8]

Living conditions at White Earth did not improve rapidly, and the number of people willing to move there reflected this state of affairs.

There were at least thirty thousand Ojibwe in Minnesota. By 1872, four years after the first people left for White Earth, only 550 Ojibwe people had settled there. By 1875, the number had only increased to eight hundred, most of whom were Mississippi Ojibwe from Crow Wing and Gull Lake, including a large number of mixed-bloods.[9]

Indian treaties themselves became a thing of the past. In 1871, a power struggle broke out between the Senate, which ratified treaties, and the House, which appropriated funds for the Office of Indian Affairs and wanted more control in the ratification process. Unable to gain that control, the House decided to end Congress's legislative power to treat with Indians.[10] New treaties with incentives for removal to White Earth could no longer be made. Congressional acts and executive orders—which were occasionally negotiated—would now serve this function, despite there still being vast stretches of unceded Indian land, including more than three million acres around Upper and Lower Red lakes in Minnesota alone. The U.S. government found other ways to get land from Indians.

Because of the reluctance of most Ojibwe to relocate, the United States issued several executive orders and congressional acts designed to concentrate them on existing reservations and vacate ceded lands. In 1872, government officials met with the Otter Tail Lake Pillagers, who had largely been left out of the treaties of 1863, 1864, and 1867. The United States appropriated twenty five thousand dollars to entice Indians already settled at White Earth to agree to include the Otter Tail Lake Pillagers on the reservation. Most relocated to Pine Point (Ponsford), Two Inlets, and Ice Cracking lakes on the southeast corner of the reservation, where most of the Pillager Band enrollees at White Earth still live today. Waabaanakwad represented the Ojibwe already settled at White Earth, but most of the payment money ended up in the hands of traders, government officials, and their families (primarily mixed-blood relocatees after the assassination).[11]

In 1873, the United States, on behalf of the Pembina Band of Ojibwe, paid twenty-five thousand dollars for a White Earth Reservation township that included the hamlet of Mahnomen and then ramped up pressure on the Pembina to relocate there. Waabaanakwad and Ojibwe leaders already at White Earth acquiesced to these changes and accepted the payments in 1876. The White Earth Reservation population almost doubled to 1,427 as a result of the new arrivals.

The United States also consulted with the Pillager, Lake Superior, and Mississippi bands at other locations with the goal of moving them to White Earth or at least to other existing reservations, thereby opening up land for logging, mining, and settlement. Most were unwilling to move, the Pillager and Lake Superior bands being particularly steadfast in their refusals. In an attempt to encourage the Mississippi Band members at Sandy Lake, Pokegama, Rabbit Lake, Mille Lacs, Crow Wing, and Gull Lake to move to Leech Lake, if not White Earth, the United States issued executive orders in 1873 and 1874 that significantly enlarged the Leech Lake Reservation. The Bois Forte Ojibwe, whose Nett Lake Reservation was established in 1866, still inhabited most of the original ceded lands. In order to consolidate them, the United States added to their reservation the spur communities at Vermilion Lake and Deer Creek by executive orders in 1881 and 1883, respectively.

On March 18, 1879, a large section was added to the northern edge of White Earth by another executive order in hopes of luring more Mississippi Ojibwe there. However, the number who moved was minimal, and the unceasing demands of whites to open the tract for settlement caused a revocation of the 1879 order on July 13, 1883.[12]

The series of presidential orders in 1873, 1874, 1879, 1881, and 1883 had limited success in concentrating and removing the Ojibwe, but the plan was not abandoned. In 1885, Bishop Henry Whipple wrote to every U.S. senator and congressman, as well as President Grover Cleveland and his administration, to push for stronger, more persistent efforts to remove all Minnesota Ojibwe to White Earth. He wrote: "The Leech Lake, Cass Lake, Winnibagoshish, Oak Point, Sandy Lake and Mille Lac Indians cannot be protected where they are at or led to civilization... There is abundant land at White Earth." Whipple hoped to bring a small group of chiefs to Washington in order to arrange more removals: "Great care must be taken to secure only those chiefs... whose influence is on the side of civilization." Whipple portrayed himself as a friend of the Indians and unabashedly criticized some of the treaties and the policy makers who engineered them, but his willingness to pick chiefs favorable to his mission, rather than chiefs who represented the views of their people, showed his true goals and character. Whipple was ultimately at the forefront of the removal and assimilation policies that impoverished and disempowered the Minnesota Ojibwe.[13]

THE NORTHWEST INDIAN COMMISSION

Bishop Whipple's efforts paid off. In 1886, Congress created the Northwest Indian Commission, which was sent to Minnesota to convince all Ojibwe except the Red Lake Band to move to White Earth. The contents of the commission's report and negotiations were to serve as the basis for further congressional action.[14]

The commissioners traveled to the major Ojibwe settlements in Minnesota, where they were showered with complaints. Substantial annuity payments had never been made. Dams on Leech Lake, Lake Winnibigoshish, Pine River, and Pokegama Falls had flooded Ojibwe villages and cemeteries and drowned most of the area's wild rice and cranberries. The Ojibwe had not been properly consulted about the dams or compensated for the tremendous damage they caused. (The Ojibwe could not sue the federal government because of sovereign immunity unless the government waived its immunity or consented to suit, so attempts to pursue a judicial remedy were denied.)[15]

In addition, the commissioners were told, lumber tycoons took advantage of laws that gave Indians rights to harvest dead and down timber on reservations by paying the Ojibwe to torch forests and cut timber. Many Ojibwe started fires and cut wood for white-owned logging companies because they were desperate for employment to meet their basic needs. Damage to wild rice, sugar maples, and berries, the decline of the fur trade, and the government's failure to pay annuities had impoverished them.[16]

The Northwest Indian Commission of 1886 uncovered notable differences in attitudes among assorted Ojibwe groups. The Grand Portage, Nett Lake, and Mille Lacs Ojibwe had no desire to move. A small number of Fond du Lac Ojibwe had already moved to White Earth, but the bulk wanted to stay at Fond du Lac under any conditions. More Mille Lacs Ojibwe had moved to White Earth, but despite government efforts fewer than 125 had moved after the initial exodus.

Grand Portage and Nett Lake Ojibwe never relocated in significant numbers. The Ojibwe on the Leech Lake Reservation and ceded lands along the Mississippi River seemed willing to move only if their concerns about annuities, dams, and timber tycoons were properly addressed. The commission also became aware of fear among Ojibwe already at White Earth that any large increases in their population would "pauperize" the reservation.[17]

When the Northwest Indian Commission submitted its report to Congress, the document was buried in committee at the end of the session. However, the findings resurfaced in 1889 and formed the substantive policy provisions of the 1889 Nelson Act, which implemented allotment for the Minnesota Ojibwe.

While the Northwest Indian Commission was meeting with the Mississippi, Lake Superior, and Pillager Ojibwe in Minnesota, another plan was being developed in Washington, DC, to wrest land from Indian control. The Dawes Act of 1887, also known as the Allotment in Severalty Act, signaled a major shift in U.S. Indian policy. It would have profound effects on the Ojibwe in Minnesota.

ALLOTMENT

The Dawes Act, which enabled allotment of Indian lands, had two underlying goals—the acquisition of Indian land and the cultural assimilation of Indian people. Farming, timber, mining, and railroad interests wanted reservation land. Missionaries wanted Indians to convert to Christianity and feared that the reservation system, by grouping Indians together, encouraged unity among native people that allowed them to keep too much of their culture. Indian control over land and cultural persistence were seen as negatives by many people, and the Dawes Act sought to change those aspects of reservation life.

The Dawes Act allowed the allotment of reservation lands to individual Indians as private land grants, thus ending the previous communal proprietorship of the land base. The Dawes Act was an "enabling" act, meaning that it set up the policy that then had to be implemented on a case-by-case basis. Carrying out the act created varying experiences with allotment—some tribes were allotted and others were not. After individual allotments were made, all "surplus" land could be sold to non-Indians, and there was a great deal of "surplus" land. The Dawes Act further stipulated that all allotments would be held in federal trust for a period of twenty-five years.

The Nelson Act of 1889 had two purposes. The first was to implement the allotment provisions of the 1887 Dawes Act for all Minnesota Ojibwe, and the second was to implement the recommendations of the Northwest Indian Commission and, specifically, to gain cession of all Minnesota Ojibwe reservations except Red Lake and White Earth and remove all Minnesota Ojibwe to those two locations. The U.S. Chippewa Commission was created to collect the necessary Ojibwe signatures to implement the Nelson Act, amend any necessary terms, and gain cessions of as much of the White Earth Reservation and unceded Red Lake land base as possible. The Nelson Act had stipulated that two-thirds of all adult Ojibwe men had to approve of the cessions and removal. The consequent negotiations created many bizarre and contradictory amendments to the act. The most significant of those was a clause permitting the Minnesota Ojibwe to take up allotments on their original reservations — essentially, making removal voluntary. Henry Rice, former trader, treaty negotiator, and senator from Minnesota, was appointed chairman of the U.S. Chippewa Commission and charged with conducting the negotiations, reservation censuses, and obtaining the necessary signatures.[18]

When the commission finally gained the necessary Ojibwe signatures, the Minnesota Ojibwe agreed to the act with the understanding that they would receive overdue annuity payments, be paid a large sum of money from the sale of nonallotted "surplus" lands, and be compensated for damages from the dams at Leech Lake, Lake Winnibigoshish, Pokegama Falls, and Pine River. The Ojibwe also accepted the Nelson Act with the understanding that they could take up allotments on their own reservations and would be under no further pressure to relocate.

Many of the Ojibwe at White Earth remembered Bagone-giizhig the Younger farming his private land grant at Gichi-mashkodeng (Big Field), near Crow Wing. The idea of private land ownership had some appeal for them, and their chief had modeled its potential. But it was the promise of quick payments for the land and reparations for the dams that convinced most Ojibwe to sign.

The misinformation given by Henry Rice and the Chippewa Commission was palpable. Annuity payments were slow in coming or

Henry M. Rice, ca. 1863. A trader, senator, and Indian Affairs officer, Rice negotiated several treaties with the Ojibwe and knew Bagone-giizhig well.

never arrived. The amount of money from sale of nonallotted Indian lands had been overstated. A congressional bill calling for $573,630 in compensation for damage caused by the dams was passed, but it in no way compensated for the full damages. Also, despite the fact that the Ojibwe were permitted to take up allotments on their original reservations, pressure continued on them to relocate.[19]

Even more important than the misinformation and manipulation that accompanied the U.S. Chippewa Commission were the devastating effects on the Ojibwe land base. Dispossession came quickly—and relentlessly. The commission succeeded in gaining a land cession equivalent to four townships from the northeast corner of the White Earth Reservation on July 29, 1889. This cession included the most valuable timberland on the reservation. A large chunk of the Grand Portage Reservation was also ceded and immediately logged off. The large unceded area surrounding Upper and Lower Red lakes was ceded at this time as well, with the provision that lands were to be held in common trust. No allotments of individual parcels were made (or have been made) at Red Lake, leaving that land base intact and tribally controlled, unlike other Ojibwe reservations in the United States. Part of the Red Lake Reservation was ceded in 1889 and retroceded in 1892, and another large section was ceded in 1904. The politics surrounding the Red Lake negotiations was fraudulent.[20]

The government's "allotment in severalty" policy began in earnest in the 1890s with tragic effects on reservation land. Through amendments to the Dawes Act of 1887 and the appropriation bill of 1904 (usually referred to as the Clapp Rider Amendment, after Minnesota's senator Moses E. Clapp), the United States manipulated the allotment policy to the greatest possible advantage of timber and mining businesses and with the greatest possible detriment to Indian people. The size of personal allotments was cut in half, and by the time this policy was reversed, most reservation land was already gone. More than five hundred people at White Earth never received the allotments they were entitled to under the Nelson Act and thus remained landless. The twenty-five-year waiting period on sale of Ojibwe allotments was shortened and in some cases ignored, creating a rapid flow of property from Indians to white land speculators and logging companies.[21]

The Burke Act of 1906 formally eliminated the twenty-five-year trust status of allotments and the nonsale provision on the land titles for mixed-blood Indians at White Earth. American policy makers argued that mixed-blood Indians, being partly white, were competent to handle their own land titles, a scam that simply served to eliminate obstacles to acquisition of Indian land. The Beaulieu, Morrison, and Fairbanks families, who had risen to power after Bagone-giizhig's death, favored the Burke Act because it removed the primary obstacle to their own land speculation. Laws regarding the cutting of timber on reservations were changed to allow logging by non-Indians on Indian land and to eliminate title restrictions on timbered allotments.[22] The Steenerson Act and further amendments to the appropriation legislation of 1904 and 1906 by Moses Clapp and others opened the door for a large-scale swindle of Indian land titles at White Earth. The power of Indian leaders to protect their people and resources had changed dramatically since 1850 when Bagone-giizhig had forced the United States to repay his band for the cutting of timber on Indian land without his permission.

In addition to these "legal" changes, there were numerous illegal abuses of the allotment system and manipulation of legal structure by land speculators, timber barons, and Indian agents. Land acquisition strategies included illegal tax forfeitures and mortgage foreclosures. In 1913, the House Committee Report on Indian Affairs, known as the Graham Report, concluded: "Considering [the Indians'] unsophisticated character, the operations of great and greedy lumber concerns and anxious speculators in farming lands, the march of settlement, and the great influence such interest could wield with the Government . . . it is but natural that results such as we found were likely to follow sooner or later. In this instance it was sooner."[23]

Allotments were easily stolen from many White Earth residents. While interviewing Joseph Auginaush in 1994, I saw a twenty-four-dollar grocery receipt responsible for loss of his family's land allotment at Roy Lake. Auginaush's father had charged food supplies at the post of a trader. The trader presented the charge slip to the allotment officer and successfully demanded title to the Auginaush land allotment. The Auginaush family was not consulted, received no notice, was not served papers, and had no hearing. There was no due process. When the family complained to the allotment officer, they were simply given the grocery receipt, which they hold today as a reminder of treachery. Many similar events occurred during the reservation allotment process, though the abuses at White Earth were among the worst.[24]

Allotment's effects were astounding. By the time allotment was complete, the White Earth Ojibwe owned only seven percent of the reservation's original land base. In a few short years, all of the Minnesota Ojibwe reservations were logged off and large sections of all but Red Lake were settled by whites. The reservation land base remains around seven percent today, and White Earth Ojibwe are a minority on their own reservation, despite significant increases in the Indian birthrate.[25]

SEEKING REDRESS: LITIGATION, ENROLLMENT,
AND INVESTIGATION

Litigation seeking redress for the abuses at White Earth was brushed under the rug in a series of investigations. A new tribal enrollment list was created in 1916 (adopted in 1920) to determine the number of full-bloods at White Earth. The Burke Act of 1906 had eliminated the twenty-five-year trust period on Indian allotments only for mixed-bloods, which meant they could sell their allotments immediately, but full-bloods had to wait and, therefore, full-bloods might be entitled to compensation for the allotment swindles.[26]

To determine the blood quantum (percent of Indian ancestry) of individuals asking for compensation, Dr. Ales Hrdlicka of the Smithsonian Museum and Dr. Albert Jenks of the University of Minnesota performed a series of cranial measurements, scratch tests (matching blood to a color chart), and tooth examinations. (A comparative sample taken from Scandinavian settlers showed some to be more Indian than the Indians.) Albert Jenks reported that Indian "noses are coarse and crudely molded rather than finely chiseled. Contrary to popular opinion, the pure Indian has slight, delicate hands and feet, the natural form of people who do little manual labor." Ranson Powell wrote to Albert Jenks during the testing process about a particularly dark Indian that he wanted stricken from the full-blood list: "I beg to hand you herewith a copy of the testimony given by Dr. Ales Hrdlicka relating to the characteristics of the pure-blood ... I note that he calls attention to the fact developed [by] his observations, that the whiskers of the pure-blood are likewise straight. Judging by the standard the darker of the two Indians I had before you the other day would be doubtful as to his blood status because of the fact that the whiskers of his is [sic] pretty curly." The *Minneapolis Journal*, perhaps with tongue in cheek, headlined an article: "1,000 Land Titles Hang by a Hair, if Curly Indians Lose."[27]

There can be no doubt about the financial agenda that motivated these eugenics investigations. The *University of Minnesota Alumni Weekly* reported on Albert Jenks's work: "So far 90% of the 300 Indians

Ojibwe Land Cessions in Minnesota, 1873-1934

CANADA

Lake of the Woods

Rainy

CEDED 1889

Red Lake

CEDED 1866

River

Bois Forte*

CEDED 1904

White Earth Addition§

Red River

NORTH DAKOTA

CEDED 1889

Leech Lake†

White Earth

Fond du Lac

Grand Portage

CEDED 1889

Lake Superior

Mille Lacs††

MINNESOTA

Mississippi

Minnesota River

River

SOUTH DAKOTA

WISCONSIN

* Nett Lake, Deer Creek, Lake Vermilion.
  The Bois Forte Reservation was
  expanded by executive orders in 1881
  and 1883.
† Leech Lake, Cass Lake, Lake
  Winnibigoshish. The Leech Lake
  Reservation was expanded by executive
  orders in 1873 and 1874.
†† Mille Lacs, Isle, Sandy Lake, Lake Lena.
  The Indian Reorganization Act (1934)
  folded Mille Lacs Lake (Neyaashiing,
  Onamia, and Vineland), Lake Lena, Isle,
  and Sandy Lake into one reservation.
  Sandy Lake had been independent since
  its inception in 1855.

IOWA

■ Reservations

§White Earth was expanded by executive order in 1879. The order was
  retracted in 1883.

miles

0   50   100

examined show unmistakable evidence of mixed-blood. The results of the government suits so far tried with aid of anthropological evidence are decidedly favorable to the citizens of Minnesota; if the defendants continue to win their cases, farming lands now valued at more than 1,500,000 [dollars] will it is conservatively estimated within ten years increase in value by improvements four hundred percent. They will be worth more than 6,000,000 [dollars] and taxable by the state."[28]

Ultimately the investigations proved to be a sham. The fraudulent eugenics tests concluded that only 126 of White Earth's 5,173 Indians were full-bloods. No land was given back, and little compensation was made. Perhaps not surprisingly, when Albert Jenks was questioned about his racist version of human origins and eugenic typing, he replied, "I accept the physical origin of man as animal ... [for] some people's ancestors but probably not mine."[29]

REMOVAL CONTINUED, 1890–1934

In addition to rapid dispossession, Minnesota Ojibwe faced mounting pressure for removal in spite of the 1889 Nelson Act's provision that allowed them to stay on their original reservations. Upset with the rapid growth of white settlements near Gull Lake, Rabbit Lake, and other locations, many Ojibwe did move to White Earth in hopes of better allotments and less interference from non-Indians, resulting in significant population growth by 1891. The United States tried to coax more migrants in 1894 by setting a removal deadline in order to receive allotments, and the deadline had some effect in encouraging migration. There was some later movement, mainly of Leech Lake and White Oak Point (Lake Pokegama) Ojibwe, but a significant number of people who moved to White Earth were unhappy there, and they returned to their original reservations. Some 1,198 new migrants moved to White Earth between the Nelson Act and 1900. Throughout the decade, pressure exerted by the government marginalized Ojibwe chiefs, who often were not consulted. Diminished ability to protect and provide meant that chiefs lost more credibility with their own people.[30]

The United States continued to exert pressure on Ojibwe people to move to White Earth. Developments at Mille Lacs Lake were especially abusive and lasted well into the twentieth century. In 1901, the local sheriff at Isle burned down around one hundred Indian houses and wigwams in hopes that the destitute Mille Lacs Ojibwe would be frightened into moving to White Earth. Similar events continued sporadically for years at Mille Lacs and other reservations.[31]

In 1926, land patents, or evidence of personal title, were finally granted at Mille Lacs; before that time, residents had to go to White Earth if they wanted to claim allotments. The denial of allotments to the Mille Lacs Ojibwe in their home community was illegal and directly contradicted the directive in the Nelson Act that they could take them at their original reservations. By the time the U.S. government consented to give land grants to Indians still living around Mille Lacs in 1926, parcel sizes had been reduced to five-acre plots and most of the Mille Lacs Ojibwe had already relocated to White Earth.

The end of removal pressure and the formal cessation of the wholesale allotment of tribal lands that had been spurred by the 1887 Dawes Act's support for privatization of common holdings finally came in 1934. That year Congress passed the Indian Reorganization Act (IRA), also known as the Wheeler-Howard Act.

TIGHTENING THE CHOKEHOLD: GOVERNMENT CONTROL AT WHITE EARTH

Josephine Warren Robinson, born in 1894, reflected on the state of affairs at White Earth after the death of Bagone-giizhig:

> The old chief didn't think it's right that the Indians should sell the allotment. Because he has already seen how much the Indians have lost to the white people coming into our country. And he was afraid that there wouldn't be any hunting rights for the Indians if they ever opened up the reservation, which he was right ... he was a pretty smart man ... So that's where all the trouble began. They wanted to get rid of him ... After this old chief was killed, well then the reservation was wide open. They were allowed to sell their property. And there was a lot of rich, rich Indians. Especially these mixed-bloods they called half-breeds, these Fairbanks and Beaulieus. And boy, they did a lot of land buying themselves. They turn around and sell their property and turn around and buy some poor Indian's property for maybe half or one-third of what they got for theirs. And they turn around and sell that, and that's how they made money ... After all the land ... was sold on the reservation ... that's when they begin to leave.[32]

Although Bagone-giizhig had been dead for twenty-five years by the time Robinson was born, she and many other White Earth Ojibwe believed that his passing had played a large role in Ojibwe political disempowerment. Traditional Ojibwe leadership paradigms were ignored by the government after removal. Waabaanakwad was still consulted about removal for the Pillager and Pembina bands in the early 1870s, but once White Earth had a critical mass of residents, he and other traditional leaders were usually pushed aside. Nonnative Indian agents ran day-to-day affairs on reservations in Minnesota and throughout the country. Courts of Indian Offenses controlled by the Office of Indian Affairs dealt with judicial issues. Enforcement of American laws and Office of Indian Affairs (OIA) administrative edicts, rules, and circulars became the domain of a law-enforcement agency called the Indian Police. The Indian Police served at the pleasure of the Indian agent and sometimes hired Indians to the force. The OIA controlled reservations until the 1934 Indian Reorganization Act. Many OIA circulars (administrative orders) were extremely oppressive: Circular 1665, issued in 1921, for example, outlawed many tribal ceremonies, feasts, and give-aways, actively suppressing freedom of religion for native people. The effects of OIA micromanagement and control were devastating to tribal culture, economy, and polity. Indian leaders, Indian ideas of justice, and Indian cultural beliefs were relegated to the margins.

While passage of the Indian Reorganization Act was a positive development for Indian self-rule, it also established quasidemocratic institutions that undermined older Indian ideas of leadership, representation, culture, and justice. The new tribal governments were an improvement, but they were riddled with major structural problems, including no proper voting and recall procedures and a judicial branch appointed by and serving at the pleasure of the chief executive. There was no balance of power or accountability woven into the new constitutional frameworks. While the Ojibwe regained and reaffirmed their sovereignty in 1934, they never regained the leadership structure that Bagone-giizhig the Elder and Bagone-giizhig the Younger worked so hard to mold. The Ojibwe leadership paradigms that produced them and that they struggled to change and strengthen were completely dismantled by the U.S. government. The ideas, culture, and practice of traditional Ojibwe leadership would never recover.

Today there are still traditional hereditary leaders, but they do not wield the same political power. Recently, some Ojibwe reservations have tried to remedy that development. At Red Lake, traditional hereditary chiefs regularly attend all tribal council meetings to advise the democratically elected tribal council and chair. This process, which is formally recognized by the tribal government, seeks to rebuild older, traditional ideas and processes of leadership at the same time that it upholds a modern, democratic ideal and empowerment of all tribal members through the voting process. Although traditional chiefs are not decision makers, they are recognized and involved in the political process and treated with great respect. (Similar developments have been discussed but not implemented at other Ojibwe reservations in Minnesota.)[33]

Despite the concerted effort to relocate and dispossess Minnesota's Ojibwe residents, they persevered. The reservations at Mille Lacs (which, after the Indian Reorganization Act, included Sandy Lake, East Lake, Isle, and Lake Lena), Nett Lake (including Deer Creek and Lake Vermilion), Grand Portage, Fond du Lac, Leech Lake, White Earth, and Red Lake survived, maintained government-to-government relations with the United States, and fought for their own best interests. In spite of systematic attempts to purloin their land, erode their sovereignty, and crush their culture, the Ojibwe of Minnesota found the economic, political, and spiritual resources necessary to live. The strong, intelligent, eloquent leadership of both Bagone-giizhigs provides inspiration and guidance for the future leaders of White Earth.

BAGONE-GIIZHIG'S FAMILY AT WHITE EARTH

Bagone-giizhig's descendants suffered in their new homeland.[34] Bagone-giizhig the Younger's two Indian wives and seven of his eight children (Louisa Roberts, Rose, Ida, Julia, Adeline, Belle or Madeline, and Ignatius Hole-in-the-Day) moved to the reservation immediately after his assassination.[35] The family had great difficulty getting the U.S. government to acknowledge their rightful claim to the personal treaty provisions Bagone-giizhig had negotiated for himself and his heirs. They repeatedly petitioned the Office of Indian Affairs and received little rectification although they relentlessly pursued legal channels from 1868 until 1924.[36] Bagone-giizhig's property was sold

and the debt claims of numerous traders satisfied without substan-
tiation although all of Bagone-giizhig's children were alive and their
locations well known. The court did not notify them about pending
land actions but simply published a notice in a Crow Wing newspaper with full knowledge that the heirs had moved to White Earth
and probably would not see the note.

Bagone-giizhig's heirs had similar trouble getting the government
to recognize their claims to the chief's private land grants around
Crow Wing and Gull Lake. The government sold the chief's lands
without the consent of heirs. Some received a settlement decades
later, but the distribution was uneven and came after some family
members had died. Bagone-giizhig's heirs were soon as impoverished as the other White Earth Ojibwe. They survived and adapted.

One son, Mino-giizhig (Fine Day), who used the English name Ignatius Hole-in-the-Day, represented the White Earth Ojibwe in diplomatic missions but was a scholar more than a diplomat. Mino-giizhig
attended St. John's College near St. Cloud, Minnesota, and studied
linguistics. He unsuccessfully aspired to a position similar to that
of his father, even boldly following his example by writing letters to
Ulysses S. Grant signed with the title "First Head Chief." Like Bagone-
giizhig's other descendants, he was defrauded by the Office of Indian
Affairs and denied an allotment at White Earth. He remained landless, struggled financially, and, like his father and grandfather, died
young.[37]

Other descendants, proud of Bagone-giizhig's role as a diplomat
and a warrior, enlisted in the U.S. Army and served in the Spanish-
American War, World War I, World War II, the Korean War, Vietnam,
the Persian Gulf wars, and Afghanistan. Joseph Woodbury, Bagone-
giizhig's child by Ellen McCarty, was adopted out after the chief's
death but returned every year to White Earth and permanently relocated there later in life. He even sought employment in the Office
of Indian Affairs.[38]

UNEARTHING MYSTERIES ABOUT BAGONE-GIIZHIG

Fascination with Bagone-giizhig ran deep in both Indian and non-
Indian communities, and it was hard to keep secrets about him buried forever. People visited his gravesite in the Crow Wing cemetery

Sister of Bagone-giizhig the Younger, ca. 1875

Mino-giizhig (Fine Day), also known as Ignatius Hole-in-the-Day, the eldest son of Bagone-giizhig the Younger, ca. 1875. As a very young man Mino-giizhig tried to assert a leadership position among the Ojibwe, writing president Ulysses S. Grant and signing his name as "First Head Chief." His attire reflects this effort here, but in later pictures he assumed the role of a scholar and usually did not display eagle feathers or a blanket.

to pay respect and satisfy their curiosity about the resting place of a great man. In 1957, almost ninety years after his assassination, John "Pete" Humphrey, a Brainerd savings-and-loan official who had been to the gravesite several times, wondered if the chief was buried with his medals, pipe, and other objects of value and historical importance. Without legal authority or family permission, he decided to investigate. He invited a Minneapolis news reporter to document his exploration of the gravesite and authenticate any relics uncovered. To their astonishment, the grave contained nothing but an empty, disintegrated wooden box.

Humphrey theorized that Bagone-giizhig the Younger's relatives had disinterred the remains and brought them to White Earth, where Dakota Indians could not desecrate them. This idea probably stems from knowledge that Bagone-giizhig the Elder's grave was desecrated by Dakota Indians in 1847. Humphrey, who was conscience-stricken that he had violated the family's wishes, now believed that the body should be protected from people like himself, but he feared legal consequences and abandoned his search.[39]

Presumed gravesite of Bagone-giizhig the Younger in the Catholic
cemetery at Crow Wing, ca. 1897

Where was Bagone-giizhig's body? Bagone-giizhig's great-great-
granddaughter, Karen Fairbanks, told me in 1992 that Bagone-giizhig's
family exhumed the body immediately after burial and transported it
to a secret location to avoid grave robbing and desecration. Although
Fairbanks did not know the exact location, she thought it was near
White Earth village and that the family, many of whom followed traditional Ojibwe religion, performed a traditional Midewiwin burial
service before reburying the body.[40]

THE LEGACY OF BAGONE-GIIZHIG

The aftermath of Chief Bagone-giizhig's death and the ensuing removal of the Ojibwe to White Earth is a tragic story. The shifts from
treaty making to executive orders and congressional acts, from trade
alliance to removal, and from tribal ownership of land to individual
allotments and sales are all part of the story of Bagone-giizhig's death
and the removal of his people to White Earth. While what happened

at White Earth was in many ways a microcosm of U.S. federal Indian policy, it was much more. It was a coup d'état staged by people who benefitted by the chief's death and the systematic dismantling of the traditional Ojibwe leadership structure that would follow.

The rise and fall of Bagone-giizhig the Elder and Bagone-giizhig the Younger is the story of Ojibwe leadership transformed from a highly structured patrilineal clan paradigm. In the new leadership dynamic, powers of oratory, diplomatic savvy, and political connections with American and Dakota leaders became paramount. Although people contested the changes to leadership patterns during their lifetimes, those transformations were too powerful for the resistance they encountered. Bagone-giizhig and his father emblematized the sweeping changes brought about by new forces in their land, but the men were also powerful agents of change themselves. Their lives embodied a critical transformation of Ojibwe politics.

Through Bagone-giizhig the Elder and Bagone-giizhig the Younger, the Ojibwe people acquired more political power than ever before. They affected a global economy in the fur trade and important political and military decisions by Great Britain, the United States, and several Indian nations. Then, the assassination of Bagone-giizhig the Younger disempowered the Ojibwe as never before. The Ojibwe were forced to leave their homes for White Earth, confined to reservations, stripped of their land base, manipulated into surrendering important attributes of their sovereignty, and pressured to cede even their Indian identity in boarding schools. The tragedy of this history leaves us astounded at the pace of change and angered at its injustice.

The lessons to be learned from the rise and fall of the Bagone-giizhig chieftainships reach even deeper. Today, their descendants struggle with epidemics of poverty, alcoholism, drug abuse, suicide, and loss of language and culture that would shock and frighten nineteenth-century Ojibwe chiefs. Bagone-giizhig's people are trying to find new solutions for their problems through tribal constitutional reform, educational reform, and cultural revival. The people of White Earth are seeking to develop a new political and social paradigm for themselves, as Bagone-giizhig did in the nineteenth century. The problems are new. The political climate is different. But the struggle is an ancient one.

An important part of building new leadership and a better life for Ojibwe people, and for their non-Indian neighbors, will be avoiding mistakes from the past, whether they were made by Bagone-giizhig, his enemies, or the U.S. government. Perhaps armed with a better understanding of the leadership paradigms transformed during Bagone-giizhig's life, we can welcome a new era in which the Ojibwe can reclaim the sovereignty, land, and political domain that Bagone-giizhig fought so hard to create and defend.

Appendix A

Participants in the Assassination of Bagone-giizhig

Beaulieu, Clement H., Sr. (Gemaa Akiwenzii)
Ruffee, Charles (Gaadookan)
Morrison, John G. (Biiyaniish)

SECONDARY CONSPIRATORS

Beaulieu, Charles
Bwaanens
Fairbanks, George
Fairbanks, Robert
MacArthur, William
Morrison, George D.
Roy, Peter (Pierre-ish)

BAGONE-GIIZHIG'S ASSASSINS

Confirmed:
Medwe-wiinind (He Who Is Heard Being Named)
Wezowiikanaage (Tail Bone)
Namewinini (Sturgeon Man)
Gebesindang (Ever Present Being)
Baadwewidang (Coming Sound)
Enami'egaabaw (He Who Stands Praying)
Naazhoobiitang (Two Waves)

Odishkwe-giizhig (End of the Day)
Dedaakamaajiiwaabe (Ebb and Flow)
Gaazhagens (Cat), aka Ondinigan (Source)
Biiwaash (Approaching Flight)

Possible:
Naawi-giizhig (Center of the Sky)
Zhiibingogwan (Shaking Feather)
Mekadewikonayed (Black Robe)

Appendix B
Principal Figures

Aazhawaa-giizhig (Crossing Sky), Mississippi Band, Rabbit Lake
Babiizigindibe (Curly Head), Mississippi Band, Sandy Lake
Bizhiki (Buffalo), Pillager Band, Leech Lake
Bookowaabide (Broken Tooth), Mississippi Band, Sandy Lake
Eshkibagikoonzh (Flat Mouth), Pillager Band, Leech Lake
Eshkibagikoonzh the Younger (Flat Mouth the Younger), or
    Niigaani-bines (Head Bird), Pillager Band, Leech Lake
Gichi-noodin (Great Wind), Mississippi Band, Gull Lake
    (brother of Bagone-giizhig the Younger)
Gwiiwizhenzhish (Bad Boy), Mississippi Band, Gull Lake,
    Mille Lacs
Ma'iingaans (Little Wolf), Mississippi Band, Gull Lake, Crow
    Wing, Mille Lacs, White Earth
Manidoowab (Sitting Spirit), Mississippi Band, Gull Lake, Crow
    Wing, White Earth
Migizi (Eagle), Mississippi Band, Mille Lacs
Mino-giizhig (Fine Day), or Ignatius Hole-in-the-Day, Mississippi
    Band, White Earth
Miskwaadesi (Painted Turtle), Mississippi Band, Crow Wing,
    White Earth
Mizhaki-giizhig (Humid Day), Mississippi Band, Crow Wing,
    White Earth
Negwanebi (Resting Feather), Mississippi Band, Mille Lacs
Niibiniishkang (He Who Treads the Earth in Summer), or Isaac
    Tuttle, Mississippi Ojibwe, Gull Lake, Crow Wing, White Earth

Niigaanigwaneb (First Seated Feather), Mississippi Band, Mille Lacs
Ojibwe (Ojibwe), Mississippi Band, Gull Lake, Crow Wing, White
Earth
Waabaanakwad (White Cloud), Mississippi Band, Gull Lake, Crow
Wing, White Earth
Waabojiig (White Fisher), Lake Superior Band, La Pointe, St. Croix
Waabojiig the Younger (White Fisher the Younger), Mississippi
Band, Sandy Lake, Gull Lake
Zoongakamig (Strong Ground), Mississippi Band, Sandy Lake,
Gull Lake

MISSIONARIES, TRADERS, PUBLIC OFFICIALS, AND OTHERS

Agidajiwekwe (Coming Over the Top of the Mountain Woman),
wife of Bagone-giizhig the Younger and mother of Ignatius
and Madeline Hole-in-the-Day
Aitkin, William, Sandy Lake and Crow Wing trader
Aspinwall, Augustus (Gus), Crow Wing and White Earth trader,
businessman
Bassett, Joel, Indian agent
Beaulieu, Claude H., trader, reverend
Beaulieu, Clement H., Sr. (Gemaa Akiwenzii), Crow Wing trader
Beaulieu, Gustave (Gus) H., White Earth trader, editor (son of
Clement)
Beaulieu, Paul H., Crow Wing trader
Biiwaabiko-giizhigookwe (Iron Sky Woman), wife of John Johnson
and niece of Bagone-giizhig the Elder
Bonga, George, Crow Wing and Leech Lake trader, interpreter
Borup, Charles, Sandy Lake tragedy special investigation
commissioner
Boutwell, William T., missionary
Brunson, Alfred, missionary, Indian agent
Cass, Lewis, governor of Michigan Territory
Copway, George (Gaagigegaabaw [Stands Forever]), missionary,
scholar
Crooks, Ramsay, American Fur Company president
Doty, James D., Schoolcraft expedition secretary
Douglass, David B., army captain
Eastman, Charles, historian

Fletcher, Jonathan, Indian agent, Ho-Chunk (Winnebago) agency
Herriman, David B., Indian agent
Hrdlicka, Ales, Smithsonian Museum
Jenks, Albert, University of Minnesota, Department of Anthropology
Jobe, A., Office of Indian Affairs, special investigation officer for
    assassination
Johnson, John (Enami'egaabaw [Stands Praying]), Gull Lake
    (St. Columba Mission) and White Earth missionary
Manypenny, George W., commissioner of Indian Affairs
McCarthy, William, Crow Wing trader
Morrill, Ashley, special Indian agent
Morrison, George D., Crow Wing and White Earth trader
Morrison, John G. (Biiyaniish), Crow Wing trader, White Earth
    police chief
Ramsey, Alexander, trader, governor of Minnesota Territory
Ramsey, Justus, Sandy Lake special investigation commissioner
    (Alexander's brother)
Rice, Henry M., trader, treaty commissioner, senator
Ruffee, Charles (Gaadookan), Crow Wing trader, businessman,
    White Earth Indian agent
Schoolcraft, Henry R., Indian agent, explorer, geologist,
    historian
Sibley, Henry H., fur trader, army officer, first governor of
    Minnesota
Snelling, Josiah, army colonel, Fort Snelling commandant
Snelling, William Joseph, writer (son of Josiah)
Spears, Julia Warren, teacher
Taliaferro, Lawrence, Indian agent
Thompson, Clark, Office of Indian Affairs, agency superintendent
Todd, John, Office of Indian Affairs
Trowbridge, Charles C., assistant to Captain Douglass, U.S. Army
Verplank, Issac A., treaty commissioner
Walker, Lucius C., Indian agent
Warren, Lyman, interpreter, La Pointe and American Fur
    Company trader
Warren, Truman A., interpreter, Crow Wing trader
Warren, William W., historian, interpreter
Watrous, John S., Office of Indian Affairs, special Indian agent
    for removal

Appendix C

Important Event Chronology

1800   Bagone-giizhig the Elder born at La Pointe, Wisconsin

1820   Bagone-giizhig the Elder moves to Sandy Lake,
        Minnesota

1825   Treaty of Prairie du Chien draws lines between Ojibwe
        and Dakota lands in Minnesota; Sandy Lake chief Curly
        Head dies; Bagone-giizhig the Elder becomes a chief at
        Sandy Lake

1827   Bagone-giizhig the Younger born

1834   John Johnson (half-Ottawa missionary) moves to
        Minnesota and soon marries Bagone-giizhig's niece,
        Biiwaabiko-giizhigookwe, and is adopted as a son by
        Bagone-giizhig

1836   Wisconsin Territory (which initially included all of
        present-day Minnesota east of the Mississippi) organized

1836–38 Bagone-giizhig the Elder, his family, and many followers
        establish new villages at Swan River, Rabbit Lake, Leaf
        River, Crow Wing, and Gull Lake; he is the undisputed
        primary chief of the newly settled area

1837   Treaty of St. Peters: the first Ojibwe land cessions in
        Minnesota, near Mille Lacs, adjacent to Bagone-giizhig's
        newly settled villages; white hamlet of Crow Wing estab-
        lished across the river from the Indian village

1847   Treaty at Leech Lake: cedes Pillager title to Long Prairie
        in preparation for moving the Ho-Chunk and Menominee
        there; Bagone-giizhig the Elder dies; Bagone-giizhig the
        Younger becomes chief at Gull Lake; Treaty of Fond du
        Lac: cedes Lake Superior and Mississippi title to Long

Prairie to enable Ho-Chunk and Menominee relocation; Bagone-giizhig the Younger's first diplomatic foray

1848   Wisconsin becomes a state

1849   Minnesota Territory formed

1850   Sandy Lake annuity tragedy: President Zachary Taylor orders Michigan and Wisconsin Ojibwe relocated to Sandy Lake, the only place they can now receive annuities, but the government feeds Indians moldy flour and bad meat, resulting in food poisoning and 550 deaths

1854   Treaty of La Pointe: cedes Arrowhead region of northeastern Minnesota

1855   Treaty of Washington, DC: cedes all Mississippi Ojibwe lands in Minnesota except for newly established reservations

1862   U.S.–Ojibwe Conflict: Bagone-giizhig manipulates other Ojibwe leaders to threaten and pressure U.S. government during U.S.–Dakota Conflict in southern Minnesota

1863   Treaty of Washington, DC: cedes Mississippi Ojibwe lands and calls for their removal to Leech Lake; the only land cession treaty affecting his people that Bagone-giizhig did not attend; "Old Crossing" Treaty: cedes northwestern Minnesota

1864   Treaty of Washington, DC: alters terms of removal order for the Mississippi Ojibwe to Leech Lake, allowing Mille Lacs Ojibwe to stay in Mille Lacs

1867   Treaty of Washington, DC: creates White Earth Reservation and calls for removal of all Ojibwe from central Minnesota

1868   Bagone-giizhig is assassinated on his way to Washington to renegotiate White Earth removal

1887   Dawes Act: enables nationwide policy of allotment

1889   Nelson Act: implements allotment of most reservations in Minnesota; gains land cessions from Red Lake

1934   Indian Reorganization Act: ends allotment, transforms the intended function of the Office of Indian Affairs from supervisory to advisory, and enables the establishment of modern tribal governments nationwide

Appendix D

More on Language

The Meaning of Ojibwe *and* Anishinaabe

The meaning of the word *ojibwe* is debated. Alexander Ramsey asserted that *ojibwe* described the contraction or narrowing of the Great Lakes at Mackinac, but no linguistic analysis supports this conclusion. He most likely confused the meaning of the place with the name of the people who lived there. Henry Schoolcraft believed that *ojibwe* was derived from *bwe* (pertaining to voice) and that it described a "peculiarity in intonation of the voice" in the Ojibwe language. George Belcourt, for whom Belcourt, North Dakota, was named, believed it was in reference to "drawling pronunciation." Peter Kelly, former grand chief of Treaty Council Three in Ontario, asserted that it was a derivation of *wajiw,* meaning "mountain" and described the original hilly homeland of the Ojibwe near Montreal. Lewis Henry Morgan wrote that the word *ojibwe* was actually a derivation of the Ojibwe word for root, *jiibik,* and signified that the Ojibwe were the "root or stem" of all people.[1]

Harold Hickerson believed that the word *ojibwe* was a derivation of the Proto-Algonquian morphemes for *crane* and *voice.* It is difficult to ascertain from his book how Hickerson arrived at this conclusion or which sources he used. The Ojibwe word for crane, *ajijaak,* sounds very different from *ojibwe.* Furthermore, *ajijaak* describes the physical appearance of the crane's long sticklike legs. Those morphemes, when broken down and rearranged (to get *ojibwe*) would not retain their reference to *crane* when attached to other morphemes. However, it is true that the crane clan was one of the traditional clans of hereditary civil chiefs in Ojibwe society. It is also true that sometimes villages and larger groups were identified by the dominant clans represented in the community.[2]

A more widely accepted explanation of *ojibwe* is that it pertains to puckering, or drawing up tight. Some have asserted that this is in reference to the "puckering of lips in speaking or drinking." William W. Warren wrote that most Ojibwe elders with whom he spoke said that the meaning of puckering is in reference to the puckered seam of the typical Ojibwe moccasin. George Copway believed that this was the origin of the word as well. Copway even claimed that it originated at a council of Indians at present-day Prairie du Chien where the entire Ojibwe delegation wore moccasins with a puckered seam. Others feel that puckering is the meaning, but in reference to the tightening of wet moccasins near fire.[3]

Warren illuminated a second conclusion as well, although it was speculative. Warren's second definition of the word *ojibwe* is that it described the process of roasting captives until puckered up, from *ojib* (to pucker) and *bwaa* (to roast). This seems unlikely, for the *aa* and *e* sounds in Ojibwe are different, nor is it historically probable. Captives were occasionally tortured by fire, but this was never a common practice. It also seems improbable that the Ojibwe would use a word laden with negative connotations as a term of self-reference. Warren also noted that "the name does not date far back," suggesting that he was not entirely convinced of this explanation.[4]

Helen Tanner believes that *ojibwe* is derived from the Ojibwe practice of writing on birch bark. Although many tribes wrote on birch bark, the custom was especially important to the Ojibwe and widely practiced. Bark writing was an identifying trademark in Ojibwe culture. Although Tanner does not provide a linguistic analysis to back up her assertion, it is valid. The *zh* sound in Ojibwe is quite similar to *j*. Therefore, *ojibwe* could easily be a derivation of *ozhi-*, pertaining to writing, as in *ozhibii'ige,* meaning "he writes." Edmund Danziger drew the conclusion that *ojibwe* means "those who make pictographs." This definition has merit as well in view of the similarity between *oji* and *ozhi.*[5]

Of all the aforementioned explanations, those referring to the puckered seam of the Ojibwe moccasin and writing practices common to the Ojibwe seem the most probable. As with many things in Ojibwe oral tradition, there may be more than one right explanation.

Ojibwe people most commonly use the term *anishinaabe* in reference to themselves. Many reputable scholars are beginning to use the term *anishinaabe* in their scholarship as well. Ojibwe elders I interviewed from White Earth and Mille Lacs, including Joseph Auginaush and Melvin Eagle, noticed and privately applauded the development. *Anishinaabe* is a term that is generally applied to all Indians. *Ojibwe* is specific only to the Ojibwe, used to distinguish them from other groups of Indians. In closely related languages like Ottawa and Potawatomi, *anishinaabe* is also used as the term of self-reference, meaning "Indian." It should be pointed out that the term *anishinaabe* means "an Indian person" but also assumes the collective singular, meaning "the Indian people." Therefore, it is not necessary to use the plural *anishinaabeg* to refer to more than one Indian. *Anishinaabeg* means "Indians." *Anishinaabe* means both "Indian" and "the Indian people."[6]

The term *anishinaabe* has even more morphological possibilities than *ojibwe.* In "The Etymology of Anishinaabe," Dennis Jones says that one explanation of *anishinaabe* is that it is derived from *anishaa* (for nothing) and *naabe* (mankind), meaning that the Indian is nothing without a spiritual life. According to Edward Benton-Banai, *anishinaabe* is derived from *ani* (from whence), *nishina* (lowered), and *abe* (the male of the species). According to Moses Tom, *anishinaabe* originated from the first word elders say when they begin a ceremony, *anishinaa,* which was also the first word the Indian spoke when he was created. William W. Warren argues that it means spontaneous man. According to Louis Councillor, *anishinaabe* is derived from *anishin* (a short form of *onizhishi,* meaning "he is good") and *aabe* (human being). He interpreted this to mean that Indians were expected to lead a good, spiritual life. Henry Schoolcraft believed that it meant common man. Peter Kelly, former grand chief of Treaty Council Three in Canada, said that *anishinaabe* means one who is humble before the creator. The oral history of Manitoulin Island postulates that it is derived from *niizh* (second, or the number two) and *naabe* (man or mankind), in reference to the second creation of man (in keeping with the traditional story of Wenabozho and the Flood, where the earth is cleansed with water and humankind starts anew). At Turtle Mountain, North Dakota, oral history provides the explanation that *anishinaabe* means a void that is filled. The most common explanation is that *anishinaabe* means original man. The morphology of *anishinaabe* and *ojibwe* explains much about Ojibwe understandings of Ojibweness, and the terms also relate directly to Ojibwe conceptions of identity and leadership.[7]

A NOTE ON COMPOUND WORDS

As with many nouns in the Ojibwe language, the terms *ojibwe* and *anishinaabe* can be compounded. *Ojibwewi-anishinaabe* and *ojibwe-wanishinaabe* both mean "an Ojibwe Indian." Both forms are still in common usage in the Ojibwe language today, although it is most common to hear *ojibwe* and *anishinaabe* used independently.

PRONUNCIATION GUIDE

The many Ojibwe personal and place-names in this book may be challenging for some readers. A basic double-vowel pronunciation guide is presented here for assistance with pronunciation and ease of reference.[8]

Letter	Ojibwe Examples	Equivalent English Sounds
a	**a**gim "count someone"	**a**bout
aa	**aa**gim "snowshoe"	f**a**ther
e	**e**mikwaan "spoon"	caf**é**
i	**i**n**i**ni "man"	p**i**n
ii	n**ii**n "me, I"	s**ee**n
o	nib**o** "he or she dies"	**o**bey
oo	**oo**dena "village"	b**oa**t, b**oo**t
b	**b**akade "he or she is hungry"	**b**ig
ch	mi**ch**aa "it is big"	sti**tch**
d	**d**ebwe "he or she tells the truth"	**d**o
g	**g**iin "you"	**g**eese
h	**h**ay' "too bad"	**h**i
'	ode**'** "his or her heart"	(uh-oh)
j	**j**iimaan "canoe"	**j**ump
k	ma**k**izin "shoe, moccasin"	pi**ck**
m	**m**iin "blueberry"	**m**an
n	**n**aa**n**an "five"	**n**ame
p	o**p**in "potato"	ri**p**
s	a**s**in "stone"	mi**ss**
sh	animo**sh** "dog"	bu**sh**
t	a**t**e "it is put somewhere"	pi**t**
w	**w**aabang "tomorrow"	**w**ay

Letter	Ojibwe Examples	*Equivalent* *English Sounds*
y	nii**y**aw "my body"	**y**ellow
z	**z**iibi "river"	**z**ebra
zh	**zh**aabonigan "needle"	mea**s**ure

The doubled vowels are separate vowel sounds, distinct from their single-vowel counterparts (hence the name double-vowel orthography). The *oo* letter is given two sounds because both appear in Ojibwe. In Mille Lacs and St. Croix the *oo* letter is usually pronounced as in *boot.* In Red Lake it is customarily pronounced as in *boat.* In Leech Lake, both are equally common. The glottal stop ['] does not have an English equivalent but loosely approximates the stop or hitch heard in the middle of the English expression "*Uh-oh.*"

Acknowledgments

I began researching Bagone-giizhig in earnest as a graduate student at the University of Minnesota in the early 1990s. While I was there this project was blessed by the guidance of many people, especially Jean O'Brien-Kehoe, Russell Menard, John Howe, and Hy Berman.

This work simply would not have been possible without the assistance of numerous Ojibwe and Dakota cultural carriers, elders, and tribal historians who contributed their knowledge about tribal languages, cultures, and history: Dora Ammann, David Aubid, Joseph Auginaush, Richard "Dick" Barber, Thomas Beardy, Edward Benton-Banai, Raining Boyd, Terrence Burnette, Albert Churchill, James Clark, William "Billy" Daniels, Melvin Eagle, George Fairbanks, Karen Fairbanks, Emma Fisher, Anna Gibbs, Brian Goodwin, Lois Goodwin, Charles Grolla, Charles "Scott" Headbird, Lawrence Henry, Susan Jackson, Daniel Jones, Dennis Jones, Nancy Jones, Floyd Jourdain, Adrian Liberty, William "Bill" May, Archie Mosay, Collins Oakgrove, Vincent Olsen, Earl Otchingwanigan (Nyholm), Margaret Porter, Connie "Babe" Rivard, Mary Roberts, Delorse Rogers, Benjamin Sam, Carolyn Schommer, Betsy Schultz, Daniel Seaboy, Luella Seelye, Marlene Stately, Frank Stech, Eugene Stillday, Thomas Stillday Jr., Leona Wakonabo, Hartley White, Walter "Porky" White, Vernon Whitefeather, and Angela Wilson. Thank you to Alfred Bush, Thomas Whitridge, and Charles Lippert for help with maps. This book was also graced by the scrutiny and editorial advice of Ann Regan, Marilyn Ziebarth, Shannon Pennefeather, David Thorstad, and Robert Treuer, all of whom made it better.

My research for this project was at times and in different ways supported financially by grants and fellowships from the MacArthur Foundation, the Committee on Institutional Cooperation, the Experienced Faculty Development Program, the Institute for the Study of World Politics, the Leech Lake Band of Ojibwe, Bemidji State University's Professional Improvement Grant Program, the Minnesota State Arts Board, the Minnesota Humanities Commission, the Minnesota Historical Society, the National Endowment for the Humanities/National Science Foundation Documenting Endangered Languages Fellowship Program, the American Philosophical Society, the Bush Leadership Fellows Program, and the John Simon Guggenheim Foundation.

Any major research and writing endeavor takes tremendous commitments of time and energy. I received unbounding support and encouragement. For that, I have a great many people to thank, not the least of which are friends Aditya Adarkar, Joseph Aitken, Dora Ammann, Brooke Ammann, Diane Amour, Donna Beckstrom, Irene and Perry Benjamin, Ab and Carol Boonswang, Michael Bowman, Benjamin Burgess, Dustin Burnette, Patrick Carriere, Brenda Child, Timothy Chow, Lee Cook, Collette "Tori" Dahlke, Donald and Priscilla Day, Paul and Betty Day, Philip Deloria, Paul DeMain, Deborah Eagle, Jamie and George "Skaff" Elias, Heid Erdrich, Louise Erdrich, Nancy Erickson, Sean Fahrlander, Judy Fairbanks, Andrew and Mary Favorite, Bruce Fetter, Donald Fixico, Henry Flocken, Anna Gibbs, Bruce Godfrey, Thomas Goldtooth, Melissa Greene, Charles Grolla, Renee Gurneau, Susan Hallett, James Hardy, Jean Higaki, Earl Hoagland, Daniel Jones, Dennis Jones, Richard and Penny Kagigebi, Shalah Kingbird, Jeremy Kingsbury, Lisa LaRonge, Bryan Lee, Adrian Liberty, Eunice Lighfeather, Eric Lin, Scott Lyons, Paul and Amy Markhoff-Johnson, Arthur and Grace Mateos, James and Betsy McDougall, Cary Miller, Leonard and Mary Moose, Archie Mosay, John Nichols, Aryani Ong, Earl Otchingwanigan (Nyholm), Keller Paap, Jon Quistgaard, Lahnah Rossbach, Skip and Babette Sandman, Thomas Saros, Robert Shimek, Kent Smith, Michael and Patty Smith, Vivasvan Soni, Daniel Stevens, Eugene Stillday, Mary Lou and Thomas Stillday Jr., Michael Sullivan, Ursula Swiney, Andrew Tallon, Audrey Thayer, Diane Thompson, David Thorstad, Isadore Toulouse, Chad Uran, Gitendra and Dilhani Uswatte, Leon "Boycee" Valliere, Linda Wade, Ted Waukey, Brendan Weickert, Colleen White, Richard White, Michael Witgen, Sumio Yamada, Daniel York, and Gene Youngdahl. I am also deeply indebted to Alfred Bush for advice, encouragement, support, and the sanctuary of his hacienda, Los Saposantos dc Calle Tapachula, La Valle de Jovel en San Cristóbal de Las Casas en Chiapas, Mexico, where I finally finished the book.

I am also always forever indebted to my greatest support base of all in my family—my parents Robert and Margaret Treuer, my siblings David, Derek, Megan, Micah, Paul, and Smith Treuer, their spouses, Gretchen Potter, Debbie, Elissa, Mary, and Ronna Treuer, my children Jordan, Robert, Maddy, Caleb, Isaac, Elias, Evan, and Mia, and my wife, Blair. Nothing would be possible without you.

Notes

Notes below use abbreviations. For full information, consult the Bibliography.

Repositories

MHS	Minnesota Historical Society
NA	National Archives
SHSW	State Historical Society of Wisconsin

ABCFMP	American Board of Commissioners for Foreign Missions Papers, MHS
AFCP	American Fur Company Papers, MHS
ARP	Alexander Ramsey Papers, MHS
BIA	Bureau of Indian Affairs
CFXGP	Charles Francis Xavier Goldsmith Papers, SHSW
CMHS	*Collections of the Minnesota Historical Society*
COIA	Commissioner of Indian Affairs
CSHSW	*Collections of the State Historical Society of Wisconsin*
DIWER	"Documents of an Investigation of the White Earth Reservation," NA and MHS
GLNP	Grace Lee Nute Papers, MHS
GPO	Government Printing Office
HWP	Henry Whipple Papers, MHS
JBP	Joel Bassett Papers, MHS
JSP	Julia A. Warren Spears Papers, MHS
LTP	Lawrence Taliaferro Papers, MHS
M	Microfilm
MRNM	Manuscripts Relating to Northwest Missions

NAMP	National Archives Microfilm Publications
OIA	Office of Indian Affairs
R	Roll
RDI	Records of the Department of the Interior
RG	Record Group

NOTES

Notes to Preface

1. Letter to editor dated June 30, 1868, anonymously authored by "B" (who claimed to have known Bagone-giizhig for fifteen years) and first published in *St. Cloud Times,* July 11, 1868.

2. Letter to editor, *St. Cloud Times,* July 11, 1868; Eastman, *Indian Heroes;* Brunson, "Sketch," 5:387–401; Clark, "Reminiscences," 5:378–86; Diedrich, *The Chiefs;* Meyer, *White Earth Tragedy;* Chute, *Legacy of Shingwaukonse;* Warren, *History;* Copway, *Life, Letters and Speeches,* 133–37.

3. Treuer, *Living Our Language.* The *Oshkaabewis Native Journal* (Bemidji State University) is the only academic journal of the Ojibwe language.

4. The Indian Reorganization Act of 1934 reestablished the right of tribes to govern themselves and removed reservations from direct control by the Office of Indian Affairs' system of Indian agents, Indian Police, and Courts of Indian Offenses. The agency's name changed from Office of Indian Affairs to Bureau of Indian Affairs in 1947. Allotment stopped with the IRA, but the policy only officially ended in 2006, when the Bureau of Land Management internally repealed it. There was no legislative reversal or termination of the Dawes Act, the original legislation that enabled allotment of Indian reservation land. On the matter of oral history being accepted as legitimate, see Wilson, *Remember This* and *In the Footsteps.*

5. Nineteenth-century and twenty-first-century Ojibwe language and culture are not identical. Other scholars have discussed the pitfall of *upstreaming,* a term developed by early anthropologists but also discussed by prominent historians of Great Lakes Indian history. See Richard White, *Middle Ground,* xiv; Schenck, *Voice of the Crane,* 8.

6. Bagone-giizhig corresponded several times with Dakota leaders such as Little Crow. Usually, he dictated his thoughts in Ojibwe, then had them translated into English and mailed. Little Crow then had Bagone-giizhig's letters translated into Dakota and relayed to him orally. For multilingual documents, see, for example, Nichols, *Statement Made by the Indians.* This petition was submitted in the Ojibwe language to U.S. government officials. Nichols reworked the translation, converting it to double-vowel orthography.

7. Warren's other writings abound in newspapers and archives. An especially useful work in following his career, thoughts, and writings is Schenck, *William Warren.*

8. William W. Warren, "Letter to the Editor," *Minnesota Democrat,* Jan. 28, 1851; Negwanebi to the President of the United States, Aug. 21, 1847, NAMP, M 234, R 389.

9. Eastman, *Indian Heroes,* 102–9.

10. Meyer, *White Earth Tragedy;* Kugel, *Main Leaders;* Schenck, *Voice of the Crane;* Chute, *Legacy of Shingwaukonse.*

11. Nichols and Nyholm, *Concise Dictionary.* See also the *Oshkaabewis Native Journal* (Bemidji State University, 1990–present), especially Treuer, "New Directions"; Vollum and Vollum, *Ojibwemowin;* and Treuer, *Living Our Language.* Several Ojibwe orthographies have been developed. They include the Frederic Baraga system, which used complicated French and Finnish writing conventions to represent Ojibwe sounds; a syllabic form of writing

Algonquian languages with unique symbols developed by missionary James Evans in the early nineteenth century, which gained wide acceptance in some Ojibwe communities, especially in Canada; a diacritic orthography; and the very inconsistent folk-phonetic system (writing it how it sounds). For the Baraga system, see Baraga, *Dictionary.* His work was also edited by a missionary named Albert Lacombe, who was familiar with the Cree language but not with Ojibwe. Lacombe altered many entries and introduced numerous inconsistencies and errors, eroding the value of Baraga's work. For information on syllabics, see Dickason, *Canada's First Nations,* 241–42; and John D. Nichols, "Teaching Northern Algonquian Syllabics for Language Awareness" (Mille Lacs: 15th Annual Native American Language Institute, Apr. 4–6, 1996).

12. The Forest County Potawatomi (Wisconsin) and the Citizen Band Potawatomi (Kansas) prefer *Potawatomi* to other spellings. William "Billy" Daniels, Forest County Potawatomi elder, affirmed this spelling when I interviewed him. The Ho-Chunk Nation of Wisconsin prefers *Ho-Chunk* to the commonly used term *Winnebago.* The Assiniboine of Fort Belknap prefer *Assiniboine* to its numerous alternate spellings. The Menominee of Wisconsin prefer *Menominee* to the published alternatives. The Grand Traverse Band (Michigan) and Oklahoma Band of Ottawa (Oklahoma) both prefer *Ottawa* to the other versions of their name.

13. Sherman Alexie (reading, Milwaukee: Schwartz Books, Mar. 1993).

Notes to Prologue

1. Letter to editor, June 30, 1868, written by "B" (who claimed to have known Bagone-giizhig for fifteen years), *St. Cloud Times,* July 11, 1868.

2. There were other men named Bagone-giizhig. In addition to Bagone-giizhig the Elder, one was famous for his role in the Battle of Sugar Point at Leech Lake in 1898 and another helped represent Red Lake during Nelson Act negotiations in 1889.

3. The primary sources of information on Bagone-giizhig's assassination are the eyewitness accounts of his cousin and bodyguard, Ojibwe. The first was given in form of an affidavit, handwritten by Indian agent Joel Bassett, signed by Ojibwe (his X mark), and archived as Ojibwe Affidavit, July 27, 1868, JBP. The second is an interview that Ojibwe gave to A. D. Prescott, published in the *St. Cloud Democrat,* July 9, 1868. Julia A. Warren Spears (missionary, historian), Augustus Aspinwall (trader), George Bonga (trader), and William Fairbanks did not witness the assassination, but they did see Bagone-giizhig immediately before his death and the assassins immediately afterward. See especially Spears, "Reminiscence of the Assassination," "Reminiscences of a Short History," "My Journey," and "Reminiscences of Hole-in-the-Day"; Augustus Aspinwall Reminiscences, 19, MHS; and Aspinwall Reminiscence, Feb. 7, 1902, in Abbe, "Remarks and Reminiscences." The U.S. government conducted two formal investigations of Bagone-giizhig's death. The first, by Indian agent Joel Bassett, is available in ten letters and reports in the JBP. The second, by Dr. A. Jobe, is archived as Jobe Report to COIA, Oct. 24, 1868, COIA Correspondence, NA. See also A. Jobe to N. G. Taylor, Oct. 24, 1868, COIA, Chippewa Agency, M R 156. Newspaper coverage on the assassination was significant, although varying widely and full of hearsay evidence. See "The Murder of Hole-in-the-Day," *St. Cloud Journal,* July 9 and Aug. 20, 1868; *Moore's Rural New Yorker,* July 11 and 18, 1868; *Minneapolis Tribune,* July 17, 1868; *St. Paul Daily Press,* July 7, 1868; *Sauk Rapids Sentinel,* July 10, 1868. Other important secondhand accounts include Draper, "A Note on Hole-in-the-Day," 5:400–401; Hall, "Hole-in-the-Day Encounter"; and Eastman, *Indian Heroes,* 102–9. When an investigation of land fraud and enrollment at White Earth began in 1911, many of the surviving businessmen, clergy, officials, and families from Crow Wing testified. In addition, the admitted assassins themselves spoke publicly for the first time. See DIWER, 111–623, especially testimonies of Medwe-ganoonind, 240–51, Enami'egaabaw, 252–59, and Mizhaki-giizhig, 272. In "Reminiscence of the Assassination," Spears claimed there were ten assassins, a discrepancy from her earlier account.

Ojibwe claimed in his affidavit that there were nine assassins. Mizhaki-giizhig testified that Naawi-giizhig, Zhiibingogwan, and Mekadewikonayed told him in 1873 that they were the primary assassins, but they were not mentioned by other assassins or witnesses as having been present for the planning or the act itself.

The names of the assassins have been spelled many ways. I have converted the folk-phonetic spellings in the original citations to the double-vowel orthography for consistency and ease of reading and translation. Melvin Eagle helped with English translations of the Indian names provided in the testimonies (phone interview, Jan. 27, 2008). Naazhoobii-tang was sometimes referred to by one of his other Indian names, Enami'egaanab (Sits Praying), or by his nickname, Gwiiwizens (Boy). Information on Ojibwe perceptions of Bagone-giizhig comes in part from interviews: Melvin Eagle, 1996, 1998, and 2005; Brian Goodwin, 1997. Ojibwe was a figure of historical importance himself; see Densmore, *Chippewa Customs,* and Treuer and Treuer, "Ojibwe."

4. This is Enami'egaabaw from Gichi-achaabaaning (Inger, MN), not John Johnson, the half-Ottawa missionary with the same Indian name. Enami'egaabaw testimony, DIWER, 252.

5. Information on the looting of Bagone-giizhig's home is from Spears, "Reminiscence of the Assassination"; Ojibwe Affidavit, July 27, 1868, JBP; and the testimonies of Medwe-ganoonind and Enami'egaabaw, DIWER, 250–51, 261. Ojibwe's affidavit provided a list of looted materials and a valuation of $1,193 (derived in an undetermined fashion). Medwe-ganoonind detailed the taking of a brass-plated rifle, a sixteen-shooter rifle, and a double-barreled shotgun, all of which he claimed to have seen at Leech Lake in the hands of the assassins immediately after the killing. Julia Warren Spears claimed that Bagone-giizhig had the revolver when he was killed and that the head assassin tried to sell it to her immediately after the event. She also claims that one of the older assassins tried to sell her the chief's watch and that she saw his bloodstained overcoat and leggings. Other accounts of the event do not put the revolver in the chief's hands when the assassination took place. All accounts validate the looting of Bagone-giizhig's house, making that the likely place where the conspirators acquired his revolver.

6. Spears, "Reminiscence of the Assassination," quote on page 2 of typed copy in the JSP. The original handwritten copy was returned to Spears after being copied by the Minnesota Historical Society. In the file are letters to her daughter, Mrs. Charles Mee, dated June 26 and July 23, 1924, that detail the document handling. Ellen McCarty appears in several sources as Bagone-giizhig's wife, but her name is presented variously as Helen Trisk, Helen Kater, and Ellen McCarthy. These references are to the same woman. In verbal Ojibwe communication, there is no "r" sound, which may have contributed to the confusion. See *Harper's New Monthly Magazine,* June 1859; *Mankato Weekly Record,* Jan. 3, 1860. The *St. Cloud Journal,* on July 9, 1868, reported that one of the assassins tried to kidnap Ellen McCarty but stopped after Ojibwe told them doing so would invoke the wrath of the white government.

7. Hole-in-the-Day to President of the United States and the COIA, June 7, 1863, COIA Correspondence, NA; *Treaty With the Chippewa—Red Lake and Pembina Bands, 1863* (Oct. 2, 1863); Kappler, *Laws and Treaties,* 853–55, 861–62. See also Blegen, *Minnesota,* 172.

8. Johnson, *Enmegahbowh's Story,* 2; "Story of Enamegahbowh's Life," in Whipple, *Lights and Shadows,* 145–47, 497–98; John Johnson, "Reminiscences," HWP, Box 3; John Johnson and Gwiiwizhenzhish (Bad Boy) to William P. Dole, Oct. 15, 1862, RDI, COIA, Chippewa Agency, M R 153. Bagone-giizhig the Elder adopted John Johnson and cultivated a brotherly relationship between Bagone-giizhig the Younger and Johnson for many years. Johnson wanted to use Bagone-giizhig to forward Johnson's advocacy for his mission and for removal, while Bagone-giizhig wanted to use Johnson to boost his status with American officials. Johnson married Biiwaabiko-giizhigookwe (Iron Sky Woman), Bagone-giizhig the Younger's first cousin. Janet Chute ably shows in *The Legacy of Shingwaukonse* how Ojibwe chief Zhingwaakoons used conversion to Christianity as a strategy to curry favor

with provincial officials and other non-Indian power brokers. While this is a useful tool in assessing relationships between tribal leaders and the clergy, I did not find that Ojibwe leaders often used conversion as a strategy (especially in Mille Lacs and Ponemah, for example). Furthermore, although Bagone-giizhig used the idea to ingratiate himself to church officials (Protestant and Catholic), it was not critical to his rise to power.

9. Article 4, *Treaty With the Chippewa of the Mississippi, 1867* (Mar. 19, 1867); Kappler, *Laws and Treaties*, 975.

Notes to Chapter 1

1. Copway, *Traditional History*, 144.

2. The Sioux organized themselves into seven primary bands, collectively known as the Oceti Sakowin. The eastern Dakota were originally the largest component, comprising four of the seven groups: Mdewakantonwan (Dwellers by Mystic Lake), Wah'petonwan (Dwellers among the Leaves), Sisitonwan (Dwellers at the Fish Grounds), and Wah'pekute (Shooters among the Leaves). The Nakota made up two more groups: Ihanktonwan (Dwellers at the End) and Ihanktonwana (Little Dwellers at the End). The westernmost Lakota initially were one band, the Titonwan (Dwellers of the Plains), although they further split into seven more subdivisions. Wilson, *Remember This*, 4–5.

3. Bagone-giizhig (Hole in the Day) of Leech Lake was a nephew to Bagone-giizhig the Elder of the Mississippi Ojibwe through marriage only.

4. Interviews, Melvin Eagle, 1996 and 1998.

5. The language material in this book comes from my own knowledge of the Ojibwe language unless otherwise noted. For a good Ojibwe dictionary, see Nichols and Nyholm, *Concise Dictionary*.

6. Diedrich, *The Chiefs*, 2; interviews, Melvin Eagle, 1997; Mary Roberts, 1992.

7. Ojibwe children were usually given names by community spiritual leaders shortly after birth. Often, youth acquired an additional name from a vision—a dream while fasting during puberty. Although this subject is documented in some primary sources, I base this explanation primarily on interviews with Ojibwe elders: Thomas Stillday Jr., 1996; Eugene Stillday, 2006; Anna Gibbs, 1998; Archie Mosay, 1994; Melvin Eagle, 2000; James Clark, 2001. See also Warren, *History*. Did Bagone-giizhig acquire his father's name as a spiritual gift on his father's deathbed or earlier in his life? Either means would have been consistent with traditional practice and belief. But it is also possible that he simply used it without acquiring it spiritually, much as he had used Gwiiwizens (Boy) as a public name before his father died.

8. Interview, Susan Jackson, 1996. Jackson and many other Ojibwe people today still avoid using their Indian names in public except at certain ceremonies. (I am not applying today's naming protocol to the past or assuming that the protocols have never changed. Jackson spoke about ancient naming practices that, in this case, have not changed dramatically.) The name *Gwiiwizhenzhish* uses the derogative *-ish*, denoting something that is either old or, in this case, naughty. The derogative is insulting when speaking to or about strangers but endearing when speaking to and about close friends and family members. *Maji-gwiiwizens* uses the preverb *maji-*, literally meaning "bad." Both were commonly used for public Ojibwe names throughout Minnesota in the nineteenth century.

9. Tanner, *Atlas*, 156; Kappler, *Laws and Treaties*, 482–86, 567–71, 648–52, 685–90, 839–42, 853–55, 862–65, 974–76; Blegen, *Minnesota*, 171–73; and Folwell, *History*, 1:320–21.

10. Copway, *Traditional History*, 144; Mason, *Schoolcraft's Expedition*, 59; Warren, *History*, 36. See Danziger, *The Chippewas*, 23; and Howard, *The Plains-Ojibwa*, 7:74.

11. Interviews, Thomas Stillday Jr., 1996; Anna Gibbs, 1994; Melvin Eagle, 1999 and 2000; James Clark, 1998; Dora Ammann, 1997; Archie Mosay, 1992 and 1994; Betsy Schultz, 1994.

12. James, *Narrative of Captivity*, 313–16; Kohl, *Kitchi-Gami*, 148–49; Warren, *History*, 141–53; Copway, *Traditional History*, 140–50.

13. The word *doodem* is given in its independent form, but it is more commonly used in its dependent (possessed) forms *indoodem* (my clan), *gidoodem* (your clan), the obviative *odoodeman* (his or her clan), and others. This helps explain the variety of divergent spellings found in missionary and fur trader references. The variety of spellings for *clan* in Ojibwe is not the result just of different orthographies but also of different noun forms.

14. The drum is put in the center of the dance area for most Ojibwe ceremonies, and dancers move clockwise around it in recognition of this understanding. Although *de* means "heart or center," *we* pertains to sound, giving the word for drum the compound meaning, "heartbeat."

15. Warren, *History*, 87; Copway, *Life, Letters and Speeches*, 15.

16. Interviews, Archie Mosay, 1994; Walter White, 1992; James Clark, 2003. Nicolas Perrot and Ruth Landes refer to use of a clan symbol as a symbol for the entire village. It is still possible that those symbols represented the chiefs of the village who spoke for everyone, rather than everyone living there. See Blair, *Indian Tribes*, 1:37, 62, 347; Landes, *Ojibwa Sociology*, 31.

17. Interviews, Archie Mosay, 1993; Thomas Stillday Jr., 1995; Warren, *History*, 35, 42, 50–52; Benton-Banai, *Mishomis Book*, 74–78.

18. Interviews, Archie Mosay, 1992; Thomas Stillday Jr., 1995; Anna Gibbs, 1995; James Clark, 1994. See also Hickerson, *Southwestern Chippewa*, 88; Bishop, *Northern Ojibwa*, 343; Cleland, *Rites of Conquest*. Different tribes have different customs. Even the closely related Potawatomi have a different one with regard to clan assignment: boys take the father's clan, girls take the mother's clan. Interview, William (Billy) Daniels, 2006.

19. Interviews, Archie Mosay, 1992; Thomas Stillday Jr., 1995; Anna Gibbs, 1995; James Clark, 1994; Joseph (Joe Maude) Auginaush, 1992; Walter (Porky) White, 1993; Edward Benton-Banai, 1989.

20. Interviews, Edward Benton-Banai, 1989; Mary Roberts, 1990; Nancy Jones, 1994.

21. William W. Warren cites five original clans (*History*, 44); Edward Benton-Banai cites seven (*Mishomis Book*, 74).

22. Interview, Thomas Beardy, 1992. My conversation with Beardy about *doodem* began as I observed his Ojibwe-language class at Lakehead University in Thunder Bay, Ontario, in June 1992. He had written on the blackboard, "Awenen gidoodem?" He asked what that meant, and I replied, "Who is your clan?" He responded, "'Who is your clan?' No. What is *clan*? It means, 'Who is your friend?'" Not only had the word changed, but the concept of clan had been erased from the collective memory of his community. Beardy took no shame or offense during our conversation. For him, the concept of clan was absent and the meaning of the word *doodem* was simply different in his part of Ojibwe country.

23. Quaife, *John Long's Voyages*, 110–12.

24. Interviews with Thomas Stillday Jr., 1995 and 1998; Anna Gibbs, 1995 and 2000; Eugene Stillday, 2006; Melvin Eagle, 2000; Archie Mosay, 1992; Edward Benton-Banai, 1989; Lawrence Henry, 1990 and 1994; Mary Roberts, 1991. See also Warren, *History*, 41–53, 87–88; and Benton-Banai, *Mishomis Book*, 74–78. Some sources, including Warren, give the word *noke* for bear, rather than *makwa*. *Noke* is usually cited as an archaic form of the same word. *Noke* was the totemic emblem of Bagone-giizhig. I suspect that *noke* referred to the grizzly bear (once common in Minnesota) and that *makwa* to the black bear, although Ojibwe speakers I interviewed have not confirmed this. *Makwa* is the accepted form for bear in all of Minnesota's Ojibwe dialects today. Knowledge and usage of *noke* is no longer common, though *noke* survives in many documents, maps, and place-names such as the Nokasippi River in central Minnesota. Nokasippi is clearly a minor distortion of *Noke-ziibi*, meaning "Bear River." *Noke* was also what Bagone-giizhig used for self-reference to his totemic emblem.

25. This concept is reinforced by all of the Ojibwe elders I interviewed on the subject, especially Anna Gibbs, 1996; Thomas Stillday Jr., 1995; Archie Mosay, 1992. See also War-

ren, *History,* 41–53; Keesing, *Kin Groups,* 60; Radcliffe-Brown, *Structure and Function,* 117; Schenck, *Voice of the Crane,* 29.

26. Interviews, Archie Mosay, 1992; David Treuer with Vernon Whitefeather, 1995; Warren, *History,* 165. Mosay and Warren attest to the origin of the *ma'iingan doodem* (wolf clan) from a Dakota man who married an Ojibwe woman. Whitefeather gives the same explanation for the origin of the *ogiishkimanisii doodem* (kingfisher clan), although he claims that that marriage occurred in Ponemah, MN. This detail helps to explain the prevalence of that clan at Red Lake and Turtle Mountain, as well as its scarcity east of Red Lake.

27. Interviews with Thomas Stillday Jr., 1995; Anna Gibbs, 1995; Eugene Stillday, 2006; Melvin Eagle, 2000; Archie Mosay, 1992. Also Warren, *History,* 41–53; Benton-Banai, *Mishomis Book,* 74–78.

28. *Medwe-ganoonind Times* 1.2 (Mar. 23, 2004): 1. I have personally met enrolled members from Red Lake who are of the *name* (sturgeon) and *adik* (caribou) clans.

29. Copway, *Traditional History,* 140; Charles Cristopher Trowbridge in Schoolcraft's Calhoun report in Williams, *Schoolcraft's Narrative Journal,* 486; Doty, "Northern Wisconsin," 197.

30. Smith, *Leadership,* 7:11.

31. Mason, *Schoolcraft's Expedition,* xvi; Buck, *Indian Outbreaks,* 19; Kohl, *Kitchi-Gami,* 270; Baraga, *Chippewa Indians,* 9; Thwaites, *Jesuit Relations,* 15:157, 38:265; Paul LeJeune in Thwaites, *Jesuit Relations,* 6:243; Warren, *History;* Copway, *Traditional History;* James, *Narrative of Captivity,* especially the section on totems, 313–16.

32. Kohl, *Kitchi-Gami,* 66; Jameson, *Winter Studies,* 136.

33. Thwaites, *Jesuit Relations,* 20:155; Blair, *Indian Tribes,* 1:145, 264; Paul LeJeune, 6:243, and Gabriel Marest, 66:221, both in Thwaites, *Jesuit Relations.*

34. Eshkibagikoonzh (Flat Mouth) in Treaty Council Minutes of 1837, *NA,* M R 234, p.12. Schoolcraft said that Eshkibagikoonzh ascended to such a high status because of his oratorical ability. See Mason, *Schoolcraft's Expedition,* 207. See also Diedrich, *The Chiefs,* 6, 10.

35. Schoolcraft Papers, Reel 4, 1827; McKenney, *Sketches of a Tour,* 315–16; Warren, *History,* 127–28, 319; Birk, *Sayer's Snake River Journal,* 46. For more information on the importance of oratory, see Stout, "Ethnohistorical Report," 97.

36. Civil chiefs grew in power throughout the French, British, and American periods because they were the intermediaries and often distributing authorities over trade goods and annuities. See Thwaites, *Jesuit Relations,* 6:243, 20:155, 66:221; Blair, *Indian Tribes,* 1:264.

37. Eshkibagikoonzh (Flat Mouth) to COIA, COIA, Letters Received, M R 234, p.387.

38. *Treaty with the Pillager Band of Chippewa Indians, 1847* (Aug. 21, 1847); Kappler, *Laws and Treaties,* 567–69; Tanner, *Atlas,* 156; Blegen, *Minnesota,* 171–73; and Folwell, *History,* 1:320–21.

39. Samuel Pond wrote that sometimes very weighty decisions, such as those regarding moving a village location, were made by the women alone, and those decisions were enforced by the women over protests by men. See Pond, *The Dakota,* 140–41.

40. Interviews, Mary Roberts, 1991; Edward Benton-Banai, 1991; Dora Ammann, 2000.

41. Interviews, Mary Roberts, 1989, 1991; Edward Benton-Banai, 1991; Dora Ammann, 2000. Numerous cultural carriers attest to this, including James Clark, 2000; Melvin Eagle, 2002; Thomas Stillday Jr., 1996; Anna Gibbs, 1996; and Mary Roberts, 1991. (All these informants are not only elders but active participants in ceremonies today.) Most civil and military councils excluded women.

42. Mittleholtz and Graves, *Historical Review,* 136 (Gaagige-ogimaansikwe also signed the Pembina Band Treaty in 1878); interview, Earl Otchingwanigan (Nyholm), 1992.

43. Meyer, *White Earth Tragedy,* 22.

44. Schoolcraft, *Indian in His Wigwam,* 73; Bray, *Journals of Nicollet,* 165. For more information on women engaging in war, see Pond, *The Dakota,* 124.

45. Interview, Mary Roberts, 1988.

46. Interviews, Archie Mosay, 1993; Earl Otchingwanigan (Nyholm), 1991, 1992, 1993. Much of the background information supplied above was relayed through Otchingwanigan (Nyholm) as well.

47. Both ɪkwekaazo and ininiikaazo are animate nouns in Ojibwe. Their plural forms are ikwekaazowag and iniiniikaazowag, respectively. Interview, Earl Otchingwanigan (Nyholm), 1991. See also Williams, Spirit and Flesh, 110.

48. The ikwekaazowag could participate in war, although there were often restrictions upon their actions. Several stories in the Ojibwe oral tradition recount the bravery of certain ikwekaazowag. Interviews, Archie Mosay; 1993; Earl Otchingwanigan (Nyholm), 1992. In 1801, for example, an ikwekaazo from Manitoba single-handedly held off a Lakota attack to cover the successful retreat of Ojibwe from their village. This event was recounted numerous times and eventually recorded by non-Indian observers, from whom the record of this event is taken. See Henry and Thompson, New Light on the Early History, 1:163–65; Williams, Spirit and Flesh, 67–68.

49. Kellogg, Early Narratives, 244n.

50. Kinietz, Chippewa Village, 155; Grant, "Saulteux Indians," 2:357, cited in Williams, Spirit and Flesh, 31.

51. McKenney, Sketches of a Tour, 315–16.

52. Kellogg, Early Narratives, 244. For details of their voyages, see Kellogg, Early Narratives, 221–81, and Thwaites, Jesuit Relations, 59:185–211. See also Folwell, History, 1:18–20.

53. Catlin, Letters and Notes, 2:214–15; interview, Earl Otchingwanigan (Nyholm), 1992; Pond, The Dakota, 124. Although Catlin's observations of the berdaches were primarily among the Dakota, this practice occurred among the Ojibwe as well. On acceptance, see especially Thwaites, Jesuit Relations, 59:129, 310; James, Narrative of Captivity, 105–6; Williams, Spirit and Flesh, 167–68. An excellent secondary account is discussed in Kugel, Main Leaders, 71–73, 92n.

54. Male leaders were called ogimaa, female leaders, ogimaakwe. Numerous interviewees attested to the balanced role of men and women in ceremonies. Interviews, Dora Ammann, 1994; Thomas Stillday Jr., 1995; Anna Gibbs, 1998; Mary Roberts, 1989.

55. Bray, Journals of Nicollet, 155.

56. Bray, Journals of Nicollet, 199–211; Warren, History, 264; Densmore, Chippewa Customs, 87–89. See also Pond, The Dakota, 93–96; Parker, Journals of Carver, 108–10.

57. Baraga, Chippewa Indians, 24, emphasis in original; William W. Warren to Alexander Ramsey, Aug. 28, 1850, ARP, R 5. For more details on "covering the dead," see Baraga, Chippewa Indians, 24; Gilman, Gilman, and Stultz, Red River Trails, 46; White, Middle Ground, 76–77, 151; Howard, The Plains-Ojibwa, 82; Wheeler-Voeglin, "Anthropological Report," 67; Mason, Schoolcraft's Expedition, 55; Evangelical Society of Missions of Lausanne, "Report of June 11, 1835," 118–19; Pond, The Dakota, 70.

58. Warren, History, 139, 264, 313; Thwaites, Jesuit Relations, 47:223; Boutwell, "Schoolcraft's Exploring Tour," 1:130–31. Among the many references to the right and ubiquity of revenge, see especially Densmore, Chippewa Customs, 132; Johnston, Ojibway Ceremonies, 59–60; Danziger, The Chippewas, 23–24, 37, 73; Bray, Journals of Nicollet, 154, 168, 277; Diedrich, The Chiefs, 2; Lund, Minnesota's Chief Flat Mouth, 19; Pond, The Dakota, 61, 69–70; Mason, Schoolcraft's Expedition, xvi, 55; Kohl, Kitchi-Gami, 67, 272; Warren, History, 264; Baraga, Chippewa Indians, 24; Howard, The Plains-Ojibwa, 81; Kellogg, French Regime, 125.

59. Thwaites, Jesuit Relations, 47:223; James, Narrative of Captivity, 113.

60. Baraga, Chippewa Indians, 24; emphasis in original.

61. Folwell, History, 1:86. For a general discussion of territorial claims in warfare, see Pond, The Dakota, 60; Schulenberg, Indians of North Dakota, 43.

62. Pond, The Dakota, 60.

63. Little Crow, as cited in Robinson, *History of the Dakota*, 111.

64. Warren, *History*, 267. For good general descriptions of *biindigodaadiwin*, see Warren, *History*, 267–69; James, *Narrative of Captivity*, 72; Hickerson, "Ethnohistory of Chippewa of Lake Superior," 48; Schulenberg, *Indians of North Dakota*, 47; Lund, *Minnesota's Chief Flat Mouth*, 22, and *Tales of Four Lakes*, 59.

65. For descriptions of scalping practices and beliefs, see Catlin, *Letters and Notes*, 1:238–40; Densmore, *Chippewa Customs*, 135; Featherstonhaugh, *Canoe Voyage*, 1:362–63; Johnston, *Ojibway Ceremonies*, 75–76; Danziger, *The Chippewas*, 24–25; Lewis, *Valley of the Mississippi*, 173–75; Pond, *The Dakota*, 130–31. Sibley, "Memoir of Jean Nicollet," 224; Howard, *The Plains-Ojibwa*, 104; Eastman, *Dahcotah*, xx. There has been some speculation that Europeans introduced scalping in North America as a form of bounty hunting. The fact that no archaeological evidence of scalping prior to contact with Europeans has been found suggests that it may not have happened in the Americas. However, many historians do not accept this theory. If scalping originated in Europe, why was it primarily practiced in North America? Early seventeenth-century documents suggest that scalping was an embedded custom when the French first entered the Great Lakes region. Samuel de Champlain, for example, reported meeting the Algonquians at Tadoussac in 1603 when they were celebrating a victory over the Iroquois and dancing with about a hundred scalps. Many have argued that Europeans transformed an older indigenous custom during the French and Indian War and other conflicts as a way to encourage Indians to kill one another and ensure that they did so. Whatever the origin, scalping was an entrenched native custom by the time Bagone-giizhig the Elder came to power. There were protocols for proper treatment of scalps. For the Ojibwe, scalping involved removing all of the hair from the forehead to the nape of the neck. Often the ears and even the cheeks were taken as well, but only from men. If someone did not have time to scalp the dead on the spot, the head was severed and taken to be scalped later. (Occasionally, when even this was not possible, a small lock of hair was cut from the head.) All scalps were tanned with the hair attached. Often they were stretched in a hoop, and they were always attached to a stick and ornamented with eagle feathers (if a man's scalp) and combs (if a woman's). If possible, the scalped person's own feathers or combs were used. Scalps could only be taken from an enemy group, not in intratribal murder.

66. Henry, *Travels and Adventures in Canada*, 203–4 (quote, p.195 of reprint); Bray, *Journals of Nicollet*, 180.

67. Bray, *Journals of Nicollet*, 275; interviews, Thomas Stillday Jr., 1994; Anna Gibbs, 1994.

68. Catlin, *Letters and Notes*, 1:245–46.

69. Mason, *Schoolcraft's Expedition*, xvi, 253, 328; Williams, *Schoolcraft's Narrative Journal*, 202–3; Kellogg, *Early Narratives*, 155.

70. Pond, *The Dakota*, 133; Sibley, "Memoir of Jean Nicollet," 223; Kohl, *Kitchi-Gami*, 67, 170. Special treatment was even given in the rare circumstances when captives were executed. Jonathan Carver mentions the Dakota practice of weeping for enemies who were about to be executed. See Parker, *Journals of Carver*, 89.

Notes to Chapter 2

1. Clark, "Reminiscences," 5:382–83. See also Lawrence Taliaferro Journal, June 12, 1827, LTP; Diedrich, *The Chiefs*, 3.

2. Exact dates are not known, although the approximate age of Bagone-giizhig appears in numerous documents once he ascended to the position of chief. Some of this information is from Lawrence Taliaferro Journal, June 5, 1827, LTP. See also Brunson, "Sketch," 5:387–401; Clark, "Reminiscences," 5:378–86.

3. Interviews with Archie Mosay, 1992; Walter "Porky" White, 1995; and other Ojibwe

spiritual leaders confirm the religious incentives behind this migration. Economically, the abundant fish, wild rice, and game around Lake Superior and beyond were sufficient to pull the Ojibwe and other groups west. Scholars place the date of Ojibwe settlement at Madeline Island, Lake Superior, anywhere from 1394 to 1600. See Benton-Banai, *Mishomis Book,* 105; Baerreis, Wheeler-Voeglin, and Wycoco-Moore, "Anthropological Report," 23; Danziger, *The Chippewas,* 27; Dunn, *The St. Croix,* 10.

4. Daniel Greysolon, Sieur Du Lhut (later corrupted into Duluth) and Nicolas Perrot offer the best accounts of this covenant. Du Lhut was present at the event. See Blair, *Indian Tribes,* 277. See also Hickerson, "Ethnohistory of Chippewa of Lake Superior," 58. Joseph Marin's journal also contains references to the Ojibwe-Dakota entente, including relevant dates, though he did not observe the diplomacy firsthand.

5. For more information, see Treuer, "Ojibwe-Dakota Relations."

6. Interview, Karen Fairbanks, 1994; Brunson, "Sketch," 5:388; Lawrence Taliaferro Journal, May 10, 1821; Sept. 2, 1825; May 28, June 5, Oct. 2, 1827; May 8, 1829, LTP; *St. Paul Pioneer and Democrat,* Apr. 28, 1856; *Minneapolis Chronicle,* May 24, 1867; Warren, *History,* 348–50. See also Diedrich, *The Chiefs,* 2.

7. Lawrence Taliaferro Journal, May 8, 1829, LTP; Brunson, "Sketch," 5:387; interview, Archie Mosay, 1995. Sandy Lake, located between Duluth and Mille Lacs Lake, is still inhabited by Ojibwe people, and since the Indian Reorganization Act of 1934 it has been incorporated into the governmental structure of the Mille Lacs Band of Ojibwe.

8. Brunson, "Sketch," 5:388.

9. Brunson, "Sketch," 5:99; Nicolay, "Hole-in-the-Day." Nicolay was private secretary to Abraham Lincoln, and he also met Bagone-giizhig the Younger in 1862 as part of commissioner of Indian Affairs William Dole's negotiating delegation that failed to resolve the standoff between Bagone-giizhig the Younger and the Americans.

10. Warren, *History,* 47. It is not clear if Babiizigindibe was impotent, if his wife or wives died, or if he had children who died. Schoolcraft claimed Babiizigindibe (Curly Head) was actually called Gichi-babiizigindibe (Big Curly Head) although this is not supported elsewhere in the record. Interview, Archie Mosay, 1990.

11. The name *Eshkibagikoonzh* literally describes a flat duck bill (mouth), rather than a flat or stern expression.

12. Baraga, *Chippewa Indians,* 45.

13. John Johnson to James Lloyd Breck, Feb. 2, 1863, HWP, Box 3.

14. Details offered here come primarily from the Doty journal, correspondence in the Cass Papers, and Lyman Warren's account in the Schoolcraft journals. See also Doty, "Northern Wisconsin"; Smith, *James Duane Doty,* 10–20; Mason, *Schoolcraft's Expedition.*

15. "General Cass," 413; Alfred Brunson to James Doty, Nov. 23, 1843, NAMP, COIA, Correspondence Files, Letters Received, M 234, R 388.

16. Kellogg, *The British Regime,* 194–95.

17. The confrontation was widely recorded in the papers and letters of Lewis Cass and in the journals of other officials present. See especially the official journal of the expedition: Doty, "Official Journal." Brunson's secondhand account gave Bagone-giizhig much attention: "Sketch," 5:88–90, 398. Some accounts claim that Bagone-giizhig intervened several hours after Cass took down the British flag, and then only to prevent bloodshed, not to protect Cass personally or to gain favor with American officials. Trowbridge claimed that Bagone-giizhig was not even present: "General Cass," 413.

18. Brunson, "Sketch," 5:90; Alfred Brunson to James Doty, Nov. 23, 1843, NAMP, COIA, Correspondence Files, Letters Received, M 234, R 388.

19. Brunson, "Sketch," 5:390; Alfred Brunson to James Doty, Nov. 23, 1843, NAMP, COIA, Correspondence Files, Letters Received, M 234, R 388. Brunson's account, although sus-

pect in many regards, may have been accurate in others. Brunson claimed that Cass gave Bagone-giizhig a medal and flag.

20. Taliaferro's copious notes, diaries, letters, and official records are among the greatest archival resources on the early American period in Minnesota, especially its intersection with the native communities there. All of his diaries and correspondence files are in MHS collections, as is an affidavit by his daughter, Mary L. Taliaferro, and his neighbor, Maria L. Rupp. Biographical sketches on Taliaferro can be found in Taliaferro, "Auto-Biography"; Babcock, "Major Lawrence Taliaferro"; Bellet, *Some Prominent Virginia Families;* Nute, "Sketch of Lawrence Taliaferro." His name was pronounced "Tä'li- vur" (Tahly-vour).

21. Meyer, *White Earth Tragedy,* 38.

22. Taliaferro was naive to think that lines could easily be drawn between Ojibwe and Dakota lands. Both groups used some areas, especially during the winter hunt. Dividing them would be very contentious. Strict boundary lines made little sense to people with a very different concept of property: Indians focused on use of the land, whites focused on ownership. Taliaferro also erred in assuming that treaty provisions could be easily enforced. Both groups contested the lines when they were finally surveyed ten years after the Treaty of 1825, sparking further tension and conflict between the two tribes. See Meyer, *White Earth Tragedy,* 38–39.

23. Large delegations of Ojibwe, Dakota, Fox, Sac, Potawatomi, Ho-Chunk, Menominee, Iowa, and Ottawa attended the conference. They were represented by important leaders such as Bookowaabide (Broken Tooth), Babiizigindibe (Curly Head), Bagone-giizhig, Little Crow, and Shakopee. Ojibwe, Dakota, and Fox delegations all made bold claims about the territory they formerly possessed and currently controlled. In this arena, the oratorical charisma of Bagone-giizhig the Elder won many important concessions from American officials, drawing lines between Ojibwe and Dakota lands much in favor of Ojibwe claims. See Indian Claims Commission, "Findings on the Chippewa Indians," 354.

24. Cass and Clark were determined to make peace between these Indian nations to enable further white settlement. They even purchased large quantities of alcohol for the treaty to encourage as many Indian delegates as possible to sign. See Meyer, *White Earth Tragedy,* 39. This practice was increasingly common in both government negotiations and private trade. See Charles W. Borup to T. Hartley Crawford, Jan. 18 and July 3, 1844, COIA, La Pointe Agency, M R 389; James P. Hayes to Henry Dodge, Aug. 15, 1846, 29th Congress, 2nd Session, House Document, No. 4, 1846, Serial 497, 258–59.

25. Brunson, "Sketch," 5:391. A slightly different version of this quote and story was printed in the *Niles Register* (Baltimore, MD: Franklin Press, 1825–26): 29:189; see also Diedrich, *The Chiefs,* 3. Whether the confrontation of 1820 had also influenced Cass's thinking is unknown. There is no doubt, however, that the Ojibwe benefited enormously from the terms of the 1825 Treaty of Prairie du Chien.

26. Copway, *Traditional History,* 64.

27. Warren, *History,* 47. There are also several notes about this transition of power in the journal of Lawrence Taliaferro, Indian agent at Fort Snelling in 1825. See LTP. Babiizigindibe's skeleton, wrapped in a blanket and adorned with an 1809 chief's medal, was unearthed in 1867 when construction workers excavated First Street in Minneapolis. Bagone-giizhig's daughter and uncle, Wemitigoozhiins (Little Frenchman), were buried at the falls in 1827 and 1830, respectively. Taliaferro Journal, May 10, 1821, Sept. 2, 1825, May 28, June 5, and Oct. 2, 1827, May 8, 1829, LTP; *St. Paul Pioneer and Democrat,* Apr. 28, 1856; *Minneapolis Chronicle,* May 24, 1867; Warren, *History,* 348–50.

28. Copway, *Traditional History,* 140; Trowbridge Journal, reprinted in Williams, *Schoolcraft's Narrative Journal,* 486.

29. Clark, "Reminiscences," 5:381.

30. Clark, "Reminiscences," 5:381–83.

31. Clark, "Reminiscences," 5:381.

32. A wealth of oral history indicates the primacy of hereditary claims to chieftain-ship and the inability of people without proper bloodlines to acquire political position. Interviews with Archie Mosay, 1992; Mary Roberts, 1995; Walter "Porky" White, 1996.

33. Brunson, "Sketch," 5:387–88. See also Diedrich, *The Chiefs*, 1.

34. Eastman, *Indian Heroes*, 104. Unbelievable though Eastman's account seems, it appears to be true. Eastman interviewed people who knew Bagone-giizhig well. Talia-ferro mentions the event in his journal, but in less detail than Eastman, so some parts of Eastman's version are difficult to confirm. Certainly, the daring ambush by Bagone-giizhig happened. Whether or not he hid behind Minnehaha Falls is harder to say. Eastman, Brunson, and Clark have all embellished the exploits of the Bagone-giizhigs. However, one time, Bagone-giizhig tried to lead war parties against Little Crow's village only to have all but a few warriors abandon him when they learned of the plan; the chief proceeded to kill someone outside the village at incredible risk. That event was widely reported in several other places. Even if some details are obscure, the fact that people believed them testifies to Bagone-giizhig's reputation.

35. For details on the treaty, see Viola, *Thomas L. McKenney*; McKenney, *Sketches of a Tour; Memoirs, Official and Personal*; and *History of Indian Tribes*.

36. Danziger, *The Chippewas*, 76; Mason, *Schoolcraft's Expedition*, xviii, including Wil-liam Joseph Snelling citation; Tanner, *Atlas*, 149; Snelling, "Running the Gauntlet," 1:366.

37. The Dakota attack on May 28, 1827, and the ensuing events described herein are detailed in the eyewitness accounts of William Joseph Snelling (son of Colonel Josiah Snel-ling) in "Running the Gauntlet," 1:442–56; *St. Paul Pioneer and Democrat*, Apr. 28, 1856; Van Cleve, "Reminiscence"; Taliaferro Journal, May 10, 1821, Sept. 2, 1825, May 28, June 5, and Oct. 2, 1827; May 8, 1829, LTP; *Minneapolis Chronicle*, May 24, 1867. See also Warren, *History*, 348–50; and Neill, "Occurrences," 2:134–35; Neill, *History of Minnesota*, 391–94; Robinson, *History of the Dakota*, 154–56; Blegen, *Minnesota*, 128; Diedrich, *The Chiefs*, 4, and *Ojibway Oratory*, 30. Colonel Josiah Snelling's son William Joseph Snelling was a sometimes con-spicuous figure in Dakota affairs between 1821 and 1828, although he served no official function, having dropped out of West Point and journeyed to Minnesota to study Indians and write. He left after his father died in 1828.

38. "Covering the dead" was a custom practiced by several tribes in the Great Lakes region in cases of murder and war. The offending party offered a tribute, a spiritual leader would pray over the offering, and bad feelings were to be laid aside between the families of the perpetrator(s) and the dead. The offended family had the final right to accept or reject whatever offerings were made by the perpetrators or their representatives. See Thwaites, *Jesuit Relations*; Warren, *History*.

39. Bagone-giizhig's spinal condition never interfered with his ability to wage war, travel, or conduct diplomacy, though it did cause him pain and complicate injuries he sustained later in life.

40. Zoongakamig speech, May 30, 1827, recorded in Josiah Snelling Journal, Snelling Papers, MHS.

41. Snelling, "Running the Gauntlet," 1:369. See also Robinson, *History of the Dakota*, 157.

42. Snelling, "Running the Gauntlet," 1:369–72.

43. Even white officers and officials were appalled at American handling of the event. Trader Henry H. Sibley, who became the first state governor of Minnesota, openly criti-cized Snelling's decisions in 1856. See Sibley, "Reminiscences," 1:388–89.

44. Bray, *Journals of Nicollet*, 12–13.

45. Taliaferro Journal, May 8, 1829, LTP; Lewis, *Valley of the Mississippi*, 118; Diedrich, *Ojibway Oratory*, 32.

46. Information on the events in 1829 is taken primarily from Taliaferro Journal, May 2, 1831, LTP.

47. Hickerson, *The Chippewa*, 97; William A. Aitkin to Ramsay Crooks, president of the American Fur Company, Oct. 12, 1836, AFCP. Aitkin wrote that he was withdrawing the American Fur Company post at Otter Tail Lake because of competition from Lake Traverse.

48. *Treaty with the Sauk and Foxes, Etc.*, July 15, 1830, in Kappler, *Laws and Treaties*, 2:305–10; Vennum, *Wild Rice*, 10; Diedrich, *The Chiefs*, 6.

49. Bray and Bray, *Nicollet on the Plains*, 125; Jenks, "Wild Rice Gatherers." See also Vennum, *Wild Rice*, 9–10. The Taliaferro journals contain several references to Ojibwe-Dakota warfare during this period. See also Hickerson, *The Chippewa*, 97–98.

50. Information on the skirmishes and village relocations from 1830 to 1835 is taken primarily from Francis Audrain to Henry Rowe Schoolcraft, June 8, 1830, AFCP; Taliaferro Journal, July 12, 1833, June 2, 1835; Miles Vineyard to Henry Dodge, July 16, 1838, COIA, Letters Received, St. Peter's Agency, R 758; Hall and Boutwell, "Report"; *St. Peter Courier*, Jan. 1, 1856; Mason, *Schoolcraft's Expedition*, xxvi, 70, 103n77, 349. For details on some the Dakota counterattacks, see Featherstonhaugh, *Canoe Voyage*, 1:223, 256, 330–31. See also Hickerson, "Mdewakanton Band," 219; Diedrich, *The Chiefs*, 6.

51. For information on Bagone-giizhig's diplomacy with Schoolcraft and Taliaferro, Schoolcraft's meeting with Eshkibagikoonzh (Flat Mouth), demarcation of the territory lines, and the 1830 smallpox epidemic at Leech Lake, see Boutwell, "Journal of Tour," July 17, 1832; Taliaferro Journal, July 12, 1833, June 2, 1835, LTP; Mason, *Schoolcraft's Expedition*, 53, 57, 73, 103; Miles Vineyard to Henry Dodge, July 16, 1838, COIA, Letters Received, St. Peter's Agency, R 758; *St. Peter Courier*, Jan. 1, 1856. See also Danziger, *The Chippewas*, 76–77. The Schoolcraft expedition of 1832 was important primarily because of the information gathered and recorded through Schoolcraft's meetings with several Ojibwe leaders. On that expedition, Ozaawindib (Yellow Head) showed Schoolcraft the source of the Mississippi River. Schoolcraft was instructed to make peace between the Ojibwe and the Dakota and to vaccinate as many Indians as possible against smallpox, a reaction in part to the epidemic that hit Leech Lake in 1830. Although Schoolcraft made some overtures toward peace and expedition physician Douglass Houghton made numerous vaccinations, Schoolcraft seized the opportunity to catapult himself to international fame as the "discoverer" of the Mississippi headwaters.

52. Taliaferro Journal, Aug. 30, 1835, LTP. There are about thirty references in his journal to the survey lines and removal of marking stakes in 1835 alone. See also Lawrence Taliaferro to William Clark, Sept. 2, 1835, and Taliaferro Journal, July 12, 1833, June 2, 1835, LTP; Mason, *Schoolcraft's Expedition*, xxvi, 103; Miles Vineyard to Henry Dodge, July 16, 1838, COIA, Letters Received, St. Peter's Agency, R 758; *St. Peter Courier*, Jan. 1, 1856. See also Dunn, *The St. Croix*, 13; Tanner, *Atlas*, 148; Folwell, *History*, 1:147n; Hickerson, "Mdewakanton Band," 287.

53. Two decades later, the oxcart road from St. Paul to Canada used the Crow Wing ford eleven miles south of Brainerd at the confluence of the Crow Wing and Mississippi rivers at the site of the original village. The geographical advantages of the place naturally brought trade and travel to Crow Wing.

54. "Story of Enamegahbowh's Life," in Whipple, *Lights and Shadows*, 145–47, 497–98; John Johnson, "Reminiscences," HWP, Box 3.

55. Alfred Brunson to Mission Board, Nov. 9, 1838, MRNM, GLNP; William Boutwell to David Greene, Nov. 8, 1837, ABCFMP; Taliaferro Journal, July 12, 1833, June 2, 1835, LTP; Mason, *Schoolcraft's Expedition*, xxvi, 103n77; Miles Vineyard to Henry Dodge, July 16, 1838, COIA, Letters Received, St. Peter's Agency, R 758; *St. Peter Courier*, Jan. 1, 1856. Helen Tanner, in her laudable work *Atlas of Great Lakes Indian History*, asserts that Babiizigindibe (Curly Head) of Sandy Lake had a permanent village established at Gull Lake by 1810

(98–99 [map 20]). She also has a village labeled "Strong Ground" placed on the north end of Sandy Lake. These labels are slightly misleading. Babiizigindibe (Curly Head) was actually a chief from Sandy Lake for two decades prior to his death after the 1825 Treaty of Prairie du Chien (Warren, *History,* 47). This assertion is supported by the observations of white traders and military officials in the area. Zebulon Pike met Babiizigindibe (Curly Head) in 1805 and described him as a Sandy Lake warrior. Actually, it was Bookowaabide (Broken Tooth) who functioned as head civil chief there at the time (Warren, *History,* 349). Zoongakamig (Strong Ground) was a mere boy in 1810. He gradually ascended to the position of *oshkaabewis* for Babiizigindibe, but that was not until after the War of 1812. Babiizigindibe was always a Sandy Laker who only wintered at Gull Lake, although he played a role in the military actions that kept the area under Ojibwe control. Zoongakamig did not ascend to a position of leadership among the Sandy Lake Ojibwe until Babiizigindibe died in 1825, and even then his position was subordinate to that of Bagone-giizhig.

56. Taliaferro, cited in Hickerson, "The Mdewakanton Band," 193; Gideon H. Pond to Ruth Pond, Mar. 16, 1836, GLNP, 3.

57. Hickerson, "The Mdewakanton Band," 210.

58. Hickerson, *The Chippewa,* 98. The Leech Lake Ojibwe (Pillagers) who settled at Otter Tail Lake moved to Pine Point on the White Earth Reservation in 1873, where their descendants still live.

59. For discussion of Ojibwe-Dakota contention for control of the Otter Tail Lake region and settlement dates, see Gilman, Gilman, and Stultz, *Red River Trails,* 42, and Hickerson, *The Chippewa,* 98, 104. Hickerson discusses intermittent warfare between the Ojibwe and Dakota in the Otter Tail Lake region through 1849. In fact, warfare continued longer than that, but territorial pressure from the Dakota had ceased to be an issue.

60. For discussion of Ojibwe dispossession of Dakota lands and joint-use areas, see Tanner, *Atlas,* 148–49, including map 28. Population estimates by Schoolcraft and Nicollet, though conservative, concur in designating Leech Lake as the largest Ojibwe community in the region and densely populated as well as a ceremonial and trade hub. See also Lund, *Tales of Four Lakes,* 27.

61. For information on the Renville-Aitkin feud and ensuing battles between the Ojibwe and Dakota from 1835 to 1837 in the following paragraphs, see William A. Aitkin to Ramsay Crooks, Oct. 12, 1836, AFCP; Major Bliss to General Gaines, May 22, 1835, GLNP; Featherstonhaugh, *Canoe Voyage,* 1:307, 340, 352, 359; Mason, *Schoolcraft's Expedition,* 54–56; Bray, *Journals of Nicollet,* 31–32, 173–74; Pond, "Indian Warfare," 3:130; *Minnesota Chronicle and Register,* May 4, June 3, and June 10, 1850; Eastman, *Dahcotah,* 192–94. The *Chronicle and Register* articles, which included a defense of Ojibwe warfare and diplomacy by William W. Warren, were essentially about Bagone-giizhig. In his letter to Crooks, Aitkin also invoked the recent death of a trader friend as a rationale for the withdrawal of the post from Otter Tail, but that reason has come into doubt and was certainly secondary. For comments on Aitkin's sentiments about the death of the trader, see William T. Boutwell (missionary) to David Green, Jan. 18, 1837, and William T. Boutwell to Henry R. Schoolcraft, Sept. 5, 1836, both GLNP. Boutwell was married to Hester Crooks, the daughter of Ramsay Crooks, whose mother was Ojibwe. The letters between Boutwell, Crooks, Green, Schoolcraft, and Aitkin must be viewed in light of the complicated marital, missionary, and economic entanglements between the parties. See also Indian Claims Commission, "Findings on the Chippewa Indians," 113; Diedrich, *The Chiefs,* 6; Hickerson, "Mdewakanton Band," 219; Folwell, *History,* 1:191. The Dakota attack at Elk Lake was especially significant in later escalations because Bagone-giizhig's relative was killed. On June 4, 1835, Bagone-giizhig visited Lawrence Taliaferro at Fort Snelling and reported the attack. See Taliaferro Journal, June 3–5, 1835, LTP.

62. Bray, *Journals of Nicollet,* 45.

63. Diedrich, *Ojibway Oratory,* 37, and *The Chiefs,* 8.

64. Bagone-giizhig the Elder, cited in Eastman, *Dahcotah,* 193; see also Diedrich, *The Chiefs,* 7.

Notes to Chapter 3

1. Clark, "Reminiscences," 5:383.

2. *Treaty With the Chippewa,* July 29, 1837 (7 Stat. 536, Ratified June 15, 1838), in Kappler, *Laws and Treaties,* 2:491–93. Separate treaties were made in 1837 with the Dakota, Ho-Chunk, and Sauk and Fox. Earlier treaties at Prairie du Chien (1825) and Fond du Lac (1827) did not involve land cessions. In addition to the treaties and their official journals, see Viola, *Thomas L. McKenney;* McKenney, *Sketches of a Tour; Memoirs, Official and Personal;* and *History of Indian Tribes.*

3. Lyman Warren was the father of Truman A. Warren (interpreter and trader), Julia Warren Spears (missionary and historian), and William W. Warren (trader, interpreter, farmer, and scholar). Lyman Warren's unscrupulous interference with payment of annuities is well documented in Taliaferro's journal and autobiography and referenced in several places in the treaty proceedings and the correspondence of missionaries and officials present. Lyman Warren and William Aitkin were close friends. Lyman's son William W. Warren married William Aitkin's daughter, Matilda Aitkin, in 1842. Lyman Warren and William Aitkin had four common grandchildren born from the union. Lyman's other children, Sophia, Julia, Charlotte, Mary, and especially Truman, factor prominently in many treaty negotiations, land contracts, annuity provision contracts, and official discourse of the Office of Indian Affairs. See J. Fletcher Williams, "Memoir of William W. Warren," 7–20, in Warren, *History,* 14.

Background information on trader claims and details on the treaty of 1837 in the next several paragraphs are taken from Schoolcraft, *Personal Memoirs,* 611; "Proceedings of a Council with the Chippewa Indians," *Iowa Journal of History and Politics* (1911): 5:408–28; Alfred Brunson to Mission Board, Nov. 9, 1838, MRNM, GLNP; William Boutwell to David Greene, Nov. 8, 1837, ABCFMP; Miles Vineyard to Henry Dodge, July 16, 1838, COIA, Letters Received, St. Peter's Agency, R 758; *St. Peter Courier,* Jan. 1, 1856; Major Bliss to General Gaines, May 22, 1835, GLNP; Pond, "Indian Warfare," 3:130; Bray, *Journals of Nicollet,* 31–32, 173–74; Hickerson, "Mdewakanton Band," 219; Featherstonhaugh, *Canoe Voyage,* 1:340; Holcombe and Hubbard, *Minnesota in Three Centuries,* 2:280.

4. Lyman Warren was not recorded as an official interpreter, but he did translate and negotiate on behalf of himself, the American Fur Company, and some of the Wisconsin Ojibwe delegations. The formal interpreters were Jean Baptiste Dubay, Peter Quinn, S. Campbell, and Stephen Bonga. See Williams, "Memoir of William W. Warren," in Warren, *History,* 14.

5. Schenck, *William Warren,* 38.

6. *Woodlands.* Many Mille Lacs elders interviewed in this video, including James Clark, Raining Boyd, Batiste Sam, and David Sam, attested to this understanding. Their statements are supported by the primary source documents cited in note 3, above.

7. Nichols, "Translation of Key Phrases." Nichols's arguments are well substantiated in other places, including Van Antwerp, "Negotiations for the Chippewa Treaty," and Auger and Beardy, *Glossary of Legal Terms.*

8. Gilman, Gilman, and Stultz, *Red River Trails,* 8; Lewis, *Valley of the Mississippi,* 56–57; Pond, *The Dakota,* 75.

9. Riggs, *Mary and I,* 70; Pond, *The Dakota,* 75.

10. Beck, *Siege and Survival,* 147–48; Clayton, "Impact of Traders' Claims," 301–9; Tanner, *Atlas,* 170.

11. The Wah'petonwan Dakota attack in the winter of 1837–38, Bagone-giizhig's counterattack in Ojibwe country on April 11, 1838, the council in July of 1838, and the surrounding events and communication are reported in William Aitkin to Boutwell, Apr. 23, 1838,

and John Aitkin to Boutwell, Apr. 25, 1838, Henry Sibley Papers, MHS; William Boutwell to David Greene, Nov. 8, 1837, ABCFMP; Miles Vineyard to Henry Dodge, July 16, 1838, COIA, Letters Received, St. Peter's Agency, R 758; Major Bliss to General Gaines, May 22, 1835, GLNP; Alfred Brunson to Mission Board, Nov. 9, 1838, MRNM, GLNP; *Minnesota Chronicle and Register,* May 4 and June 3, 1850 (William W. Warren's version); *St. Peter Courier,* Jan. 1, 1856; Pond, "Indian Warfare," 3:130; Bray, *Journals of Nicollet,* 31–32, 173–74; Featherston-haugh, *Canoe Voyage,* 1:340; Kohl, *Kitchi-Gami,* 350–54; Schoolcraft, *Personal Memoirs,* 611; Brunson, "Sketch," 5:392; Riggs, *Mary and I,* 70; "Proceedings of a Council With the Chippewa Indians." See also Holcombe and Hubbard, *Minnesota in Three Centuries,* 2:280; Diedrich, *Dakota Oratory,* 33, 41, and *The Chiefs,* 8; Folwell, *History,* 1:150–51; and Hickerson, "Mdewakanton Band," 219.

12. *Biindigodaadiwin* was a common practice in which Ojibwe and Dakota people gathered in joint-use areas to share harvest time, literally entering one another's lodges. See Warren, *History,* 267–69; James, *Narrative of Captivity,* 72; Hickerson, "Ethnohistory of Chippewa of Lake Superior," 48; Schulenberg, *Indians of North Dakota,* 47; Lund, *Minnesota's Chief Flat Mouth,* 22, and *Tales of Four Lakes,* 59.

13. Some have claimed that Bagone-giizhig planned another attack for later that spring when they could catch the Wah'petonwan off guard and do more damage, but Bagone-giizhig's plan for an attack materialized long after he had accepted the Dakota offer of peace.

14. Brunson, "Sketch," 5:392. Although some accounts claim that the event took place at Lac qui Parle, Sauk Lake, or present-day Benson, MN, Pond's report of the location seems the most accurate since he buried the dead the next day. Some sources claim that a young boy escaped capture. See Neill, *History of Minnesota,* 454–56

15. Brunson, "Sketch," 5:393–94.

16. Bray and Bray, *Nicollet on the Plains,* 298.

17. Bray and Bray, *Nicollet on the Plains,* 279.

18. For Ojibwe-Dakota warfare outside of Bagone-giizhig's actions during this period, see Pond, "Indian Warfare," 3:130; Meyer, *White Earth Tragedy,* 61; Neill, "Battle of Lake Pokegama," 1:141.

19. Details of the events on Aug. 2–3, 1838, here and below, are from Taliaferro Journal, Aug. 2–8, 1838, LTP; William Aitkin to William T. Boutwell, Apr. 23, 1838, and John Aitkin to William T. Boutwell, Apr. 25, 1838, Henry Sibley Papers, MHS; Pond, "Indian Warfare," 3:130; Brunson, "Sketch," 5:395. A good secondary account can be found in Folwell, *History,* 1:151–54.

20. Taliaferro Journal, Aug. 3–8, 1838, LTP.

21. The meeting in 1839 and subsequent Dakota attacks were reported in Taliaferro Journal, June 21–July 3, 1839, LTP; Taliaferro to Hole-in-the-Day, June 18, 1839; Taliaferro to Henry Dodge, June 10, 17, 25, 26, 1838; Taliaferro to Robert Lucas, June 17, 24, and 26, 1839; and Taliaferro to Major Daniel P. Bushnell (U.S. Sub-Indian agent, La Pointe), July 1, 1839, all in Taliaferro Letter Book, B, LTP; *St. Paul Pioneer Press,* May 14, 1898 (Henry H. Sibley's account); William Aitkin to Henry H. Sibley, Oct. 12, 1839, Henry H. Sibley Papers, MHS; Pond, *The Dakota,* 135–36; Pond, "Indian Warfare," 3:131–33; Riggs, *Mary and I,* 42, 289–91; John Johnson, "Sioux-Chippewa Peace Treaty," in Clark Papers, MHS; Johnson, *Enmegahbowh's Story,* 45–56; Evangelical Society of Missions of Lausanne, "Report of June 11, 1835" 58; Copway, *Traditional History,* 58–59. Good secondary accounts can be found in Folwell, *History,* 1:154–58; Lewis, *Valley of the Mississippi,* 199–201; Meyer, *White Earth Tragedy,* 61, 64; Dunn, *The St. Croix,* 14–15, 115–16; Danziger, *The Chippewas,* 77; Diedrich, *Dakota Oratory,* 36, and *The Chiefs,* 9; Lund, *Tales of Four Lakes,* 72; Tanner, *Atlas,* 150; Blegen, *Minnesota,* 131–32, 148, and "War on the Minnesota Frontier," 15–16; Hickerson, *The Chippewa,* 90; Hughes, *Indian Chiefs of Southern Minnesota,* 38–39. Diedrich claims only seven hundred Ojibwe were present and that they were protesting the move of the annuity station rather than

expecting payments. It seems unlikely that so many would come to stage a protest with no expectation of payment or provision. Taliaferro's correspondence and journal suggest that the Ojibwe were misled to believe they would receive the annuities at Fort Snelling.

22. Diedrich claims the men were from Leech Lake (*The Chiefs*, 9), but other sources suggest they were from Bagone-giizhig's band. One account claims the man they killed was an elderly spiritual leader (Lewis, *Valley of the Mississippi*, 200). Another claims that the Dakota casualty was the son of a chief (Diedrich, *The Chiefs*, 9). Most of the other accounts, including Taliaferro, claim that the man they murdered was a young but respected Dakota hunter and that another, younger boy witnessed the event and reported it to the chief in his village near Lake Calhoun.

23. Shakopee as cited in Diedrich, *The Chiefs*, 9.

24. Copway, *Traditional History*, 58–59. Aitkin and other traders used alcohol to obtain the best price for furs by dealing with Indians when they were intoxicated. Official correspondence through the Indian agency at La Pointe frequently reported such details, including a letter from Charles W. Borup, who wrote that Aitkin sent his traders "continually in the lodges on Indian land where they get all the furs by taking the Indians to Aitkin's house and giving whiskey there." See Charles W. Borup to T. Hartley Crawford, Jan. 18 and July 3, 1844, COIA, La Pointe Agency, M R 389; James P. Hayes to Henry Dodge, Aug. 15, 1846, 29th Congress, 2nd Session, House Document, No. 4, 1846, Serial 497, 258–59.

25. Evangelical Society of Missions of Lausanne, "Report of June 11, 1835," 58. For information on the abandonment of Lake Calhoun and Lake Harriet, see Riggs, *Mary and I*, 42; Meyer, *White Earth Tragedy*, 64; Tanner, *Atlas*, 150; Folwell, *History*, 1:196; Lund, *Tales of Four Lakes*, 72; Blegen, *Minnesota*, 148.

26. Nute, "Sketch of Lawrence Taliaferro."

27. Interviews, Melvin Eagle, 2006, and Archie Mosay, 1994; Danziger, *The Chippewas*, 77.

28. Rev. B. T. Kavenaugh to Secretary, Nov. 5, 1839 and May 1, 1840, GLNP; Rev. B. T. Kavenaugh to Daniel P. Bushnell (U.S. Sub-Indian agent, La Pointe), July 26, 1841, 27th Congress, 2nd Session, Senate Doc. No. 1, 1841–42, Serial 395, 315. See also Diedrich, *The Chiefs*, 9.

29. Primary sources for Bagone-giizhig's attacks in 1841–42 are *Chronicle and Register*, June 3, 1850 (William W. Warren's account); Rev. B. T. Kavenaugh to E. Ames, June 18, 1841, Gideon Pond to Samuel Pond, June 26, 1842, and William T. Boutwell to Samuel Pond, Feb. 3 and June 29, 1842, all GLNP; Pond, "Indian Warfare," 3:133; Nicolay, "Hole-in-the-Day," 186. See also Diedrich, *The Chiefs*, 9.

30. Henry Blatchford, U.S. interpreter for the treaty, reported Bagone-giizhig's arrival in Journal of the 1842 Treaty, May 3, 1843. John Johnson was also there and deeply impressed, according to his later account, available in John Johnson to Henry B. Whipple, Dec. 1, 1898, HWP. Other firsthand accounts include L. H. Wheeler to David Greene, May 3, 1843, ABCFMP; Gideon Pond to Samuel Pond, June 26, 1842, and William T. Boutwell to Samuel Pond, Feb. 3 and June 29, 1842, GLNP; Pond, "Indian Warfare," 3:133. See also Cleland, "The 1842 Treaty," 36–37; Diedrich, *The Chiefs*, 9–10.

31. Brunson, "Sketch," 5:397. On song, see Densmore, *Chippewa Music*, 2:123.

32. John Johnson to Henry B. Whipple, Dec. 1, 1898, HWP.

33. Alfred Brunson to James Doty, Nov. 23, 1843, NAMP, COIA, Correspondence Files, Letters Received, M 234, R 388; Brunson, "Sketch," 5:398.

34. Eyewitness accounts of the battles in the 1840s include Pond, "Indian Warfare," 3:133–34; William T. Boutwell to Samuel Pond, June 29, 1842, Samuel Pond Papers, MHS; Larpenteur, "Recollections"; Sharp, "Tenting on Pokegama Lake"; Neill, "Battle of Lake Pokegama," 142–45. Neill gives a detailed description of skirmishes between the Ojibwe and Dakota in the early 1840s, including the death of two of Little Crow's sons in a daring attack by two Ojibwe warriors on an armed war party of over one hundred Dakota and several retaliatory attacks by the Dakota at and around the mission at Lake Pokegama. The Pond letters and article are firsthand accounts of other events during this time period

as well as the attack at Pokegama. Secondary accounts are available in Nute, "Missionaries Among the Sioux and Chippewa," GLNP; Danziger, *The Chippewas*, 74; Blegen, *Minnesota*, 146; Folwell, *History*, 1:179–81; Meyer, *White Earth Tragedy*, 62, 69; Dunn, *The St. Croix*, 21; Diedrich, *The Chiefs*, 9.

35. Clark, "Reminiscences," 5:383.

36. Brunson, "Sketch," 5:390; Diedrich, *The Chiefs*, 10; interviews, James Clark, 1994; Raining Boyd, 1994; Melvin Eagle, 1994 and 2006.

37. Copway, *Life, Letters and Speeches*, 136.

38. Copway, *Life, Letters and Speeches*, 137.

39. Johnson, *Enmegahbowh's Story*, 1, 2.

40. See Charles W. Borup to T. Hartley Crawford, Jan. 18 and July 3, 1844, COIA, La Pointe Agency, M R 389; James P. Hayes to Henry Dodge, Aug. 15, 1846, 29th Congress, 2nd Session, House Document, No. 4, 1846, Serial 497, 258–59.

41. Many missionaries and government officials wrote about Bagone-giizhig's alcohol abuse and Zoongakamig's death from alcohol poisoning. See Clark, "Reminiscences," 5:384; Lanman, *Summer in the Wilderness*, 70; Riggs, *Tah-koo Wah-kan*, 444; Schoolcraft, *Indian Tribes*, 1:166–67; Eastman, *Dahcotah*, 195–96, 205.

42. The skirmishes in 1844–45 are documented in *Chronicle and Register*, June 3, 1850; E. Ely to D. Greene, Sept. 21, 1843, and T. Hartley Crawford to Jackson Kemper, Oct. 5, 1843, MRNM, GLNP; Ezekial Gear to Jackson Kemper, Aug. 17, 1843, GLNP; *Spirit of Missions*, 460–61; Pond, "Indian Warfare," 3:134; Eastman, *Dahcotah*, 195–96. Secondary accounts are available in Diedrich, *Ojibway Oratory*, 43, and *The Chiefs*, 13.

43. The attempts to remove the Menominee and Ho-Chunk are well documented in the treaty materials and the journals of the commissioners. See also Folwell, *History*, 1:308–20; Tanner, *Atlas*, 156, 164.

44. Henry M. Rice to William Medill, Feb. 16, 1847, COIA Correspondence, NA; *Prairie du Chien Patriot*, May 11, 1847. There are also references to Bagone-giizhig's efforts to gain Ho-Chunk support for relocation to Minnesota at the treaty negotiations with the Ho-Chunk. (Bagone-giizhig attended but was not a signatory.) See Treaty Journal, Jan. 23, 1847, COIA, Winnebago Agency, R. 931. His role is also referred to in the later 1855 Treaty Negotiations Journal, James F. Sutherland Papers, MHS.

45. The details of Bagone-giizhig the Elder's death were reported in *Minnesota Chronicle and Register*, June 10, 1850; *Patriot*, June 8, 1847; *Minnesota Pioneer*, Dec. 26, 1849 (includes William W. Warren's account); *Minneapolis Tribune*, July 1, 1868; Clark, "Reminiscences," 5:384; Eastman, *Dahcotah*, 205; Lanman, *Summer in the Wilderness*, 70; Riggs, *Tah-koo Wah-kan*, 444; Schoolcraft, *Indian Tribes*, 1:166–67. See also Carl Zappfe, "Chiefs 'Hole-in-the-Day,'" *Cass County Independent* (Walker, MN), Aug. 28, 1975. Warren reported that the accident happened at Royalton, MN, rather than Little Falls and that oxen rather than horses drew the cart.

46. This quote was printed in each of the newspaper articles and the Eastman version, all listed in the above note.

Notes to Chapter 4

1. Eastman, *Indian Heroes*, 105.

2. Nicolay, "Hole-in-the-Day," 191.

3. For information on Bagone-giizhig the Younger fasting, see Lanman, *Summer in the Wilderness*, 71. For his first scalping, see Brunson, "Sketch," 5:392; Diedrich, *The Chiefs*, 14. For his bear cubs, see Eastman, *Indian Heroes*, 103–4. Keeping bear cubs for pets was rare but not unprecedented. Gladys Shingobe Ray, an elder from White Earth, kept them as a child, even after they got quite large. Eastman's adulation of Bagone-giizhig the Younger, like the obvious admiration expressed by Brunson, Clark, and others, suggests the possibility they embellished their accounts of Bagone-giizhig's childhood.

4. Eastman, *Indian Heroes*, 103.

5. Traditional Ojibwe mourning practice demanded a ghost feed four days after burial, when the soul arrived in the spirit world. Gwiiwizens and other close family members would have blackened their faces with charcoal for an entire year and refrained from braiding their hair. At the end of mourning, the family would have a feast to "wash off their sadness," remove the charcoal, and re-braid their hair. They also would have restrained from eating traditional foods until each came into season and had been fed to the family members in ceremony. Interviews, Archie Mosay, 1994; Earl Nyholm, 1994; David Aubid, 1996. See also Diedrich, *The Chiefs*, 15.

6. *Minnesota Pioneer*, Dec. 26, 1849 (includes William W. Warren's account); *Minneapolis Tribune*, July 1, 1868; Diedrich, *The Chiefs*, 15.

7. Rev. Claude H. Beaulieu as cited in Eastman, *Indian Heroes*, 103.

8. Spears, "Reminiscences of a Short History."

9. Brunson, "Sketch," 5:399.

10. *New York Tribune*, 1851 (reprinted in *CSHSW*, 5:408–9); *Prairie du Chien Courier*, Mar. 25, 1858; Nicolay, "Hole-in-the-Day," 191; "Death of Hole-in-the-Day the Younger," *St. Paul Pioneer Press*, June 30, 1868.

11. "Death of Hole-in-the-Day the Younger," *St. Paul Pioneer Press*, June 30, 1868; Warren, *History*, 497–98; *Minnesota Pioneer*, Dec. 26, 1849; *Minneapolis Tribune*, July 1, 1868; Holcombe, *Apostle of the Wilderness*, 87.

12. Neill, "History of the Ojibways," 5:497–98. See also Diedrich, *The Chiefs*, 16.

13. "Death of Hole-in-the-Day the Younger," *St. Paul Pioneer Press*, June 30, 1868.

14. Nagonaby et al. to the President of the United States of America, Aug. 21, 1847, NAMP, M 234, R 389; interviews, Melvin Eagle, 2000, and Jean Skinaway-Lawrence, 2010. (The double-vowel spelling is Negwanebi, which I use throughout the text. Citations, however, are given in the original form and spelling, hence the variation.) Negwanebi complained bitterly to the COIA but received no remedy. His opinions are well detailed in another dictated letter: Naguonabe to John Livermore, Nov. 14, 1848, NA and Records Service, Correspondence of the COIA and Related Records, Letters Received 1824–81, NAMP, RG 75, M 234, R 390. See also Tanner, "Mille Lacs Band," 471.

15. "Death of Hole-in-the-Day the Younger," *St. Paul Pioneer Press*, June 30, 1868.

16. In fact, the main body of chiefs, warriors, and headmen who signed the treaty did so on August 2, 1847. Bagone-giizhig signed it the next day with William Aitkin and D. T. Sloan as witnesses, rather than William W. Warren, Peter Marksman, and Smith Hovers, who had witnessed all the other signatures. See *Treaty with the Chippewa of the Mississippi and Lake Superior*, Aug. 2, 1847 (9 Stat. 904, Ratified Apr. 3, 1848, Proclaimed Apr. 7, 1848), in Kappler, *Laws and Treaties*, 2:567–69. See also Diedrich, *The Chiefs*, 16.

17. Johnson, *Enmegahbowh's Story*, 2. Schenck's *The Voice of the Crane Echoes Afar* ably shows how Ojibwe identity shifted from a focus on clan and village to a more malleable notion that transcended locale and broadened throughout the fur-trade era. This argument seems to support Bagone-giizhig the Younger's assertion of authority beyond his own village. Although Schenck overstates the role of outside forces as primary agents of change in Ojibwe leadership patterns, she provides evidence that shows how the Ojibwe were agents of their own cultural and political transformation.

18. Nicolay, "Hole-in-the-Day," 187.

19. Cleland, "Mille Lacs Chippewa," 75–76.

20. Information on Ojibwe-Dakota warfare in the later 1840s is taken primarily from Henry M. Rice to W. Medill, June 4, 1848, COIA, Winnebago Agency, M R 932; *Minnesota Chronicle and Register*, June 10 and 13, 1850; *Boston Daily Journal*, Aug. 1, 1848; Tanner, "History of Fort Ripley," 10:198–99; Daniels, "Reminiscences of Little Crow," 12:520–23; Brunson, "Sketch," 5:399. Good secondary accounts are available in Dunn, *The St. Croix*, 16; Buck, *Indian Outbreaks*, 19; Meyer, *White Earth Tragedy*, 105; Diedrich, *The Chiefs*, 19.

21. Bagone-giizhig the Younger, in 1855 Treaty Negotiations Journal, James F. Sutherland Papers, MHS. See also Diedrich, *The Chiefs,* 19–20.

22. Eastman, *Indian Heroes,* 103; *Harper's New Monthly Magazine,* June 1959; *Mankato Weekly Record,* Jan. 3, 1860; *Minnesota Pioneer,* Apr. 16, 1867; *Cass County Independent,* Aug. 28, 1976; Augustus Aspinwall Reminiscences, 19, MHS; Frances Densmore, "A Short History of the Indians in Minnesota for Use in School" (1941) 98, microfilm, WPA Papers, MHS. Erlenmon, Calin, and Ohbezzum died young. Louisa Roberts had four children: Joseph, Allan, Mary, and Millie. Rose Hole-in-the-Day died before she could have children. Ida Hole-in-the-Day married Peter Jourdan and had two children, both of whom died before coming of age. Julia Hole-in-the-Day married John Fairbanks and died before having children. John Fairbanks then married his dead wife's sister, Adeline Hole-in-the-Day. They had five children: Charles, Carrie, Robert, George, and Joseph. Belle (also known as Madeline) Hole-in-the-Day married William Warren (grandson of William W. Warren) and had two children. Ignatius had two children: Willie Hole-in-the-Day and Maggie Hole-in-the-Day, who later married Charles Vanoss and had five children of her own. Joseph Woodbury, Bagone-giizhig's son with Helen McCarty, later returned to White Earth. He had three children by his first marriage — Clarence, Harry, Gladdy — and one more by his second. Bagone-giizhig's descendents number in the hundreds today. J. H. Hinton to C. C. Daniels, Attorney in Charge of White Earth Land Matters, June 26, 1914, COIA, Correspondence File, NA; *St. Paul Dispatch,* Oct. 11, 1875; *Brainerd Dispatch,* Aug. 28, 1885, Nov. 30 and Dec. 14, 1888; *Cass County Independent,* Aug. 28, 1975; Coleman, LaBud, and Humphrey, *Old Crow Wing,* 31; Diedrich, *The Chiefs,* 53–54; *Minnesota Pioneer,* Aug. 3, 1865. Edwin Clark Papers, MHS, has several references as well. There are numerous additional references in the probate correspondence after Bagone-giizhig's death. See Isabelle Hole-in-the-Day to E. S. Parker, COIA, Dec. 7, 1869, W. F. Campbell to COIA, Nov. 6, 1895, W. F. Campbell to M. R. Baldwin, June 20, 1894, Joseph Hole-in-the-Day Woodbury to Senator Knute Nelson, Apr. 22, 1897, M. R. Baldwin, and COIA to Knute Nelson, Apr. 22, 1897, Marshall A. Spooner to Charles A. Fairbanks, May 30, 1914, J. H. Hinton to COIA, Aug. 19, 1914, Harry P. Woodbury to J. H. Hinton, June 20, 1914, E. P. Wakefield to Charles Vanoss, Feb. 3, 1914, J. H. Hinton to Madeline Fairbanks, or Ke-we-tah-be-quay, Jan. 1, 1915, Superintendent to Commissioner, Sept. 18, 1915, Assistant Commissioner to John R. Howard, Aug. 13, 1915, Memorandum from Chief of Land Contracts, June 30, 1915, J. H. Hinton to COIA, June 25 and 29, 1915, J. H. Hinton to C. C. Daniels, Attorney in Charge of White Earth Land Matters, June 26, 1914, C. C. Daniels to J. H. Hinton, June 22, 1914, R. C. Bell, Special Assistant to Attorney General to John H. Hinton, Aug. 1, 1916, P. R. Wadsworth to COIA, Mar. 4, 1921, Adeline Hole-in-the-Day Fairbanks to Halvor Steenerson, Feb. 21, 1921, Cato Sells, COIA to Halvor Steenerson, Feb. 21, 1921, and Halvor Steenerson to Commissioner, Feb. 19, 1921, all COIA Correspondence, NA; Morrison County, Probate Order: In the Matter of the Estate of Hole-in-the-Day, Deceased, Nov. 27, 1869; W. F. Campbell to H. Smith, Secretary of the Interior, June 20, 1894, Department of the Interior Correspondence File, NA; Knute Nelson to Secretary of the Interior, Apr. 27, 1897, Secretary of the Interior, Correspondence File, NA

23. Johnson, *Enmegahbowh's Story,* 2. The mission was located at Lot 42, Mission Point, Gull Lake, and was formally bequeathed by Chief Gwiiwizhenzhish (Bad Boy), not Chief Bagone-giizhig. The land was part of Gwiiwizhenzhish's private scrip, but it was indeed Bagone-giizhig who originally encouraged the construction of the mission and school at Gull Lake. Bagone-giizhig himself left Gull Lake to build a new house for himself on his land opposite the village at Crow Wing a couple of years after enticing Johnson to set up the mission at Gull Lake.

24. James Bassett testimony, DIWER, 117.

25. Ma'iingaans testimony, DIWER, 134. Julia Warren Spears claimed that Bagone-giizhig did not drink much, especially early in his chieftainship. ("Reminiscences of a Short History"). Ma'iingaans also asserted that Bagone-giizhig felt used by the traders.

The chief knew he was doing them a tremendous favor, and he wanted to maintain the appearance of civilized decadence, drinking with the traders, but he deeply distrusted their motives from the very beginning.

26. Eastman, *Indian Heroes,* 106; Nicolay, "Hole-in-the-Day," 187. There was a Major H. Day who spent time in central Minnesota as well, but the voter registration of H. Day appears to be that of Bagone-giizhig.

27. "Death of Hole-in-the-Day the Younger," *St. Paul Pioneer Press,* June 30, 1868.

28. *Prairie du Chien Courier,* Mar. 25, 1858; Eastman, *Indian Heroes,* 106. Bagone-giizhig's abilities in English were severely limited, however. In 1863, Charles E. Mix (commissioner of Indian Affairs in 1858) reported to William P. Dole (commissioner of Indian Affairs from 1861 to 1865) that when Bagone-giizhig tapped him on the shoulder to initiate a conversation without an interpreter they were unable to exchange words, and "consequently nothing more than a *how* was uttered." Charles E. Mix to William P. Dole, June 3, 1863, COIA Correspondence, NA.

29. Information on the Fairbanks killing and its aftermath is primarily from Jonathan E. Fletcher to William Medill, May 29, 1849, NAMP, M 842, R 1; Jonathan E. Fletcher to William Medill, Feb. 12, 1849, COIA, Winnebago Agency, M R 392; Alexander Ramsey to W. Medill, July 9, 1849, COIA, Minnesota Superintendency; Clement Beaulieu to J. Livermore, Jan. 10, 1849 and Feb. 14, 1849, COIA, Winnebago Agency, M R 392; William Fairbanks testimony, DIWER, 111–623; Nicolay, "Hole-in-the-Day," 188. A newspaper in St. Paul reported that Bagone-giizhig was showing off his revolver in the bar when it discharged; see "Death of Hole-in-the-Day the Younger," *St. Paul Pioneer Press,* June 30, 1868. Bagone-giizhig did frequently show off his marksmanship, once shooting prairie chickens in dramatic demonstration for white traders; see Nicolay, "Hole-in-the-Day," 188. Bagone-giizhig kept a revolver with him at all times, forgetting to carry one only once, in 1868, when he was assassinated.

30. William Fairbanks testimony, DIWER, 111–623. Fairbanks, who testified years later, had great disdain for Bagone-giizhig's offer to "cover the dead." He held the chief responsible and called him a lawless miscreant. His proposed adoption never took place. Interestingly, the Ojibwe custom of "covering the dead" was refused by the mixed-blood family in part because they felt the offer to be insincere but also because they claimed they did not participate in Indian protocol for addressing war and murder. Nevertheless, the Fairbanks family was later implicated in Bagone-giizhig's assassination conspiracy, which raises a question about how far the family had really strayed from older Ojibwe beliefs about murder and revenge. Alexander Ramsey voiced a disdainful opinion of the chief after the Fairbanks killing as well, but it did not translate into official action; see Alexander Ramsey to W. Medill, July 9, 1849, COIA, Minnesota Superintendency.

31. David B. Herriman to Willis A. Gorman, Oct. 17, 1855, 34th Congress, 1st Session, House Executive Documents, 1855–56, Serial 840, 370–72. The Dakota and Ho-Chunk turned to commercial agriculture in even greater numbers than the Ojibwe.

32. Bagone-giizhig's petition and Fletcher's letter of support are contained in Jonathan E. Fletcher to T. Harvey, July 25, 1848, with Chippewa Petition Enclosed, COIA, Winnebago Agency, M R 392. Additional information on the government response can be found in *Boston Daily Journal,* Aug. 1 and 10, 1848.

33. Ramsey, Bagone-giizhig, John B. S. Todd, and John S. Watrous communicated extensively about the timber dispute by letter. See especially John B. S. Todd to Alexander Ramsey, Nov. 11, 1850, Hole-in-the-Day to John Todd, Nov. 11, 1850, enclosed with Todd to Ramsey, Nov. 11, 1850, Todd to Adjutant General, Mar. 15, 1850, all Letters Received, Sandy Lake Subagency, BIA, RG 75, NA; Alexander Ramsey to John Todd, Nov. 15, 1850, 1:275, Alexander Ramsey to John S. Watrous, Nov. 15 and Dec. 23, 1850, 1:276, 287, Alexander Ramsey to Hole-in-the-Day, Dec. 13, 1850, 1:284, all Letters Sent, Minnesota Superintendency, BIA, RG 75, NA; Hole-in-the-Day to Alexander Ramsey, Nov. 17, 1850, John S. Watrous to Alexander Ramsey, Nov. 19, 1850, both Letters Received, Minnesota Superintendency, BIA, RG 75, NA;

Isaac A. Verplank to COIA, Aug. 2, 1847, Ratified Treaty File Number 250, BIA, RG 75, NA. See also Alexander Ramsey diaries, vol. 19, Nov. 14, 1850, MHS, M 203, R 38; *Minnesota Chronicle and Register,* Dec. 2, 1850. Neill, "History of the Ojibways," 5:498; "Death of Hole-in-the-Day the Younger," *St. Paul Pioneer Press,* June 30, 1868. A good secondary account is available in Kvasnicka, "The Timber Is Mine." On Dec. 2, 1850, the *Minnesota Chronicle and Register* erroneously reported that John Watrous had retrieved the cattle, based no doubt on his own assertions to that effect. Bagone-giizhig's claim seems much more probable considering how difficult it would have been for a white man with limited Ojibwe language skills to even find the Indians who had the cattle, much less negotiate for their return. Watrous, moreover, had a motive to appear helpful to the governor, even if by making a false claim, because he was being held responsible for much of the mounting crisis at Sandy Lake. He needed to divert the negative attention of the governor's office. Henry Rice substantiated Bagone-giizhig's claim, as does the correspondence from Ramsey, the first territorial governor of Minnesota. Captain John B. S. Todd, stationed in Minnesota and Dakota Territory until 1855, later became delegate for Dakota Territory and was promoted to general for the Union Army during the Civil War. (The Office of Indian Affairs was located in the Department of War during this period, which is why their documents involve military personnel.)

34. Hole-in-the-Day to John Todd, Nov. 11, 1850, enclosed with Todd to Ramsey, Nov. 11, 1850, Letters Received, Sandy Lake Subagency, BIA, RG 75, NA; Alexander Ramsey to John S. Watrous, Nov. 15, 1:275–76, Letters Sent, Minnesota Superintendency, BIA, RG 75, NA.

35. Alexander Ramsey to Hole-in-the-Day, Dec. 13, 1850, Letters Sent, 1:284, Minnesota Superintendency, BIA, RG 75, NA.

36. Alexander Ramsey to John S. Watrous, Dec. 23, 1850, 1:287, Letters Sent, Minnesota Superintendency, BIA, RG 75, NA. See also Alexander Ramsey diaries, vol. 19, Nov. 14, 1850, MHS, M 203, R 38.

37. Interviews, Melvin Eagle, 1998 and 2000; Thomas Stillday Jr., 1996; Charles W. Borup to T. Hartley Crawford, Jan. 18 and July 3, 1844, COIA, La Pointe Agency, M R 389; James P. Hayes to Henry Dodge, Aug. 15, 1846, 29th Congress, 2nd Session, House Document, No. 4, 1846, Serial 497, 258–59.

38. The Sandy Lake Annuity Fiasco was widely reported in the correspondence of government officials and Ojibwe chiefs, including Bagone-giizhig. I used for primary reference Bagone-giizhig, letter to editor, *Minnesota Democrat,* July 15, 1851; Bagone-giizhig, Open Letter to William W. Warren, *Minnesota Pioneer,* Jan. 16, 1851; William W. Warren, letter to editor, *Minnesota Democrat,* Jan. 28, 1851; Sela Wright to J. Bardwell, Feb. 1, 1851, MRNM, GLNP; *Minnesota Democrat,* Jan. 21 and Dec. 10, 1851; *Minnesota Pioneer,* Nov. 21, 1850; William W. Warren to George P. Warren, June 24, 1852, CFXGP, 1:4; William W. Warren to Alexander Ramsey, Jan. 21, 1851, enclosed with Ramsey to Luke Lea, Jan. 28, 1851, M1171, NAMP, M 234, R 767:133–34; John S. Watrous to Alexander Ramsey, Dec. 22, 1851, MHS M203, R 6; Alexander Ramsey diaries, vol. 21, Jan. 8–9, 1851, MHS, M 203, R 38; Eshkibagikoonzh (Flat Mouth) Speech at Sandy Lake, Transcribed, Translated and Sent to Alexander Ramsey, Dec. 3, 1850, ARP, R 5; Spears, "My Journey," "Reminiscence of the Assassination," "Reminiscences of a Short History," and "Reminiscences of Hole-in-the-Day," 1. See also Tanner, *Atlas,* 167; Diedrich, *Ojibway Oratory,* 48–51, and *The Chiefs,* 21–22.

39. Spears, "My Journey." Julia Warren Spears's youngest sister, Sophia Warren, was among those infected with measles.

40. *Minnesota Pioneer,* Nov. 21, 1850. Some reports said the Ojibwe contracted dysentery as well as food poisoning, which has somewhat similar symptoms. Food poisoning is caused by bacteria, usually E. coli or salmonella; symptoms include vomiting and diarrhea. Dysentery, with similar symptoms but including blood, is caused by yet another infection, either bacterial or viral, and is communicable on its own. Either way, the Ojibwe held the government responsible for the deaths.

41. Eshkibagikoonzh (Flat Mouth) speech at Sandy Lake, transcribed, translated and sent to Alexander Ramsey, Dec. 3, 1850, ARP, R 5.

42. The letters and speeches of Bagone-giizhig and William W. Warren speak for themselves, but there is also a great secondary source discussion of them in Schenck, *William Warren*, 102–8.

43. Alexander Ramsey diaries, vol. 21, Jan. 8–9, 1851, MHS, M 203, R 38; John S. Watrous to Alexander Ramsey, Dec. 22, 1851, MHS, M 203, R 6.

44. William W. Warren to Alexander Ramsey, Jan. 21, 1851, enclosed with Ramsey to Luke Lea, Jan. 28, 1851, M 1171, NAMP, M 234, R 767:133–34.

45. Bagone-giizhig, Open Letter to William W. Warren, *Minnesota Pioneer*, Jan. 16, 1851.

46. William W. Warren, letter to editor, *Minnesota Democrat*, Jan. 28, 1851; William W. Warren to George P. Warren, Jan. 15, 1851, CFXGP, 1:4.

47. William W. Warren to George P. Warren, Jan. 15, 1851, CFXGP, 1:4; Spears, "Reminiscences of a Short History" and "Reminiscence of the Assassination."

48. William W. Warren to Alexander Ramsey, Aug. 11, 1850, NAMP, COIA, Correspondence Files, Letters Received, M 234, R 390; Alexander Ramsey to Luke Lea, Aug. 16, 1850, NAMP, COIA, Correspondence Files, Letters Received, M 234, R 390.

49. Bagone-giizhig, letter to editor, *Minnesota Democrat*, July 15, 1851.

50. Primary sources on the June 10, 1850, peace conference and the 1850s Ojibwe-Dakota skirmishes described here are Jonathan E. Fletcher to William W. Warren, Mar. 30, 1850, COIA, Field Office Records, NAMP, M 842, R 2; Alexander Ramsey to Orlando Brown, June 15, 1850, Captain John B. S. Todd to Alexander Ramsey, Aug. 11, 1850, and Alexander Ramsey to Orlando Brown, June 15 and July 13, 1850, all NAMP, COIA, Correspondence Files, Letters Received, M 234, R 438; William W. Warren to Alexander Ramsey, Aug. 28, 1850, ARP, R 5; William W. Warren to Alexander Ramsey, May 14 and 19, 1850, NAMP, COIA, Field Office Records, M 842, R 2; Alexander Ramsey to Luke Lea, June 3, 1850, NAMP, Correspondence of the COIA, Letters Received, M 234, R 438; Captain John B. S. Todd to Alexander Ramsey, May 27, 1850, NAMP, Correspondence of the COIA, Letters Received, M 234, R 2; Alexander Ramsey to Luke Lea, Aug. 16 and Sept. 24, 1850, COIA, Minnesota Superintendency, NAMP, COIA, Correspondence Files, Letters Received, M 234, R 438; Cathcart, "Sheaf of Remembrances," 529 (one of the two women attending the June 10, 1850, peace conference); Densmore, *Chippewa Music*, 2:70–71 (Ojibwe's [Bagone-giizhig's cousin's] version of May 1850 attack); *Minnesota Pioneer*, Apr. 10, May 16 and 23, and June 13, 1850; *New York Tribune*, 1851, excerpts of which were reprinted in *CSHSW* 5:408–9; *Weekly Minnesotian*, Oct. 21, 1854; *Minnesota Democrat*, Oct. 18, 1854; *St. Anthony Falls Minnesota Republican*, Oct. 19, 1854, and Feb. 5, 1858; *Minnesota Chronicle and Register*, Apr. 6 and 13, May 4 and 16, and June 3, 10, 17 and 18, 1850; *Pioneer and Democrat*, Jan. 15 and 19 and Feb. 3, 1858; *St. Cloud Visitor*, May 27, 1858; *St. Cloud Democrat*, May 17, 1860; *Goodhue County Republican* (Red Wing), May 18, 1860; Eastman, *Indian Heroes*, 106; Nicolay, "Hole-in-the-Day," 188; Tanner, "History of Fort Ripley," 10:198–99; Daniels, "Reminiscences of Little Crow," 12:520–23; Neill, *History of Minnesota*, 530; Williams, "History of the City of St. Paul." Williams describes scuffles and gunfights between the Ojibwe and the Dakota in downtown St. Paul in full view of many white settlers and officials, including Theodore Borup and George H. Oakes. He details the frustration of town and army officials at being unable to quell the animosities, though these were mere skirmishes and fights. See also Buck, *Indian Outbreaks*, 19; Meyer, *White Earth Tragedy*, 105; Dunn, *The St. Croix*, 15–16, 21–22; Tanner, *Atlas*, 156; Folwell, *History*, 1:258–59, 1:305–7; Diedrich, *The Chiefs*, 21, 25–29, *Ojibway Oratory*, 46, and *Dakota Oratory*, 42; Lund, *Tales of Four Lakes*, 73–76; Hickerson, *The Chippewa*, 104.

51. *Minnesota Chronicle and Register*, Apr. 6 and 13, May 4, and June 3 and 10, 1850.

52. William W. Warren to Alexander Ramsey, May 14, 1850, NAMP, COIA, Field Office Records, M 842, R 2.

53. William W. Warren to Alexander Ramsey, May 19, 1850, NAMP, COIA, Field Office Records, M 842, R 2.

54. *Minnesota Chronicle and Register*, June 10, 1850.

55. Thwaites, *Jesuit Relations;* Catlin, *Letters and Notes.*

56. Eastman, *Indian Heroes*, 106; *New York Tribune*, 1851 (reprinted in *CSHSW* 5:408–9).

57. For details on Bagone-giizhig's speech, monetary request, and overture, see Alexander Ramsey to Orlando Brown, June 15, 1850, NAMP, COIA, Correspondence Files, Letters Received, M 234, R 438.

58. The Dakota killed four children at Otter Tail Lake in August 1850, the same summer the peace conference was held. Captain John B. S. Todd to Alexander Ramsey, Aug. 11, 1850, NAMP, COIA, Correspondence Files, Letters Received, M 234, R 438; William W. Warren to Alexander Ramsey, Aug. 28, 1850, ARP, R 5.

59. Nicolay, "Hole-in-the-Day," 188.

60. For information on the pre-treaty Indian-white political environment in Minnesota in 1854 and Bagone-giizhig's involvement with politicians and missionaries, see *Weekly Minnesotian*, Oct. 21, 1854; *Minnesota Democrat*, Oct. 18, 1854; *St. Anthony Falls Minnesota Republican*, Oct. 19, 1854; and David Herriman to Willis Gorman, May 29, 1854, enclosed with Willis Gorman to COIA, June 5, 1854, M1101, NAMP, M 234, R 150. See also Dunn, *The St. Croix*, 21–22; Tanner, *Atlas*, 156; Folwell, *History*, 1:305–7; Diedrich, *The Chiefs*, 25–29.

61. David Herriman to Willis Gorman, May 29, 1854, enclosed with Willis Gorman to COIA, June 5, 1854, M1101, NAMP, M 234, R 150.

62. *Treaty with the Chippewa Indians, 1854* (Sept. 30, 1854), and *Treaty with the Chippewa Indians, 1855* (Feb. 22, 1855); Kappler, *Laws and Treaties*, 2:648–51, 2:685–90; David Herriman to Willis Gorman, May 29, 1854, enclosed with Willis Gorman to COIA, June 5, 1854, M1101, NAMP, M 234, R 150; George C. Whiting to George W. Manypenny, Feb. 20, 1856, NAMP, RG 75, M 234, R 151:0158–59; James Lloyd Breck to William Chauncey Langdon, Sept. 30, 1857, Protestant Episcopal Church Papers, MHS, Box 46, vol. 42; Major H. Day to George W. Manypenny, Apr. 26, 1856, NAMP, RG 75, M 234, R 151:8–9; *Weekly Minnesotian*, Oct. 21, 1854; *Minnesota Democrat*, Oct. 18, 1854; *St. Anthony Falls Minnesota Republican*, Oct. 19, 1854; *Galena Daily Advertiser*, Mar. 20, 1855; *Washington Evening Star*, Feb. 17, 1855; *Minnesota Weekly Times*, Jan. 17, 1855. Useful secondary sources include Kvasnicka, "From Wilderness to Washington," 3:56–7; Dunn, *The St. Croix*, 21–22; Tanner, *Atlas*, 156; Folwell, *History*, 1:305–7; Diedrich, *The Chiefs*, 25–29.

63. Major H. Day to George W. Manypenny, Apr. 26, 1856, NAMP, RG 75, M 234, R 151:8.

64. George C. Whiting to George W. Manypenny, Feb. 20, 1856, NAMP, RG 75, M 234, R 151:0158–59; James Lloyd Breck to William Chauncey Langdon, Sept. 30, 1857, Protestant Episcopal Church Papers, MHS, Box 46, vol. 42.

65. Ma'iingaans testimony, DIWER, 136. Bagone-giizhig built his new house next to trader Clement Beaulieu at Gichi-mashkodeng (Big Field). He lived there from 1855 until it was burned in 1862. When he rebuilt, he moved back across the river, closer to the tribal village.

66. David B. Herriman to Willis A. Gorman, Oct. 17, 1855, 34th Congress, 1st Session, House Executive Documents, 1855–156, Serial 840, 370–72.

Notes to Chapter 5

1. Kohl, *Kitchi-Gami*, 352.

2. Bagone-giizhig as cited by Daniel Mooers in *Minneapolis Times*, Sept. 22, 1897.

3. I use the term *U.S.–Dakota Conflict of 1862* intentionally. Many historians of the event, such as Duane Schultz, C. M. Oehler, Kenneth Carley, and Hank H. Cox have termed the event "The Great Sioux Uprising of 1862." However, the term *Sioux* is corrupted from an Ojibwe word meaning "snake." A conflict between two sovereign nations can hardly be termed an "uprising." And most importantly, I cannot see what is so *great* about the events in 1862.

4. There are numerous references to communication between Bagone-giizhig and Little Crow about joint diplomatic and possible joint military action. See especially Clark Thompson in Winchell, *Aborigines of Minnesota,* 655; Captain Francis Hall to Alexander Ramsey, Aug. 23, 1862, Minnesota Governor's Archives, MHS, file 255; Johnson, *Enmegahbowh's Story,* 18; Jackson, "Enmegahbowh."

5. Major Edwin Clark, letter to editor, *Minneapolis Journal,* Dec. 4, 1916.

6. Wilson, *Remember This* and *In the Footsteps;* Gibson, *American Indian;* Meyer, *History of the Santee;* Anderson and Woolworth, *Through Dakota Eyes;* Anderson, *Little Crow* and *Kinsmen;* Schultz, *Over the Earth,* 28; Radin, *Winnebago Tribe;* Carley, *Dakota War,* originally published as *The Sioux Uprising of 1862;* Cox, *Lincoln and the Sioux Uprising;* Oehler, *Great Sioux Uprising;* Monjeau-Marz, *Dakota Indian Internment.*

7. Andrew Myrick as cited in Schultz, *Over the Earth,* 28.

8. For estimates on Ojibwe populations, see Tanner, *Atlas,* 65–66. For estimates on Dakota populations, see Upham, "Groseilliers and Radisson," 504. Most population estimates were based on the number of warriors, with at least five or six citizens for every Indian warrior. Sometimes the number was as high as eight. Population estimates were usually conservative.

9. Kohl, *Kitchi-Gami,* 352. Kohl identified the leader as "Wapeassina."

10. Kohl, *Kitchi-Gami,* 353.

11. The conversation between Bagone-giizhig and surveyor was recorded by Kohl, *Kitchi-Gami,* 350–54.

12. Randall, *History of the Chippewa Valley,* 33; *Minnesota Pioneer,* Mar. 13, 1850. Information on Indian-white tension and violence in the 1850s is taken primarily from William W. Warren to George P. Warren, Mar. 31, 1850, CFXGP, 1:4; *Minnesota Pioneer,* Mar. 13, 1850; Randall, *History of the Chippewa Valley,* 33–35.

13. *The Union* as cited in Dunn, *The St. Croix,* 17. The retained usufructary rights of the Ojibwe, affirmed in the Treaty of 1837, are not well understood by most Minnesotans, as demonstrated by widespread resistance to the exercise of off-reservation fishing rights throughout the treaty area. Eventually, those claims were contested and appealed to the U.S. Supreme Court (Aug. 13, 1990); the decision, rendered on March 24, 1999, upheld unfettered Indian rights to harvest game, fish, and rice on all of Lake Mille Lacs and the 1837 treaty area. *Minnesota, et al, Petitioners v. Mille Lacs Band of Chippewa, et al.,* Opinion of the Supreme Court of the United States (Opinion Number 97–1337), Mar. 24, 1999, written by Sandra Day O'Connor. In addition to its formal publication in the record of the Supreme Court, a copy of the entire opinion is given in McClurken, *Fish in the Lakes,* 525–46.

14. Details of the Cornstalk War are taken from *Pioneer and Democrat,* Aug. 25, Sept. 1, 3, 4, and 13, 1857; Dunn, *The St. Croix,* 17–19; Folwell, *History,* 1:325–26.

15. Interview, Danny Seaboy, 2007. Seaboy is Inkpaduta's grandson and carries the same name.

16. Information on the 1857 killing of the German settler and its aftermath, including the Johnson and Beaulieu fallout, is primarily from Tanner, "History of Fort Ripley," 10:194–95; Johnson, "Indian Disturbances of 1857," Clark Papers, MHS; Johnson, *Enmegahbowh's Story,* 7–9; *Little Falls Northern Herald,* Aug. 19, 1857; Robert D. Pomeroy, "Morrison County's Only Lynching," Aug. 16, 1962, unpublished, MHS; *Little Falls Transcript,* Feb. 13, 1880. John Johnson gave the name of the German settler as Fritz but did not provide a last name.

17. John Johnson translated his name as "The One Who Stands before His People," in John Johnson to Nathan Richardson, Feb. 15, 1902, Clark Papers, MHS; Johnson, *Enmegah-bowh's Story,* 9–10. "Stands Praying" is a more literal translation, as *anami'e* and its changed form *enami'e* clearly pertain to prayer.

18. Tanner, "History of Fort Ripley," 10:197.

19. Many white people developed conspiracy theories after the violence in 1862. By 1858, according to Daniel Buck (a U.S. soldier in 1862 and a virulent racist), "The Chippewas

seemed to have a secret understanding with the Sioux that they would join in common cause in a war against the whites." Buck, *Indian Outbreaks,* 175. Although this was a post-conflict theory about what was happening before the hostilities, it echoes a broader feeling among whites and Indians alike that tensions were very high in the late 1850s.

20. Information about the annuity embezzlements of Lucius C. Walker and David B. Herriman in the 1850s and early 1860s and Bagone-giizhig's response and communications with Thompson and William P. Dole is taken from Hole-in-the-Day to William P. Dole, June 11 and 19, 1862, COIA, Chippewa Agency; Hole-in-the-Day to William P. Dole, June 14, 1862, NAMP, RG 75, M 234, R 153:0049–50; Affidavit of J. Ross Browne, Mar. 2, 1855, NAMP, RG 75, M 234, R 150:0166; Charles E. Mix, Report of the Northern Superintendency, Nov. 14, 1862, COIA, Reports, NA; David B. Herriman to Major G. W. Patten, Sept. 5, 1855, NAMP, RG 75, M 234, R 150:0347–48; David B. Herriman to Willis A. Gorman, July 18, 1854, NAMP, RG 75, M 234, R 150:0105; David B. Herriman to Willis A. Gorman, July 2, 1855, NAMP, RG 75, M 234, R 150:0280; David B. Herriman to Willis A. Gorman, Oct. 29, 1854, NAMP, RG 75, M 234, R 150:0120; E. Steele Peake to Henry B. Whipple, Sept. 12, 1862, HWP; George C. Whiting to George W. Manypenny, Feb. 20, 1856, NAMP, RG 75, M 234, R 151:0155–58; J. D. Fuller to Alfred B. Greenwood, June 11, 1860, NAMP, RG 75, M 234, R 152:0150; J. W. Lynde to William J. Cullen, Nov. 15, 1858, NAMP, RG 75, M 234, R 152:0050; John Johnson to George C. Whiting, Sept. 15, 1855, NAMP, RG 75, M 234, R 151:0173; Lucius C. Walker to Beaulieu Brothers, Feb. 17 and 22, 1862, COIA, Chippewa Agency; Mah yah chew a we tong, Ke be twa ge schick and Kah yah ge was kung to our Father, Dec. 26, 1855, NAMP, RG 75, M 234, R 150:0331–34; Memorial of the Undersigned Chiefs and Delegates of Mississippi Bands of Chippewa Indians, Dec. 24, 1855, NAMP, RG 75, M 234, R 150:0325–30; William J. Cullen to James W. Denver, Dec. 8, 1858, NAMP, RG 75, M 234, R 152:0049; Willis A. Gorman to George W. Manypenny, July 28, 1855, NAMP, RG 75, M 234, R 150:0288; Willis A. Gorman to George W. Manypenny, May 28, 1854, NAMP, RG 75, M 234, R 150:0087; Report of the COIA, Nov. 26, 1862 (p.20), COIA, Reports, NA; Flandrau, "Journal of a Voyage," Aug. 26, 1858; Clement Beaulieu in *Affairs at White Earth Reservation, Minnesota* (Washington, DC: GPO, 1887), 25 (Beaulieu estimated Walker's take of the annuity theft at more than eight thousand dollars); *Pioneer and Democrat,* June 6, 1862; Daniel Mooers, *Minneapolis Times,* Sept. 22, 1897. See also Diedrich, *The Chiefs,* 32. A good discussion of the nationwide problems with annuity payments during the Civil War is available in Nichols, *Lincoln and the Indians,* 72–74.

21. J. D. Fuller to Alfred B. Greenwood, June 11, 1860, NAMP, RG 75, M 234, R 152:0150.

22. Charles E. Mix, Report of the Northern Superintendency, Nov. 14, 1862, COIA, Reports, NA.

23. Copway, *Life, Letters and Speeches,* 137.

24. Gwiiwizhenzhish (Bad Boy), quote from Special File 201, COIA, as cited in Diedrich, *Ojibway Oratory,* 75.

25. Goiffon, "Autobiography," 42, 45; Tanner, "History of Fort Ripley," 10:198–99.

26. John Johnson to Henry Whipple, Aug. 25, 1862, HWP, Box 3; Report of the COIA, Nov. 26, 1862 (p.14), COIA, Reports, NA, 15; Johnson, *Enmegahbowh's Story,* 18; Johnson, "Indian Outbreak of 1862," Clark Papers, MHS.

27. Eastman, *Indian Heroes,* 107.

28. William P. Dole (COIA), Major Alfred Brunson, Alexander Ramsey, Ashley Morrill, and other officials reported widespread Ojibwe depredations through December 1862. Missionaries, including Henry Whipple and John Johnson, also wrote about the plunderings and causes of the conflict in their journals and correspondence. Most of the background information discussed below, including details on the attempt to arrest Bagone-giizhig and the burning of his house, is taken from Ashley C. Morrill, Special Indian agent, Report to Clark W. Thompson, Superintendent of Indian Affairs, Aug. 18, 1862, Report Number 5, COIA, Reports, NA; Ashley C. Morrill to Clark W. Thompson, Aug. 18, 1862, in House Executive Documents, 1862–63, 2:217; Charles E. Mix, Report of the Northern Superintendency,

Nov. 14, 1862, COIA, Reports, NA; Captain Francis Hall to Alexander Ramsey, Aug. 23, 1862, Minnesota Governor's Archives, MHS, file 255; COIA Report, Nov. 26, 1862 (p.14), COIA, Reports, NA; E. Steele Peake to Henry Whipple, Sept. 12 and 19, 1862, John Johnson to Henry Whipple, Aug. 25, Sept. 6, and 29, 1862, and John Johnson to James Lloyd Breck, Oct. 3, 1862, all HWP, Box 3; E. Steele Peake, "Reminiscences of Gull Lake Mission," Protestant Episcopal Church Papers, MHS, Box 13 (Subject Files); Ezekial Gear to Henry Whipple, Sept. 5, 9, and 11, 1862, HWP; Hole-in-the-Day to William P. Dole, June 11 and 19, 1862, and Lucius C. Walker to Beaulieu Brothers, Feb. 17 and 22, 1862, COIA, Chippewa Agency; Alexander Ramsey in *Pioneer and Democrat*, Sept. 19, 1862; Ashley Morrill in *Pioneer and Democrat*, Sept. 16, 1862; Augustus Aspinwall in *Pioneer and Democrat*, Sept. 21, 1862; Francis Hall in *Pioneer and Democrat*, Aug. 26, 1862; *Pioneer and Democrat*, June 6 and Aug. 27, 1862; *St. Cloud Democrat*, Aug. 21, 1862; *St. Paul Daily Press*, Sept. 9, 1862; Sweet, "Incidents of the Threatened Outbreak," 6:403–4; Abbe, "Remarks and Reminiscences"; Clement Beaulieu in *Affairs at White Earth Reservation, Minnesota*, (Washington, DC: GPO, 1887), 25; Daniel Mooers, *Minneapolis Times*, Sept. 22, 1897; Whipple, "Civilization and Christianization," 932, and *Lights and Shadows*, 317; Statement of John Johnson, 1862, NAMP, RG 75, M 234, R 153:304; Johnson, "Indian Outbreak of 1862," Clark Papers, MHS; Johnson, *Enmegahbowh's Story*, 11–24; Jackson, "Enmegahbowh"; *Minnesota in the Civil and Indian Wars*, 2:190–91. In addition to the regular military and government reports, Alfred Brunson wrote a Paper in December 1862 which was later read and published in Military Order of the Loyal Legion and Neill, *Glimpses of the Nation's Struggle*. That paper describes Brunson bringing a detachment of sixteen troops from Fort Ripley to the Indian agency at Ottertail City and finding the doors destroyed by axes, the safe looted, and the building vandalized. These statements are substantiated by the official report from the COIA (Report of the COIA, Nov. 26, 1862, COIA, Reports, NA, 16–17). See also Winchell, *Aborigines of Minnesota*, 654–55; Nichols, *Lincoln and the Indians*, 72–74; Diedrich, *The Chiefs*, 32–37, *Ojibway Oratory*, 71–76, and "Chief Hole-in-the-Day"; Buck, *Indian Outbreaks*, 177–80; Lund, *Tales of Four Lakes*, 79–80; and Smith, *Leadership*, 7:21.

29. Bishop Henry Whipple, as cited in Winchell, *Aborigines of Minnesota*, 655. It is unclear from the text and note in this publication if Whipple's comments were provided directly to the author or appeared in some other publication, although I have found no other such reference in the Whipple Papers.

30. Spears, "Reminiscences of a Short History." John Johnson's reports of Indian enlistment payments to traders, the intoxication of those being signed up, and his acceptance of bribes and hush money are reported in Johnson, "Indian Outbreak of 1862," Clark Papers, MHS; Johnson, *Enmegahbowh's Story*, 12–13, 17.

31. Bagone-giizhig cited in Spears, "Reminiscences of a Short History." This same statement was quoted almost verbatim in Maajiigaabaw's (Starts Standing) speech at the Crow Wing meeting in September 1862. See Mah-che-carbo Speech in "Minutes of Council Held at Crow Wing, Sept. 1862, between Major Ashley C. Morrill and the Pillager Chiefs and Braves," enclosed with Ashley C. Morrill, Special Indian agent, Report to Clark W. Thompson, Superintendent of Indian Affairs, Aug. 18, 1862, Report Number 5, COIA, Reports, NA, also appended to the Congressional Record as "Minutes of a Council Held at Crow Wing, Sept. 1862," in 37th Congress, 3rd Session, House Executive Document, 1862–63, Serial 1157, 2:220.

32. Some of the Mille Lacs warriors may have tried to join Bagone-giizhig before their chiefs intervened. Maude Kegg reported her grandmother's firsthand observation: "Miish iidog imaa neyaashiing imaa enda-baapinkamigiziwag giiwenh ingiw oshki-ininiwag debibinaawaad iniw odayiwaan. Mii iwidi waa-apa'igowaad iwidi endanakandenig wii-o-naadamawaawaad iniw anishinaaben miigaanimind." Translation: "At Neyaashiing [Vineland] the young men are in a state of excitement and are catching their horses. They want to ride to where the action is and go help the Indians in the war." Kegg, "Nookomis Gaa-inaajimotawid," 8–9.

33. Interview, Albert Churchill, 1998; Spears, "Reminiscences of a Short History." Churchill spoke at length about the original Chief Bizhiki, who commanded the respect of Ojibwe leaders and people. Because of his age and reputation, he would have been given greater deference than most other Ojibwe chiefs present. Even if Bizhiki did not do most of the talking, his nod of approval, disposition, and body language would influence others. Churchill carried this opinion of Bizhiki (from Leech Lake) generations after Bizhiki had died, even though Churchill was from the greater Lake Lena area (on the Minnesota side of the St. Croix River). In 1847, Bizhiki was a young chief who signed the treaty as "warrior."

34. Chief Bizhiki Speech in "Minutes of Council Held at Crow Wing, Sept. 1862, between Major Ashley C. Morrill and the Pillager Chiefs and Braves," enclosed with Ashley C. Morrill, Special Indian agent, Report to Clark W. Thompson, Superintendent of Indian Affairs, Aug. 18, 1862, Report Number 5, COIA, Reports, NA, also appended to the Congressional Record as "Minutes of a Council Held at Crow Wing, Sept. 1862," in 37th Congress, 3rd Session, House Executive Document, 1862–63, Serial 1157, 2:220.

35. Melvin Eagle, grandson of Chief Migizi, attested to this in several interviews, as did Mille Lacs elders James Clark and Raining Boyd. See also interviews with Batiste Sam and David Sam in *Woodlands,* a compilation of filmed oral histories by the Mille Lacs Band of Ojibwe.

36. Winchell, *Aborigines of Minnesota,* 655; Sweet, "Incidents of the Threatened Outbreak," 6:403–4; Report of the COIA, Nov. 26, 1862, COIA, Reports, NA, 17.

37. Kugel, *Main Leaders;* "Death of the Younger Hole-in-the-Day," *St. Paul Pioneer Press,* June 30, 1868.

38. Information on John Johnson's panic during the U.S.–Ojibwe Conflict and the death of his children is taken from *Enmegahbowh's Story,* 20, 23, 27–28; Johnson, "Indian Outbreak of 1862," Clark Papers, MHS; Johnson, "Removal to White Earth in 1868," Clark Papers, MHS; Report of the COIA, Nov. 26, 1862, COIA, Reports, NA, 16; Sweet, "Incidents of the Threatened Outbreak," 6:403–4.

39. *Pioneer and Democrat,* Aug. 26, 1862; COIA, Reports (1862), 14–15, 73, 77. Evidence is clear in the newspaper article and in the official Indian affairs report that it was a suicide. However, Thomas B. Walker believed that Lucius Walker's death was a homicide. See Walker, "Memories of Early Life," 462; Nicolay, "Hole-in-the-Day," 189. The official report reads, "He had evidently become deranged and committed suicide" (Report of the COIA, Nov. 26, 1862, COIA, Reports, NA, 14). See also Diedrich, "Chief Hole-in-the-Day," 194.

40. Report of the COIA, 1862 (Washington, DC: GPO, 1863) 15.

41. Details on the council at Crow Wing and its aftermath, including Bagone-giizhig's meetings with Ashley Morrill, William Dole, Alexander Ramsey, and Henry Rice, are taken primarily from "Minutes of Council Held at Crow Wing, Sept. 1862, between Major Ashley C. Morrill and the Pillager Chiefs and Braves," enclosed with Ashley C. Morrill, Special Indian agent, Report to Clark W. Thompson, Superintendent of Indian Affairs, Aug. 18, 1862, Report Number 5, COIA, Reports, NA, also appended to the Congressional Record as "Minutes of a Council Held at Crow Wing, Sept. 1862," in 37th Congress, 3rd Session, House Executive Document, 1862–63, Serial 1157, 2:220; Report of the COIA, Nov. 26, 1862, COIA, Reports, NA, 20; John Johnson to Henry Whipple, Aug. 25, 1862, Ezekial G. Gear to Henry Whipple, Aug. 27, 1862, and John Johnson to J. Lloyd Breck, Sept. 6, 1862, all HWP, Box 3; Gwiiwizhenzhish (Bad Boy) and John Johnson to William P. Dole, Oct. 15, 1862, NAMP, RG 75, M 234, R 153:25; Ashley C. Morrill to Clark W. Thompson, Aug. 18, 1862, in House Executive Document, 1862–63, 2:217; Ezekial Gear to Henry Whipple, Sept. 11, 1862, and E. Steele Peake to Henry Whipple, Sept. 12, 1862, both HWP; Whipple, "Civilization and Christianization," 932; Ashley Morrill in *Pioneer and Democrat,* Sept. 16, 1862; Augustus Aspinwall in *Pioneer and Democrat,* Sept. 21, 1862; Augustus Aspinwall Reminiscence, Feb. 7, 1902, in Abbe, "Remarks and Reminiscences"; Alexander Ramsey in *Pioneer and Democrat,* Sept. 19, 1862; Francis Hall in *Pioneer and Democrat,* Aug. 26, 1862; *St. Cloud Democrat,* Aug. 21,

1862; *St. Paul Daily Press,* Sept. 9, 1862; interviews, Melvin Eagle, 1998 and 2000; Winchell, *Aborigines of Minnesota,* 654; Johnson, *Enmegahbowh's Story,* 18–24; Abbe, "Remarks and Reminiscences"; *Pioneer and Democrat,* Aug. 27, 1862; Sweet, "Incidents of the Threatened Outbreak," 6:403–4. Good secondary accounts are available in Nicolay, "Hole-in-the-Day," 188–89; Brunson, "Sketch"; Draper, "A Note on Hole-in-the-Day," 5:401; Spears, "Reminiscences of a Short History"; *Minnesota in the Civil and Indian Wars,* 2:190–91; Hall, "Hole in the Day Encounter"; Meyer, *White Earth Tragedy,* 43–45; Diedrich, *The Chiefs,* 34.

42. John Johnson to Henry Whipple, Aug. 25, 1862, HWP, Box 3; Gwiiwizhenzhish (Bad Boy) and John Johnson to William P. Dole, Oct. 15, 1862, NAMP, RG 75, M 234, R 153:25.

43. Sweet, "Incidents of the Threatened Outbreak," 6:403–4; Augustus Aspinwall Reminiscence, Feb. 7, 1902, in Abbe, "Remarks and Reminiscences."

44. Report of the COIA, Nov. 26, 1862, COIA, Reports, NA, 18; trader Daniel Mooers as cited in *Minneapolis Times,* Sept. 22, 1897.

45. Joshua R. Giddings, U.S. Consul General, British North America Provinces to William H. Seward, Aug. 29, 1862, Correspondence File, COIA, Northern Superintendency, NA.

46. The September 15 special commissioners included missionary Frederick Ayer, E. A. C. Hatch, and Judge Cooper of St. Paul. Commissioner Dole argued that the terms of the treaty were granted while the government was under duress and wrote, "It ought not be ratified...leaders of this outbreak shall be exonerated from punishment." Report of the COIA, Nov. 26, 1862, COIA, Reports, NA, 20; *Treaty of September 15, 1862 with Chippewas of the Mississippi, Pillager and Winnebagosh Bands,* COIA, Reports, 1862, NA.

47. Ashley C. Morrill, Special Indian agent, Report to Clark W. Thompson, Superintendent of Indian Affairs, Aug. 18, 1862, Report Number 5, COIA, Reports, NA.

48. *Treaty with the Chippewa, Mississippi, and Pillager and Lake Winnibigoshish Bands, 1864,* Article 3, awards "five thousand dollars to chief Hole-in-the-Day, for depredations committed in burning his house and furniture in 1862." Kappler, *Laws and Treaties,* 862–65. See also Winchell, *Aborigines of Minnesota,* 655.

49. Hole-in-the-Day to President of the United States and the COIA, June 7, 1863, COIA Correspondence, NA. This important letter includes Bagone-giizhig's issues with the recent treaty, the earliest known discussion of removal to White Earth, and the chief's offer to represent the government in obtaining land cessions from the Red Lake Ojibwe. Julia Warren Spears confirmed Bagone-giizhig's assertion about the arsonists, although she did not divulge their names, "Reminiscences of a Short History."

50. Article 3, *Treaty with the Chippewa, Mississippi, and Pillager and Lake Winnibigoshish Bands, 1864.* Copies of treaties are available in many forms, including Kappler, *Laws and Treaties,* 2:862–65. See also Winchell, *Aborigines of Minnesota,* 655. Bagone-giizhig built his house on the Crow Wing village side. His relationship with Clement Beaulieu had obviously soured, and he didn't trust him as a neighbor. He needed the loyal support of his people more than his business connections with white and mixed-blood traders.

51. Winchell, *Aborigines of Minnesota,* 655; John Johnson and Gwiiwizhenzhish (Bad Boy) to William P. Dole, Oct. 15, 1862, NAMP, RG 75, M 234, R 153:26.

52. "Petition of the Mille Lacs Chiefs," NAMP, RG 76, M 234, R 153:408. The rifts between Ojibwe leaders in Minnesota and emergence of the oppositional dynamic in their diplomacy is reported in John Johnson to Henry Whipple, Feb. 16 and 28, 1863, and John Johnson to J. Lloyd Breck, Feb. 1, 16, and 28, 1863, all HWP, Box 3; Clark W. Thompson to William P. Dole, Oct. 28, 1863, NAMP, RG 75, M 234, R 153:0361; Shob aush Kung to Clark W. Thompson, Aug. 21, 1864, NAMP, RG 75, M 234, R 154:92–93; Edwin Clark to Dennis N. Cooley, Nov. 3, 1866, NAMP, RG 75, M 234, R 155:262; Joel B. Bassett to Charles E. Mix, Dec. 13, 1867, JBP; "Petition of the Mille Lacs Chiefs," NAMP, RG 76, M 234, R 153:408. Kugel devotes a chapter in *To Be the Main Leaders of Our People,* 55–99, to rifts in Ojibwe leadership and divisions between civil and military leaders. Although she casts Bagone-giizhig primarily as a war leader, the book is excellent and meticulously researched. Gwiiwizhenzhish (Bad Boy), the most

high profile of the people who relocated, continued to be recognized as a chief when he settled at Mille Lacs—a remarkable accomplishment given the deeply entrenched leadership structure there. His relocation may have also been a strategy to resist removal from central Minnesota. See John Johnson to Henry Whipple, Feb. 16 and 28, 1863, HWP, Box 3.

53. Kugel's perspective on how Ojibwe chiefs like Bagone-giizhig the Younger used an oppositional dynamic with the Americans, while chiefs from Mille Lacs used conciliatory diplomacy, is well developed in *To Be the Main Leaders of Our People*. She concludes that as long as Ojibwe leaders employed both strategies, both techniques could succeed, but in the absence of one dynamic, the other lost its power.

54. Meyer, *White Earth Tragedy*, 240. Ojibwe resentment of Dakota war refugees was most pronounced among the plains Ojibwe. At the Peguis community, a ninety-year-old chief encouraged an attack on the Dakota refugee villages on the Red River. There were also isolated reports of murders instigated by Ojibwe. No evidence suggests that either group carried on serious military campaigns. See Dickason, *Canada's First Nations*, 266; Schultz, *Over the Earth*, 268, 270. Fannie Johns of Red Lake, MN, Charles Grolla of Nett Lake, and other Ojibwe interviewees have attested to the entrenched distrust and resentment of Dakotas long after the period of military clashes between the tribes (interview, Charles Grolla, 2005). Fannie Johns, who adopted Grolla as a grandson, recalled living in one of the original villages in the Old Crossing (1863) treaty area, and she retained a deep distrust of the Dakotas until her death in 2003.

55. Howard, *The Plains-Ojibwa*, 7:22.

56. I interviewed several drum keepers from St. Croix, Mille Lacs, and White Earth, including Archie Mosay, 1992; Melvin Eagle, 1995; Albert Churchill, 1993; and Benjamin Sam, 1993. They attest to the approximate date and the details of the drum's origin and purpose. See also Vennum, *Ojibwa Dance Drum*. Ojibwe-Dakota cultural exchange includes transmission of the Ojibwe's primary religious society, the Midewiwin, which the Dakota called the wakan dance. See Treuer, *Ojibwe in Minnesota*, 20, 89n15; interview, Archie Mosay, 1994; Pond, *The Dakota*, 86–99, 110–11, 159–61.

57. The treaty period continued into the twentieth century. Canada's Rocky Boy Ojibwe-Cree were not settled on a reservation until 1917 and not fully recognized until 1935. See Schultz, *Over the Earth*, 279; Ewers, "Ethnological Report," 160.

Notes to Chapter 6

1. Bagone-giizhig, "Letter to the editor," *Minnesota Democrat*, July 15, 1851.

2. John G. Morrison testimony, DIWER, 493, 568.

3. Wilson, *Remember This* and *In the Footsteps*; Meyer, *History of the Santee*; Schultz, *Over the Earth*, 28; Gibson, *American Indian*; Radin, *Winnebago Tribe*. The Ho-Chunk were completely removed from southern Minnesota. Small numbers of Dakota stayed on as squatters, but most were relocated to Santee, Nebraska, or took refuge in other U.S. and Canadian Indian communities.

4. George Bonga to Henry Whipple, Aug. 12, 1866, HWP, Box 4. White and mixed-blood fear of the Ojibwe permeates correspondence after 1862. See Henry Bartling to R. B. Van Valkenburgh, Acting COIA, Oct. 12, 1865, NAMP, RG 75, M 234, R 154:131; James Harlan to Dennis N. Cooley, Oct. 26, 1865, NAMP, RG 75, M 234, R 154:223

5. COIA, Annual Report, 1863: 449. See also Folwell, *History*; Meyer, *White Earth Tragedy*.

6. Kappler, *Laws and Treaties*, 2:482–86; Folwell, *History*, 4:190; Tanner, *Atlas*, 156. The most notable exception was the opening of legal liquor trade in Ojibwe country. Sale of alcohol was illegal on Indian land, but the 1837 land cession technically became the property of the United States, and traders quickly exploited this by selling liquor to Ojibwe and Dakota people along the Mississippi River.

7. Nichols, *Lincoln and the Indians*, 72–74; *Treaty With the Chippewa, 1837* (July 29, 1837); Kappler, *Laws and Treaties*, 491–93.

8. Article 4, *Treaty With the Pillager Band of Chippewa Indians, 1847* (Aug. 21, 1847); Kappler, *Laws and Treaties*, 567–71. See also Tanner, *Atlas*, 156; Blegen, *Minnesota*, 171–73; Folwell, *History*, 1:320–21.

9. *Treaty with the Chippewa of the Mississippi and Lake Superior*, Aug. 2, 1847 (9 Stat. 904, Ratified Apr. 3, 1848, Proclaimed Apr. 7, 1848), in Kappler, *Laws and Treaties*, 2:567–69.

10. *Treaty with the Chippewa Indians, 1854* (Sept. 30, 1854) and *Treaty with the Chippewa Indians, 1855* (Feb. 22, 1855); Kappler, *Laws and Treaties*, 648–51, 685–90. Background information on the treaties is discussed in detail above. See also David Herriman to Willis Gorman, May 29, 1854, enclosed with Willis Gorman to COIA, June 5, 1854, M1101, NAMP, M 234, R 150; *Galena Daily Advertiser*, Mar. 20, 1855; *Weekly Minnesotian*, Oct. 21, 1854; *Minnesota Democrat*, Oct. 18, 1854; *St. Anthony Falls Minnesota Republican*, Oct. 19, 1854; *Washington Evening Star*, Feb. 17, 1855; *Minnesota Weekly Times*, Jan. 17, 1855; Kvasnicka, "From Wilderness to Washington," 3:56–57; Dunn, *The St. Croix*, 21–22; Tanner, *Atlas*, 156; Folwell, *History*, 4:190–91 and 4:305–7; Diedrich, *The Chiefs*, 25–29; Blegen, *Minnesota*, 172.

11. Information on the treaties, article provisions, and immediate aftermath are taken from *Treaty with the Chippewa of the Mississippi and the Pillager and Lake Winnibigoshish Bands, 1863* (Mar. 11, 1863); Kappler, *Laws and Treaties*, 839–42; Bagone-giizhig Affidavit in JBP; *Minnesota Pioneer*, Apr. 16 and Aug. 27, 1867. See also Diedrich, *The Chiefs*, 39; Folwell, *History*, 4:194. During negotiations, the Ojibwe living at Lake Winnibigoshish were usually considered a separate band (with a separate reservation initially), but occasionally they were lumped together with the Pillager Band during negotiations and eventually in assignment of reservations. Sometimes it is difficult to discern the difference between the bands in nineteenth-century diplomacy records because Ojibwe within the Cass Lake–Lake Winnibigoshish–Leech Lake triangle were all termed Pillager Band members.

12. *Treaty With the Chippewa—Red Lake and Pembina Bands, 1863* (Oct. 2, 1863); Kappler, *Laws and Treaties*, 853–55, 861–62. See also Blegen, *Minnesota*, 172.

13. Hole-in-the-Day to President of the United States and the COIA, June 7, 1863, COIA Correspondence, NA.

14. Aazhawaa-giizhig (Crossing Sky), along with Gwiiwizhenzhish (Bad Boy), had begun to undermine and eventually oppose Bagone-giizhig when he moved from Gull Lake to his private land parcel in 1855. Since Bagone-giizhig was not party to the Leech Lake removal treaty in 1863, Aazhawaa-giizhig and the other signers received most of the blame for the loss of their reservations at Rabbit Lake, Pokegama, and Gull Lake, strengthening Bagone-giizhig's return to the position of chief diplomat for the Mississippi Ojibwe. The murders of the chiefs are reported in Ashley C. Morrill, Indian agent, to Clark W. Thompson, Superintendent of Indian Affairs, May 7, 1863, COIA, Correspondence File, NA; Bagone-giizhig Affidavit in JBP; *Minnesota Pioneer*, Apr. 16 and Aug. 27, 1867. See also Diedrich, *The Chiefs*, 39.

15. COIA, Annual Report, 1863: 449. Bagone-giizhig's reaction to the 1863 treaty, including his formal correspondence on it, is available in Hole-in-the-Day to President Abraham Lincoln, June 7, 1863, 38th Congress, 1st Session, House Documents, 1863–64, Serial 1182, 3:448–51; Bagone-giizhig Affidavit in JBP; *Minnesota Pioneer*, Apr. 16 and Aug. 27, 1867, and May 5, 1864; *Minneapolis State Atlas*, May 4, 1864; *Washington Evening Star*, Apr. 26, 1864; Alexander Ramsey to William P. Dole, Oct. 1863, House Document, 38th Congress, 1st Session, Serial 1182, 553–54; John Johnson to Henry B. Whipple, Apr. 28, 1864, HWP.

16. *Treaty with the Chippewa, Mississippi, Pillager, and Lake Winnibigoshish Bands, 1864* (May 7, 1864); Kappler, *Laws and Treaties*, 862–65. See also Folwell, *History*, 4:194. On the way to Washington, Bagone-giizhig and others were taken to Niagara Falls by buggy so that they could cross a new suspension bridge. They instead wanted to cross the river by canoe, and

they made a great scene, offering tobacco and saying good-bye to one another, apparently believing that the bridge was dangerous; Draper, "A Note on Hole-in-the-Day," 5:408–9.

17. Article 12, *Treaty With the Chippewa, Mississippi, and Pillager and Lake Winnibigoshish Bands, 1864* (May 7, 1864); Kappler, *Laws and Treaties,* 865.

18. The status of the Mille Lacs Ojibwe was ambiguous between 1855 and 1934, when it was again formally recognized and organized as a sovereign nation in the eyes of the federal government. However, the separate and autonomous Ojibwe communities at Sandy Lake, East Lake, Lake Lena, and Isle were not recognized as independent under the Indian Reorganization Act of 1934. They were simply lumped together with Mille Lacs as separate communities within the same reservation. The IRA directly contradicted and demolished the long-standing separation of those communities in all previous treaties and federal negotiations. Sandy Lake, which had always been a separate and sovereign group with its own leadership tradition, now found itself a numerically smaller and a less integral part of a larger Indian political structure. Its traditional leaders no longer made primary decisions about their community. The only venue for sovereign representation came through the auspices of the Mille Lacs government, where it had a district representative but not autonomous control. The IRA thus created intratribal tensions at the same time that it reaffirmed the land tenure and sovereignty of Mille Lacs and the surrounding Ojibwe communities. The issue of independence for various Indian communities that are part of the Mille Lacs Indian Reservation is still unresolved for many Indians enrolled at Mille Lacs, although changes in the current political configuration of the reservation now seem unlikely. Interview, David Aubid, 1997; Treuer, *Ojibwe in Minnesota,* 42.

19. John Johnson to Henry Whipple, July 7, 1864, HWP, Box 3.

20. These missionaries and clergymen refer often in their journals, correspondence, and speeches to their efforts at promoting relocation and concentration of the Ojibwe. George Copway devotes nearly a third of his published correspondence to the subject in *Life, Letters and Speeches.* See also Folwell, *History,* 4:193. William W. Warren had also been a staunch advocate for Ojibwe removal before and during his service to the government during the Sandy Lake annuity fiasco in 1850.

21. Warren, *History,* 267–69; Hickerson, *The Chippewa,* 73. Report of Ashley C. Morrill, Aug. 18, 1862, as cited in Winchell, *Aborigines of Minnesota,* 656.

22. Henry Whipple to COIA, Mar. 14, 1866, NAMP, M 234, R 599:1408–17.

23. Information on the White Earth removal treaty and communication around it is taken primarily from *Treaty with the Chippewa of the Mississippi, 1867* (Mar. 19, 1867); Kappler, *Laws and Treaties,* 974–76; Bagone-giizhig Affidavit, JBP; John Johnson to Edwin A. Hatch, Sept. 13, 1867, HWP; *Minnesota Pioneer,* Aug. 27, 1867; *St. Cloud Times,* July 11, 1868. See also Diedrich, *The Chiefs,* 45; Folwell, *History,* 4:195–96.

24. Article 4, *Treaty with the Chippewa of the Mississippi, 1867* (Mar. 19, 1867); Kappler, *Laws and Treaties,* 975.

25. Eastman, *Indian Heroes,* 106; Spears, "Reminiscences of a Short History," 5. Ellen McCarty appears in several sources as Bagone-giizhig's wife, but her name is presented variously as Helen Trisk, Helen Kater, and Ellen McCarthy. Details on her meeting with Bagone-giizhig, affair, trip to Minnesota, and wedding are taken from Nicolay, "Hole-in-the-Day," 186–91; *Harper's New Monthly Magazine,* June 1859; *Mankato Weekly Record,* Jan. 3, 1860; Eastman, *Indian Heroes,* 106–7; Spears, "Reminiscences of a Short History," 5. See also Diedrich, *The Chiefs,* 54. Eastman records that McCarty actually caught up with him in St. Paul, although stronger sources suggest it was Chicago, even if they were first seen together in St. Paul. Joseph Woodbury, as Bagone-giizhig's child was named after his adoption, found his way back to White Earth as an adult and served as one of Eastman's primary informants.

26. Information on the rift between Bagone-giizhig, Waabaanakwad, and the other Mississippi chiefs as well as the initial move to White Earth is taken primarily from

Bagone-giizhig Affidavit, JBP; *Minnesota Pioneer,* Aug. 27, 1867; *St. Cloud Times,* July 11, 1868; John Johnson to Edwin A. Hatch, Sept. 13, 1867, HWP; Spears, "Reminiscences of a Short History"; Gilfillan, "Ne-bun-esh-kunk," 195–96; John G. Morrison testimony, DIWER, 494–95; Charles W. Borup to T. Hartley Crawford, Jan. 18 and July 3, 1844, RDI, COIA, La Pointe Agency, M R 389; James P. Hayes to Henry Dodge, Aug. 15, 1846, 29th Congress, 2nd Session, House Document, No. 4, 1846, Serial 497, 258–59; Meyer, *White Earth Tragedy,* 47; Diedrich, *The Chiefs,* 46.

27. Gilfillan, "Ne-bun-esh-kunk," 195–96, as cited in Diedrich, *The Chiefs,* 46.

28. Aspinwall claimed $1,124.99 in travel expenses forwarded to Bagone-giizhig against the chief's estate, which was surely exaggerated. Augustus Aspinwall Reminiscences, 17, MHS.

29. Peter Roy served as interpreter for some treaty negotiations between the Mississippi Ojibwe and the U.S. government. He may have translated some of Bagone-giizhig's personal correspondence as well. He was called Pierre-ish by many of the Crow Wing Indians (Pierre is the French version of Peter). The –ish suffix is from Ojibwe, a derogative meaning "That Old Pierre." He later moved to White Earth. His numerous descendants are among the larger families on the reservation today. He was present at a meeting in June 1866 with Clement Beaulieu and Charles Ruffee of relevance in later investigations. See Diedrich, *The Chiefs,* 47.

30. Details of the assassination are provided above, pages 3–6. See Ojibwe Affidavit, July 27, 1868, and Joel Bassett report, JBP; Ojibwe interview with A. D. Prescott, *St. Cloud Democrat,* July 9, 1868; Spears, "Reminiscence of the Assassination," "Reminiscences of a Short History," "My Journey," and "Reminiscences of Hole-in-the-Day," Augustus Aspinwall Reminiscences, 19, MHS; Augustus Aspinwall Reminiscence, Feb. 7, 1902, in Abbe, "Remarks and Reminiscences"; Jobe Report to COIA, Oct. 24, 1868, COIA Correspondence, NA. See also A. Jobe to N. G. Taylor, Oct. 24, 1868, COIA, Chippewa Agency, M R 156; "The Murder of Hole-in-the-Day," *St. Cloud Journal,* July 9, 1868; *Moore's Rural New Yorker,* July 11 and 18, 1868; *Minneapolis Tribune,* July 17, 1868; *St. Paul Daily Press,* July 7, 1868; *Sauk Rapids Sentinel,* July 10, 1868; *St. Cloud Journal,* Aug. 20, 1868; Draper, "A Note on Hole-in-the-Day," 5:400–401; Hall, "Hole-in-the-Day Encounter"; Eastman, *Indian Heroes,* 102–9; Diedrich, *The Chiefs,* 51; DIWER, 111–623, especially the testimonies of Medwe-ganoonind, 240–51, Enami'egaabaw, 252–59, and Mizhaki-giizhig, 272. Most of the assassins were Pillager Band Ojibwe from Leech Lake.

31. Bagone-giizhig's burial at the Catholic cemetery in Crow Wing, officiated by Father Francis Pierz, was reported in Coleman, LaBud, and Humphrey, *Old Crow Wing,* 33, 36; "The Murder of Hole-in-the-Day," *St. Cloud Journal,* July 9, 1868; Spears, "Reminiscences of a Short History," 6.

32. Bassett's ten different letters and reports related to Bagone-giizhig, his assassination, and the formal investigation of the event are in the JBP. Bassett also collected and handwrote Ojibwe's affidavit, signed by Ojibwe (his X mark) and archived as Ojibwe Affidavit, July 27, 1868, JBP, version of the assassination. The subsequent Jobe investigation also reported on the earlier investigation by Bassett. See A. Jobe to N. G. Taylor, Oct. 24, 1868, COIA, Chippewa Agency, M R 156. See also Diedrich, *The Chiefs,* 51.

33. Jobe's investigation was presented in Jobe Report to COIA, Oct. 24, 1868, COIA Correspondence, NA. See also A. Jobe to N. G. Taylor, Oct. 24, 1868, COIA, Chippewa Agency, M R 156.

34. Jobe Report to COIA, Oct. 24, 1868, COIA Correspondence, NA, 21. Emphasis in original. The typed reprint in the Commissioner's Correspondence file did not show the emphasis, but it is obvious in Jobe's original handwritten report. The original is also in the COIA correspondence file.

35. A. Jobe to N. G. Taylor, Oct. 24, 1868, COIA, Chippewa Agency, M R 156. Jobe's original report also detailed Ruffee's charges against Bassett. Jobe Report to COIA, Oct. 24, 1868, COIA Correspondence, NA, 14.

36. Letter to editor, June 30, 1868, by anonymous author "B," *St. Cloud Times,* July 11, 1868.

37. Jobe Report to COIA, Oct. 24, 1868, COIA Correspondence, NA, 14, 19. Jobe reported that Eshkibagikoonzh (Flat Mouth) was coached "and encouraged by the principal assassins of Hole in the Day" throughout his interview. Jobe Report to COIA, Oct. 24, 1868, COIA Correspondence, NA, 14, 19.

38. Mizhaki-giizhig testimony, DIWER, 273.

39. Namewinini speech in "Message from the President of the United States, Transmitting Communication from the Secretary of the Interior, with Papers Relating to Chippewa Indians in Minnesota," Executive Document Number 115, 49th Congress, 2nd Session (1887), 98.

40. DIWER, 111–623. For information on the failure of the conspirators to pay the assassins, see especially the testimony of Enami'egaabaw and Mizhaki-giizhig, 255, 273. See also A. Jobe to N. G. Taylor, Oct. 24, 1868, COIA, Chippewa Agency, M R 156.

41. Morrison testimony, DIWER, 493, 568; Augustus Aspinwall Reminiscences, 17, MHS. See also references to Bagone-giizhig in Aspinwall testimony, DIWER, 111–623.

42. The two children died from exposure while Johnson carried them by canoe on the evening of August 17, 1862, from his mission to Fort Ripley. He blamed Bagone-giizhig for trying to initiate hostilities and threatening his family, which precipitated his panic. Johnson later wrote to Commissioner William P. Dole that he would not be safe in Ojibwe country until Bagone-giizhig was "disposed of." See John Johnson and Gwiiwizhenzhish (Bad Boy) to William P. Dole, Oct. 15, 1862, RDI, COIA, Chippewa Agency, M R 153.

43. Meyer, *White Earth Tragedy.*

44. Henry B. Whipple to A. Jobe, Aug. 4, 1868, COIA Correspondence, NA. Also relevant in this letter is a detailed description of the political infighting in the Indian Affairs Office over Charles Ruffee's bid for the position of Indian agent.

45. There are numerous references to Ruffee's feud and trade politics in the correspondence of traders and government officials in the 1860s. See "Statement of B. Daggett," Jobe Report to COIA, Oct. 24, 1868, Henry B. Whipple to A. Jobe, Aug. 4, 1868, and Letter, Peter Roy to Henry B. Whipple, Sept. 26, 1868, Washington DC, all COIA Correspondence, NA.

46. Peter Roy to Henry B. Whipple, Sept. 26, 1868, Washington DC: COIA Correspondence, NA.

47. DIWER, 84, 117–21, and Ma'iingaans testimony, 134; Spears, "Reminiscences of a Short History." Information on Bagone-giizhig's brawls, including the fight and the incident with Gaa-kanawaab (see below) is taken primarily from Ma'iingaans testimony, DIWER, 131–45; Spears, "Reminiscences of a Short History"; Hole-in-the-Day to President Abraham Lincoln, June 7, 1863, 38th Congress, 1st Session, House Documents, 1863–64, Serial 1182, 3:448–51; Bagone-giizhig Affidavit in JBP; *Minnesota Pioneer,* Apr. 16 and Aug. 27, 1867 and May 5, 1864; *Minneapolis State Atlas,* May 4, 1864; *Washington Evening Star,* Apr. 26, 1864; Alexander Ramsey to William P. Dole, Oct. 1863, House Document, 38th Congress, 1st Session, Serial 1182, 553–54; John Johnson to Henry B. Whipple, Apr. 28, 1864, HWP. Melvin Eagle (grandson of Chief Migizi on his father's side and Ma'iingaans on his mother's side) has no knowledge of this event but says that Bagone-giizhig had frequent, sometimes violent disagreements with traders late in his life; interview, Melvin Eagle, 2006. See also Meyer, *White Earth Tragedy,* 45. Bagone-giizhig's barroom killing of John Fairbanks Jr. is detailed above, page 97.

48. Spears, "Reminiscences of a Short History."

49. There are several independent sources of information on the conspirators' communications. See Spears, "Reminiscences of a Short History"; DIWER, 111–623, especially Gaagigeyaash testimony, 220–29; Eastman, *Indian Heroes,* 102–9. See also Meyer, *White Earth Tragedy,* 46; Diedrich, *The Chiefs,* 46–47. The Gaagigeyaash testimony is the primary source on the first known meeting of the conspirators.

50. Gaagigeyaash testimony, DIWER, 222–23, 236. Bwaanens was named in several of the 1911 testimonies and referred to as Charles Beaulieu in one of them, although I could not confirm that Bwaanens was Charles Beaulieu. Mizhaki-giizhig testified that the assassins were promised two thousand dollars each, but other eyewitness accounts from Ma'iingaans, Enami'egaabaw, and Medwe-ganoonind put the figure at one thousand.

51. Medwe-ganoonind testimony, DIWER, 241–42. The primary source on the second known meeting of the conspirators is Medwe-ganoonind testimony, DIWER, 240–51.

52. Information on the names and identities of the actual assassins and their presentation herein is cited in this book's Prologue (above). Enami'egaabaw is from Gichiachaabaaning (Inger, MN), not John Johnson, the half-Ottawa missionary with the same Indian name.

53. Enami'egaabaw testimony, DIWER, 253–54.

54. Densmore, *Chippewa Customs;* Treuer and Treuer, "Ojibwe."

Notes to Epilogue

1. Augustus Aspinwall Reminiscences, 17, MHS.

2. Longfellow, "The Song of Hiawatha," *Poems and Other Writings,* 256–57.

3. Interviews, Karen Fairbanks, 1992; Brian Goodwin, 1994.

4. James Bassett testimony, DIWER, 84.

5. Williams, "Memoir of William W. Warren," 7–20, in Warren, *History.* Sophia Warren had been infected with measles during the Sandy Lake tragedy in 1850 but apparently survived and migrated to White Earth with the rest of her family.

6. *Report in the Matter of the Investigation of the White Earth Reservation,* 62nd Congress, 3rd session, House Reports, Report Number 1336, Serial 6336 (Washington, DC: GPO, submitted Jan. 16, 1913), 17. James M. Graham, representative from Illinois, was chairman of the subcommittee that provided oversight of the investigation.

7. Meyer, *White Earth Tragedy,* 48; DIWER, 118.

8. Meyer, *White Earth Tragedy,* 48.

9. Information on Ojibwe population in Minnesota and at White Earth is from "Findings of the Northwest Indian Commission," *Senate Executive Documents,* 49th Congress, 2nd session, Serial 2449 (Washington, DC: GPO), 115:1–82; *House Journal,* 50th Congress, 1st session, Serial 2529 (Washington, DC: GPO), 204, 789, 999; Tanner, *Atlas,* 65–66; Upham, "Groseilliers and Radisson," 504; Meyer, *White Earth Tragedy,* 48, 55.

10. Treuer, *Ojibwe in Minnesota,* 35; St. Germain, *Indian Treaty-Making Policy.* The decision itself was only possible when Indian nations could be treated as subjects of American policy rather than as independent nations.

11. Information on the executive orders used to relocate the Otter Tail Lake Pillagers and Pembina Band members to White Earth in 1872–73 (here and below) and enlarge the reservations at Leech Lake and Bois Forte is from COIA, *Statutes at Large,* 17:189, 539 and 18:173–74. See also Folwell, *History,* 4:197–98, 4:257; Ebbott, *Indians in Minnesota,* 27; Meyer, *White Earth Tragedy,* 49.

12. Information on the 1879 White Earth addition and 1883 retrocession is taken from *Chippewa Indians in Minnesota,* 51st Congress, 1st session, *House Executive Documents,* Serial 2747 (Washington, DC: GPO), 247:2–3, 14–15, 25, 95–110. See also Folwell, *History,* 4:233.

13. Whipple, *Lights and Shadows,* 314. Whipple's other letters advocating greater effort at removal can be found in *Senate Executive Documents,* 49th Congress, 1st session, Serial 2333 (Washington, DC: GPO), vol. 44; *Senate Executive Documents,* 49th Congress, 2nd session, Serial 2449 (Washington, DC: GPO), 115:53; COIA, *Statutes at Large,* 24:44. See also Folwell, *History,* 4:201. Whipple is sometimes lauded—incorrectly—as a hero who defended Indians from politicians by advocating assimilation and relocation. Early historians such as William W. Folwell repeated that impression, as have more recent explorations of his life such as a Minnesota Public Radio piece that aired in November 1994.

14. "Findings of the Northwest Indian Commission," *Senate Executive Documents*, 49th Congress, 2nd session, Serial 2449 (Washington, DC: GPO), 115:1–82. The commission findings include complaints about flooding from the dams, annuity fraud, railroad and timber speculation, and resistance to removal. See also Folwell, *History*, 4:209–11.

15. Pillagers scoffed at the fifteen thousand dollars offered as compensation, for the damage was widespread, severe, and long lasting. They have yet to be adequately compensated. See Chief of Engineers, *Reports*, Serial 1447 (Washington, DC: GPO: 1870), 282–89; "Damages to Chippewa Indians," *House Executive Documents*, 48th Congress, 1st session, Serial 2200 (Washington, DC: GPO), 76:1–21; "Findings of the Northwest Indian Commission," *Senate Executive Documents*, 49th Congress, 2nd session, Serial 2449 (Washington, DC: GPO), 115:1–82; Folwell, *History*, 4:210.

16. *Congressional Record*, 50th Congress, 2nd session, 273, 396–400, 829 (includes testimony for the Nelson Act about exploitative lumber harvest in Minnesota); Folwell, *History*, 4:224.

17. "Findings of the Northwest Indian Commission," *Senate Executive Documents*, 49th Congress, 2nd session, Serial 2449 (Washington, DC: GPO), 115:1–82; Folwell, *History*, 4:205, 208; interview, Lois Goodwin, 2006; Meyer, *White Earth Tragedy*, 57, 59, 61.

18. Primary records about the Nelson Act of 1889, its incorporation of Northwest Commission findings, implementation of Dawes allotment provisions, redress for damages caused by dams, and the unique situation at Red Lake are in government findings of the Northwest Indian Commission, the debate over the act, and the legislation itself. See "Findings of the Northwest Indian Commission," *Senate Executive Documents*, 49th Congress, 2nd session, Serial 2449 (Washington, DC: GPO), 115:1–82; *House Journal*, 50th Congress, 1st session, Serial 2529 (Washington, DC: GPO), 204, 789, 999; *Congressional Record*, 50th Congress, 1st session, 1886–89, 1971, 9129–31, 9353, 9616; Chief of Engineers, *Reports*, Serial 1447 (Washington, DC: GPO, 1870), 282–89; "Damages to Chippewa Indians," *House Executive Documents*, 48th Congress, 1st session, Serial 2200 (Washington, DC: GPO), 76:1–21. See also Folwell, *History*, 4:219–35.

19. *Chippewa Indians in Minnesota*, 51st Congress, 1st session, *House Executive Documents*, Serial 2747 (Washington, DC: GPO), 247:1–12 (includes a full report from Henry Rice on flooding from dams, survey problems, and abortive legislation on arrearages and compensation); Folwell, *History*, 4:234.

20. *Chippewa Indians in Minnesota*, 51st Congress, 1st session, *House Executive Documents*, Serial 2747 (Washington, DC: GPO), 247:2–3, 14–15, 25, 95–110; Folwell, *History*, 1:325, 4:231–33. See map of the retrocession area in Folwell, *History*, 4:298.

21. *Report in the Matter of the Investigation of the White Earth Reservation*, 62nd Congress, 3rd session, House Reports, Serial 6336 (Washington, DC: GPO, submitted Jan. 16, 1913), 1336:524–649; Folwell, *History*, 4:265–68. For information on the evolution of allotment implementation in Minnesota, see Meyer, *White Earth Tragedy*, 51–52, 64–65.

22. This was achieved most notably through the Clapp Rider legislation and the Steenerson Act. See *Congressional Record*, 56th Congress, 1st session, 56, 2566; *Congressional Record*, 58th Congress, 2nd session, 685, 3660, 4413, 5546, 5825; COIA, *Statutes at Large*, 33:539; *Chippewa Indians in Minnesota*, 51st Congress, 1st session, *House Executive Documents*, Serial 2747 (Washington, DC: GPO), 247:822–27; Folwell, *History*, 4:266–67.

23. *Report in the Matter of the Investigation of the White Earth Reservation*, 62nd Congress, 3rd session, House Reports, Report Number 1336, Serial 6336 (Washington, DC: GPO, submitted Jan. 16, 1913), 5. This report is sometimes referred to as the Graham Report.

24. Interview, Joseph Auginaush, 1994.

25. Interview, Winona LaDuke, Nov. 28, 1994. See also Meyer, *White Earth Tragedy*, 229.

26. Information on allotment litigation at White Earth, the Jenks and Hrdlicka tests, and tribal rolls is from Records of the U.S. Attorney, U.S. Department of Justice, "Land Allotment Fraud Cases at White Earth, Deposition Testimony," NA (Chicago Regional

Branch), 11; Hrdlicka, "Anthropology of the Chippewa," 198–227; Albert Jenks to William Folwell, May 21, 1926, William Watts Folwell Papers, MHS; "Professor Jenks Returns to the University," *University of Minnesota Alumni Weekly* 15.21 (Feb. 21, 1916): 12; Ranson J. Powell to Albert Jenks, Nov. 16, 1914, Powell Papers, MHS; "Popular Picture of Indian Upset by Investigation, Eagle Beak Nose Belongs Not to Red Man, but to Fiction," *Minneapolis Journal*, Apr. 9, 1916, 3; *Minneapolis Journal*, May 1 and 5, 1918, 12; *Minneapolis Tribune*, Nov. 1 and 13, 1920. For reliable secondary sources, see a fantastic article on eugenics testing and compilation of blood-quantum records at White Earth in Beaulieu, "Curly Hair and Big Feet," 281–314. See also Folwell, *History*, 4:291–93.

27. Records of the U.S. Attorney, U.S. Department of Justice, "Land Allotment Fraud Cases at White Earth, Deposition Testimony," NA (Chicago Regional Branch), 11; Ranson J. Powell to Albert Jenks, Nov. 16, 1914, Powell Papers, MHS; "1,000 Land Titles Hang by a Hair, if Curly Indians Lose," *Minneapolis Journal*, June 24, 1915, 1.

28. "Professor Jenks Returns to the University," *University of Minnesota Alumni Weekly* 15.21 (Feb. 21, 1916): 12.

29. "Popular Picture of Indian Upset by Investigation, Eagle Beak Nose Belongs Not to Red Man, but to Fiction," *Minneapolis Journal*, Apr. 9, 1916, 3.

30. Information on the policy and practice of removal to White Earth from 1890 to 1934 is taken from Meyer, *White Earth Tragedy*, 56, 61; *Woodlands*; Ebbott, *Indians in Minnesota*, 34; interviews, Melvin Eagle, 2008; James Clark, 2002.

31. *Woodlands*; Ebbott, *Indians in Minnesota*, 34; interviews, Melvin Eagle, 2008; James Clark, 2002.

32. Cynthia Kelsey interview with Josephine Warren Robinson, Aug. 9, 1968, ms. 190, American Indian Oral History Research Project, part 2, University of South Dakota, New York Times Oral History Program, 20–21, as cited in Meyer, *White Earth Tragedy*, 224.

33. Interviews, Floyd Jourdain, 2005; William May, 2006.

34. Information on the Bagone-giizhig genealogy and the plight of his descendants after removal is taken from J. H. Hinton to C. C. Daniels, Attorney in Charge of White Earth Land Matters, June 26, 1914, COIA, Correspondence File, NA; *St. Paul Dispatch*, Oct. 11, 1875; *Brainerd Dispatch*, Aug. 28, 1885, Nov. 30 and Dec. 14, 1888; *Cass County Independent*, Aug. 28, 1975. See also Warren, *History*, 14; Coleman, LaBud, and Humphrey, *Old Crow Wing*, 31; Diedrich, *The Chiefs*, 53–54.

35. Children Erlenmon, Calin, and Ohbezzum died young. Please refer to Chapter 4, note 22, above, for details on members of Bagone-giizhig's descendants.

36. The correspondence files of the COIA have numerous letters and petitions from Bagone-giizhig's heirs and their attorneys. Isabelle Hole-in-the-Day, Joseph Woodbury, and their attorneys W. F. Campbell and Marshall A. Spooner wrote most of the petitions. Special Indian agent J. H. Hinton wrote many of the replies, as did the staff and eventually various commissioners in the Indian Affairs Office. Please refer to Chapter 4, note 22, above, for details on this correspondence.

37. Ignatius Hole-in-the-Day, First Head Chief, Ma-ni-to-wab, et al, to Ulysses S. Grant, Oct. 1, 1874, NAMP, RG 75, M 234, R 162:252–53. For information on denial of allotment to Ignatius Hole-in-the-Day, see E. P. Wakefield to Charles Vanoss, Feb. 3, 1914, COIA Correspondence, NA.

38. Joseph Hole-in-the-Day Woodbury to Senator Knute Nelson, Apr. 22, 1897, and M. R. Baldwin, COIA to Knute Nelson, Apr. 22, 1897, both COIA Correspondence, NA; Knute Nelson to Secretary of the Interior, Apr. 27, 1897, Secretary of the Interior, Correspondence, NA.

39. In 1980, Humphrey confided to Robert Treuer about his attempt to dig in Bagone-giizhig's grave site and his genuine remorse. While I was unable to trace the Humphrey family, Treuer's excellent notes from his typed and dated interviews, as well as copies of his correspondence with Humphrey, validate Humphrey's story.

40. Interview, Karen Fairbanks, 1992. I was unable to corroborate Fairbanks's story in other oral or archival sources, but she was a reliable source of information. During the interview in 1992, I learned for the first time about Bagone-giizhig's body being moved after its initial internment. Discovery of Robert Treuer's correspondence and field notes from his Humphrey interview give some confirmation that the chief's family had moved his body.

Notes to Appendix D

1. Alexander Ramsey and George A. Belcourt as cited in Upham, "Groseilliers and Radisson," 529; Mason, *Schoolcraft's Expedition,* 59; Schoolcraft, *American Indians,* 136, 205; Peter Kelly (speech, University of Minnesota Native Languages Conference, Shakopee, MN, Mar. 16, 1996); Lewis Henry Morgan, *Systems of Consanguinity and Affinity of the Human Family* (Amsterdam: Anthropological Publications, [1871] 1970), 287, as cited in Schenck, *Voice of the Crane,* 22.

2. Hickerson, *The Chippewa,* 44.

3. Upham, "Groseilliers and Radisson," 529; Warren, *History,* 36. See also Baerreis, Wheeler-Voeglin, and Wycoco-Moore, "Anthropological Report," 23; Copway, *Traditional History,* 30.

4. Warren, *History,* 36. *Bwaa* is the correct double-vowel orthography equivalent to *bwa,* as it appears in the Warren orthography, *History,* 37.

5. Tanner, *Atlas,* 4; Danziger, *The Chippewas,* 7. The morphological components of *ozhibii'ige* are known to everyday speakers of Ojibwe. However, this word is similarly glossed in Nichols and Nyholm, *Concise Dictionary,* and in Baraga, *Dictionary.*

6. Interviews, Joseph Auginaush, 1996; Melvin Eagle, 1996. This is common knowledge to speakers of Ojibwe. However, I also had several discussions with Earl Otchingwanigan (Nyholm) and other speakers about the appropriate use of the label and term *anishinaabe.* Interview, Earl Otchingwanigan (Nyholm), 1992.

7. Jones, "Etymology of Anishinaabe"; Benton-Banai, *Mishomis Book,* 3; Henry R. Schoolcraft as cited in Warren, *History,* 56; Peter Kelly (speech, University of Minnesota Native Languages Conference, Shakopee, MN, Mar. 16, 1996); interviews, Earl Otchingwanigan (Nyholm), 1992; Danziger, *The Chippewas,* 7.

8. Pronunciation chart adapted from Nichols and Nyholm, *Concise Dictionary,* xxiv–xxvii.

Bibliography

This bibliography lists the major archival collections housing most of the correspondence, journals, and notes about the Bagone-giizhigs, as well as oral history interviews with knowledgeable tribal elders, historians, and descendants of all the Ojibwe leaders mentioned in this book. The bibliography also lists newspapers that followed their activities, as well as books and articles with significant references to them, to Ojibwe history, and to the Ojibwe language.

ARCHIVAL COLLECTIONS CITED

Iowa State Historical Society
    Collections (published series)
Library of Congress
    Henry Rowe Schoolcraft Papers
Minnesota Historical Society (MHS) Archive
    Abbe Abby Fuller and Family Papers
    Abraham M. Fridley and Family Papers
    Alexander Ramsey Papers
    American Board of Commissioners for Foreign Missions Papers
    American Fur Company Papers
    Augustus Aspinwall Reminiscences
    Charles Eugene Flandrau Family Papers
    Collections of the Minnesota Historical Society (published series)
    Douglass Houghton Diaries
    Edwin Clark Papers
    Grace Lee Nute Papers
    Henry Benjamin Whipple Papers
    Henry H. Sibley Papers
    James F. Sutherland Papers
    Jedediah D. Stevens Diaries (Grace Lee Nute Papers)
    Joel B. Bassett Papers
    Josiah Snelling Papers

Julia Warren Spears Papers
Lawrence Taliaferro Papers
Manuscripts Relating to Northwest Missions (Grace Lee
 Nute Papers)
Mary Spears Papers
Pond Family Papers
Protestant Episcopal Church Papers
Ranson J. Powell Papers
William Watts Folwell and Family Papers
National Archives
 Congressional Record
 Files of the Department of the Interior
  Commissioner of Indian Affairs Correspondence Files
  Commissioner of Indian Affairs Reports
  Indian Agent Report Files
  Office/Bureau of Indian Affairs Classified Files
  Office/Bureau of Indian Affairs Correspondence Files
  Office/Bureau of Indian Affairs Segregated Files
 House Correspondence Files
 House Executive Documents
 Presidential Correspondence Files
 Senate Correspondence Files
 Senate Executive Documents
 Works Progress Administration Papers
National Museum of the American Indian
 Photo Archives
North Dakota Historical Society
 North Dakota Historical Collections (published series)
State Historical Society of Wisconsin (SHSW)
 Charles Francis Xavier Goldsmith Papers
 Collections of the State Historical Society of Wisconsin
  (published series)

INTERVIEWEES CITED

Ammann, Dora. St. Croix Band of Ojibwe, Wisconsin. Tribal Elder, Mide-ogimaakwe. Interviews conducted in Ojibwe and in English, 1991–2008.
Aubid, David. Mille Lacs Band of Ojibwe, Minnesota. Tribal Elder. Interviews conducted in Ojibwe, 1992–2007.
Auginaush, Joseph (Joe Maude). White Earth Band of Ojibwe, Minnesota. Tribal Elder. Interviews conducted in Ojibwe 1992–97.
Barber, Richard (Dick). Lac Courte Oreilles Band of Ojibwe, Wisconsin. Tribal Elder, Mide-oshkaabewis. Interviews conducted in Ojibwe, 1991–96.
Beardy, Thomas. Bearskin Lake Oji-Cree, Ontario. Tribal Elder. Interviews conducted in Ojibwe and English, 1992.
Benton-Banai, Edward. Lac Courte Oreilles Band of Ojibwe, Wisconsin. Tribal Elder, Mide-ogimaa. Interviews conducted in Ojibwe, 1986–2007.
Boyd, Raining. Mille Lacs Band of Ojibwe, Minnesota. Tribal Elder, Drum Chief. Interviews conducted in Ojibwe, 1992–2004.

Burnette, Terrence. White Earth Band of Ojibwe. Drum Chief. Interviews conducted in Ojibwe, 1992–2007.

Churchill, Albert. Mille Lacs Band of Ojibwe, Minnesota. Tribal Elder, Drum Chief, Mide-ogimaa. Interviews conducted in Ojibwe, 1992–2001.

Clark, James. Mille Lacs Band of Ojibwe, Minnesota. Tribal Elder. Interviews conducted in Ojibwe, 1992–2007.

Daniels, William (Billy). Forest County Potawatomi, Wisconsin. Tribal Elder, Drum Chief. Interview conducted in Ojibwe and Potawatomi, 2006. (The languages are closely related, so we were able to comprehend each other without difficulty.)

Eagle, Melvin. Mille Lacs Band of Ojibwe, Minnesota. Tribal Elder, Drum Chief, Hereditary Chief. Interviews conducted in Ojibwe, 1992–2008.

Fairbanks, George. White Earth Band of Ojibwe, Minnesota. Tribal Elder. Interviews conducted in Ojibwe, 1996–2006.

Fairbanks, Karen. White Earth Band of Ojibwe, Minnesota. Tribal Elder. Interviews conducted in English, 1991–95.

Fisher, Emma. Leech Lake Band of Ojibwe, Minnesota. Tribal Elder. Interviews conducted in Ojibwe, 1991–96.

Gibbs, Anna. Red Lake Band of Chippewa, Minnesota. Tribal Elder, Mide-ogimaakwe. Interviews conducted in Ojibwe, 1991–2007.

Goodwin, Brian. White Earth Band of Ojibwe, Minnesota. Interviews conducted in English, 1991–98.

Goodwin, Lois. White Earth Band of Ojibwe, Minnesota. Tribal Elder. Interviews conducted in English, 2004–7.

Grolla, Charles. Bois Forte Band of Ojibwe, Minnesota. Interviews conducted in English, 2004–7.

Headbird, Charles (Scott). Leech Lake Band of Ojibwe, Minnesota. Tribal Elder. Interviews conducted in Ojibwe, 1991–95.

Henry, Lawrence. Roseau River First Nation, Manitoba. Tribal Elder. Interviews conducted in Ojibwe, 1986–1996.

Jackson, Susan. Leech Lake Band of Ojibwe, Minnesota. Tribal Elder. Interviews conducted in Ojibwe, 1991–2001.

Jones, Daniel. Nigigoonsiminikaaning First Nation, Ontario. Interviews conducted in Ojibwe, 1991–2008.

Jones, Dennis. Nigigoonsiminikaaning First Nation, Ontario. Interviews conducted in Ojibwe, 1991–2008.

Jones, Nancy. Nigigoonsiminikaaning First Nation, Ontario. Tribal Elder. Interviews conducted in Ojibwe, 1991–2007.

Jourdain, Floyd. Red Lake Band of Chippewa, Minnesota. Tribal Chair. Interviews conducted in English, 1992–2003.

LaDuke, Winona. White Earth Band of Ojibwe, Minnesota. Executive Director, White Earth Land Recovery Project. Interviews conducted in English, 1994.

Liberty, Adrian. Leech Lake Band of Ojibwe, Minnesota. Drum Chief. Interviews conducted in Ojibwe, 1992–2008.

May, William. Red Lake Band of Chippewa, Minnesota. Tribal Elder. Interviews conducted in English, 2005–7.

Mosay, Archie. St. Croix Band of Ojibwe, Wisconsin. Tribal Elder, Drum Chief, Mide-ogimaa. Interviews conducted in Ojibwe, 1991–96.

Oakgrove, Collins. Red Lake Band of Chippewa, Minnesota. Tribal Elder. Interviews conducted in Ojibwe, 1992–2008.

Olsen, Vincent. White Earth Band of Ojibwe, Minnesota. Drum Chief. Interviews conducted in English, 1992–2007.

Otchingwanigan (Nyholm), Earl. Keweenaw Bay Band of Ojibwe, Michigan. Tribal Elder, Professor of Ojibwe Emeritus, Bemidji State University. Interviews conducted in Ojibwe and English, 1991–2000.

Porter, Margaret. Red Lake Band of Chippewa, Minnesota. Tribal Elder. Interviews conducted in Ojibwe, 1988–2007.

Rivard, Connie. St. Croix Band of Ojibwe, Wisconsin. Tribal Elder. Interviews conducted in Ojibwe, 1992–2007.

Roberts, Mary. Roseau River First Nation, Manitoba. Tribal Elder, Mide-ogimaakwe. Interviews conducted in Ojibwe and English, 1986–1996.

Rogers, Delorse. St. Croix Band of Ojibwe, Wisconsin. Tribal Elder. Interviews conducted in Ojibwe, 1992–2003.

Sam, Benjamin. Mille Lacs Band of Ojibwe, Minnesota. Tribal Elder. Drum Chief. Interviews conducted in Ojibwe, 1992–96.

Schommer, Carolyn. Dakota, Granite Falls, Minnesota. Tribal Elder. Interviews conducted in English, 1992–94.

Schultz, Betsy. St. Croix Band of Ojibwe, Wisconsin. Tribal Elder. Interviews conducted in Ojibwe and English, 1992–2001.

Seaboy, Daniel. Dakota, Sisseton, South Dakota. Tribal Elder. Interviews conducted in English, 2006–7.

Skinaway-Lawrence, Jean. Sandy Lake Band of Ojibwe, Minnesota. Tribal Member. Interviews conducted in English, 2010–11.

Stech, Frank. White Earth Band of Ojibwe, Minnesota. Drum Chief. Interviews conducted in English, 1992–2007.

Stillday, Eugene. Red Lake Band of Chippewa, Minnesota. Tribal Elder. Interviews conducted in Ojibwe, 1995–2008.

Stillday, Thomas, Jr. Red Lake Band of Chippewa, Minnesota. Tribal Elder, Mide-ogimaa. Interviews conducted in Ojibwe, 1992–2008.

White, Hartley. Leech Lake Band of Ojibwe, Minnesota. Tribal Elder. Interviews conducted in Ojibwe, 1992–2007.

White, Walter (Porky). Leech Lake Band of Ojibwe, Minnesota. Tribal Elder. Interviews conducted in Ojibwe, 1986–2001.

Whitefeather, Vernon. Red Lake Band of Chippewa, Minnesota. Tribal Elder. Interviews conducted in Ojibwe with David Treuer, 1995.

Wilson, Angela. Dakota, Granite Falls, Minnesota. Interviews conducted in English, 1991–97.

NEWSPAPERS CITED

Boston Daily Journal
Brainerd Dispatch
Cass County Independent
Chronicle and Register [St. Paul]
Galena Daily Advertiser
Goodhue County Republican
Harper's New Monthly Magazine
Little Falls Northern Herald
Little Falls Transcript
Mankato Weekly Record
Medwe-ganoonind Times
Minneapolis Chronicle
Minneapolis Journal
Minneapolis State Atlas

Minnesota Chronicle and Register
Minnesota Democrat
Minnesota Pioneer
Minnesota Weekly Times
Moore's Rural New Yorker
New York Tribune
Pioneer and Democrat
Prairie du Chien Courier
Prairie du Chien Patriot
The Progress [White Earth]
St. Anthony Falls Minnesota Republican
St. Anthony Falls Republican
St. Cloud Democrat
St. Cloud Journal
St. Cloud Times
St. Cloud Visitor
St. Paul Daily Press
St. Paul Dispatch
St. Paul Pioneer and Democrat
St. Paul Pioneer Press
St. Peter Courier
Sauk Rapids Sentinel
The Tomahawk [White Earth]
The Union
University of Minnesota Alumni Weekly
Washington Evening Star
Weekly Minnesotian

WORKS CONSULTED

Abbe, Abby Fuller. "Remarks and Reminiscences of Mrs. Abby Fuller Abbe on Hole-in-the-Day and the Sioux Outbreak, 1862." Fuller and Family Papers, Box 1, Minnesota Historical Society Archives (hereinafter MHS Archives).

Adams, Arthur T. *The Explorations of Pierre Esprit Radisson from the Original Manuscript in the Bodleian Library and the British Museum.* Minneapolis, MN: Ross and Haines, 1967.

Allen, Robert S. *The British Indian Department and the Frontier in North America, 1755–1830.* Canadian Historic Sites no. 14. Ottawa, ON: Queens Printer, 1976.

———. *His Majesty's Indian Allies: British Indian Policy in the Defense of Canada, 1774–1815.* Toronto: Dundurn Press, 1992.

America's Lost Landscape: The Tallgrass Prairie. Video documentary. Cedar Falls, IA: New Light Media, 2004.

Anderson, Gary Clayton. *Kinsmen of Another Kind: Dakota-White Relations in the Upper Mississippi Valley, 1680–1862.* Lincoln: University of Nebraska Press, 1984.

———. *Little Crow: Spokesman for the Sioux.* St. Paul: Minnesota Historical Society Press (hereinafter, MHS Press), 1986.

Anderson, Gary Clayton, and Alan Woolworth, eds. *Through Dakota Eyes: Narrative Accounts of the Minnesota Indian War of 1862.* St. Paul: MHS Press, 1988.

Auger, Donald J., and Thomas Beardy. *Glossary of Legal Terms Translated Into Northwestern Ojibwe.* Thunder Bay, ON: Nishnawbe-Aski Legal Services Corporation, 1993.

Auginaush, Joseph. "Anishinaabe Izhichigewin Geyaabi Omaa Ayaamagad." Edited by Anton Treuer. *Oshkaabewis Native Journal* (Bemidji, MN: Indian Studies Publications, Bemidji State University) 3 (Spring 1996): 39.

———. "Gaa-jiikajiwegamaag Ingii-tazhi-ondaadiz Wiigiwaaming." Edited by Anton Treuer. *Oshkaabewis Native Journal* 4 (Spring 1997): 14–23.

———. "Gii-pakitejii'iged Wenabozho." Edited by Anton Treuer. *Oshkaabewis Native Journal* 4 (Spring 1997): 36–37.

Axtell, James. "Ethnohistory: An Historian's Viewpoint." In *The European and the Indian: Essays in Ethnohistory of Colonial North America.* New York: Oxford University Press, 1981.

Babcock, Willoughby M., Jr. "Major Lawrence Taliaferro, Indian Agent." *Mississippi Valley Historical Review* 2 (December 1924): 358–75.

Baerreis, David A., Erminie Wheeler-Voeglin, and Remedios Wycoco-Moore. "Anthropological Report on the Chippewa, Ottawa, and Potawatomi Indians in Northeastern Illinois and the Identity of the Mascoutens." In *Indians of Northeastern Illinois.* New York: Garland Publishing, 1974.

Bailey, Kenneth P. *Journal of Joseph Marin, August 7, 1753–June 20, 1754.* San Marino, CA: Huntington Library, 1975.

Baker, James H. "The Sources of the Mississippi: Their Discoverers, Real and Pretended." *Collections of the MHS* 6 (1887): 311–53.

Baraga, Frederic. *Chippewa Indians in 1847.* New York: Studia Slovenica, 1976.

———. *A Dictionary of the Ojibway Language.* St. Paul: MHS Press, 1992.

———. *The Diary of Bishop Frederic Baraga: First Bishop of Marquette, Michigan.* Edited by Regis M. Walling and Rev. N. Daniel Rupp. Detroit, MI: Wayne State University Press, 1990.

Bardon, Richard, and Grace Lee Nute, eds. "A Winter in the St. Croix Valley, 1802–1803: A Fur Trader's Reminiscences by George Nelson." *Minnesota History* 28 (1943): 142–59, 225–40.

Bartlett, William W. "Chief Hole-in-the-Day: Quite a Remarkable Man—and Knew It" (untitled newspaper), May 13, 1928. Eau Claire, WI. MHS Archives.

———. "Rice Lake Scene of All-Day Battle Between Ojibways and Sioux in 1798; Former, tho [*sic*] Outnumbered, Finally Win" (untitled newspaper), May 8, 1928. Eau Claire, WI. MHS Archives.

Beaulieu, David L. "Curly Hair and Big Feet: Physical Anthropology and the Implementation of Land Allotment on the White Earth Chippewa Reservation." *American Indian Quarterly* 8 (Fall 1984): 281–314.

Beck, David. *Siege and Survival: History of the Menominee Indians, 1634–1856.* Lincoln: University of Nebraska Press, 2002.

Belcourt, George A. "A Sketch of the Red River Mission." *Collections of the MHS* 1 (1902): 121–40.

Bellet, Louise du. *Some Prominent Virginia Families.* Lynchburg, VA: N.p., 1907.

Beltrami, J. C. *A Pilgrimage in Europe and America.* Vol. 2. London: Hunt and Clarke, 1828.

Benton-Banai, Edward. *The Mishomis Book: The Voice of the Ojibway.* Hayward, WI: Indian Country Communications, 1988.

Berthoud, E. L. "Manuscript on Verendrye." Unpublished, undated. MHS Archives.

Biggar, H. P. *The Voyages of Jacques Cartier.* Ottawa, ON: F. A. Acland, 1924.

———. *The Works of Samuel de Champlain.* 6 vols. Toronto: Champlain Society, 1922.

Birk, Douglas A. *John Sayer's Snake River Journal, 1804–1805.* Minneapolis: Institute for Minnesota Archaeology, 1989.

Bishop, Charles Aldrich. "The Northern Chippewa: An Ethnohistorical Study." PhD diss., State University of New York, 1969.

———. *The Northern Ojibwa and the Fur Trade: An Historical and Ecological Study.* Toronto: Holt, Rinehart and Winston, 1974.

Blackbird, Andrew J. *Complete Both Early and Late History of the Ottawa and Chippewa Indians.* Harbor Springs, MI: Babcock and Darling, 1897.

Blair, Emma Helen. *The Indian Tribes of the Upper Mississippi Valley and Region of the Great Lakes as Described by Nicolas Perrot, French Commandant of the Northwest; Bacqueville de La Potherie, French Royal Commissioner to Canada; Morrell Marston, American Army Officer; and Thomas Forsyth, United States Agent at Fort Armstrong.* 2 vols. Cleveland, OH: Arthur H. Clark, 1912.

Blegen, Theodore C. "Armistice and War on the Minnesota Frontier." *Minnesota History* 24 (1943): 11–25.

———. *Minnesota: A History of the State.* Minneapolis: University of Minnesota Press, [1963] 1975.

———. "Two Missionaries in the Sioux Country; The Narrative of Samuel Pond." *Minnesota History* 21 (1940): 15–32, 158–75, 272–83.

Boutwell, William T. "Journal of Tour with H. R. Schoolcraft." Unpublished, 1838. Grace Lee Nute Papers. MHS Archives.

———. "Schoolcraft's Exploring Tour of 1832." Vol. 1. Received July 2, 1833. Grace Lee Nute Papers. MHS Archives. Published in *Collections of the Minnesota Historical Society* 1 (1902): 121–40.

Bray, Edmund C., and Martha Coleman Bray. *Joseph N. Nicollet on the Plains and Prairies: The Expeditions of 1838–39 with Journals, Letters, and Notes on the Dakota Indians.* St. Paul: MHS Press, 1976.

Bray, Martha Coleman. *The Journals of Joseph N. Nicollet: A Scientist on the Mississippi Headwaters with Notes on Indian Life, 1836–37.* Translated by André Fertey. St. Paul: MHS Press, 1970.

Brown, Jennifer S. H., and Elizabeth Vibert. *Reading Beyond Words: Contexts for Native History.* Orchard Park, NJ: Broadview, 1996.

Brunson, Alfred. "Early History of Wisconsin." *Collections of the State Historical Society of Wisconsin* (hereinafter *Collections of the SHSW*) 4 (1859): 229–51.

———. "Sketch of Hole-in-the-Day." *Collections of the SHSW* 5 (1869): 387–401.

———. *A Western Pioneer or Incidents of the Life and Times of Rev. Alfred Brunson.* Cincinnati, OH: Hitchcock and Walden, 1879.

Buck, Daniel. *Indian Outbreaks.* Minneapolis, MN: Ross and Haines, 1965.

Burpee, Lawrence J. *Journals and Letters of Pierre Gaultier de Varennes de La Vérendrye and His Sons with Correspondence between the Governors of Canada and the French Court, Touching the Search for the Western Sea.* Toronto: Champlain Society, 1968.

Calloway, Colin G. *The American Revolution in Indian Country: Crisis and Diversity in Native American Communities.* New York: Cambridge University Press, 1995.

———. *Crown and Calumet: British-Indian Relations, 1783–1815.* Norman: University of Oklahoma Press, 1987.

———. *First Peoples: A Documentary Survey of American Indian History.* Boston: Bedford-St. Martin's Press, 2004.

———. *New Directions in American History.* Norman: University of Oklahoma Press, 1988.

———. *New Worlds for All: Indians, Europeans, and the Remaking of Early America.* Baltimore, MD: Johns Hopkins University Press, 1997.

———. *One Vast Winter Count: The Native American West before Lewis and Clark.* Lincoln: University of Nebraska Press, 2003.

Carley, Kenneth. *The Dakota War of 1862.* St. Paul: MHS Press, 2001. (Reprint of *The Sioux Uprising of 1862.* St. Paul: MHS Press, 1976.)

Catlin, George. *Letters and Notes on the Manners, Customs, and Conditions of North American Indians.* 2 vols. New York: Dover Publications, 1973.

Cathcart, Rebecca. "A Sheaf of Remembrances," *Collections of the MHS* 15 (1915): 515–52.

Champagne, Antonio. "Grand Rapids: An Old Historical Spot." Lecture, Manitoba Historical Society, November 20, 1962. MHS Archives.

Champe, John L. "Yankton Chronology." *Sioux Indian III.* New York: Garland Publishing, 1974.

Chute, Janet. *The Legacy of Shingwaukonse: A Century of Native Leadership.* Toronto: University of Toronto Press, 1998.

Clark, James. "Ayaabadak Ishkode." Edited by Anton Treuer. *Oshkaabewis Native Journal* 5 (Fall 1998): 14–17.

———. "Baa Baa Makade-maanishtaanish." Edited by Anton Treuer. *Oshkaabewis Native Journal* 5 (Fall 1998): 30–31.

———. "Dibaakonigewinini Miinawaa Anishinaabe." Edited by Anton Treuer. *Oshkaabewis Native Journal* 5 (Fall 1998): 8–9.

———. "Gaa-ina'oonind Anishinaabe." Edited by Anton Treuer. *Oshkaabewis Native Journal* 5 (Fall 1998): 54–59.

———. "Gaazhagens Minnawaa Naazhaabii'igan." Edited by Anton Treuer. *Oshkaabewis Native Journal* 5 (Fall 1998): 32–33.

———. "Gibaakwa'igan Dazhi-anishinaabeg." Edited by Anton Treuer. *Oshkaabewis Native Journal* 5 (Fall 1998): 24–29.

———. "Gidinwewininaan." Edited by Anton Treuer. *Oshkaabewis Native Journal* 5 (Fall 1998): 42–49.

———. "Ikwabin." Edited by Anton Treuer. *Oshkaabewis Native Journal* 5 (Fall 1998): 40–41.

———. "Inday." Edited by Anton Treuer. *Oshkaabewis Native Journal* 5 (Fall 1998): 18–23.

———. "Jiigibiig Nenaandago-ziibiing." Edited by Anton Treuer. *Oshkaabewis Native Journal* 5 (Fall 1998): 34–39.

———. "Mawadishiwewin." Edited by Anton Treuer. *Oshkaabewis Native Journal* 5 (Fall 1998): 50–53.

———. "Mawinzowin." Edited by Anton Treuer. *Oshkaabewis Native Journal* 5 (Fall 1998): 10–13.

Clark, James, and Raining Boyd. "Naawi-giizis Miinawaa Gimiwan." Edited by Anton Treuer. *Oshkaabewis Native Journal* 6 (Spring/Fall 2003): 32–37.

Clark, Julius T. "Reminiscences of the Chippewa Chief, Hole-in-the-Day." *Collections of the SHSW* 5 (1869): 378–86.

Clark, William, and Lewis Cass. "Journal of Proceedings at Prairie du Chien." Office of Indian Affairs, August 1825. Office of Indian Affairs, Segregated File. National Archives.

Clayton, James L. "The Impact of Traders' Claims on the American Fur Trade." In David M. Ellis, ed. *The Frontier in American Development: Essays in Honor of Paul Wallace Gates.* Ithaca. NY: Cornell University Press, 1969.

Cleland, Charles E. "The 1842 Treaty of La Pointe," 36–37. In James M. McClurken, ed. *Fish in the Lakes, Wild Rice, and Game in Abundance: Testimony on Behalf of the Mille Lacs Ojibwe Hunting and Fishing Rights.* East Lansing: Michigan State University Press, 2000.

———. "The Mille Lacs Chippewa in the 1850s: A Rise to Prominence." In James M. McClurken, ed. *Fish in the Lakes, Wild Rice, and Game in Abundance: Testimony on Behalf of the Mille Lacs Ojibwe Hunting and Fishing Rights.* East Lansing: Michigan State University Press, 2000.

———. *Rites of Conquest: The History and Culture of Michigan's Native Americans.* Ann Arbor: University of Michigan Press, 1992.

Clifton, James A. *The Prairie People: Continuity and Change in Potawatomi Indian Culture.* Lawrence, KS: Regents Press, 1977.

Coleman, Bernard, Ellen Frogner, and Estelle Eich. *Ojibwa Myths and Legends.* Minneapolis, MN: Ross and Haines, 1962.

Coleman, Bernard, Verona LaBud, and John Humphrey. *Old Crow Wing, History of a Village.* Minnesota: self-published, 1967.

————. *Where the Water Stops: Fond du Lac Reservation.* Duluth, MN: College of St. Scholastica, 1967.

Copway, George. *Life, Letters and Speeches.* Lincoln: University of Nebraska Press, 1997. Originally published in 1847 as *The Life, History and Travels of Kah-ge-ga-gah-bowh,* expanded and republished in 1850 as *The Life, Letters and Speeches of Kah-ge-ga-gah-bowh or G. Copway, Chief Ojibway Nation.* New York: S. W. Benedict, 1850.

————. *The Traditional History and Characteristic Sketches of the Ojibway Nation.* London: Charles Gilpin, 1850. Reprinted in the United States as *Indian Life and Indian History, by an Indian Author: Embracing the Traditions of the North American Indians Regarding Themselves, Particularly of That Most Important of All the Tribes, the Ojibways.* Boston: Albert Cosby and Company, 1858.

Coues, Elliott. *The Expeditions of Zebulon Montgomery Pike.* 2 vols. New York: Dover Publications, 1987.

————. *New Light on the Early History of the Greater Northwest: The Manuscript Journals of Alexander Henry, Fur Trader of the Northwest Company and David Thompson, Official Geographer and Explorer of the Same Company, 1799–1814.* 3 vols. New York: Francis P. Harper, 1897. Reprinted in two volumes by Ross and Haines, 1965.

Cox, Hank H. *Lincoln and the Sioux Uprising of 1862.* Nashville, TN: Cumberland House, 2005.

Cox, Isaac J. *The Journeys of Robert Cavelier de LaSalle.* 2 vols. New York: A. S. Barnes, 1905.

Curot, Michel. "A Wisconsin Fur-Trader's Journal, 1803–1804." *Collections of the SHSW* 20 (1911): 396–471.

Daniels, Asa W. "Reminiscences of Little Crow." *Collections of the MHS* 12 (1908): 513–30.

Danziger, Edmund Jefferson, Jr. *The Chippewas of Lake Superior.* Norman: University of Oklahoma Press, 1979.

Deloria, Philip. *Playing Indian.* New Haven, CT: Yale University Press, 1998.

Deloria, Vine. *Custer Died for Your Sins.* New York: Macmillan, 1969.

Denevan, William M. *The Native Population of the Americas in 1492.* Madison: University of Wisconsin Press, 1992.

Densmore, Frances. *Chippewa Customs.* St. Paul: MHS Press, 1979.

————. *Chippewa Music.* 2 vols. Minneapolis, MN: Ross and Haines, 1973.

————. *How Indians Use Wild Plants for Food, Medicine and Crafts.* New York: Dover Publications, 1974.

Dewdney, Sydney. *The Sacred Scrolls of the Southern Ojibway.* Toronto: University of Toronto Press, 1975.

Diamond, Jared. "Speaking with a Single Tongue." *Discover* (February 1993): 78–85.

Dickason, Olive Patricia. *Canada's First Nations: A History of Founding Peoples from Earliest Times.* Norman: University of Oklahoma Press, 1992.

————. *The Myth of the Savage and the Beginnings of French Colonialism in the Americas.* Edmonton: University of Alberta Press, 1984.

Diedrich, Mark. "Chief Hole-in-the-Day and the Chippewa Disturbance: A Reappraisal." *Minnesota History* 50 (Spring 1989):193–203.

————. *The Chiefs Hole-In-The-Day of the Mississippi Chippewa.* Rochester, MN: Coyote Books, 1986.

————. *Dakota Oratory: Great Moments in the Recorded Speech of the Eastern Sioux, 1695–1874.* Rochester, MN: Coyote Books, 1989.

————. *Famous Chiefs of the Eastern Sioux.* Rochester, MN: Coyote Books, 1987.

————. *Ojibway Oratory: Great Moments in the Recorded Speech of the Chippewa, 1695–1889.* Rochester, MN: Coyote Books, 1989.

"Documents of an Investigation of the White Earth Reservation." Records of the Department of the Interior, Commissioner of Indian Affairs. Classified Files: White Earth 83129–1911–211. National Archives. Also cataloged as "Records of Investigation of White Earth Mixed Bloods, 1911–1915," MHS Archives.

Doty, James D. "Northern Wisconsin in 1820." *Collections of the SHSW* 7 (1876): 195–206.
———. "Official Journal, 1820: Expedition with Cass and Schoolcraft." *Collections of the SHSW* 8 (1895): 163–246.
Dowd, Gregory E. *A Spirited Resistance: The North American Indian Struggle for Unity, 1745–1815.* Baltimore, MD: Johns Hopkins University Press, 1992.
Draper, Lyman C. "A Note on Hole-in-the-Day." *Collections of the SHSW* 5 (1868): 400–401.
———. "Additional Note on Hole-in-the-Day." *Collections of the SHSW* 5 (1868): 408–9.
Dunn, James Taylor. *The St. Croix: Midwest Border River.* St. Paul: MHS Press, 1979.
Dunning, R. W. *Social and Economic Change among the Northern Ojibwa.* Toronto: University of Toronto Press, 1959.
Eagle, Melvin. "Gekendaasojig." Edited by Anton Treuer. *Oshkaabewis Native Journal* 5 (Spring 1998): 8–86.
"Early Days at Fort Snelling." *Collections of the MHS* 1 (1902): 345–49.
Eastman, Charles A. *Indian Heroes and Great Chieftains.* Boston: Little, Brown and Company, 1918.
Eastman, Mary. *Dahcotah; or, Life and Legends of the Sioux around Fort Snelling.* Minneapolis, MN: Ross and Haines, 1962.
Ebbott, Elizabeth. *Indians in Minnesota.* Minneapolis: University of Minnesota Press, 1985.
Eby, Cecil. *That Disgraceful Affair, the Black Hawk War.* New York: W. W. Norton and Co., 1973.
Echo-Hawk, Roger. "Ancient History in the New World: Integrating Oral Traditions and Archaeology in Deep Time." *American Antiquity* 65 (April 2000): 267–90.
Edmunds, Russell David. *The Potawatomis: Keepers of the Fire.* Norman: University of Oklahoma, 1978.
Evangelical Society of Missions of Lausanne. "Report of June 11, 1835: The Mission of Canada." Grace Lee Nute Papers. MHS Archives.
Ewers, John C. "Ethnological Report on the Chippewa Cree Tribe of the Rocky Boy Reservation and the Little Shell Band of Indians." *Chippewa Indians VI.* Indian Claims Commission. New York: Garland Publishing, 1974.
Featherstonhaugh, George W. *A Canoe Voyage up the Minnay Sotor with an Account of the Lead and Copper Deposits in Wisconsin; of the Gold Region in the Cherokee Country; and Sketches of Popular Manners.* 2 vols. St. Paul: MHS Press, 1970.
Fisher, Emma. "Gii-agaashiinyiyaan." Edited by Anton Treuer. *Oshkaabewis Native Journal* 3 (Spring 1996): 51.
———. "Gii-kikinoo'amaagoziyaan." Edited by Anton Treuer. *Oshkaabewis Native Journal* 3 (Spring 1996): 63–64.
———. "Gii-kinjiba'iweyaan." Edited by Anton Treuer. *Oshkaabewis Native Journal* 3 (Spring 1996): 79–80.
———. "Indayag." Edited by Anton Treuer. *Oshkaabewis Native Journal* 2 (Fall 1995): 75–77.
———. "Indinawemaaganag." Edited by Anton Treuer. *Oshkaabewis Native Journal* 4 (Fall 1997): 52–53.
Fixico, Donald. *Rethinking American Indian History.* Albuquerque: University of New Mexico Press, 1997.
Flandrau, Charles E. "Journal of a Voyage from Chippewa Agency to the Source of the Mississippi River." Charles Eugene Flandrau Family Papers. Vol. 23. MHS Archives.
Folwell, William W. *A History of Minnesota.* 4 vols. St. Paul: MHS Press, 1956.
Foss, Rose. "Aadizookewin." Edited by Gilles Delisle. *Oshkaabewis Native Journal* 3 (Spring 1996): 54–55.
———. "Baapaase." Edited by Gilles Delisle. *Oshkaabewis Native Journal* 3 (Spring 1996): 60–61.
———. "Gookooko'oo Miinawaa Ikwezens." Edited by Gilles Delisle. *Oshkaabewis Native Journal* 3 (Spring 1996): 84–87.

———. "Ikwe Miinawaa Ogwizisan." Edited by Gilles Delisle. *Oshkaabewis Native Journal* 3 (Spring 1996): 72–73.

———. "Ishkode Gii-kimooding." Edited by Gilles Delisle. *Oshkaabewis Native Journal* 4 (Spring 1997): 56–58.

———. "Wenabozho Gii-ondaadizid." Edited by Gilles Delisle. *Oshkaabewis Native Journal* 4 (Spring 1997): 51–53.

———. "Wenabozho Miinawaa Bine." Edited by Gilles Delisle. *Oshkaabewis Native Journal* 4 (Spring 1997): 43–44.

———. "Wenabozho Miinawaa Onibwaakaaminan." Edited by Gilles Delisle. *Oshkaabewis Native Journal* 4 (Spring 1997): 33–34.

"The Fox and Ojibwa War." *Collections of the MHS* 1 (1902): 283–85.

Fritzen, John. "The History of Fond du Lac and Jay Cooke State Park." Unpublished, 1964. MHS Archives.

Gates, Charles M. *Five Fur Traders of the Northwest, Being the Narrative of Peter Pond and the Diaries of John Macdonell, Archibald N. McLeod, Hugh Faries, and Thomas Connor.* St. Paul: MHS Press, 1933.

Gibbs, Anna C. "Aaniing Wenji-mawid Maang." Edited by Anton Treuer. *Oshkaabewis Native Journal* 7 (Spring 2010): 72–75.

———. "Ajidamoo Miinawaa Aandegwag." Edited by Anton Treuer. *Oshkaabewis Native Journal* 7 (Spring 2010): 28–29.

———. "Akiwenzii Miinawaa Gaag." Edited by Anton Treuer. *Oshkaabewis Native Journal* 7 (Spring 2010): 42–43.

———. "Anishinaabe-waaboowayaan." Edited by Anton Treuer. *Oshkaabewis Native Journal* 7 (Spring 2010): 76–77.

———. "Bashkwegino-makizin Waabigwaniins." Edited by Anton Treuer. *Oshkaabewis Native Journal* 7 (Spring 2010): 86–89.

———. "Enaadizookaazod Mikinaak." Edited by Anton Treuer. *Oshkaabewis Native Journal* 7 (Spring 2010): 82–85.

———. "Ezhi-ganoonad Gibiibiiyensim Anishinaabemong." Edited by Anton Treuer. *Oshkaabewis Native Journal* 7 (Spring 2010): 110–19.

———. "Gaa-ondinang Dakwaanowed Makwa." Edited by Anton Treuer. *Oshkaabewis Native Journal* 7 (Spring 2010): 68–71.

———. "Gaa-ondinang Mikinaak Odashwaan Imaa Obikwanaang." Edited by Anton Treuer. *Oshkaabewis Native Journal* 7 (Spring 2010): 34–37.

———. "Gaa-ondinang Ojiishigid Wiigwaasi-mitig." Edited by Anton Treuer. *Oshkaabewis Native Journal* 7 (Spring 2010): 66–67.

———. "Gaag Miinawaa Wiikenh." Edited by Anton Treuer. *Oshkaabewis Native Journal* 7 (Spring 2010): 24–27.

———. "Gii-wiindaawasod awe Waawaabiganoojiinh." Edited by Anton Treuer. *Oshkaabewis Native Journal* 7 (Spring 2010): 58–59.

———. "Ma'iingan Miinawaa Animosh." Edited by Anton Treuer. *Oshkaabewis Native Journal* 7 (Spring 2010): 96–99.

———. "Migizi." Edited by Anton Treuer. *Oshkaabewis Native Journal* 7 (Spring 2010): 104–9.

———. "Na'aangabiyaan Niga-waaboozagoodoo." Edited by Anton Treuer. *Oshkaabewis Native Journal* 7 (Spring 2010): 48–49.

———. "Nenabozho Miinawaa Ditibidaabaan." Edited by Anton Treuer. *Oshkaabewis Native Journal* 7 (Spring 2010): 38–41.

———. "Nenabozho Miinawaa Gaag." Edited by Anton Treuer. *Oshkaabewis Native Journal* 7 (Spring 2010): 44–45.

———. "Nenabozho Miinawaa Ojiiwaaman." Edited by Anton Treuer. *Oshkaabewis Native Journal* 7 (Spring 2010): 50–57.

——. "Nitam Memengwaag." Edited by Anton Treuer. *Oshkaabewis Native Journal* 7 (Spring 2010): 90–93.

——. "Nursery Rhymes." Edited by Anton Treuer. *Oshkaabewis Native Journal* 7 (Spring 2010): 102–3.

——. "Onaabani-giizis: Miigaadiwaad Ziigwan Miinawaa Biboon." Edited by Anton Treuer. *Oshkaabewis Native Journal* 7 (Spring 2010): 94–95.

——. "Waabooz Gaa-ondinang Gii-kinwaanig Otawagan." Edited by Anton Treuer. *Oshkaabewis Native Journal* 7 (Spring 2010): 62–65.

——. "Wenji-anishinaabewiyang." Edited by Anton Treuer. *Oshkaabewis Native Journal* 7 (Spring 2010): 30–33.

——. "Wenji-beshizhid Agongos." Edited by Anton Treuer. *Oshkaabewis Native Journal* 7 (Spring 2010): 78–81.

——. "Wenji-waabishkizid a'aw Zhingos." Edited by Anton Treuer. *Oshkaabewis Native Journal* 7 (Spring 2010): 60–61.

——. "Wiigwaasi-jiimaan Nagamon." Edited by Anton Treuer. *Oshkaabewis Native Journal* 7 (Spring 2010): 100–101.

——. "Ziinzibaakwad." Edited by Anton Treuer. *Oshkaabewis Native Journal* 7 (Spring 2010): 46–47.

Gibson, Arrell M. *The American Indian: Prehistory to the Present.* Lexington, MA: D. C. Heath, 1980.

——. *Harlow's Oklahoma History.* Norman, OK: Harlow, 1972.

Gilfillan, J. A. "Ne-bun-esh-kunk, the Ideal Soldier." In *Red Man.* Carlisle Indian Industrial School (January 1913).

Gilman, Carolyn. *The Grand Portage Story.* St. Paul: MHS Press, 1992.

Gilman, Rhoda R., Carolyn Gilman, and Deborah M. Stultz. *The Red River Trails: Oxcart Route between St. Paul and the Selkirk Settlement, 1820–1870.* St. Paul: MHS Press, 1979.

Goggleye, George, Sr. "Anishinaabemowin." Edited by Anton Treuer. *Oshkaabewis Native Journal* 6 (Spring/Fall 2003): 22–25.

Goiffon, Joseph. "Autobiography: 1824–25." Unpublished. Translated by Charlotte Huot. Grace Lee Nute Papers. MHS Archives.

Grant, Peter. "The Saulteux Indians about 1804." In L. R. Masson, ed., *Les Bourgeois de la Compagnie du Nord-Ouest.* 2 vols. Quebec: Imprimerie, 1890.

Greenblatt, Stephen. *Marvelous Possessions: The Wonder of the New World.* Chicago: University of Chicago Press, 1991.

Grim, John A. *The Shaman: Patterns of Religious Healing among the Ojibway Indians.* Norman: University of Oklahoma Press, 1983.

Hagan, William T. *The Sac and Fox Indians.* Norman: University of Oklahoma Press, 1989.

Hall, Stephen P. "The Hole-in-the-Day Encounter." *Minnesota Archeologist* 36 (1977): 77–96.

Hall, Stephen P., and William T. Boutwell. "Report to the Prudential Committee of the American Board for Foreign Missions." February 7, 1833. Grace Lee Nute Papers, MHS Archives.

Headbird, Scott. "Waawaabiganoojiish." Edited by Anton Treuer. *Oshkaabewis Native Journal* 2 (Fall 1995): 81–82.

Henry, Alexander. *Travels and Adventures in Canada and the Indian Territories between the Years 1760 and 1776.* Ann Arbor, MI: University Microfilms, [1809] 1966.

Henry, Alexander, and David Thompson. *New Light on the Early History of the Greater Northwest.* Edited by Elliott Coues. New York: Harper, 1897.

Hexom, Charles Philip. *Indian History of Winneshiek County.* Decorah, IA: A. K. Bailey and Son, 1913.

Hickerson, Harold. *The Chippewa and Their Neighbors: A Study in Ethnohistory.* Prospect Heights, IL: Waveland Press, [1970] 1988.

———. "Ethnohistory of Chippewa in Central Minnesota." In *Chippewa Indians IV.* Indian Claims Commission. New York: Garland Publishing, 1974.

———. "Ethnohistory of Chippewa of Lake Superior." In *Chippewa Indians III.* Indian Claims Commission. New York: Garland Publishing, 1974.

———. "The Genesis of a Trading Post Band: The Pembina Chippewa." *Ethnohistory* 3 (1956): 289–345.

———. "Land Tenure of the Rainy Lake Chippewa at the Beginning of the 19th Century." *Smithsonian Contributions to Anthropology* 2 (1967).

———. "Mdewakanton Band of Sioux Indians." In *Sioux Indians I.* Indian Claims Commission. New York: Garland Publishing Co., 1974.

———. *The Southwestern Chippewa: An Ethnohistorical Study.* Memoir 92. American Anthropological Association, 1962.

Hilger, Inez. M. *Chippewa Child Life and Its Cultural Background.* St. Paul: MHS Press, 1992.

Hill, Alfred J. "The Geography of Perrot; So Far as It Relates to Minnesota and the Regions Immediately Adjacent." *Collections of the MHS* 2 (1860–67): 200–15.

Holcombe, Return I., and Lucius Hubbard. *Minnesota in Three Centuries, 1655–1908.* 2 vols. Mankato: Publishing Society of Minnesota, 1908.

Holcombe, Theodore I. *An Apostle of the Wilderness.* New York: Thomas Whittaker, 1903.

Houghton, Douglass. Diary: June 23–August 25, 1832. MHS Archives.

Howard, James H. *The Canadian Sioux.* Lincoln: University of Nebraska Press, 1984.

———. *The Plains-Ojibwa or Bungi.* Reprints in *Anthropology.* Vol. 7. Vermillion: University of South Dakota Press, 1977.

Hoxie, Frederick E. *American Nations: Encounters in Indian Country, 1850 to the Present.* Lincoln: University of Nebraska Press, 1984.

———. *A Final Promise: The Campaign to Assimilate the Indians, 1880–1920.* New York: Routledge, 2001.

Hoxie, Frederick E., and Harvey Markowitz. *Native Americans: An Annotated Bibliography.* Pasadena, CA: Salem Press, 1991.

Hoxie, Frederick E., Ronald Hoffman, and Peter J. Albert, eds. *Native Americans and the Early Republic.* Charlottesville: United States Capitol History Society–University Press of Virginia, 1999.

Hrdlicka, Ales. "Anthropology of the Chippewa." *Holes Anniversary Volume: Anthropological Essays.* Washington, DC: 1916.

Hughes, Thomas. *Indian Chiefs of Southern Minnesota.* Minneapolis, MN: Ross and Haines, 1969.

Hurt, Wesley R. "Dakota Sioux Indians." *Sioux Indians II.* New York: Garland Publishing, 1974.

Indian Claims Commission. "Commission Findings on the Chippewa Indians." *Chippewa Indians VII.* New York: Garland Publishing, 1974.

———. "Commission Findings on the Sioux Indians." *Sioux Indians IV.* New York: Garland Publishing, 1974.

Jackson, Donald. *Black Hawk: An Autobiography.* Urbana: University of Illinois, 1964.

Jackson, Leroy. *Enmegahbowh—A Chippewa Missionary.* Bismarck: North Dakota Historical Collections, 1908.

Jackson, Susan. "Aabadak Waaboozoo-nagwaaganeyaab." Edited by Anton Treuer. *Oshkaabewis Native Journal* 4 (Spring 1997): 38–41.

———. "Chi-achaabaan Naanaagadawendamaan." Edited by Anton Treuer. *Oshkaabewis Native Journal* 4 (Spring 1997): 24–29.

Jacobs, Sue-Ellen, Wesley Thomas, and Sabine Lang. *Two Spirit People: Native American Gender Identity, Sexuality, and Spirituality.* Urbana: University of Illinois Press, 1997.

Jacobs, Wilbur R. *Dispossessing the American Indian: Indians and Whites on the Colonial Frontier.* New York: Scribner, 1972.

————. *Wilderness Politics and Indian Gifts: The North Carolina Frontier, 1748–1763.* Lincoln: University of Nebraska Press, 1950.

James, Edwin, ed. *A Narrative of the Captivity and Adventures of John Tanner during Thirty Years Residence among the Indians in the Interior of North America.* London: Carvill, 1830. Reprint, Minneapolis, MN: Ross and Haines, 1956.

Jameson, Anna. *Winter Studies and Summer Rambles in Canada.* 3 vols. New York: Wiley and Putnam, 1839.

Jenks, Albert E. "The Wild Rice Gatherers of the Upper Great Lakes: A Study in American Primitive Economics." *Nineteenth Annual Report of the Bureau of American Ethnology* 2 (1897–98): 1013–137. Washington, DC: GPO, 1900.

Johnson, John. *Enmegahbowh's Story: An Account of the Disturbances of the Chippewa Indians at Gull Lake in 1857 and 1862 and Their Removal in 1868.* Minneapolis, MN, 1904.

Johnston, Basil. *Ojibway Ceremonies.* Lincoln: University of Nebraska Press, 1990.

————. *Ojibway Heritage.* Lincoln: University of Nebraska Press, 1990.

Jones, Dennis. "The Etymology of Anishinaabe." *Oshkaabewis Native Journal* 2 (Fall 1995): 45–46.

Jourdain, Robert. "Mezinaanakwad." Edited by Anton Treuer. *Oshkaabewis Native Journal* 6 (Spring/Fall 2003): 6–15.

Kane, Lucile M., June D. Holmquist, and Carolyn Gilman. *The Northern Expeditions of Stephen H. Long: The Journals of 1817 and 1823 and Related Documents.* St. Paul: MHS Press, 1978.

Kappler, Charles J. *Laws and Treaties.* 2 vols. Washington, DC: GPO, 1904.

Keating, William H. *Narrative of an Expedition to the Source of the St. Peters River.* 2 vols. London: George B. Whittaker, 1825.

Keesing, Roger M. *Kin Groups and Social Structure.* New York: Holt, Rinehart, and Winston, 1975.

Kegg, Maude. "Nookomis Gaa-inaajimotawid." *Oshkaabewis Native Journal* 1 (1990).

————. *Portage Lake: Memories of an Ojibwe Childhood.* Edmonton: University of Alberta Press, 1991.

Kellogg, Louise Phelps. *The British Regime in Wisconsin and the Old Northwest.* Madison: State Historical Society of Wisconsin Press, 1935.

————. *Early Narratives of the Northwest, 1634–1699.* New York: Charles Scribner's Sons, 1917.

————. *The French Regime in Wisconsin and the Northwest.* Madison: State Historical Society of Wisconsin Press, 1925.

Kessing, Felix M. *The Menomini Indians of Wisconsin: A Study of Three Centuries of Cultural Contact and Change.* Madison: University of Wisconsin Press, 1987.

Kinietz, Vernon W. *Chippewa Village.* Bloomfield, MI: Cranbrook Press, 1947.

————. *The Indians of the Western Great Lakes, 1615–1750.* Ann Arbor: University of Michigan Press, 1940. Repaginated and reprinted 1965, 1972.

Kinzie, Juliette. *Wau-Bun, the Early Days in the Northwest.* Chicago: Lakeside Press, 1932.

Knuth, Helen E. "Economic and Historical Background of Northeastern Minnesota Lands: Chippewa Indian of Lake Superior." *Chippewa Indian III.* Indian Claims Commission. New York: Garland Publishing, 1974.

Kohl, Johann Georg. *Kitchi-Gami: Life among the Lake Superior Ojibway.* St. Paul: MHS Press, 1985 (1860).

Kugel, Rebecca. *To Be the Main Leaders of Our People: A History of Minnesota Ojibwe Politics, 1825–1898.* East Lansing: Michigan State University Press, 1998.

Kvasnicka, Robert M. "From Wilderness to Washington — and Back Again: The Story of the Chippewa Delegation of 1855." *Kansas Quarterly* 3 (Fall 1971): 56–63.

————. *Hole-in-the-Day.* Milwaukee, WI: Raintree, 1990.

———. "The Timber Is Mine," *Prologue: The Journal of the National Archives* 3 (Spring 1971): 21–26.

Landes, Ruth. *Ojibwa Sociology.* New York: Columbia University Press, 1937.

Lanman, Charles. *A Summer in the Wilderness.* New York: Appleton, 1847.

Larpenteur, Auguste L. "Recollections of the City and People of St. Paul, 1843–1898." *Collections of the MHS* 9 (1901): 363–94.

Lewis, Henry. *The Valley of the Mississippi Illustrated.* Translated by Hermina Poatgieter. St. Paul: MHS Press, 1967.

Longfellow, Henry Wadsworth. *Poems and Other Writings.* New York: Library of America, 2000.

Losure, Mary. "Saving Ojibwe." National Public Radio broadcast, December 26, 1996.

Lund, Duane R. *Lake of the Woods: Yesterday and Today.* Staples, MN: Nordell Graphic Communications, 1975.

———. *Lake of the Woods II: Featuring Translations of Pierre La Vérendrye's Diaries and Father Alneau's Letters.* Staples, MN: Nordell Graphic Communications, 1984.

———. *Minnesota's Chief Flat Mouth of Leech Lake.* Staples, MN: Nordell Graphic Communications, 1983.

———. *The North Shore of Lake Superior: Yesterday and Today.* Staples, MN: Nordell Graphic Communications, 1993.

———. *Our Historic Boundary Waters: From Lake Superior to Lake of the Woods.* Staples, MN: Nordell Graphic Communications, 1980.

———. *Tales of Four Lakes: Leech Lake, Gull Lake, Mille Lacs Lake, the Red Lakes, and the Crow Wing River.* Staples, MN: Nordell Graphic Communications, 1977.

Lynd, James W. "History of the Dakotas." *Collections of the MHS* 2 (1860–67): 143–75.

Mackenzie, Alexander. *Voyages from Montreal on the River St. Laurence through the Continent of North America to the Pacific Oceans in the Years 1789 and 1793 with a Preliminary Account of the Rise, Progress, and Present State of the Fur Trade of That Country.* Rutland, VT: Charles E. Tuttle, 1971.

Malhiot, Francois V. "A Wisconsin Fur-Trader's Journal, 1804–1805." *Collections of the SHSW* 19 (1910): 163–233.

Mancall, Peter C., and James H. Merrell. *American Encounters: Natives and Newcomers from European Contact to Indian Removal, 1500–1850.* New York: Routledge, 2000.

Margry, P. *Découvertes et Établissements des Francais dans l'Ouest et dans le Sud de l'Amérique Septentrionale, 1614–1754: Mémoires et Documents Originaux.* 6 vols. Paris, 1886.

Martin, Calvin. *The American Indian and the Problem of History.* New York: Oxford University Press, 1987.

———. *Keepers of the Game: Indian-Animal Relationships and the Fur Trade.* Berkeley: University of California Press, 1978.

Mason, Philip P. *Schoolcraft's Expedition to Lake Itasca: The Discovery of the Source of the Mississippi.* East Lansing: Michigan State University Press, 1993.

———. *Schoolcraft's Ojibwa Lodge Stories: Life on the Lake Superior Frontier.* East Lansing: Michigan State University Press, 1997.

Masson, L. R. *Les Bourgeois de la Compagnie du Nord-Ouest: Récits de Voyages, Lettres et Rapports Inédits Relatifs au Nord-Ouest Canadien.* 2 vols. New York: Antiquarian Press, 1960.

McCann, Helen. "The Cass Lake Indian Mission." November 1937. Grace Lee Nute Papers. MHS Archives.

McClurken, James M., ed. *Fish in the Lakes, Wild Rice and Game in Abundance: Testimony on Behalf of the Mille Lacs Ojibwe Hunting and Fishing Rights.* East Lansing: Michigan State University Press, 2000.

McDonald, T. H. *Exploring the Northwest Territory: Sir Alexander Mackenzie's Journal of a Voyage by Bark Canoe from Lake Athabasca to the Pacific Ocean in the Summer of 1789.* Norman: University of Oklahoma Press, 1966.

McKenney, Thomas L. *History of Indian Tribes of North America: With Biographical Sketches and Anecdotes of the Principal Chiefs.* 3 vols. Philadelphia: E.C. Biddle, 1836–44.

———. *Memoirs, Official and Personal: Thomas L. McKenney.* Lincoln: University of Nebraska Press, 1973. Originally published as McKenney, Thomas L. *Memoirs, Official and Personal: With Sketches of Travels Among the Northern and Southern Indians; Embracing a War Excursion, and Descriptions of Scenes Along the Western Borders.* 2 vols. New York: Paine and Burgess, 1846.

———. *Sketches of a Tour to the Lakes, of the Character and Customs of the Chippeway Indians and of Incidents Connected with the Treaty of Fond du Lac.* Minneapolis, MN: Ross and Haines, 1959. Originally published as McKenney, Thomas L. *Sketches of a Tour of the Lakes, of the Character and Customs of the Chippeway Indians, and of Incidents Connected with the Treaty of Fond du Lac.* Baltimore, MD: Fielding Lucas, 1827.

McLachlan, Honora C. "The Cadotte Family and the Fur Trade of the Northwest, 1760–1810." Undated. Grace Lee Nute Papers. MHS Archives.

McNally, Michael D. *Ojibwe Singers: Hymns, Grief, and a Native Culture in Motion.* New York: Oxford University Press, 2000.

Merrell, James H. *The Indians' New World: Catawbas and Their Neighbors from European Contact through the Era of Removal.* Chapel Hill: University of North Carolina Press, 1989.

Meyer, Melissa L. *The White Earth Tragedy: Ethnicity and Dispossession at a Minnesota Anishinaabe Reservation, 1889–1920.* Lincoln: University of Nebraska Press, 1994.

Meyer, Roy W. *History of the Santee Sioux: United States Indian Policy on Trial.* Lincoln: University of Nebraska Press, 1993.

Military Order of the Loyal Legion of the United States and Edward D. Neill. *Glimpses of the Nation's Struggle. [1st]-6th Series. Papers read before the Minnesota commandery of the military order of the loyal legion of the United States [1887]-1903/08.* St. Paul. MN: Commandery of the military order, 1909.

Minnesota in the Civil and Indian Wars, 1861–1865. 2 vols. St. Paul: Minnesota State Board of Commissioners, 1890.

Mittelholtz, Erwin F., and Rose Graves. *Historical Review of the Red Lake Indian Reservation: Centennial Souvenir Commemorating a Century of Progress, 1858–1958.* Bemidji, MN: General Council of the Red Lake Band of Chippewa Indians and the Beltrami County Historical Society, 1957.

Monjeau-Marz, Corinne L. *The Dakota Indian Internment at Fort Snelling, 1862–1864.* St. Paul, MN: Prairie Smoke Press, 2005.

Moose, Leonard L., et al. *Aaniin Ekidong: Ojibwe Vocabulary Project.* St. Paul: Minnesota Humanities Center, 2009.

Morrison, William. "Who Discovered Itasca Lake?" *Collections of the MHS* 1 (1902): 343–44.

Mosay, Archie. "Apane Anishinaabe Ogaganoonaan Manidoon." Edited by Anton Treuer. *Oshkaabewis Native Journal* 3 (Fall 1996): 20–25.

———. "Gaa-amwaawaad Animoonsan." Edited by Anton Treuer. *Oshkaabewis Native Journal* 3 (Fall 1996): 58–61.

———. "Gaa-pazhiba'wid Niijanishinaabe." Edited by Anton Treuer. *Oshkaabewis Native Journal* 3 (Fall 1996): 54–57.

———. "Gaa-tazhi-ondaadiziyaang." Edited by Anton Treuer. *Oshkaabewis Native Journal* 3 (Fall 1996): 18–19.

———. "Mii Gaa-pi-izhichigewaad Mewinzha." Edited by Anton Treuer. *Oshkaabewis Native Journal* 3 (Fall 1996): 26–35.

———. "Mii Sa Iw." Edited by Anton Treuer. *Oshkaabewis Native Journal* 2 (Fall 1995): 95.

———. "Nandawaaboozwe Makadewiiyaas Miinawaa." Edited by Anton Treuer. *Oshkaabewis Native Journal* 3 (Fall 1996): 50–51.

———. "Nitamising Gaa-waabamag Makadewiiyaas." Edited by Anton Treuer. *Oshkaabewis Native Journal* 3 (Fall 1996): 48–49.

———. "Waabooz Gaa-piindashkwaanind." Edited by Anton Treuer. *Oshkaabewis Native Journal* 3 (Spring 1996): 37.

———. "Wayeshkad Gaa-waabamag Aadamoobii." Edited by Anton Treuer. *Oshkaabewis Native Journal* 3 (Fall 1996): 46–47.

———. "Wenabozho Gaa-giishkigwebinaad Zhiishiiban." Edited by Anton Treuer. *Oshkaabewis Native Journal* 3 (Fall 1996): 62–67.

Neill, Edward D. "Battle of Lake Pokegama." *Collections of the MHS* 1 (1902): 141–45.

———. "Dakota Land and Dakota Life." *Collections of the MHS* 1 (1902): 205–40.

———. *History of Minnesota.* New York: Arno Press, [1858, 1883], 1975.

———. "History of the Ojibways and Their Connection with Fur Traders, Based upon Official and Other Records." *Collections of the MHS* 5 (1885): 395–510.

———. "Occurrences in and around Fort Snelling, from 1819 to 1840." *Collections of the MHS* 2 (1860–67):102–42.

Nelson, George. *My First Years in the Fur Trade: The Journals of 1802–1804.* St. Paul: MHS Press, 2002.

Nesper, Larry. *The Walleye War: The Struggle for Ojibwe Spearfishing and Treaty Rights.* Lincoln: University of Nebraska Press, 2002.

Nichols, David. *Lincoln and the Indians.* Columbia: University of Missouri Press, 1978.

Nichols, John D., ed. *Statement Made by the Indians: A Bilingual Petition of the Chippewas of Lake Superior, 1864.* London: University of Western Ontario, Centre for Research and Teaching of Canadian Native Languages, 1988.

———. "The Translation of Key Phrases in the Treaties of 1837 and 1855," 514–24. In James M. McClurken, ed. *Fish in the Lakes, Wild Rice, and Game in Abundance: Testimony on Behalf of the Mille Lacs Ojibwe Hunting and Fishing Rights.* East Lansing: Michigan State University Press, 2000.

Nichols, John D., and Earl Nyholm (Otchingwanigan). *A Concise Dictionary of Minnesota Ojibwe.* Minneapolis: University of Minnesota Press, 1995.

———. *Ojibwewi-ikidowinan: An Ojibwe Word Resource Book.* Bemidji, MN: Bemidji State College Indian Studies, 1979.

Nicolay, John George. "Hole-in-the-Day." *Harper's New Monthly Magazine* (January 1863): 186–91.

Nute, Grace Lee. "Alexander Faribault." Unpublished, July 5, 1926. MHS Archives.

———. *Documents Relating to Northwest Missions, 1815–1827.* MHS Archives, 1942.

———. "Early American Explorers of the Northwest." *Hamline Radio Hour* 24 (November 6, 1928). MHS Archives.

———. "The History of Missions in the Central Northwest." Unpublished, May 21, 1929. MHS Archives.

———. "Missionaries Among the Indians of the Northwest." *Hamline Radio Hour* 28 (November 27, 1928). MHS Archives.

———. "Missionaries Among the Sioux and Chippewa." *Hamline Radio Hour* 26 (November 20, 1928). MHS Archives.

———. "The Site of the Sioux Villages at Mille Lacs Lake in the Time of Father Hennepin." Unpublished, February 18, 1941. Grace Lee Nute Papers. MHS Archives.

———. "Sketch of Lawrence Taliaferro." Unpublished, 1933. Grace Lee Nute Papers. MHS Archives.

———. "Sketch of Samuel W. Pond." Unpublished, undated. MHS Archives.

———. "Some Famous Minnesota Fur-Traders." Unpublished, 1924. MHS Archives.

Oakgrove, Collins. "Bebaamosed Miinawaa Gawigoshko'iweshiinh." Edited by Anton Treuer. *Oshkaabewis Native Journal* 4 (Fall 1997): 40–45.

———. "Bijiinag Anishinaabe Gaa-waabamaad Chimookomaanan." Edited by Anton Treuer. *Oshkaabewis Native Journal* 4 (Fall 1997): 24–27.

———. "Gaa-aakozid Akiwenzii." Edited by Anton Treuer. *Oshkaabewis Native Journal* 4 (Fall 1997): 48–49.

———. "Wenji-nibwaakaad Nenabozho." Edited by Anton Treuer. *Oshkaabewis Native Journal* 4 (Fall 1997): 32–35.

———. "Zhaawanoowinini Indizhinikaaz." Edited by Anton Treuer. *Oshkaabewis Native Journal* 4 (Fall 1997): 16–17.

Oehler, C. M. *The Great Sioux Uprising.* New York: Oxford University Press, 1959.

Parker, John, ed. *The Journals of Jonathan Carver and Related Documents.* St. Paul: MHS Press, 1976.

Parkman, Francis. *La Salle and Discovery of the Great West.* New York: New American Library, 1963.

The Permanent Home of the Pine: A Pictoral History of the People and Culture of Cass Lake and the Surrounding Area. Cass Lake, MN: Cass Lake Civic and Commerce Association, 1988.

Pond, Samuel W. *The Dakota or Sioux in Minnesota: As They Were in 1834.* St. Paul: MHS Press, 1986.

———. "Indian Warfare in Minnesota." *Collections of the MHS* 3 (1880): 129–38.

"Proceedings of a Council with the Chippewa Indians." *Iowa Journal of History and Politics* 5 (1911): 408–28.

Prucha, Francis Paul. *Documents of United States Indian Policy.* Lincoln: University of Nebraska Press, 1975.

Quaife, Milo Milton. *Chicago and the Old Northwest, 1673–1835.* Chicago: University of Chicago, 1913.

———. *John Long's Voyages and Travels in the Years 1768–1788.* Chicago: Lakeside, [1791] 1922.

Radcliffe-Brown, A. R. *Structure and Function in Primitive Society.* New York: Free Press, 1952.

Radin, Paul. *The Winnebago Tribe.* Lincoln: University of Nebraska Press, 1970.

Randall, Thomas E. *History of the Chippewa Valley.* Eau Claire, WI: Free Press, 1875.

Red Lake Band of Chippewa Indians. *Open House.* Red Lake, MN: Red Lake Band of Chippewa Indians, 1959.

Richter, Daniel K. *Facing East From Indian Country: A Native History of America.* Cambridge, MA: Harvard University Press, 2001.

———. *The Ordeal of the Longhouse: The Peoples of the Iroquois League in the Era of European Colonization.* Chapel Hill: University of North Carolina Press, 1992.

Richter, Daniel K., and James H. Merrell. *Beyond the Covenant Chain: The Iroquois and the Neighbors in Indian North America, 1600–1800.* Syracuse, NY: Syracuse University Press, 1987.

Riggs, Stephen R. *A Dakota-English Dictionary.* St. Paul: MHS Press, 1992.

———. *Mary and I: Forty Years with the Sioux.* Minneapolis, MN: Ross and Haines, 1969.

———. *Tah-koo Wah-kan; or, the Gospel among the Dakotas.* Boston: Congregational Sabbath School and Publishing Society, 1869.

Ritzenthaler, Robert E. *Building a Chippewa Birchbark Canoe.* Milwaukee, WI: Milwaukee Public Museum Publications, 1984.

———. "Chippewa Preoccupation with Health: Change in a Traditional Attitude Resulting From Modern Health Problems." PhD diss., Columbia University, 1949.

Ritzenthaler, Robert E., and Pat Ritzenthaler. *The Woodland Indians of the Western Great Lakes.* Garden City, NY: Natural History, 1970.

Robinson, Doane. *A History of the Dakota or Sioux Indians: From Their Earliest Traditions and First Contact with White Men to the Final Settlement of the Last of Them upon Reservations and the Consequent Abandonment of the Old Tribal Life*. Minneapolis, MN: Ross and Haines, 1967.

Roy, Arthur J., and Donald Freeman. *Give Us Good Measure: An Economic Analysis of Relations between the Indians and the Hudson's Bay Company before 1763*. Toronto: University of Toronto Press, 1978.

St. Germain, Jill. *Indian Treaty-Making Policy in the United States and Canada, 1867–1877*. Lincoln: University of Nebraska Press, 2001.

Satz, Ronald N. *Chippewa Treaty Rights: The Reserved Rights of Wisconsin's Chippewa Indians in Historical Perspective*. Wisconsin Academy of Sciences, Arts and Letters 79 (1991).

Schaefer, Francis J. "Discovery of Fort St. Charles on the Lake of the Woods and the Remains of J. B. de La Vérendrye, J. P. Aulneau de la Touche, S. J. and Their Nineteen Companions." Unpublished, undated. MHS Archives.

Schenck, Theresa M. *The Voice of the Crane Echoes Afar: The Sociopolitical Organization of the Lake Superior Ojibwa, 1640–1855*. New York: Garland, 1997.

———. *William Warren: The Life, Letters, and Times of an Ojibwe Leader*. Lincoln: University of Nebraska Press, 2007.

Schlarman, J. H. *From Quebec to New Orleans: Fort de Charles*. Belleville, IL: Beuchler, 1929.

Schmalz, Peter S. *The Ojibwa of Southern Ontario*. Toronto: University of Toronto Press, 1991.

Schoolcraft, Henry Rowe. *Algic Researches: Indian Tales and Legends*. 2 vols. New York: Harper, 1839.

———. *The American Indians, Their History, Condition and Prospects, from Original Notes and Manuscripts*. Buffalo, NY: G. H. Derby, 1851. (Originally published 1844–45 in eight separate issues titled *Onéotá*.)

———. *The Indian in His Wigwam or Characteristics of the Red Race of America*. Buffalo, NY: W. H. Graham, 1848.

———. *The Indian Tribes of the United States: Their History, Antiquities, Customs, Religion, Arts, Language, Traditions, Oral Legends, and Myths*. Edited by Francis S. Drake. 2 vols. Philadelphia: J. B. Lippincott and Company, [1852] 1883.

———. *Narrative Journal of Travels: Through the Northwestern Regions of the United States Extending from Detroit Through the Great Chain of American Lakes to the Sources of the Mississippi River in the Year 1820*. Edited by Mentor L. Williams. East Lansing: Michigan State University Press, [1951] 1992.

———. *Personal Memoirs*. Philadelphia: Lippincott, Grambo and Company, 1851.

Schulenberg, Raymond F. *Indians of North Dakota*. Bismarck: State Historical Society of North Dakota Press, 1956.

Schultz, Duane. *Over the Earth I Come: The Great Sioux Uprising of 1862*. New York: St. Martin's Press, 1992.

Sharp, S. Freightner. "Tenting on Pokegama Lake." Unpublished, undated. MHS Archives.

Sharrock, Floyd W., and Susan R. Sharrock. "History of the Cree Indian Territorial Expansion from the Hudson Bay Area to the Interior Saskatchewan and Missouri Plains." *Chippewa Indians VI*. Indian Claims Commission. New York: Garland Publishing, 1974.

Sheldon, E. M. *The Early History of Michigan from the First Settlement to 1815*. New York: A. S. Barnes, 1956.

Sibley, Henry H. "Memoir of Jean Nicollet." *Collections of the MHS* 1 (1902): 146–56.

———. "Reminiscences: Historical and Personal." *Collections of the MHS* 1 (1902): 374–96.

Slotkin, Richard. *The Fatal Environment: The Myth of the Frontier in the Age of Industrialization, 1800–1890*. New York: Atheneum, 1985.

Smith, Alice Elizabeth. *History of Wisconsin: Volume I, From Exploration to Statehood.* Madison: State Historical Society of Wisconsin Press, 1973.

———. *James Duane Doty: Frontier Promoter.* Madison: State Historical Society of Wisconsin, 1954.

Smith, James G. E. *Leadership among the Southwestern Ojibwa.* Ottawa, ON: National Museums of Canada, *Publications in Ethnology* 7 (1973).

Snelling, William J. "Running the Gauntlet." *Collections of the MHS* 1 (1902): 360–73.

Spears, Julia Warren. "My Journey with the Chippewa Indians." September 1921. Julia Warren Spears Papers. MHS Archives.

———. "Reminiscence of the Assassination of Hole-in-the-Day." Undated. Julia Warren Spears Papers. MHS Archives.

———. "Reminiscences of a Short History of the Chippewa Chief Hole-in-the-Day." July 1922. Julia Warren Spears Papers. MHS Archives.

———. "Reminiscences of Hole-in-the-Day." Julia Warren Spears Papers. MHS Archives.

"Speech of Sundry Chippeway Chiefs Met in Council at Snake River," September 25, 1837. American Fur Company Papers. MHS Archives.

The Spirit of Missions. New York: Board of Missions of the Protestant Episcopal Church, 1843.

Steck, Francis Borgia. *The Joliet-Marquette Expedition, 1673.* Quincy, IL: Franciscan Fathers, 1928.

Stevens, Frank E. *The Black Hawk War.* Chicago: Frank E. Stevens, 1903.

Stevens, Jedediah D., Diary: September 9, 1829, to April 2, 1830. Grace Lee Nute Papers. MHS Archives.

Stillday, Thomas J. "Bajaaganish Miinawaa Makizinish (Version 1)." Edited by Anton Treuer. *Oshkaabewis Native Journal* 7 (Fall 2009): 32–35.

———. "Bajaaganish Miinawaa Makizinish (Version 2)." Edited by Anton Treuer. *Oshkaabewis Native Journal* 7 (Fall 2009): 36–39.

———. "Gidaan." Edited by Anton Treuer. *Oshkaabewis Native Journal* 7 (Fall 2009): 20–23.

———. "Gookooko'oo Otawagaang." Edited by Anton Treuer. *Oshkaabewis Native Journal* 7 (Fall 2009): 24–27.

———. "Nenabozho Agoozid." Edited by Anton Treuer. *Oshkaabewis Native Journal* 7 (Fall 2009): 96–99.

———. "Obaashiing." Edited by Anton Treuer. *Oshkaabewis Native Journal* 7 (Fall 2009): 42–95.

———. "Opichi." Edited by Anton Treuer. *Oshkaabewis Native Journal* 7 (Fall 2009): 28–31.

———. "Waabikwed." Edited by Anton Treuer. *Oshkaabewis Native Journal* 7 (Fall 2009): 40–41.

Stone, William L. *The Life and Times of Sir William Johnson.* Albany, NY: J. Munsell, 1865.

Stout, David B. "Ethnohistorical Report on the Saginaw Chippewa." *Chippewa Indian v. Indian Claims Commission.* New York: Garland Publishing, 1974.

Sweet, George W. "Incidents of the Threatened Outbreak of Hole-in-the-Day and Other Ojibways at the Time of the Sioux Massacre of 1862." *Collections of the MHS* 6 (1894): 401–8.

Taliaferro, Lawrence. "Auto-Biography of Maj. Lawrence Taliaferro." *Collections of the MHS* 6 (1894): 189–255.

Tanner, George C. "History of Fort Ripley, 1849 to 1859, Based on the Diary of Rev. Solon W. Manney, D.D., Chaplain of This Post from 1851 to 1859." *Collections of the MHS* 10 (1905): 179–202.

Tanner, Helen Hornbeck, ed. *Atlas of Great Lakes Indian History.* Norman: University of Oklahoma Press, 1987.

———. "The Chippewa of Eastern Lower Michigan." *Chippewa Indians v. Indian Claims Commission.* New York: Garland Publishing, 1974.

———. "The Mille Lacs Band and the Treaty of 1855." In James McClurken, ed. *Fish in the Lakes, Wild Rice and Game in Abundance: Testimony on Behalf of the Mille Lacs Ojibwe Hunting and Fishing Rights.* East Lansing: Michigan State University Press, 2000.

Thomas, David Hurst. *Skull Wars: Kennewick Man, Archaeology, and the Battle for Native American Identity.* New York: Basic, 2000.

Thornton, Russell. *American Indian Holocaust and Survival: A Population History since 1492.* Norman: University of Oklahoma Press, 1987.

Thwaites, Reuben Gold. *Father Louis Hennepin's A New Discovery of a Vast Country in America.* Toronto: Coles, 1974.

———. *The French Regime in Wisconsin.* Madison: State Historical Society of Wisconsin, 1902–8.

———. *The Jesuit Relations and Allied Documents.* 73 vols. New York: Pageant Book Company, 1959.

Treuer, Anton S. "Akiwenziiyan Gaa-miinaad Nagamon Zagime." *Oshkaabewis Native Journal* 3 (Spring 1996): 59.

———. "Anishinaabewisijigewin: Preserving, Learning and Teaching Ojibwe." *Oshkaabewis Native Journal* 6 (Spring/Fall 2003): 3–5.

———. "Building a Foundation for the Next Generation: A Path for Revival of the Ojibwe Language." *Oshkaabewis Native Journal* 3 (Spring 1996): 3–7.

———. "Full Circle: From Disintegration to Revitalization of Otterskin Bag Use in Great Lakes Tribal Culture." *Princeton University Library Chronicle* 67 (Winter 2006): 358–65.

———. "Gaa-izhinikaanaad Asaawen." *Oshkaabewis Native Journal* 3 (Spring 1996): 75.

———. "Gaayosejig." *Oshkaabewis Native Journal* 2 (Fall 1995): 73.

———. "Ge-onji-aabadak Anishinaabe-Inwewinan." *The American Indian Quarterly: Special Issue: Indigenous Languages and Indigenous Literatures.* Edited by David Treuer. 30 (Winter/Spring 2006): 87–90.

———. "Giniigaan-ayi'iiminaan." *Oshkaabewis Native Journal* 6 (Spring/Fall 2003): 84–119.

———. "Healing is a Two-Way Street," *Newsline,* February 26, 1992, 16.

———. "The Importance of Language: A Closer Look." *Oshkaabewis Native Journal* 4 (Spring 1997): 3–12.

———. "Jean Baptiste Faribault." *American National Biography.* Cary, NC: Oxford University Press, 1999. Vol. 7: 712–13.

———. "Keeping Legends Alive: Niibaa-giizhig and Anishinaabe-bimaadiziwin." *Oshkaabewis Native Journal* 3 (Fall 1996): 3–14.

———. *Living Our Language: Ojibwe Tales and Oral Histories.* St. Paul: MHS Press, 2001.

———. "Miskobines Manoominike." *Oshkaabewis Native Journal* 2 (Fall 1995): 85.

———. "Naawi-giizis." *Oshkaabewis Native Journal* 5 (Fall 1998): 3–5.

———. "Nagamotawag Indaanis." *Oshkaabewis Native Journal* 3 (Spring 1996): 45–46.

———. "New Directions in Ojibwe Language Study." *Oshkaabewis Native Journal* 2 (Fall 1995): 3–6.

———. "Noopinadoon Gide' Waa-izhichigeyan." *Oshkaabewis Native Journal* 3 (Spring 1996): 83.

———. *Ojibwe in Minnesota.* St. Paul: MHS Press, 2010.

———. "Ojibwe Language." *Dictionary of American History.* New York: Charles Scribner's Sons, 2004.

———. "Ojibwe-Dakota Relations: Diplomacy, War and Social Union, 1679–1862." MA thesis, University of Minnesota, 1994.

———. *Omaa Akiing.* Princeton, NJ: Western Americana Press, 2002.

———. "Our Mission: Preserve and Revitalize." *Oshkaabewis Native Journal* 4 (Fall 1997): 3–5.

———. "The Pilgrim's Shame: How Our Schools and Our Culture Perpetuate Misconceptions about Native Americans." *Nassau Herald,* April 18, 1991, 15.

———. "Revitalizing Ojibwe Language and Culture" Radio interview. WOJB 88.9, March 8, 1997, Reserve, WI.

———. "Traditional Anishinaabe Learning: Melvin Eagle and the Art of Gikendaasowin." *Oshkaabewis Native Journal* 5 (Spring 1998): 3–6.

———. "Transcription Notes for 'Gekendaasojig.'" *Oshkaabewis Native Journal* 5 (Spring 1998): 89–96.

———. "Waasabiikwe." *Oshkaabewis Native Journal* 7 (Spring 2010): 9–20.

———. "The War Is Over: Native Americans at Princeton." *The Progressive Review* (November 1990): 5.

———. "Wezaawibiitang." *Oshkaabewis Native Journal* 7 (Fall 2009): 3–14.

———. "What's in a Name: The Meaning of Ojibwe." *Oshkaabewis Native Journal* 2 (Fall 1995): 39–41.

———. "Wii-ani-miigaading," *'A 'A Arts.* Honolulu, HI: Pualei Circle, June 2003.

———. "Wii-ani-miigaading." *Chain.* Edited by Jena Osman and Juliana Spahr. Honolulu, HI: S. Press Distribution, 2003, 249.

———. "Zaaga'ang Awiiya." *Oshkaabewis Native Journal* 4 (Spring 1997): 35.

Treuer, Anton S., and David R. Treuer. "A Day in the Life of Ojibwe." *Making Minnesota Territory, 1849–1858.* Edited by Anne Kaplan and Marilyn Ziebarth. St. Paul: MHS Press, 1999: 20–22.

———. "A Day in the Life of Ojibwe," *Minnesota History* 56 (Winter 1998–99): 172–74.

Treuer, Anton S., and Thomas J. Stillday. "Bawatig." Edited by Anton Treuer. *Oshkaabewis Native Journal* 7 (Fall 2009): 100–131.

Treuer, David R., ed. *The American Indian Quarterly: Special Issue: Indigenous Languages and Indigenous Literatures* 30 (Winter/Spring 2006).

Trowbridge, Charles. "General Cass at Ste. Marie, 1820." *Collections of the SHSW* 5 (1867): 68–69.

Upham, Warren. "Groseilliers and Radisson, the First White Men in Minnesota, 1655–56, and 1659–60, and Their Discovery of the Upper Mississippi River." Part 2. *Collections of the MHS* 10 (1905): 449–594.

———. *Minnesota Place Names: A Geographical Encyclopedia.* St. Paul: MHS Press, [1969] 2001.

Usner, Daniel H. *American Indians in the Lower Mississippi Valley: Social and Economic Histories.* Lincoln: University of Nebraska Press, 1998.

Valentine, J. Randolph. *Nishnaabemwin Reference Grammar.* Toronto: University of Toronto Press, 2001.

Van Antwerp, Ver Planck. "Negotiations for the Chippewa Treaty of July 29, 1837." In Ronald N. Satz, *Chippewa Treaty Rights.* Wisconsin Academy of Sciences, Arts, and Letters 79 (1991): 131–53.

Van Cleve, Charlotte O. "A Reminiscence of Fort Snelling." *Collections of the MHS* 3 (1880): 76–81.

Van Kirk, Sylvia. *Many Tender Ties: Women in Fur-Trade Society.* Norman: University of Oklahoma Press, 1980.

Vansina, Jan. *Oral Tradition as History.* Madison: University of Wisconsin Press, 1985.

Vecsey, Christopher. *Traditional Ojibwa Religion and Its Historical Changes.* Philadelphia: American Philosophical Society, 1983.

Vennum, Thomas, Jr. *The Ojibwa Dance Drum: Its History and Construction.* St. Paul: MHS Press, [1989] 2009.

———. *Wild Rice and the Ojibway People.* St. Paul: MHS Press, 1988.

Viola, Herman J. *Thomas L. McKenney: Architect of America's Early Indian Policy: 1816–1830.* Chicago: The Swallow Press [Sage Books], 1974.

Vollum, Judith, and Thomas Vollum, *Ojibwemowin.* St. Paul, MN: Ojibwe Language Publishing, 1994.

Walker, Thomas B. "Memories of the Early Life and Development of Minnesota," *Collections of the MHS* 15 (1915): 455–78.

Warner, Robert M. "Economic and Historical Report on Northern Michigan." *Chippewa Indian v. Indian Claims Commission.* New York: Garland Publishing, 1974.

Warner, Robert M., and Lois J. Groesbeck. "Historical Report on the Sault Ste. Marie Area." *Chippewa Indian v. Indian Claims Commission.* New York: Garland Publishing, 1974.

Warren, William W. "Answers to Inquiries Respecting the History, Present Condition and Future Prospect of the Ojibwas of Mississippi and Lake Superior." *Minnesota Pioneer,* December 5, 12, 19, and 26, 1849.

———. "A Brief History of the Chippewa." *Minnesota Democrat,* February 11, 18, 25, March 4, 11, 25, and April 1, 1851.

———. *History of the Ojibway People.* St. Paul: MHS Press, 1984. Originally published as *History of the Ojibways Based upon Traditions and Oral Statements,* 1885.

———. "Letter to the Editor." *Minnesota Pioneer,* March 13, 1850. (Warren signed the letter "O-jib-way.")

———. "Letters to the Editor." *Minnesota Democrat.* January 28, November 29, December 31, 1851, and January 14, 1852.

———. "Oral Traditions Respecting the History of the Ojibwa Nation." In Henry Rowe Schoolcraft, ed. *The Indian Tribes of the United States: Their History, Antiquities, Customs, Religion, Arts, Language, Traditions, Oral Legends, and Myths.* Edited by Francis S. Drake. 2 vols. Philadelphia: J. B. Lippincott and Company, 1883 [1852] 2: 135–67.

———. "Pillagers, or Mukkundwas." *Indian Tribes of the United States.* Edited by Henry Rowe Schoolcraft. 5 (1855): 184–91.

———. "Sioux and Chippewa Wars." *Minnesota Chronicle and Register.* June 3 and 10, 1850.

Weatherford, Jack. *Indian Givers: How the Indians of the Americas Transformed the World.* New York: Fawcett Columbine, 1988.

———. *Native Roots: How the Indians Enriched America.* New York: Fawcett Columbine, 1991.

Wedel, Mildred Mott. "LeSueur and the Dakota Sioux." In *Aspects of Upper Great Lakes Anthropology.* St. Paul: MHS Press, 1974.

Wheeler-Voegelin, Erminie. "An Anthropological Report on Indian Use and Occupancy of Northern Michigan." *Chippewa Indians v. Indian Claims Commission.* New York: Garland Publishing, 1974.

Whipple, Delores. "Mezinaashiikwe." Edited by Anton Treuer. *Oshkaabewis Native Journal* 6 (Spring/Fall 2003): 26–31.

Whipple, Henry B. "Civilization and Christianization of the Ojibways in Minnesota." *Collections of the MHS* 9 (1901): 129–42.

———. *Lights and Shadows of a Long Episcopate.* New York: Macmillan, 1899.

White, Hartley. "Onizhishin O'ow Bimaadiziwin." Edited by Anton Treuer. *Oshkaabewis Native Journal* 4 (Fall 1997): 6–15.

———. "Zhaawanose." Edited by Anton Treuer. *Oshkaabewis Native Journal* 6 (Spring/Fall 2003): 16–21.

White, Richard. *The Middle Ground: Indians, Empires and Republics in the Great Lakes Region, 1650–1815.* New York: Cambridge University Press, 1991.

White, Walter. "Gaagoons Indigoo." Edited by Anton Treuer. *Oshkaabewis Native Journal* 3 (Spring 1996): 69.

———. "Gegwe-dakamigishkang Gaagiigido." Edited by Anton Treuer. *Oshkaabewis Native Journal* 2 (Fall 1995): 91–94.

———. "Ogii-izhinaazhishkawaan Bwaanan." Edited by Anton Treuer. *Oshkaabewis Native Journal* 3 (Spring 1996): 49–50.

White Crow, Doris. "Nisidotawiminaagozi Anishinaabe." Edited by Anton Treuer. *Oshkaabewis Native Journal* 6 (Spring/Fall 2003): 38–43.

Willand, Jon. *Lac Qui Parle and the Dakota Mission.* Madison, MN: Lac qui Parle County Historical Society, 1964.

Williams, Fletcher J. "A History of the City of Saint Paul, and of the County of Ramsey, Minnesota." *Collections of the MHS* 4 (1876):336–38.

Williams, Mentor L. *Schoolcraft's Narrative Journal of Travels: Through the Northwestern Regions of the United States Extending from Detroit through the Great Chain of American Lakes to the Sources of the Mississippi River in the Year 1820.* East Lansing: Michigan State University Press, [1951] 1992.

Williams, Walter. *The Spirit and the Flesh: Sexual Diversity in American Indian Culture.* Boston: Beacon Press, 1992.

Williamson, John P. *An English-Dakota Dictionary.* St. Paul: MHS Press, 1992.

Willison, Charles C. "The Successive Chiefs Named Wabasha." *Collections of the MHS.* 12 (1908): 503–12.

Wilson, Angela. *In the Footsteps of Our Ancestors: The Dakota Commemorative Marches of the 21st Century.* St. Paul, MN: Living Justice Press, 2006.

———. "The Power of the Spoken Word: Native Oral Traditions in American Indian History." In Donald Fixico, *Rethinking American Indian History.* Albuquerque: University of New Mexico Press, 1997.

———. *Remember This: Dakota Decolonization and the Eli Taylor Narratives.* Lincoln: University of Nebraska Press, 2005.

Winchell, Newton H. *The Aborigines of Minnesota: A Report Based on the Collections of Jacob V. Brower, and on the Field Surveys and Notes of Alfred J. Hill and Theodore Lewis.* St. Paul: MHS Press, 1911.

Woodlands: The Story of the Mille Lacs Ojibwe. Oral history video documentary. Onamia, MN: Mille Lacs Band of Ojibwe, 1994.

Woolworth, Alan R. "Ethnohistorical Report on the Yankton Sioux." In *Sioux Indians III.* New York: Garland Publishing, 1974.

Zapffe, Carl Andrew. *Indian Days in Minnesota's Lake Region: A History of the Great Sioux-Ojibwe Revolution, from Invasion to the Intertribal Boundary of 1825.* Brainerd, MN: Historic Heartland Association, 1991.

Index

Page numbers in *italics* indicate graphics.

The Assassination of Hole in the Day is set in the Cambria typeface family. Book design by Daniel Leary; typesetting by Allan S. Johnson, Phoenix Type, Appleton, Minnesota. Printed by Sheridan Books, Ann Arbor, Michigan.